Literature for Youth
Series Editor: Edward T. Sullivan

Disabilities and Disorders in Literature for Youth

A Selective Annotated Bibliography for K–12

Alice Crosetto
Rajinder Garcha
Mark Horan

Literature for Youth, No. 12

The Scarecrow Press, Inc.
Lanham • Toronto • Plymouth, UK
2009

Published by Scarecrow Press, Inc.
A wholly owned subsidiary of The Rowman & Littlefield Publishing Group, Inc.
4501 Forbes Boulevard, Suite 200, Lanham, Maryland 20706
http://www.scarecrowpress.com

Estover Road, Plymouth PL6 7PY, United Kingdom

British Library Cataloguing in Publication Information Available

Library of Congress Cataloging-in-Publication Data
Crosetto, Alice, 1954-
 Disabilities and disorders in literature for youth : a selective annotated bibliography for K-12 / Alice Crosetto, Rajinder Garcha, Mark Horan.
    p. cm. — (Literature for youth ; no. 12)
 Includes bibliographical references and index.
 ISBN 978-0-8108-5977-7 (cloth : alk. paper) — ISBN 978-0-8108-6962-2 (ebook : alk. paper)
 1. Disabilities—Juvenile literature--Bibliography. 2. People with disabilities—Juvenile literature—Bibliography. I. Garcha, Rajinder. II. Horan, Mark, 1949- III. Title. Z6122.
C76 2009
 [HV1568]
 016.3624—dc22
                                                                      2009014734

∞™ The paper used in this publication meets the minimum requirements of American National Standard for Information Sciences—Permanence of Paper for Printed Library Materials, ANSI/NISO Z39.48-1992.

Printed in the United States of America

To my father,
Carl P. Crosetto,
who taught me to respect all individuals,
and to my sister Norma,
who will always be one of those good-looking Crosetto girls. *AC*

To my grandsons,
Nicholas Scott and Christopher Robert Mocerino,
who hold a special place in my heart. *RG*

To my nephew,
Steven Earle Enders, "Power Up, Dude!"
to my gracious sisters, and to the light of my life, S.W.S. *MH*

Contents

Acknowledgments

The authors acknowledge the following individuals who provided assistance and support while preparing this annotated bibliography. The following authors made a special effort to provide their books which would not have been available otherwise:

Vanita Oelschlager for *My Grampy Can't Walk* and *Let Me Bee.*

Barbara Esham for *Stacey Coolidge's Fancy-Smancy Cursive Handwriting; Mrs. Gorski, I Think That I Have the Wiggle Fidgets; Last to Finish: A Story about the Smartest Boy in Math Class;* and *If You're so Smart, How Come You Can't Spell Mississippi?*

Our gratitude goes to Keith Myles, on behalf of the Autism Asperger Publishing Company, for providing these books: *My Strange and Terrible Malady; In His Shoes: A Short Journey through Autism;* and *Arnie and His School Tools: Simple Sensory Solutions That Build Success.* These titles would not have been accessible otherwise.

In addition, the authors thank Forest Zhang, IBBY Deputy Director of Administration, for providing a complimentary copy of the *Outstanding Books for Young People with Disabilities 2009.*

We thank the members of the OhioLINK libraries, the staff of the Toledo-Lucas County Public Library, Norma Wheller, and Sheila Randel for providing resources for this bibliography. In addition, we extend our appreciation to our colleague Laura Kinner for proofreading certain chapters in this manuscript.

Every attempt has been made by the authors to ensure accuracy and consistency regarding information provided in this book. However, the authors apologize for any inaccuracies, omissions, or any inconsistencies herein. The discretion of teachers, parents, and librarians should be used to consider carefully the resources that they can use for educational purposes.

Foreword

To truly know the human condition, we have to take into account the range of human circumstances that today we call *disability*. The human experience is fundamentally an embodied one: to be human is to have a body, is to *be* a body in a profound way. We are not just bodies, of course: we are mind, we are spirit, we are the past and the hope for the future. But without bodies, we simply do not exist. And bodies come in a wide variety of shapes, sizes, colors, manners, and degrees of function.

Disability is one of those concepts that initially seems straightforward, even obvious. But like so much in this intricate and interconnected world, when we look more closely, we see that what seemed simple is anything but. When we look closely, we see that the web of common assumptions around disability misleads us as to the very nature of what we thought we were looking at. When we talk about disability, disorder, or impairment, it is easy to think that we are talking about clear and certain diagnostic categories that describe objectively verifiable conditions of disease, deformity, or malfunction. But when we look closely, we can see that the ways we are talking and thinking are based on decisions that others in society have made about how to divide up humanity, about what bodies, functions, and behaviors are appropriate, acceptable, or normal, and which are inadequate, insufficient, or invalid. Disability is not a fixed or self-evident thing; like so much of our world, it is a product of social processes, processes that manage to keep themselves hidden by masquerading as natural and normal (which are themselves arguable concepts: Where do we draw the line between the natural and the unnatural? Are tools natural? Why is it important to compare ourselves to a norm?).

We can divide up bodies and ways of moving through the world into diagnostic categories. And that can provide some useful information; the experience of being blind, for example, is different in important ways from experiences of mental illness, of mobility impairment, of autism. Yet starting with diagnostic categories hides from view crucial insights about what it means to differ in the ways that we call *disability*. It hides from view the most penetrating insight of the disability movement that began to take hold in the middle part of the twentieth century: that the social deficits that accompany disability are separate from the bodily facts of disability. An enduring image illustrates this distinction: picture a woman in a wheelchair at the foot of the stairs leading to the library. Is it her inability to walk that keeps her out of the library? Or is the decision whether to climb the stairs a necessary part of entering the library? This image can help us understand the distinction scholars draw between *impairment* and *disability*: *impairment* refers to the functional differences and limitations that impact how disabled people* live in the world; *disability* refers to the social implications of those differences. Making this distinction allows us to start to see how people who have impairments have been made into second-class citizens (or worse).

But wait, you might think—we have ramps, we have elevators, we have disabled kids in classes—that picture no longer obtains. And the notable successes of the disability rights movement have made important differences in access to public services and places. But what about private places, the places where most of us live most of our lives? How about the restaurant where your friends are planning to gather? What about your home and the homes of your friends? Access is a complex and nuanced thing, a nut we are only beginning to crack.

Distinguishing impairment from disability is an important part of moving from a diagnosis-centered medical model to a more inclusive and aware sociocultural perspective on disability. Calling the biophysical/pathological orientation "medical" is not to minimize important contributions from health professionals and those in the helping fields, not to suggest that all health professionals operate with those blinders on, but to recognize that this focus on personal deficits minimizes the personhood of disabled people, positioning them as victims, as not fully competent members of society, even as potential threats. This is not merely a matter of mistaking part of the puzzle for the whole: the diagnosis focus considers disabled people to have diminished capacity to participate in society, to make meaningful decisions about their own lives, to contribute to the greater whole. The diagnosis focus means that it is remarkably difficult to see disabled people as whole human beings.

Enter works of the imagination. By creating worlds that reflect life as it really is lived for readers and viewers, literature and other works of art can open windows onto lives too often lived in the shadows. Through the imagination, we can learn to shed our own blinders. Through the imagination, we can feel what it

---

*I use the phrase "disabled people" instead of the people-first phrase "people with disabilities" in order to characterize disability as a social process rather than simply an embodied condition. This is in keeping with the call from Simi Linton and others to center disabled experience and claim a political identity for disabled people. See *Claiming Disability: Knowledge and Identity* by Simi Linton (New York: NYU Press, 1998).

might be like to live on the other side of the divide. Through the imagination, we can begin to envision what life might be like if we could tear down the invisible walls that divide us, if we could truly embrace diversity in all its many aspects, if we could recognize the many ways that disability enriches our lives. There is no better teacher than disability to foster flexible thinking, adaptability, creativity, and persistence. Disability presents not threat but opportunity—opportunity to reach students previously marginalized, opportunity to learn new ways of thinking and moving through the world, opportunity to expand the realm of the possible.

Disabilities and Disorders in Literature for Youth: A Selective Annotated Bibliography for K–12 offers a useful tool in moving toward that promise. Though the book is organized by diagnostic category, it offers a wealth of useful texts that can help students and all of us move beyond simple "awareness" and into the richer space of imagining a better tomorrow. Education, ultimately, is about change; this book can help us move toward positive change.

Disability ultimately can never be contained within categories because it always surprises. Despite the claims of prognostication, disability describes the life that is not predictable, the life that is always something more, something less, something different from the norm, than what is expected. And it is this element of the unexpected that you will be asking the readers to bring to the text. So even though they are "normally" taught to think within categories, an engaged reading, one truly informed by the richness that is disability, would require that they think outside the expected. Thinking outside the boxes—what more can anyone ask of an education?

Jim Ferris, Ph.D.
Ability Center of Greater Toledo Endowed Chair in Disability Studies
The University of Toledo

Introduction

One in five Americans currently lives with at least one disability or disorder. This represents almost 50 million individuals.[1] Some disabilities and disorders are obvious, such as the use of a wheelchair or a hearing aid; others are not, such as having an eating disorder or Asperger's syndrome. While some individuals may live with a disability or a disorder throughout their entire lives, others may experience one at some time.

Studies reveal that approximately 17 percent of children in the United States have a developmental disability.[2] Developmental disabilities include autism spectrum disorders (ASDs), intellectual disabilities, cerebral palsy, attention-deficit/hyperactivity disorder (AD/HD), hearing loss, and vision impairment.[3] In addition, about 20 percent of children in the United States are estimated to have mental disorders with some mild, functional impairment. These mental disorders include anxiety disorders, bipolar disorders, eating disorders, and schizophrenia.[4]

Educators and professionals who are responsible for teaching students with disorders and disabilities and for providing services and support for them need reliable and updated resources. The Individuals with Disabilities Education Act (IDEA), with its subsequent amendments and revisions, mandates that schools provide education to children with disabilities in general education classrooms. The resources identified in this book can play an integral role in the process of inclusion. For example, educators can benefit by using some of the strategies and suggestions offered in the resources specifically identified for them. In addition, educators can use the fiction and nonfiction titles listed in this book for building a successful inclusive curriculum.

Parents and guardians need to understand and address questions, concerns, and fears regarding the affect of a disability or disorder on family members, particularly siblings, and they should be aware of the existence of reliable and current resources. The resources specifically identified for parents in this guide provide successful strategies for parental advocacy, practical intervention, and effective communication in order to help their children improve their behavior, interact with others, and develop self-help skills. In addition, parents will benefit from resources that address their role in working with school personnel to identify strategies for academic success and in working with health personnel to explore treatment options.

In order to have an understanding of the challenges faced by classmates and by other individuals with disabilities or disorders and to interact effectively with them, nondisabled students need to have the opportunity to learn about disabilities and disorders. The resources in this bibliography specifically identified for students at various grade levels provide information that can help them develop character, empathy, and respect for others with disabilities or disorders.

Students with disabilities or disorders need to have their social, educational, and emotional concerns addressed. The resources listed in this bibliography provide information that students with disabilities or disorders can identify with, and the characters and situations in some of the resources can help build self-respect and enhance self-esteem.

During the course of this project, the authors discovered several challenges. Since there were so many disabilities and disorders, it was challenging to decide which ones to include. Once it was decided which specific disabilities and disorders to include, it was challenging to determine where they would fall in terms of categorizing. The three categories selected for this book were emotional, learning, and physical. Since some of the entries qualified for more than one of these categories, it was decided to create a fourth category, namely, multiple disabilities. The literature review revealed that some of the disabilities and disorders were not classified consistently. For example, autism was sometimes referred to as an emotional disorder, and in other sources, it was categorized as a learning disability. Vision and hearing impairments, although directly connected with physical limitations, were, in some cases, identified as developmental disabilities. Also, variant spellings and abbreviations for certain disabilities and disorders were encountered, such as, Asperger's syndrome versus Asperger syndrome; Down syndrome versus Down's syndrome; and attention-deficit/hyperactivity disorder referred to as AD/HD, ADD, or ADHD/ADD. In addition, locating the most current materials in some of the categories was difficult; specifically, there was a dearth of current fiction and nonfiction books regarding physical disabilities. There was also a lack of material in the area of eating disorders for elementary and middle school grade levels. The majority of valuable websites for K–12 students were embedded within larger websites, which made their identification rather challenging.

This reference book provides resources to help educators, professionals, parents, siblings, guardians, as well as students, understand, and therefore be well informed regarding various disabilities and disorders faced by children today.

METHODOLOGY

Identification of the resources selected for this publication was based on a comprehensive literature survey. Materials were evaluated based on positive reviews in standard selection tools such as *Booklist, Children's Literature, Doody's Review, Kirkus Reviews, KLIATT, Library Journal, Publishers Weekly, School Library Journal, Signpost,* and *VOYA (Voices of Youth Advocates)* and the availability of the materials. In the case of media resources, due to their limited availability, descriptive media summarizations from print material and websites were used. Most of the resources included in this bibliography were published primarily from 2000 to the present. However, in some circumstances, due to the lack of current titles, certain resources were included that were published prior to 2000. The authors felt it was important to include these older, yet valuable, entries, particularly in the area of physical disabilities.

The following resources were used for identifying books, media, and journals/magazines for this bibliography: *A to Zoo: Subject Access to Children's Picture Books* (7th edition, 2006); *Best Books for Children: Preschool through Grade 6* (8th edition, 2006); *Best Books for Middle School and Junior High Readers: Grades 6–9* (2004); *Best Books for Middle School and Junior High Readers: Grades 6–9. Supplement to the First Edition* (2006); *Best Books for High School Readers: Grades 9–12* (2004); *Best Books for High School Readers: Grades 9–12. Supplement to the First Edition* (2006); Books in Print (online), Films for the Humanities & Sciences, OhioLINK (the consortium of academic libraries in Ohio), Public Broadcasting Service (PBS), Ulrich's Periodicals Directory (online), WorldCat, and a variety of online bibliographies.

Balancing the entries with respect to the grade level was taken into account. Due to the lack of resources in some subject areas, relevant to grade level, there was a disparity of entries.

NOTES

1. Matthew Brault, "Disability Status and the Characteristics of People in Group Quarters: A Brief Analysis of Disability Prevalence among the Civilian Noninstitutionalized and Total Populations in the American Community Survey, February 2008," U.S. Census Bureau, http://www.census.gov/hhes/www/disability/GQdisability.pdf.

2. Coleen A. Boyle and José F. Cordero, "Birth Defects and Disabilities: A Public Health Issue for the 21st Century," *American Journal of Publish Health* 95, no. 11 (November 2005): 1884–1886.

3. Marshalyn Yeargin-Allsopp, Carolyn Drews-Botsch, and Kim Van Naarden Braun, "Epidemiology of Developmental Disabilities," in *Children with Disabilities*, 6th edition, ed. Mark L. Batshaw, Louis Pellegrino, and Nancy J. Roizen, 231–243 (Baltimore: Paul Brookes Publishing, 2007).

4. U.S. Office of the Surgeon General, "Mental Health: A Report from the Surgeon General, Chapter 2: Epidemiology of Mental Illness," http://www.surgeongeneral.gov/library/mentalhealth/chapter2/sec2_1.html.

Scope and Arrangement of Material

This publication is aimed primarily at students, educators, librarians, parents, school media specialists, and other professionals who are interested in identifying helpful resources regarding disabilities and disorders. The publication covers resources for students from K–12 grade levels. In addition, this guide also includes resources for educators, parents, and other professionals. At the time of this writing, the literature review revealed that there was no existence of a reference guide in English that included all of the following: Internet sites; journals and magazines; media; resources for the specific grade levels, K–12; resources for educators, professionals and parents; general reference resources; and identification of award-winning titles. This selective bibliography consists of four major headings: Emotional, Learning, Physical, and Multiple Disabilities. Each of the subsections under these headings is further categorized into fiction and nonfiction.

Complete annotated entries provide information in the following sequence:

Chapter 1: Emotional
        Depression
          Fiction
          Nonfiction
        Depression-Related Disorders
          Fiction
          Nonfiction
        Eating Disorders
          Fiction
          Nonfiction
        Mental Illness
          Fiction
          Nonfiction

Physical
Blindness and Visual Impairments
Deafness and Hearing Impairments
Mobility Impairments
Multiple Physical Disabilities

ENTRIES

Annotations provide a complete bibliographical description, including author's name, title, place of publication, publisher, year, pagination, ISBN, and illustrator, if applicable. Series and awards are identified at the end of the entries. The grade levels for each entry are indicated as best suited (e.g., K–2, 4–6, 9–12). In addition, resources are identified for appropriate levels, such as Teens/Educators/Parents, Educators/Professionals, Parents, and Educators/Parents. Positive reviews from standard selection tools, such as *School Library Journal*, are included when available.

Media resources, in addition to the above bibliographic description and levels, include format (i.e., VHS or DVD), running time, and closed-captioning feature.

Internet resources are categorized similar to the print resources, and include URLs. Journals/Magazines provide URLs and ISSNs, when available.

APPENDICES

There are two appendices. Appendix A includes awards and distinctions given for books and media. Appendix B includes a calendar of observances related to various disabilities and disorders.

INDICES

The indices include an author index, an illustrator/photographer index, a title index, a series index, a book and media award index, a grade/level index, and a subject index.

Chapter 1

Emotional

This chapter provides 159 fiction and nonfiction resources regarding emotional disorders and disabilities. Sixty-three of the resources are explicitly for the high school grade level; seventy-seven are for the middle school grade level, sixteen are for the elementary grade level, and three entries are for teens/educators/parents. The chapter is subdivided into the following five headings: Depression, Depression-Related Disorders, Eating Disorders, Mental Illness, and Multiple Emotional Disabilities.

DEPRESSION

Fiction

1. *Breaking Trail.* Bell, Joanne. Toronto, Ontario: Broundwood Books, 2005. 135 pp. ISBN: 0888996306. Grades 5–7.

Young Becky's teenage world is changing due to her father's deep depression. Since her father is no longer the family leader, Becky tries to keep herself and the family going as she relies on all the good, strong memories of her father in better times. As the family sets off for their annual vacation at their Yukon Territory cabin, Becky learns to be resourceful for herself and her family. "Their dependence on and loyalty to the sled dogs also makes this an appealing story for animal lovers." *School Library Journal*

2. *Emo Boy: Vol. 1, Nobody Cares about Anything Anyway, So Why Don't We All Just Die?* Edmond, Steve. San Jose, CA: SLG Publishing, 2006. [170] pp. ISBN: 9781593620530. Grades 10–12.

Emo Boy is a graphic novel about a teenage boy and all the dark, depressing fears of being a teenager. Emo Boy lives with a high school classmate, Maxine, and her mother for most of his life. The black and white graphics add to the dark and hopeless atmosphere of the text. Poor Emo Boy has no family, is unpopular, and unloved. Not only does he need to deal with things, such as pondering suicide and questioning his sexual identity, but he also has emo super powers that only seem to bring destruction and disaster, causing everyone to hate him more than they already do. Due to the contents, such as his first love suffering a head explosion, the football team wanting him dead, and getting an F in English, this story should be appropriate for mature readers.

3. *Letters from Rapunzel.* Holmes, Sara Lewis. New York: HarperCollins Publishers, 2007. 184 pp. ISBN: 0060780738; ISBN2: 9780060780739. Grades 7–9.

Cadence's father is a creative writing and poetry professor. At 12 years old, she is trying to understand her father's hospitalization due to the "The Evil Spell"—her name for clinical depression. She uses her exceptional writing talent to compose this first-person narrative in letters to an unknown person at P.O. Box 5667 who just might have the answer to her father's situation. Agitated by her schoolteachers' demands, her mother who is too busy as a nurse to talk to her, and the continued nonresponse from Box 5667, Cadence slowly finds the inner strength and knowledge to find some resolution. This easy-to-read story with a very likable character will certainly help other readers who find themselves in situations they can neither control nor understand. "The novel could be therapeutic for those children who must deal with the far-reaching effects of a parent's illness while experiencing the universal angst of adolescence." *School Library Journal*

4. *Remote Man.* Honey, Elizabeth. New York: Alfred A. Knopf, 2002. 260 pp. ISBN: 0375814132. Grades 6–10.

Ned, a 13-year-old, has his world turned upside down when his mother falls into a deep depression. To combat the depression, Ned's mother decides that they should move to America and stay with a colleague's mother. Ned is able to maintain his old friends and meet new ones by using the Internet. With the help of his new American friend, Ned discovers the antics and dangers of an international smuggling gang. "The characters are lovingly portrayed in this most enjoyable read." *School Library Journal*

5. *Damage.* Jenkins, A. M. (Amanda McRaney). New York: HarperCollins, 2001. 186 pp. ISBN: 0060291001. Grades 10–12.

Austin Reid, a high school senior, football star, popular with both the guys and the girls, is experiencing depression, serious enough that he contemplates suicide.

His relationship with his new girlfriend, Heather, has its ups and downs. Jenkins portrays the treatment of depression and its resolution realistically—there are no magic wands that can make his problems go away. As the story ends, Austin is still concerned about his depression. "A brave, truthful, stylistically stunning young adult novel." *School Library Journal*

6. *Saving Francesca.* Marchetta, Melina. New York: Alfred A. Knopf: Distributed by Random House, 2004. 243 pp. ISBN: 0375829822. Grades 9–12.

Francesca, a 16-year-old known as Frankie, begins the new school year as one of the few girls in a predominantly all-boys school. She needs the love and support of her mother now more than ever. However, her mother, once the center and heart of the family, has fallen into a crippling depression. Frankie finds her inner strength not only for herself but also for her younger brother. This is a very realistic portrayal of the challenges faced by all teenagers in school. "[T]he book also has great characterizations, witty dialogue, a terrific relationship between Francesca and her younger brother, and a sweet romance. Teens will relate to this tender novel and will take to heart its solid messages and realistic treatment of a very real problem. " *School Library Journal*

7. *Under the Wolf, Under the Dog.* Rapp, Adam. Cambridge, MA: Candlewick Press, 2004. 310 pp. ISBN: 0763618187. Grades 10–12.

Sixteen years old and living at a facility for problem teenagers, Steve Nugent experiences life's lowest lows and loses on every level. His father's depression, his mother's recent death due to breast cancer, and the discovery of his older brother's death by suicide bring about Steve's depression. While in this facility, Steve's friendship with several of the other teenagers provides Steve with some hope for his future. "Rapp offers teens well-constructed peepholes into harsh circumstances, with a bit of hope tinting the view." *School Library Journal* 2006 Schneider Family Book Award in the Teen category.

8. *The Black Box: A Novel.* Schumacher, Julia. New York: Delacorte Press, 2008. 168 pp. ISBN: 0385735421; ISBN: 9780385735421. Grades 7–12.

Lena's 16-year-old sister Dora is diagnosed with chronic depression and has to be hospitalized. Fourteen-year-old Lena assumes the responsibility of taking care of Dora because her parents, who constantly argue, are in denial and are having a difficult time in coping with Dora's disorder. Lena, who is caught between helping her sister and maintaining the family secret regarding the depression, finds support from her friend, Jimmy. Eventually Lena realizes that Dora has to help herself. The author explores various treatment options for depression, the impact that depression has on the family, and the cultural stigma of hospitalization. "The writing is spare, direct, and honest. Written in the first person, this is a readable, ultimately uplifting book about a difficult subject." *School Library Journal*

9. *It's Kind of a Funny Story.* Vizzini, Ned. New York: Miramax Books/Hyperion Books for Children, 2006. 444 pp. ISBN: 0786851961. Grades 9–12.

Craig Gilner is a depressed 15-year-old who, despite therapy sessions, medication, and supportive parents, checks himself into a hospital one evening after contemplating suicide. Once admitted in the hospital, Craig begins to understand his mental state and all the stress with which he has been dealing, such as the feelings for his friends and coping at the prestigious private school he has been attending. The fact that the author himself spent time in a psychiatric hospital makes the reader feel that the scenes and other individuals in the hospital, drawn from actual experience, make them more credible and realistic. "This book offers hope in a package that readers will find enticing, and that's the gift it offers." *Booklist*

10. *The Opposite of Music.* Young, Janet Ruth. New York: Atheneum Books for Young Readers, 2007. 346 pp. ISBN: 1416900403; ISBN2: 9781416900405. Grades 9–12.

Billy's father has been diagnosed with clinical depression. His mother is not satisfied with the doctor's treatment, so she decides that she and 15-year-old Billy can effectively treat him at home. After only a few months, Billy and his mother realize that professional medical attention is needed. Readers who experience the challenges of being caretakers of their parents should be able to identify with the characters in this story. "Attention to medical detail and advocacy for counseling will definitely put this title on bibliotherapy lists." *School Library Journal*

Nonfiction

11. *Why Are You So Sad? A Child's Book about Parental Depression.* Andrews, Beth; illustrated by Nicole Wong. Washington, DC: Magination Press, 2002. 32 pp. ISBN: 1557988366. Grades 1–4.

This is an excellent resource for young children of parents who are experiencing varying types of depression. The author has written this interactive text in order to engage the reader with the many self-help options. The introductory chapter provides good definitions for the various types of depression. The rest of the chapters discuss steps that can be taken by children facing specific challenges of having a depressed parent, such as how a parent may act or what the parent may say and what the parent needs to do to get better. Children should benefit from the suggestions listed in the chapter that addresses what they can do for themselves. The author's twofold message for children attempts to help them during this challenging time. The first message is that depression is an illness not caused by the child, and second, the parent still loves the child.

12. *Coping with Depression and Other Mood Disorders.* Gelman, Amy. Series: Coping. New York: Rosen Publishing Group, 1999. 106 pp. ISBN: 0823929736. Grades 7–9.

This volume, one of the titles in the Coping series, addresses the various issues and concerns associated with individuals who suffer from clinical depression. The author uses realistic scenarios to illustrate the key concepts in each chapter. The chapters "Physical Causes of Depression" and "Emotional Causes and Risk Factors" provide insightful information. Since most teenagers experience mood swings during their teenage years, the information in this book is greatly appreciated. A glossary, additional reading material, and an index are included.

13. *The Truth about Fear and Depression.* Kittleson, Mark J. Series: Facts on File, The Truth About. New York: Facts on File, 2005. 164 pp. ISBN: 0816053014; ISBN13: 9780816053018. Grades 9–12.

The introductory chapter of this volume of the Facts on File, The Truth About series, provides a good overview of mental health and mental disorders, particularly the symptoms and effects of fear, anxiety, and depression in teenagers. The A–Z guide follows and contains twenty-two entries such as anxiety disorders, causes and symptoms of depression, posttraumatic stress disorder, rehabilitation, and treatment of anxiety disorders and depression. Reading lists are scattered throughout the book. An extensive glossary, hotlines, help websites, and an index are included.

14. *Taking Depression to School.* Korb-Khalsa, Kathy L. Series: Special Kids in School. Plainview, NY: JayJo Books, 2002. [27] pp. ISBN: 1891383221. Grades 1–3.

Emily tells her story about her sad, upset, and scary feelings in an honest, first-person narrative in this volume of the Special Kids in School series. After visiting a psychiatrist and a therapist, Emily learns that she has childhood depression. She learns what she needs to do in order to handle her depression. "Depression Kids' Quiz!" and "Ten Tips for Teachers" are excellent sections for younger readers and for teachers. A list of additional reading material and organizations is included. Color illustrations complement the text.

15. *Teen Depression.* Martin, Michael. Series: Diseases and Disorders. Detroit: Thomson/Gale, 2005. 96 pp. ISBN: 1590185021; ISBN2: 9781590185025. Grades 9–12.

In this title, part of the Diseases and Disorders series, the author provides clear explanation of the causes, symptoms, diagnoses, and treatment of teen depression. New ideas including techniques and medication for treatment and prevention of teen depression are presented as well. Black and white illustrations, annotated bibliographies, detailed indexes, and lists of organizations to contact for additional information are included. "[P]rovide[s] the kind of information that a student may need either for an assigned research project or for personal enlightenment and assistance. Highly recommended." *Library Media Connection*

16. *Youth with Depression and Anxiety: Moods that Overwhelm.* McIntosh, Kenneth and Phyllis Livingston. Series: Helping Youth with Mental, Physical, and Social Challenges. Philadelphia, PA: Mason Crest Publishers, 2008. 128 pp. ISBN: 1422201422; ISBN2: 9781422201428. Grades 8–12.

Part of the series titled Helping Youth with Mental, Physical, and Social Challenges, this book describes the story about Ashley who finds it very difficult to cope with life due to bleak moods and extreme anxiety that she goes through. Her best friend's death, which is suspected as a suicide, makes Ashley wonder if suicide is the only way that she too can find freedom from her problems. Information regarding treatment of depression is provided. A glossary, a list of books for additional information, including websites, a bibliography, color photographs, and an index are included.

17. *Living with Depression.* Miller, Allen R. Series: Teen's Guides. New York: Facts on File, 2008. 202 pp. ISBN: 0816063451; ISBN2: 9780816063451. Grades 9–12.

This title in the series Teen's Guides provides information for teens regarding depression, which affects one in eight teens. Written by a licensed psychologist, the following topics are examined: defining depression; bipolar disorder and the blues; getting a diagnosis and treatment options; psychotherapy and antidepressants; helping yourself or friends; paying for care; and looking toward the future. Case studies are used for illustrating and understanding depression. One of the chapters is most beneficial in discussing how depression leads to other issues, such as anxiety/panic attacks, eating disorders, posttraumatic stress disorder (PTSD), self-abuse (cutting), and bullying. Two appendices are included: Appendix 1 contains an extensive list of associations and resources related to depression; Appendix 2 contains a list of drug company patient-assisted programs. A glossary, additional reading materials, and an index are included. "[T]he text is appealing, well-organized, and accessible for the teen reader." *VOYA*

18. *Depression.* Moragne, Wendy. Series: Twenty-First Century Medical Library. Brookfield, CT: Twenty-First Century Books, 2001. 112 pp. ISBN: 0761317740. Grades 7–10.

This title in the Twenty-First Century Medical Library series uses the stories of seven teenagers to illustrate the multifaceted nature of depression. Each chapter begins with a detailed account of one of the teenagers and addresses the following concerns: "What Is Depression?"; "Signs and Symptoms"; "Diagnosis and Treatment"; "Suicide and Its Prevention"; "Family, Friends, and School"; "The Power of Self-Esteem." An in-depth glossary, additional resources, including a list of organizations, and an index are included.

19. *Depression.* Peacock, Judith. Series: Perspectives on Mental Health. Mankato, MN: LifeMatters, 2000. 64 pp. ISBN: 0736804358. Grades 4–8.

This title in the Perspectives on Mental Health series provides a good overview of depression for middle school readers. Each chapter begins with a chapter overview. Brief case studies are used to illustrate key concepts. The text is straightforward and understandable. Chapter topics include the following: defining various types of depression, getting help, and how depression is diagnosed and treated. The last chapter, "Staying Well," has excellent suggestions for helping the reader who may be experiencing depression or who knows someone suffering from depression. Color photographs, text boxes containing basic information and case studies, a glossary, additional reading material, websites, and an index are included.

20. *When Life Stinks: How to Deal with Your Bad Moods, Blues, and Depression.* Piquemal, Michel with Melissa Daly; illustrated by Olivier Tossan. New York: Amulet Books, 2004. 112 pp. ISBN: 0810949326. Grades 6–10.

This invaluable book should help young readers understand their personal feelings, particularly negative moods. In covering a wide range of adolescent feelings, the authors discuss the following topics: leaving childhood, adolescent blues, and dealing with parents and teachers. Poems written by teenagers that reflect their feelings and how they handle challenging situations often experienced during the teenage years are sprinkled throughout the chapters. A straightforward and nonthreatening discussion of depression makes this a helpful resource for this age level. Color illustrations, additional reading material, support groups, websites, hotlines, and an index are included. "This reassuring book will help readers to distinguish between age-appropriate feelings and more serious mood disturbances." *School Library Journal*

21. *Depression.* Roy, Jennifer Rozines. Series: Health Alert. New York: Benchmark Books, 2005. 64 pp. ISBN: 0761418008. Grades 4–7.

This title in the Health Alert series provides a very good introduction on the subject of depression for middle school students. The introductory chapter provides information in order to understand depression. "The History of Depression" is an excellent chapter that traces depression throughout Western civilization and highlights famous individuals who have had depression. The chapter "Living with Depression" covers treatment options and suggestions for coping with depression and reaching out for support. Color photographs, graphics, text boxes, a glossary, additional reading material, organizations, hotlines, websites, and an index are included. This book is a good resource that demystifies depression.

22. *Depression.* Willis, Laurie. Series: Social Issues First Hand. Detroit: Greenhaven Press, 2008. 147 pp. ISBN: 0737738367; ISBN: 9780737738360. Grades 10–12.

This title in the Social Issues First Hand series provides useful information regarding depression, which is one of the most common mental illnesses affecting 20 million Americans each year. The four chapters cover the following topics: depression; living with depression; getting help; and how depression affects others. The personal narratives cover individuals within a wide range of ages, professions, and situations to illustrate depression-related issues. The last section details treatment options including medication, hospitalization, and electroconvulsive therapy. A list of organizations, including annotations, additional resources, and an index, are included.

23. *Teens, Depression, and the Blues: A Hot Issue.* Winkler, Kathleen. Series: Hot Issues. Berkeley Heights, NJ: Enslow Publishers, 2000. 64 pp. ISBN: 0766013693. Grades 5–8.

The introductory chapter in this book, one of the titles in the Hot Issues series, tells the stories of Kelly and Annie who have clinical depression. This mental condition affects about a million and half individuals each year. Using their stories and scenarios taken from their lives, the author explores, explains, and illustrates the causes of depression and the various types of depression, including clinical depression. The chapter on suicide provides information that is most beneficial for this age group. The concluding chapters provide suggestions for treatment options and for helping friends who have been experiencing depression. Color photographs, a glossary, support organizations, additional reading material, and an index are included.

24. *Depression.* Zucker, Faye. Series: Life Balance. New York: F. Watts, 2003. 80 pp. ISBN: 053112259X. Grades 4–7.

This title in the Life Balance series provides thorough coverage on the topic of depression. Chapter topics include signs and symptoms of depression, treatment options and living with depression, as well as severe depression and suicide. The author includes several helpful features such as a table that lists many myths and facts about the various types of depression, a listing of literature titles that feature characters who are depressed, and suggestions for finding the right psychotherapist. An extensive glossary, a list of additional resources, websites, organizations, and an index are included.

DEPRESSION-RELATED DISORDERS

Fiction

25. *Things Hoped For.* Clements, Andrew. New York: Philomel Books, 2006. 167 pp. ISBN: 039924350X. Grades 10–12.

A gifted 17-year-old violinist, Gwen, has moved from her family's home in West Virginia to live with her grandfather in Manhattan so that she can study music at a prestigious music school. As Gwen prepares for the all-important auditions, her already stressful situation worsens because her grandfather mysteriously disappears. With the help and friendship of a fellow music student, Gwen discovers her own inner strength and determination. "This offers a riveting story line, engaging characters, and intriguing insights into the development of musical artistry." *Booklist*

26. *Mr. Worry.* Hargreaves, Roger. Series: Mr. Men and Little Miss. Manchester, UK: World International, 1990. [31] pp. ISBN: 0749800119. Grades K–3.

This is one of the titles in the classic series Mr. Men and Little Miss in which Mr. Worry does nothing but worry. He worries about himself and everything he does and he worries about all his friends and the things that they do. One day Mr. Worry meets a Wizard who helps him get rid of all Mr. Worry's worries. Mr. Worry is happy, but only for a short time until he starts worrying about having nothing to worry about. This color illustrated reading book should spark discussion among younger readers.

27. *Hunger Moon.* Lamstein, Sarah. Asheville, NC: Front Street Books, 2004. 109 pp. ISBN: 1932425055. Grades 4–8.

This is an excellent glimpse into the dysfunctional family of 12-year-old Ruth during the early 1950s. Her parents, owners of a not-so-profitable business, are distant and angry because of the mental and physical limitations of one of Ruth's younger brothers, Eddy. Ruth's two other brothers are too young to understand their mother's frustration and often semiviolent screaming and physical actions. Their father's passive and nonemotional dynamics with the children and, at times, explosive behavior contribute to the hardships faced by the children.

In the beginning of the story, Ruth is angry because Eddy's behavior demands the entire family's attention. This affects her behavior in school and toward the family as a whole. Ruth becomes Eddy's champion toward the end of the story when she realizes that she may be the only person in the family who can bring about a change for the good.

28. *Buried.* MacCready, Robin Merrow. New York: Speak, 2008. 198 pp. ISBN: 0142411418; ISBN: 9780142411414. Grades 11–12.

Seventeen-year-old Claudine has spent her life coping with her alcoholic mother. Claudine receives support from her friends at the Teens of Alcoholics group, but now, even those friends cannot help her. One morning Claudine discovers that their trailer has been trashed and her mother is gone. Claudine tells everyone, including one of her mother's boyfriends and her mother's boss, that her mother has entered a rehabilitation facility. Claudine has developed a mental disorder due to her mother's irresponsible behavior. "Well-done and recommended for both reluctant and serious young readers." *Kirkus Reviews*

29. *Let Me Bee.* Oelschlager, Vanita; illustrated by Kristin Blackwood. Akron, OH: Vanita Books, 2008. [40] pp. ISBN: 9780980016215. Grades PreK–3.

In this excellent story about being afraid, a young boy is always worried about being stung by a bee. One young bee is afraid of the young boy because of the boy's larger size. This story reveals that both the young boy and the bee need to learn about each other in order to understand that their fears are unnecessary. Young readers should enjoy the two pages of jokes related to bees. The creative three-dimensional illustrations are exceptional and complement the text, which is told in verse.

30. *The Next-Door Dogs.* Rodowsky, Colby F.; illustrated by Amy June Bates. New York: Farrar Straus and Giroux, 2005. 103 pp. ISBN: 0374364109. Grades 1–4.

Sara is 9 years old and terrified of dogs. She does not know what to do when her new neighbor moves in next door with two large dogs. Sara wants to be friends with her neighbor but cannot overcome her fear of dogs. One day when the neighbor has an accident, Sara is forced to face her fear of dogs in order to help her neighbor. This easy-to-read story should help younger readers understand their fears and how to resolve them. "Any children with fears of their own will relate to Sara and root for her in this difficult situation. Transitional readers will enjoy this tight, compact story with a fully realized protagonist and a subtle message." *School Library Journal*

Nonfiction

31. *Drug Therapy and Anxiety Disorders.* Brinkerhoff, Shirley. Series: Psychiatric Disorders: Drugs and Psychology for the Mind and Body. Philadelphia,
PA: Mason Crest Publishers, 2008. 128 pp. ISBN: 1422203859; ISBN:
9781422203859. Grades 10–12.

This title in the Psychiatric Disorders: Drugs and Psychology for the Mind
and Body series provides thorough coverage of how drug therapy can help those
individuals who suffer from anxiety disorders. The following topics are discussed
in seven chapters: identifying those who suffer from anxiety disorders, defining
anxiety disorders, the history of psychiatric drugs, treatment options, how drugs
work, risks and side effects, including alternative treatments. Case studies and
in-depth explanations of the various anxiety disorders provide substantial information. Color photographs, illustrations, text boxes, additional reading material,
and an index are included.

32. *What to Do When You're Scared & Worried: A Guide for Kids.* Crist, James
J. Minneapolis: Free Spirit Publishing, 2004. 122 pp. ISBN: 1575421534.
Grades 5–8.

Psychologist James Crist uses his own experience from years of counseling
both children and adults to compile this easy-to-read, self-help guide for younger
teenagers in order to help them deal with fears and worries. The content of this
comprehensive work is divided into two parts. The chapters in the first part focus on questions that children have about everyday concerns and fears, such as
identifying fear and coping with their feelings. The chapters in the second part
address the more serious anxieties, such as handling separation and panic attacks.
Crist also includes advice for coping with obsessive-compulsive behavior and
posttraumatic stress disorders. A section for parents, additional resources, support organizations, and an index are included. "This title will empower children
and help them to understand, confront, and master troubling emotions." *School
Library Journal*

33. *Balancing Act: A Teen's Guide to Managing Stress.* Esherick, Joan. Series:
The Science of Health: Youth and Well-Being. Philadelphia, PA: Mason
Crest Publishers, 2005. 128 pp. ISBN: 1590848535. Grades 8–10.

This volume, one of the titles in the Science of Health: Youth and Well-Being
series, focuses on how teens can manage situations that produce stress. Chapters
include "Stressed to the Max," "The Causes of Stress," "How Stress Affects
Your Body, Mind, and Emotions," and "How Stress Affects Your Relationships."

There are two very helpful chapters about how teens can handle stress. This very readable text contains reflections from teens about their stressful situations. Color text boxes, graphics, photographs, an extensive list of organizations and websites, additional resources, a glossary, and an index are included.

34. *Stress Management.* Gregson, Susan R. Series: Perspectives on Mental Health. Mankato, MN: LifeMatters, 2000. 64 pp. ISBN: 0736804323. Grades 4–8.

This title in the Perspectives on Mental Health series provides a good introduction to the concept of stress for young readers. The straightforward text is divided into six manageable chapters and includes the topics: the various types of stress, the causes of stress, activities that will reduce stress, and suggestions that can help individuals manage the stress in their lives. In the last chapter, the author presents the story of a teenager that illustrates how she deals with stressful events and people at home and at school. Color photographs, text boxes that contain basic information and case studies, a glossary, additional resources, websites, and an index are included.

35. *What to Do When You Worry too Much: A Kid's Guide to Overcoming Anxiety.* Huebner, Dawn; illustrated by Bonnie Matthews. Series: What-to-Do-Guides for Kids. Washington, DC: Magination Press, 2006. 80 pp. ISBN: 1591473144; ISBN13: 9781591473145. Grades 3–6.

Huebner, a clinical psychologist, has written this guide as part of the What to Do series. This excellent resource for younger readers provides suggestions and advice for coping with daily situations, involving family, friends, and school, that cause anxiety. Introductory chapters pose the questions: "Are You Growing Worries?" "What Is a Worry?" and "How Do Worries Get Started?" Additional topics include how to make worries go away, spending less time on worries, and keeping worries away. Each chapter contains activities that children can do, such as list the people you know who worry a lot, write down one of your worries, and draw what your worry bully looks like. Black and white illustrations, graphics, and instructions for parents and caregivers are included.

36. *What to Do When Your Temper Flares: A Kid's Guide to Overcoming Problems with Anger.* Huebner, Dawn; illustrated by Bonnie Matthews. Series: What-to-Do-Guides for Kids. Washington, DC: Magination Press, 2008. 95 pp. ISBN: 1433801345; ISBN: 9781433801341. Grades 3–6.

This workbook, written by a clinical psychologist, provides cognitive behavioral techniques that help children resolve anger issues. An introductory section for parents and caregivers explains the techniques that should help children understand and gain control over their thoughts, while learning how to deal with anger. Topics include secrets about anger, recognizing situations that trigger anger, and anger-dousing methods. Fun exercises are provided throughout the guide. Black and white illustrations are included.

37. *Anxiety Disorders.* Hyman, Bruce M. and Cherry Pedrick. Series: Twenty-First Century Medical Library. Minneapolis: Twenty-First Century Books, 2006. 96 pp. ISBN: 0761328270; ISBN: 9780761328278. Grades 7–10.

This title in the Twenty-First Century Medical Library series uses firsthand stories of eight teenagers to illustrate the various types of anxiety disorders. The chapters include the following topics: panic and fear; rituals, trauma, and worry; treatment options; stress management; and beating an anxiety disorder. Each chapter begins with a detailed account of one of the teenagers who has one of the disorders, followed by definitions, causes, medications, and behavior therapy pertaining to the particular disorder. The final chapter presents brief updates of each teenager. A glossary and additional resources, including organizations, websites, online chat sites, a list of further reading materials, a bibliography, and an index, are included. "This excellent book provides a first step in recognizing behaviors in ourselves and others and in encouraging professional help for those who need it." *Children's Literature*

38. *Obsessive-Compulsive Disorder.* Hyman, Bruce M. and Cherry Pedrick. Series: Twenty-First Century Medical Library. Minneapolis: Twenty-First Century Books, 2009. 95 pp. ISBN: 0822585790; ISBN: 9780822585794. Grades 7–10.

This title in the Twenty-First Century Medical Library series provides an overview of obsessive-compulsive disorder (OCD), which can develop in childhood, adolescence, or young adulthood, and affects approximately 2.5 percent of the population. The introduction provides brief scenarios of nine teenagers who have OCD, such as difficulty in taking tests, intense anxiety and self-consciousness about appearance, excessive hand-washing, rigid behavior, excessive collecting of things, and keeping areas organized. The first four chapters explore the following topics regarding OCD: defining OCD, the symptoms of OCD, treatment options, and the impact on family and friends. The last chapter, "Living with OCD," provides an update of the teenagers who are mentioned throughout the book. Black and white illustrations and photographs, a glossary, and additional resources, including mental health organizations and websites, further reading lists, and an index, are included.

39. *Coping with Anxiety and Panic Attacks.* Lee, Jordan. Series: Coping. New York: Rosen Publishing, 2000. 106 pp. ISBN: 0823932028. Grades 7–9.

This second edition of one of the titles in the Coping series is divided into four chapters: "The Six Types of Anxiety Disorders," "What Causes These Disorders?" "Managing Everyday Anxiety," "Treating Anxiety Disorders." The author includes scenarios to illustrate key points throughout this readable and nonthreatening text. A glossary, contact information for support groups, additional reading material, and an index are included. "This book is readable and well organized; its clear style, realistic examples, and practical advice guarantee its usefulness for both self-help and reports." *School Library Journal*

40. *Stress and Depression.* Lennard-Brown, Sarah. Series: Health Issues. Austin, TX: Raintree Steck-Vaughn, 2001. 64 pp. ISBN: 0739844199; ISBN: 9780739844199. Grades 8–10.

Written specifically for young adults, this title, part of the Health Issues series, explores the link between stress and change, which could be physical, psychological, spiritual, or social. The introductory chapter explains what happens when an individual is stressed and suffers from depression. Symptoms and causes of depression are discussed. A practical way to cope with depression, including information about medication and counseling, are presented as well. There is also a discussion of type A and type B personalities. Almost every page features color photographs and text boxes related to various issues discussed. Additional resources, including films and cartoons, a glossary, and an index, are included. "This book could be very helpful for individuals having difficulty with stress, especially in this uncertain time." *Parent Council Reviews*

41. *The Feelings Book: The Care & Keeping of Your Emotions.* Madison, Lynda; illustrated by Norm Bendell. Series: American Girl Library. Middleton, WI: Pleasant Company, 2002. 104 pp. ISBN: 1584855282. Grades 5–9.

A wide range of emotions that teenage girls experience is explored in this title from the American Girl Library series. This resource provides comprehensive coverage of issues and concerns that girls encounter during their teenage years, which is usually the most difficult time in their lives. Emotions range from being anxious to feeling unsafe. Young girls should benefit greatly from the section "How a Girl's Body Reacts to the Messages Received by the Brain," which includes topics such as, why do you cry, feeling out of control, and what can you do. An additional important section titled "Help" provides useful and practical resolutions for being scared, anxious, sad, and grief-ridden. The author places interactive quizzes throughout the book followed by helpful answers. The abundant color illustrations depict a variety of girls from various ethnic backgrounds. "Filled with good, reliable advice for readers dealing with the new surge of emotions, it will be a positive addition to adolescent-psychology shelves." *School Library Journal*

42. *Stress Relief: The Ultimate Teen Guide.* Powell, Mark; illustrated by Kelly Adams. Series: It Happened to Me. Lanham, MD: Scarecrow Press, 2007. 99 pp. ISBN: 0810858061; ISBN2: 9780810858060. Grades 9–12.

This title in the It Happened to Me series is an excellent updated resource for today's teenager. The text is written in readable, nonthreatening language. The first section explores various types of stress. The second section explains why people have stress. The third section gives numerous suggestions regarding coping with stress associated with everyday situations. Black and white photographs, graphics, text boxes, extensive additional resources and reading material, websites, and index are included.

43. *Feeling Better: A Kid's Book about Therapy.* Rashkin, Rachel. Washington, DC: Magination Press, 2005. 48 pp. ISBN: 1591472377. Grades 4–7.

Told in a journal format, 12-year-old Maya explains her ups and downs, both at school and with her friends. After discussing the idea of therapy with her, Maya's parents decide that she would benefit from visiting a therapist. Reluctant at first, Maya gradually understands the important and healing role of visiting a therapist. This very positive representation of the benefits of therapy should calm any fears or apprehension young teenagers may have. Upbeat black and white drawings throughout the book illustrate the various stages that Maya undergoes during therapy. "Clearly written and well-organized, this realistic book uses the device of a journal to elucidate the therapy process. This title gently encourages kids who are struggling with issues to seek help." *School Library Journal*

44. *Coping with Post-Traumatic Stress Disorder.* Simpson, Carolyn and Dwain Simpson. Series: Coping. New York: Rosen Publishing Group, 1997. 129 pp. ISBN: 0823920801. Grades 7–9.

This volume, one of the titles in the Coping series, is most useful today, particularly in light of such tragic events as 9/11. The first part of this book addresses the numerous situations and causes of posttraumatic stress disorder (PTSD), such as natural disasters, rape, sexual and physical trauma, wars, and captivity. The second part addresses how to secure treatment for PTSD. Other topics covered are the negative and positive ways of coping with PTSD, how to build a support system, how to choose the right therapist, as well as accepting the need for hospitalization, and getting on with one's life. The epilogue contains suggestions and guidelines for the reader who might know someone who has suffered from PTSD. A glossary, additional reading material, and an index are included. This is a highly recommended title.

45. *Coping with Your Emotions: A Guide to Taking Control of Your Life.* Tym, Kate and Penny Worms. Chicago: Raintree, 2005. 48 pp. ISBN: 1410905756. Grades 7–9.

Adolescents experience a wide range of emotions such as depression, fear, shyness, jealousy, envy, and love. This book provides a good explanation of various emotions and offers helpful tips for dealing with each of them. Case studies are included for study and possible discussion starters. A personality quiz is provided for the reader to discover how to handle some emotionally charged scenarios. A glossary, an index, and "The-Get-Real-Advice-Directory," which provides further reading and help lines, are included. Very colorful layout and color photographs on every page hold the reader's interest.

EATING DISORDERS

Fiction

46. *Mercy, Unbound.* Antieau, Kim. New York: Simon Pulse, 2006. 165 pp. ISBN: 1416908935; ISBN2: 9781416908937. Grades 9–12.

Mercy is 15 years old and seems to be well adjusted. However, she is convinced that she is an angel who does not need to eat. Her father, a university professor, and her mother, an environmental attorney, are supportive, but remain ineffective in helping Mercy address and overcome her anorexia. Mercy tries to understand the major concerns in her life such as her parents' diverse views on religion and the challenges that come from her mother's Jewish family, including grandparents who survived the Holocaust. "[M]any readers will want this for the family story and for the teen talk, which is fast, frank, and irreverent." *School Library Journal*

47. *Massive.* Bell, Julia. New York: Simon Pulse, 2002. 261 pp. ISBN: 1416902074; ISBN2: 9781416902072. Grades 9–12.

Carmen is 14 years old and does not know what to do when her mother leaves her stepfather, the only father Carmen has ever known. Carmen and her mother move to her mother's hometown where her grandparents and the estranged sister of her mother still live. Not only is Carmen challenged in her new school, but her mother's anorexia and obsession with Carmen's weight is spiraling out of control. "Bell does a masterful job of describing what anorexia looks like from the outside." *Booklist*

48. *Life in the Fat Lane.* Bennett, Cherie. New York: Delacorte Press, 1998. 260 pp. ISBN: 0786228873. Grades 9–12.

Lara, a 16-year-old and one of the prettiest and most popular girls at school, is kind to everyone—at least that is what she thinks. One day after being crowned the homecoming queen, Lara starts gaining weight. Although she does not have an eating disorder, her condition is mysterious. The reader gradually learns the truth about her parents and her relationships with her family and friends. Not until the family moves to another state and Lara experiences life as an overweight individual does she come to realize what is important. The value of this text is in her honest feelings and reactions to others who react to her new physical appearance of being overweight. "Readers will be totally caught up in Lara's struggle to find her true self under all that weight." *Booklist* "[T]he author lays out the issues with unusual clarity, sharp insight, and cutting irony." *Kirkus Reviews*

49. *Leaving Jetty Road.* Burton, Rebecca. New York: Alfred A. Knopf, 2006. 248 pp. ISBN: 037593488X. Grades 9–12.

Nat, Lise, and Sofia are three best friends in Australia who grow apart during their senior year of high school as each embark on a different path. Each girl's subtle narration of her eating disorder reminds the reader how persuasive an eating disorder can be and how friends and family react when someone they know develops an eating disorder. Two of the friends provide first-person narratives in alternate chapters. Lise's narrations regarding her anorexia are especially poignant. "[T]his [is a] well-written, never-didactic novel." *Booklist*

50. *Faded Denim.* Carlson, Melody. Colorado Springs, CO: THINK Books, 2006. 215 pp. ISBN: 1576835375. Grades 9–12.

Emily is a 17-year-old who wants to lose some weight. She develops an eating disorder that occupies most of her time and energy. Her friends as well as her personal belief in God finally help her to take control of her life.

51. *Nothing.* Friedman, Robin. Woodbury, MN: Flux, 2008. 232 pp. ISBN: 073871304X; ISBN: 9780738713045. Grades 9–12.

High school senior Parker Rabinowitz is under multiple pressures: pleasing his wealthy and demanding parents, maintaining his straight-A grade record, being accepted into Princeton, being voted as the sexiest student in the high school, and dealing with his non-Jewish girlfriend. He reacts to all these pressures by developing bulimia. Danielle, Parker's 14-year-old sister, narrates her story of how she lives in Parker's shadow, at home, at school, and even with her own friends. Danielle discovers that Parker is bulimic and tries to help him. "Parker's negative body image and need for control will be familiar to teen readers, but the callous dismissal of his few attempts to discuss his worries says worlds about social expectations about teen boys." *Kirkus Reviews*

52. *Perfect.* Friend, Natasha. Minneapolis: Milkweed Editions, 2004. 172 pp. ISBN: 1571316523. Grades 8–11.

Isabelle is 13 years old and uses bulimia in order to cope with the loss of her father whose sudden death two years earlier changed her life. Her mother is not able to cope very well with this loss either. Isabelle thinks that bulimia is her solution to the challenges in her life because she discovers in her therapy group that the most popular girl in school is also experiencing this eating disorder. Isabelle thinks that in sharing this eating disorder, she is creating a lasting bond of friendship with her. This story contains very honest and realistic dialogue and situations for young girls facing problems and who turn to bulimia as an answer. "A satisfying novel that addresses common teen issues." *School Library Journal*

53. *Looks.* George, Madeleine. New York: Viking, 2008. 240 pp. ISBN: 0670061670; ISBN: 9780670061679. Grades 9–12.

Meghan Ball and Aimee Zorn, who are complete opposites, start the new year at high school. Meghan is extremely overweight, and Aimee is anorexic. Aimee's anorexia creates a strained relationship with her mother and overshadows her interactions with her classmates. When Aimee is betrayed by the same girl who betrayed Meghan years earlier, they decide to teach her a lesson. The author portrays realistic challenges encountered at high schools, such as students feeling that they are outcasts, teachers struggling to teach defiant students, and coaches focusing on athletics and ignoring academics. Aimee's attempts to maintain a paternal relationship with her mother's ex-live-in boyfriend is poignant. "Despite the loose ends, the story will make readers think about the various issues touched upon, and it is difficult to put down." *School Library Journal*

54. *Upstream: A Novel.* Hoekstra, Molly. Greensboro, NC: Tudor Publishers, 2001. 221 pp. ISBN: 0936389869. Grades 8–12.

Kathryn is a 16-year-old who spends one summer in a hospital in order to overcome her anorexia. Her father has died and Kathryn has been more of an adult than her mother, who is a soap opera actress. Kathryn and the other characters in this novel, as well as the events and the setting, provide very realistic and credible portraits of the challenges teenagers face in order to treat eating disorders. "The resulting tale creates multidimensional understanding of those who suffer from the disorder." *School Library Journal*

55. *Skinny.* Kaslik, Ibi. New York: Walker & Company, 2006. 244 pp. ISBN: 0802796087. Grades 9–12.

This is a story of 22-year-old Giselle who spirals out of control in her inability to manage her anorexia. Her sister Holly, who is eight years her junior and a natural-born athlete, battles for acceptance at school in her own way. Both sisters are trying to cope with the relationships between members of their family, which has been strained since the death of their father several years ago. The author uses a unique format by having the sisters tell their respective feelings of what they are experiencing, in alternate chapters. This realistic story reveals the sincere and insightful concerns that children of immigrant parents experience, and the challenges that all family members face. "[O]lder readers will likely connect with the raw emotions and intelligent insights into a family's secrets, pain, and enduring love." *Booklist*

56. *What Happened to Lani Garver.* Plum-Ucci, Carol. San Diego, CA: Harcourt, 2002. 307 pp. ISBN: 0152168133. Grades 9–12.

Sixteen-year-old Claire has been dealing with the complications associated with her leukemia treatment. In addition, Claire develops an eating disorder. When a new student, Lani, moves to town, Claire develops a deep friendship with the androgynous Lani. Claire has to evaluate her personal beliefs and her relationships with her friends. A terrible experience at the hands of bigoted individuals provides a surprise ending. "Outstanding writing, strong characterization, and riveting plot development make this title rise above many recent coming-of-age stories." *School Library Journal*

57. *How I Live Now.* Rosoff, Meg. New York: Wendy Lamb Books, 2004. 194 pp. ISBN: 0385746776; ISBN2: 9780385746779. Grades 9–12.

At age 15, Daisy leaves Manhattan and her father and his new pregnant wife and moves to England to be with her mother's younger sister and her never-before-seen cousins. Her aunt and cousins are unaware of her eating disorder. Daisy discovers an inner strength with the help of her relationship with her cousin Edmond. Her life changes once again when the country is attacked and occupied by an unnamed aggressor. Daisy and her cousins are forced to live in this hostile environment and plan for an unknown future.
2005 Michael L. Printz Medal winner.

58. *More Than You Can Chew.* Tokio, Marnelle. Toronto, Ontario: Tundra Books, 2003. 234 pp. ISBN: 0887766390. Grades 9–12.

This semiautobiographical account of a high school senior's bout with anorexia is at times humorous, at times hopeless, and at times very real. As Marty prepares to graduate, her interactions with her boyfriend who is critical of her,

her combatant divorced parents, a too-busy, alcoholic mother and a remote father, make her spiral into the dark abyss of anorexia. When she is sent to a treatment facility, her interactions with fellow inmates and the staff portray the real challenges of individuals dealing with anorexia. This realistic story portrays the challenges, both positive and unfortunate, that teenagers face as they try to recover from anorexia. "Marty's struggles as she learns to take things 'one day at a time' will satisfy teens' voracious appetites for novels about the disordered and disturbed." *Booklist*

59. *Full Mouse, Empty Mouse: A Tale of Food and Feelings.* Zeckhausen, Dina; illustrated by Brian Boyd. Washington, DC: Magination Press, 2007. 37 pp. ISBN: 1433801329; ISBN2: 9781433801327. Grades K–3.

The author, a practicing therapist specializing in eating disorders, weaves this wonderful story about a topic that is usually reserved for older readers. In this story, mice children, Billy Blue and his sister Sally Rose, have been experiencing overwhelming stressful situations. They handle their stress differently; Billy Blue overeats, and Sally Rose, on the other hand, does not eat. In spite of the fact that their parents are caring and understanding, the mice children still develop eating disorders. Their kind Aunt Lou offers them suggestions for handling stress that does not involve eating. An extensive "Note to Parents" containing excellent suggestions and discussion questions and websites are included. The exceptional color illustrations complement this story, which is told in verse. This is a must title for every elementary school library. "Provides a wonderful way to open the door for conversations about food and feelings that could lead to greater health and happiness for readers of all ages." National Eating Disorders Association

Nonfiction

60. *What Do I Have to Lose: A Teen's Guide to Weight Management.* Bauchner, Elizabeth. Series: The Science of Health: Youth and Well-Being. Philadelphia: Mason Crest Publishers, 2005. 128 pp. ISBN: 1590848551. Grades 8–10.

This excellent volume, one of the titles in the Science of Health: Youth and Well-Being series, examines the information that teenagers need to have in order to maintain healthy weight. The eight chapters cover major concerns and issues that are involved in developing healthy weight management, including combating the negative images of overweight individuals, that society and the media portray. Chapter topics, such as needing to lose weight, are excellent starting points for group discussion. Additional chapter topics focus on the positive aspects of weight management. For example, Chapter 7, "How Can I Avoid Eating Disorders?" provides suggestions that teenagers can follow. Case studies are used to illustrate the key concepts regarding healthy weight, and text boxes scattered throughout the book contain personal reflections from teenagers on weight management. Graphics and photographs, an extensive listing of organizations and websites, additional resources, a glossary, and an index are included.

61. *Eating Disorders.* Bjorklund, Ruth. Series: Health Alert. New York: Marshall Cavendish Benchmark, 2005. 64 pp. ISBN: 0761419144. Grades 4–7.

This title in the Health Alert series provides thorough coverage of eating disorders for younger teens. The author uses case studies to discuss the various topics associated with eating disorders. The chapter topics cover all aspects of eating disorders, such as what they are and the various treatment options. Chapter 3 stands out because it provides an exceptional look at eating disorders throughout history. One of the end sections, "Reaching Out," provides excellent suggestions for approaching a friend who has an eating disorder. A glossary, color photographs, graphics, additional reading material, websites, and an index are included.

62. *Drug Therapy and Eating Disorders.* Brinkerhoff, Shirley. Series: Psychiatric Disorders: Drugs and Psychology for the Mind and Body. Philadelphia: Mason Crest Publishers, 2004. [128] pp. ISBN: 159084565X. Grades 8–10.

This volume, one of the titles in the Psychiatric Disorders: Drugs and Psychology for the Mind and Body series, details how eating disorders can be treated with drug therapy. Each of the six chapters begins with an email conversation that introduces some of the challenges associated with an eating disorder. The introductory chapter, "The Disorder and History of Drug," is a good springboard for the other chapters that discuss drug use in combating eating disorders. Chapter 5, "Risks and Side Effects," is especially important for teenagers. Color photographs, illustrations, text boxes, additional reading material, and an index are included.

63. *Eating Disorders.* Bryan, Jenny. Series: Talking Points. Austin, TX: Raintree Steck-Vaughn, 2000. 64 pp. ISBN: 0817253211. Grades 7–9.

This volume, one of the titles in the Talking Points series, is one of the best resources on the topic of eating disorders aimed for the middle school reader. The chapters are divided into manageable topics, such as defining eating disorders, anorexia, bulimia, and compulsive eating. The author has excellently balanced informative text with pleasant illustrations. Color illustrations, graphics, text boxes, black and white photographs, a glossary, additional reading material, resources that provide useful addresses of support groups, and an index are included.

64. *Bulimia Nervosa: The Secret Cycle of Bingeing and Purging.* Burby, Liza
    N. Series: Teen Health Library of Eating Disorder Prevention. New York:
    Rosen Publishing Group, 1998. 64 pp. ISBN: 0823927628. Grades 5–8.

This volume, one of the titles in the Teen Health Library of Eating Disorder
Prevention series, contains the chapters: "The Hidden Disease," "What Is Bulimia?" "Why Do People Develop Bulimia?" "How Bulimia Affects the Body
and Mind," "Recovering from Bulimia and Developing a Positive Body Image."
Quotes from teens who have eating disorders are sprinkled throughout the chapters in italics. Suggestions for those with this eating disorder and for concerned
friends, a glossary, a list of organizations including websites for the United States
and Canada, additional reading material, and an index are included.

65. *Understanding Weight and Depression.* Clarke, Julie M. and Ann Kirby-
    Payne. Series: A Teen Eating Disorder Prevention Book. New York: Rosen
    Publishing Group, 2000. 118 pp. ISBN: 0823929949. Grades 7–10.

This title in the Teen Eating Disorder Prevention Book series provides a good, basic overview of how personal weight issues lead to depression among teenagers. The
introductory chapter examines the relationship of one's body and one's mind as well
as the myth of body image versus body reality. Additional chapter topics include the
dangers of dieting, identifying eating disorders, becoming depressed, and preventing suicide. The last chapter provides teenagers helpful suggestions and valuable
advice that they need for living healthy and living happy. Case studies that illustrate
key concepts are scattered throughout this book. A glossary, support organizations,
hotlines, websites, additional reading material, and an index are included.

66. *You Remind Me of You.* Corrigan, Eireann. New York: Scholastic, 2002.
    123 pp. ISBN: 0439297710. Grades 10–12.

Corrigan's autobiographical account of her teenage years, told in quasi-prose
form, provides a glimpse into the dark and secretive world of eating disorders.
Daniel, Corrigan's teenage boyfriend, is so troubled that he attempts suicide, but
fortunately survives. His suicide attempt becomes the turning point in Corrigan's
life that empowers her to get control of her own eating disorder. Teenage girls
should identify with Corrigan's honest account of her interactions with friends
and her battle with anorexia. "The unusual and effective format sharpens each
word, making readers savor and thoughtfully examine each poetic piece . . . this
book complements the many fiction and non-fiction works on the topic." *School
Library Journal*

67. *Anorexia and Bulimia.* Cotter, Alison. Series: Diseases and Disorders. San
    Diego, CA: Lucent Books, 2002. 112 pp. ISBN: 156006725X. Grades 6–9.

This title in the Diseases and Disorders series provides comprehensive coverage in six chapters. The first two chapters are: "What Are Anorexia and Bulimia?" and "Psychological and Biological Causes." Chapter 3, "Societal Pressures," is especially relevant for the middle school age group. The remaining chapters cover dangers, treatment and recovery, and prevention tips. The text is easy to read while providing all important concepts in manageable sections. Black and white photographs, graphics, and text boxes are used throughout the book. An extensive list of organizations, a section listing websites, and an index are included.

68. *Insatiable: The Compelling Story of Four Teens, Food and Its Power.* Eliot, Eve. Deerfield Beach, FL: Health Communications, 2001. 284 pp. ISBN: 1558748180. Grades 9–12.

The author uses her own experiences with an eating disorder to tell this revealing story about the highs and lows, mostly lows, of four high school teens and their interactions with their families, friends, and classmates at school. Each girl develops an eating disorder for different reasons: one binges, one is bulimic, and two are anorexic. This is a very interesting and very identifiable story for teenagers who often feel shame, fear, and confusion compelling them to use, or refuse, food in misguided attempts to feel safe and in control of their lives. "This novel by a well-known therapist who specializes in food addictions demonstrates the pervasiveness of the disorder." *School Library Journal*

69. *Youth with Eating Disorders: When Food Is an Enemy.* Flynn, Noa. Series: Helping Youth with Mental, Physical, and Social Challenges. Philadelphia, PA: Mason Crest Publishers, 2008. 128 pp. ISBN: 1422201449; ISBN2: 9781422201442. Grades 8–12.

Part of the series titled Helping Youth with Mental, Physical, and Social Challenges, this book contains stories about Susan who has struggled with her weight most of her life, and Brooke who feels overweight and struggles with food. Information regarding treatment of eating disorders is provided. A glossary, a list of books for additional information including websites, color photographs, and an index are included. "[V]olumes in this series are very informative and engaging. The clever manner in which the chapters first present a part of the story and end with facts about the topic allow readers to gain valuable information without feeling bogged down by facts." *VOYA*

70. *Am I Fat? The Obesity Issue for Teens.* Gay, Kathlyn. Series: Issues in Focus Today. Berkeley Heights, NJ: Enslow Publishers, 2006. 112 pp. ISBN: 0766025276. Grades 7–9.

As one of the titles in the Issues in Focus Today series, this work provides thorough coverage of one of today's most serious health concerns, obesity. Chapter topics include causes of obesity, health risks, and diets, including weight loss surgery. Chapter notes provide extensive resources, as do the listings of associations, books, and websites. A brief glossary and an index are included. The larger, colorful photographs provide good visuals throughout the book. This is a very pleasing and welcoming book for the middle school age group. "[U]seful and timely addition[s]. . . . This information lays a solid foundation on which to tackle the topic of unhealthy weight-loss strategies." *School Library Journal*

71. *Eating Disorders: Anorexia, Bulimia, and Binge Eating.* Gay, Kathlyn. Series: Diseases and People. Berkeley Heights, NJ: Enslow Publishers, 2003. 112 pp. ISBN: 0766018946. Grades 7–10.

This volume, one of the titles in the Diseases and People series, addresses three eating disorders: anorexia, bulimia, and binge eating. The chapter titled "The Enemy Is Food" provides examples of current celebrities who have one of these disorders and a brief story of their battles with eating disorders. The chapter titled "The History of Anorexia and Bulimia" provides excellent coverage of historical figures who developed eating disorders for religious reasons, such as St. Catherine of Siena. The questions and answers section is very helpful. A timeline listing individuals who have had eating disorders, black and white photographs, a glossary, support groups and organizations, websites, additional reading material, and an index are included.

72. *Eating Disorders: A Hot Issue.* Goodnough, David. Series: Hot Issues. Berkeley Heights, NJ: Enslow Publishers, 1999. 64 pp. ISBN: 0766013367. Grades 5–8.

This title in the Hot Issues series is a straightforward overview of eating disorders. The introductory chapter contains the case studies of three teenage girls who have eating disorders. Chapter topics include insight into anorexia, bulimia, and other eating disorders as well as how to cope with these disorders. The chapter "Not Just a Celebrity Sickness" provides valuable insight into who develops eating disorders and the reasons behind developing them. The author uses real stories that have tragic consequences to illustrate the destructive nature of eating disorders. Color photographs, text boxes, a glossary, additional reading material, organizations, websites, and an index are included. "[A] concise and clear account of anorexia nervosa, bulimia, and binge eating." *School Library Journal*

73. *Let's Talk about Being Overweight.* Gordon, Melanie Apel. Series: Let's Talk Library. New York: PowerKids Press, 2000. 24 pp. ISBN: 0823954137. Grades 1–4.

This volume, one of the Let's Talk Library series, contains ten, one-page chapters about being overweight. Chapter topics are "How Did I Gain Weight," "The Food You Eat," and "Staying Healthy and Fit." Color photographs, a short glossary, and an index are included.

74. *Bulimia.* Graves, Bonnie B. Series: Perspectives on Mental Health. Mankato, MN: LifeMatters, 2000. 64 pp. ISBN: 0736804307; ISBN2: 9780736804301. Grades 4–8.

This well-organized volume is one of the titles in the Perspectives on Mental Health series. The first chapter addresses how teenagers use food as a solution to various situations and a substitute for uncontrollable feelings. The next chapter discusses why teenagers feel the importance of being thin. The last three chapters provide a realistic look at the following topics: facing the dangerous consequences of bulimia, choosing a healthier lifestyle, and getting the appropriate support needed to overcome this eating disorder. Suggestions for providing assistance to friends who have bulimia are also listed. Color photographs, a glossary, useful addresses and websites, and an index are included.

75. *Eating Disorders: A Handbook for Teens, Families, and Teachers.* Heller, Tania. Jefferson, NC: McFarland & Company, 2003. 174 pp. ISBN: 0786414782. Teens/Educators/Parents.

The author of this book has compiled an excellent resource written in first-person narrative from her own experience as a medical director at an eating disorders center. This comprehensive guide covers topics such as what eating disorders are and who develops them, warning signs and complications, treatment options, and recovery. The chapters are subdivided into manageable and easy-to-read subsections. The chapter devoted to eating disorders among males provides excellent insight for this often overlooked topic. Case studies are used throughout to illustrate specific concerns and issues. The last chapter, "Questions and Answers," provides a nonthreatening format to convey essential information. Appendix A is a "Quick Reference Guide" and Appendix B contains a list of national organizations and their contact information. A bibliography and an index are included.

76. *Want Fries with That? Obesity and the Supersizing of America.* Ingram, Scott. New York: Franklin Watts, 2005. 128 pp. ISBN: 0531167569. Grades 8–12.

This fact-filled book addresses one of the country's most serious and current health concerns, obesity. Topics include the obesity crisis, what people eat, how obesity affects mind and body, and treatment options. The personal stories of Morgan Spurlock, from the 2004 documentary, Super Size Me, and Patrick

Deuel, whose weight had ballooned to over 1,000 pounds, illustrate this nation's current epidemic, obesity. The black and white photographs, red and black graphics, and tables present a powerful visual message for younger readers as well as important information about nutrition and dieting. An extensive glossary, additional reading material, and websites are included. "[L]ibraries may want to purchase it because of the timely information offered and the increasing number of students researching this topic for reports and debates." *Booklist*

77. *Eating Disorders.* Keel, Pamela K. Series: Psychological Disorders. New York: Chelsea House Publishers, 2006. 111 pp. ISBN: 0791085406. Grades 7–9.

This title in the Psychological Disorders series examines the symptoms, causes, and effects of eating disorders. The introductory chapter provides brief definitions for anorexia, bulimia, binge eating, and other eating disorders not otherwise specified. A two-page overview of the life of St. Catherine of Siena, focusing on her self-imposed starvation, provides a glimpse of one of the few historical examples of girls or women and their unusual eating habits. In the following three chapters the author uses case studies to illustrate the emotional, cognitive, behavioral, and interpersonal effects, as well as warning signs of anorexia, bulimia, and eating disorders. The remaining chapters examine the causes, treatment options, and future ways in which the health and medical profession may be able to help individuals. Color photographs, abundant color graphics of the human anatomy, text boxes that contain essential facts, a glossary, additional reading material, websites, and an index are included.

78. *The Truth about Eating Disorders.* Kittleson, Mark J., editor. Series: Facts on File, The Truth About. New York: Facts on File, 2005. 166 pp. ISBN: 0816063006. Grades 9–12.

The introductory chapter of this volume of the Facts on File, The Truth About series provides a good overview of behaviors associated with eating disorders and specific issues, such as warning signs, the impact of body image, diagnosing eating disorders, and their physical, social, health, and long-term effects. The A–Z guide follows and contains twenty-two entries such as diet pills, eating disorders in men and boys, fad diets, and peer pressure. Graphics featuring essential information such as the food guide pyramid and body mass index and reading lists are scattered throughout the chapters. An extensive glossary, hotlines, help sites, and index are included.

79. *The Beginner's Guide to Eating Disorders Recovery.* Kolodny, Nancy J. Carlsbad, CA: Gurze Books, 2004. 228 pp. ISBN: 093607745X. Grades 9–12.

Teenagers can use this excellent self-help guide to get control of their eating disorders. This resource, written by a therapist with over twenty years of experience working in the field of eating disorders, provides the latest information on eating disorders in two parts: Part I explains what eating disorders are. Part II details steps for recovery. The author uses straightforward text and employs case studies to illustrate key concepts. In addition, tables containing information and personal poems written by teenagers are scattered throughout the work. The author encourages both men and women to take charge of their lives. Suggested reading material, a list of definitions about anorexia and bulimia, and an index are included.

80. *Eating Disorders Information for Teens: Health Tips about Anorexia, Bulimia, Binge Eating, and Other Eating Disorders.* Lawton, Sandra Augustyn, editor. Series: Teen Health. Detroit: Omnigraphics, 2005. 337 pp. ISBN: 0780807839. Grades 9–12.

This volume, one of the titles in the Teen Health series, provides one of the most comprehensive resources about eating disorders available today. The book's subtitle reflects the in-depth coverage: health tips about anorexia, bulimia, binge eating, and other eating disorders, including information on the causes, prevention, and treatment of eating disorders as well as other issues such as maintaining healthy eating and exercise habits. This work includes rarely addressed issues, such as boys and athletes dealing with eating disorders. An impressive directory of organizations that deal with eating disorders and index complete the work. "Divided into well-organized sections, this comprehensive volume [is] . . . A solid addition for any non-fiction or reference collection." *School Library Journal*

81. *The Ultimate Weight Solution for Teens: The 7 Keys to Weight Freedom.* McGraw, Jay. New York: Free Press, 2003. 293 pp. ISBN: 0743257472. Grades 8–12.

This upbeat approach for combating eating challenges, written by the son of the popular talk show host Dr. Phil, entertains while providing helpful suggestions and guidelines for teenagers. Jay, an accomplished author in his own right, addresses topics of maintaining healthy weight issues in eleven brief chapters. Chapter topics include "The Solution You've Been Looking For," "Get-With-It Goals," "Mastery over Food and Impulse Eating," and "Your Circle of Support." Jay includes plenty of case studies and success stories in this self-help book. Lists of suggestions, quizzes, activities, a relaxation script, Jay's portion power plan foods, fast food choices, workout diary, and a listing of helpful organizations are included.

82. *Preventing Eating Disorders among Pre-Teen Girls: A Step-by-Step Guide.* Menassa, Beverly Neu. Westport, CT: Praeger, 2004. 113 pp. ISBN: 0865693323. Teens/Educators/Parents.

The author, a mental health counselor, writes this guide for young college women, but younger teenagers can also benefit from it. The introductory chapters, which contain a literature review, risk factors of having eating disorders, and suggestions for using this guide, provide useful information for teenagers, professionals, and counselors. Chapter 4 includes the details necessary for professionals who want to conduct group sessions, such as focus, objectives, as well as the activities, questions, group discussion starters and suggestions, and homework assignments. The appendices contain forms and questionnaires, websites, nutritional assistance, breathing and meditation exercises, and resource materials for parents and guardians. Additional reading material and an index are included.

83. *Coping with Eating Disorders.* Moe, Barbara. Series: Coping. New York: Rosen Publishing Group, 1999. 133 pp. ISBN: 0823929744. Grades 7–9.

This revised title in the Coping series provides good coverage of various types of eating disorders. The author uses case studies to illustrate the key concepts in each chapter. One chapter addresses family factors and influences that can lead a teenager to develop an eating disorder. One chapter discusses a variety of emotions experienced by teenagers with eating disorders. A glossary, a list of organizations in the United States and Canada, hotlines, websites, newsgroups, additional reading material, and an index are included.

84. *Understanding Eating Disorder Support Groups.* Moehn, Heather. Series: A Teen Eating Disorder Prevention Book. New York: Rosen Publishing Group, 2000. 138 pp. ISBN: 0823929922. Grades 7–10.

This title in the Teen Eating Disorder Prevention Book series provides a good, basic overview of eating disorders and the various support options available to teenagers. The topics covered in the chapters in the first part of this book are anorexia, bulimia, binge eating, and compulsive exercise disorder. The topics in the second part focus on available support concerns, such as how to ask for support, treatment options, and support groups. One of the most valuable chapters in this book is "Supporting a Friend," which provides suggestions and advice for readers who want to help their friends who have an eating disorder. A glossary, support organizations, hotlines, websites, additional reading material, and an index are included.

85. *What's Eating You? A Workbook for Teens with Anorexia, Bulimia & Other Eating Disorders.* Nelson, Tammy. Oakland, CA: Instant Help Books, 2008. 112 pp. ISBN: 1572246073; ISBN: 9781572246072. Grades 9–12.

The main topics covered in this book are regarding the prevention and treatment of eating disorders in teenagers. The workbook contains thirty-seven activities, such as draw your feelings, family dinner table, your food plan, family patterns, and whose body is this. Each activity includes questions and exercises. By completing the worksheets, one will learn how to eat in healthy ways and how to stay in balance, physically and emotionally, how to correct eating behaviors that are dysfunctional, and how to deal with stress and frustrations that often lead to eating disorders.

86. *Over It: A Teen's Guide to Getting Beyond Obsessions with Food and Weight.* Normandi, Carol Emery and Laurelee Roark. Novato, CA: New World Library, 2001. 187 pp. ISBN: 1577311485. Grades 9–12.

This is one of the best self-help resources written by the founders of a national nonprofit organization that provides support for teens with eating disorders and body image disturbance. The first chapter, "Getting Over the Obsession with Food and Weight," sets the tone for the entire book with its informal and straightforward text. Case scenarios are used to illustrate issues and concerns. The chapter "Trusting Your Process" explains the authors' treatment for recovery. This is a very valuable and self-empowering resource that should attract teenager readers. An appendix includes a section for parents and a list of organizations and websites. Black and white graphics and an index are included.

87. *Starving to Win: Athletes and Eating Disorders.* O'Brien, Eileen. Series: Teen Health Library of Eating Disorder Prevention. New York: Rosen Publishing Group, 1998. 64 pp. ISBN: 0823927644. Grades 5–8.

This title in the Teen Health Library of Eating Disorder Prevention series focuses on a topic that is often not discussed, that is, the experiences of young athletes who develop eating disorders. The stories of Gina, Nikki, and Theo are used throughout the book to illustrate how athletes develop eating disorders and are affected by various eating disorders. Chapter topics include the consequences of young athletes' eating disorders and possible treatment options that can ensure their successful recovery. Young readers should identify with the readable language and the nonthreatening approach that the author takes in addressing the impact eating disorders have in the sports world. Color photographs, a glossary, a list of organizations in the United States and Canada, additional reading materials, and an index are included.

88. *When the Mirror Lies: Anorexia, Bulimia and Other Eating Disorders.* Orr, Tamra. Danbury, CT: Franklin Watts, 2007. 144 pp. ISBN: 0531167917; ISBN2: 9780531167915. Grades 9–12.

Orr uses case studies to illustrate the devastating effects on those who have eating disorders. This informal text contains chapter topics that address distorted body image, physical and mental effects, and treatment options. Black and white photographs, graphics, and text boxes titled "Weighty Words" provide additional information. A glossary, additional reading material, a directory of support groups and organizations, and an index are included. "Readers who are suffering from eating disorders will feel comforted and hopefully inspired to seek more support, while those who are trying to learn more about the topic will come away with a clearer understanding of its complexities." *School Library Journal*

89. *Teens, Health & Obesity.* Owens, Peter. Series: The Gallup Youth Survey: Major Issues and Trends. Broomall, PA: Mason Crest Publishers, 2004. 112 pp. ISBN: 1590848721. Grades 9–12.

This volume, one of the titles in the Gallup Youth Survey: Major Issues and Trends series, explains that obesity has become an increasing health concern among adolescents and is increasing at an alarming rate. The author uses the data collected from three Gallup polls to explore the reasons behind this health concern. This information is divided into manageable sections and includes unhealthy eating habits and their consequences during the teen years, common eating disorders, the importance of one's body image, and options for combating obesity. Additional topics explored are how obesity and overweight individuals are viewed in the media and society as a whole and the latest information regarding the scientific aspect of weight and metabolism. Color photographs, graphics, a glossary, Internet resources, additional reading material, and an index are included. This title, as with the other titles in this series, contains up-to-date information and is highly recommended.

90. *Compulsive Overeating.* Peacock, Judith. Series: Perspectives on Mental Health. Mankato, MN: LifeMatters, 2000. 64 pp. ISBN: 0736804374; ISBN2: 9780736804370. Grades 4–8.

This volume is one of the titles in the Perspectives on Mental Health series. The introductory chapter defines compulsive overeating. The next two chapters address individuals who are liable to be at risk and reasons why eating disorders develop. The remaining topics deal with facing the dangerous consequences of compulsive overeating, choosing a healthier lifestyle, and getting appropriate support needed to overcome the eating disorder. Suggestions for providing assistance to friends who have bulimia are also listed. Color photographs, a glossary, useful addresses and websites, and an index are included.

91. *Addictions and Risky Behaviors: Cutting, Bingeing, Snorting, and Other Dangers.* Rebman, Renee C. Series: Issues in Focus Today. Berkeley Heights, NJ: Enslow Publishers, 2006. 104 pp. ISBN: 0766021653. Grades 7–9.

This volume, one of the titles in the Issues in Focus Today series, provides excellent coverage of several addictions including drug, alcohol, eating disorders, and Internet obsession. The layout with color photos and off-set text make this an attractive read for this age group. A glossary, an index, and additional information that lists Internet addresses are included.

92. *Bulimia.* Ruggiero, Adriane. Series: At Issue: Health. Detroit: Greenhaven Press, 2008. 98 pp. ISBN: 0737736739; ISBN: 9780737736731. Grades 9–12.

This book in the At Issue: Health series contains twelve chapters on various aspects and issues pertaining to bulimia. Written by medical and health professionals, as well as educators, the chapters cover the following topics: causes of bulimia; experiencing shame; the element of self-harm; the impact of athletics; the role of the Internet; treatment options including antidepressants; hospitalization; and behavior therapy. The final chapter explores the question, "Should insurers pay for bulimics' hospitalization and treatment programs?" which is an important issue for parents. A list of organizations to contact, a bibliography, and an index are included. "[P]rovide[s] a variety of carefully chosen contrasting opinions for class discussions and debates as well as individual research." *KLIATT*

93. *Dealing with the Stuff That Makes Life Tough: The 10 Things That Stress Girls Out and How to Cope with Them.* Rutledge, Jill Zimmerman. Chicago: Contemporary Books, 2004. 228 pp. ISBN: 0071423265. Grades 8–10.

Psychotherapist Jill Rutledge used her own experience as well as twenty years of counseling young girls to compile this resource. Each chapter examines different causes of stress, such as body image, panic attacks, depression, and the blues. Rutledge uses actual case studies from her own private practice to illustrate the stress causes as well as the tactics that can be used to calm down and control a stressful situation. The last chapter contains additional resources, such as books, fiction and nonfiction; articles, media (CDs and films) suggestions, and websites. "[A]necdotes . . . are broad in scope and right on target." *School Library Journal*

94. *Eating Disorders.* Savage, Lorraine. Series: Perspectives on Diseases and Disorders. Detroit: Thomson Gale, 2008. 144 pp. ISBN: 0737738723; ISNB: 9780737738728. Grades 10–12.

This title in the Perspectives on Diseases and Disorders series provides useful information for teen readers regarding eating disorders. The first chapter presents an overview of eating disorders, including symptoms, causes, treatments, severity of eating disorders, binge eating, and eating disorders particularly in males. The next chapter covers several current controversies associated with eating disorders such as the contributions of mental illness, genetic and family factors, the role of the fashion industry, and the Internet. The last chapter contains personal stories that should benefit readers. Color photographs and graphics, a glossary, chronology, a list of organizations to contact for additional information, print resources, and an index are included.

95. *Coping with Compulsive Eating.* Simpson, Carolyn. Series: Coping. New York: Rosen Publishing Group, 1997. 89 pp. ISBN: 0823925161. Grades 7–9.

This title in the Coping series focuses on compulsive eating. The author addresses the emotional reasons, the components and factors of this specific eating disorder, as well as the physical and social challenges and complications. Readers should find the chapter about the various types of compulsive eating very informative. The chapter titled "When Something Is Physically Wrong" provides useful information. The author uses case studies to illustrate the key concepts in each chapter. A guide for eating healthy, a glossary, a list of contact information for organizations, a list of hotlines, websites, additional reading material, and an index are included.

96. *Understanding Compulsive Eating.* Simpson, Carolyn. Series: A Teen Eating Disorder Prevention Book. New York: Rosen Publishing Group, 2000. 118 pp. ISBN: 0823929892. Grades 7–10.

This title in the Teen Eating Disorder Prevention Book series provides a good, basic overview of compulsive eating. The introductory chapter identifies and provides definitions for various eating disorders. The following chapters discuss topics such as compulsive eating, causes and solutions, and getting help. The last chapter, "Dealing with Compulsive Eating," is specifically for the individual who has an eating disorder. A glossary, a list of American and Canadian support organizations, websites, additional reading material, and an index are included.

97. *Anorexia Nervosa: When Food Is the Enemy.* Smith, Erica. Series: Teen Health Library of Eating Disorder Prevention. New York: Rosen Publishing Group, 1999. 64 pp. ISBN: 0823927660. Grades 5–8.

This resource, one of the titles in the Teen Health Library of Eating Disorder Prevention series, contains the chapters "Anorexia Is an Eating Disorder," "The Beginnings of Anorexia," "Am I at Risk?" and "The Quest for Thinness and

Choosing Health." There are text boxes and full-page color photographs of boys and girls providing a most up-to-date look. Quotes from teens affected with this eating disorder are sprinkled throughout the chapters in italics. Suggestions for those with this eating disorder and for concerned friends, a glossary, a list of organizations including websites in the United States and Canada, additional reading material, and an index are included.

98. *Nutrition and Eating Disorders.* Smolin, Lori A. and Mary B. Grosvenor. Philadelphia: Chelsea House, 2005. 164 pp. ISBN: 0791078515. Grades 8–12.

This excellent resource written by two nutritionists emphasizes that the key to dealing with or preventing eating disorders for teenagers is to develop and maintain healthy eating habits. There are two table of contents that provide easy access to the information: the first is a skeletal overview of the book's material, and the second is a detailed listing of all subsections and topics. The chapter topics include understanding food and the value of nutrition, accepting one's body image, and specific eating disorders. Thought-provoking questions sprinkled throughout the book engage young readers in examining their own beliefs and actions regarding nutrition. "Fact Boxes" highlight issues and information of related interest. Appendices contain nutritional and dietary statistics, an extensive glossary of nutritional terms, additional reading material, websites, and an index. Color photographs, graphics, tables, and text boxes are included.

99. *Understanding Anorexia Nervosa.* Stanley, Debbie. Series: A Teen Eating Disorder Prevention Book. New York: Rosen Publishing Group, 1999. 104 pp. ISBN: 0823928772. Grades 7–10.

This title in the Teen Eating Disorder Prevention Book series provides a good, basic overview of anorexia nervosa. The introductory chapters identify and provide a definition for anorexia and address the facts and myths associated with anorexia. The following chapters discuss topics such as other eating disorders and related conditions, causes for developing anorexia, treatment options, getting help, and prevention strategies. The final chapter, titled "Whose Life Is It Anyway? Healthy Ways to Assert Yourself," contains excellent suggestions and advice. Case studies are used to illustrate key concepts. A glossary, a list of American and Canadian support organizations, websites, additional reading material, and an index are included. "The brisk, readable text is broken up with attractive shaded insets and bulleted items." *School Library Journal*

100. *Understanding Bulimia Nervosa.* Stanley, Debbie. Series: A Teen Eating Disorder Prevention Book. New York: Rosen Publishing Group, 1999. 129 pp. ISBN: 0823928780. Grades 7–10.

This title in the Teen Eating Disorder Prevention Book series provides a good, basic overview of bulimia nervosa. The introductory chapter defines bulimia and identifies the role that society, the media, and one's family play in an individual's developing bulimia. The following chapters discuss topics such as who has bulimia, helping yourself and helping others, coping with society's pressure to have the perfect body, and other eating disorders and related conditions. The final chapter titled "Your Health: A Reality Check" contains excellent suggestions for teenagers to take charge of their eating habits and their health. Case studies are used to illustrate key concepts. A glossary, a list of American and Canadian support organizations, websites, additional reading material, and an index are included.

101. *Understanding Sports and Eating Disorders.* Stanley, Debbie. Series: A Teen Eating Disorder Prevention Book. New York: Rosen Publishing Group, 2000. 118 pp. ISBN: 0823929930. Grades 7–10.

This title in the Teen Eating Disorder Prevention Book series provides a good, basic overview of the often overlooked topic regarding athletes who develop eating disorders in order to enhance their performance in sports. The introductory chapter identifies and provides definitions of specific eating disorders. The chapter devoted to the myths about eating disorders is especially enlightening. The chapter titled "Building Up, Tearing Down" addresses the specific issues and concerns of athletes who develop eating disorders. In addition, teenage athletes share their unique experiences with eating disorders, as well as examining the roles that their coaches and teammates play, both in developing and overcoming their eating disorders. A glossary, support organizations, hotlines, websites, additional reading material, and an index are included.

102. *Teens with Eating Disorders.* Stewart, Gail. Series: The Other America. San Diego, CA: Lucent Books, 2001. 112 pp. ISBN: 1560067640. Grades 8–12.

As one of the books in the Other America series, this title profiles four individuals, now in their twenties, who tell their own stories about their struggles with eating disorders, specifically anorexia and bulimia, during their teen years. The four young adults reveal very personal information about the everyday challenges that they experienced and encountered due to their eating disorders, including their successes and failures in controlling the disorder. In addition, the experiences they shared with both family members and friends reveal how these relationships have enabled some of them to live successful and fulfilling lives. Black and white photographs of three of the individuals (one individual requested anonymity), suggestions for getting involved, additional reading material, and an index are included. The reader should enjoy the epilogue, which provides updated information on the profiled individuals.

103. *Eating Disorders.* Strada, Jennifer L. Series: Lucent Overview Series. San Diego, CA: Lucent Books, 2001. 96 pp. ISBN: 1560066598. Grades 7–9.

This title in the Lucent Overview series offers a fairly good overview of eating disorders regarding the following topics: food obsession, food effects, risk factors, treatment options, and prevention steps. The author uses straightforward text that contains personal reflections as well as comments from teenagers about their experiences with different types of eating disorders. Graphics, cartoons, text boxes, black and white photographs, a list of support groups and organizations, additional reading material, and an index are included. "Whether for younger or older readers, this is an unsensationalized, easy-to-understand overview that makes the core issue clear." *Booklist*

104. *Eating Disorders.* Trueit, Trudi Strain. Series: Life Balance. New York: F. Watts, 2003. 80 pp. ISBN: 0531122182. Grades 4–7.

This volume in the Life Balance series addresses the need to understand the importance of identifying and accepting one's body image. Trueit illustrates that having a poor body image can lead to eating disorders, in particular, anorexia and bulimia. In addition to providing important warning signs and symptoms of these disorders, she also includes suggestions for getting help, resolving conflict, and ways to booster one's body image. Graphics, an extensive glossary, additional reading material, videos, websites, organizations, and an index are included.

105. *Teen Eating Disorders.* Vollstadt, Elizabeth Weiss. Series: Lucent Teen Issues. San Diego: Lucent Books, 1999. 112 pp. ISBN: 1560065168. Grades 6–9.

As part of the Lucent Teen Issues series, this is a good introduction to the complicated issues associated with eating disorders. The information of this text, divided into manageable sections, addresses the following topics that teenagers encounter: society's pressure to be thin, causes of eating disorders, eating disorders in males, the dangers associated with eating disorders, treatment options, and suggestions for preventing teenagers from developing eating disorders. Black and white photographs, a glossary, research sources, support organizations, additional reading material, and an index are included.

106. *Eating Disorders.* Warbrick, Caroline. Series: Just the Facts. Chicago: Heinemann Library, 2003. 56 pp. ISBN: 1588106780. Grades 7–9.

This title in the Just the Facts series provides a good overview of eating disorders. The introductory chapters contain overall and specific descriptions of the various eating disorders. Following chapters are most beneficial for the middle school reader because they address specific concerns of adolescence, social pressures, and emotions. The author covers in separate chapters the topics of the warning signs of eating disorders and tips for helping oneself. The final chapters offer treatment options and advice for recovering from various eating disorders. Text boxes, some containing quotes, a glossary, additional reading material, and an index are included.

107. *Anorexia.* Watson, Stephanie. Series: Danger Zone: Dieting and Eating Disorders. New York: Rosen Publishing Group, 2007. 64 pp. ISBN: 140421996X. Grades 7–9.

This volume, one of the titles in the Danger Zone: Dieting and Eating Disorders series, provides clear and concise information about anorexia in six chapters that can be personally used by teenagers in order to understand and cope with this eating disorder. The introductory chapter defines anorexia nervosa and its causes. Additional chapters contain the following topics: individuals at risk, the obsession to be thin, and steps to take in order to get happy. The last chapter, titled "Diagnosing Anorexia and Choosing a Recovery Plan," is particularly valuable for teenage readers in order to begin a recovery program. The author includes brief text about celebrities who have anorexia. A glossary, suggested reading material, resources, and an index are included.

108. *Binge Eating.* Watson, Stephanie. Series: Danger Zone: Dieting and Eating Disorders. New York: Rosen Publishing Group, 2007. 64 pp. ISBN: 1404219986. Grades 7–9.

This volume, one of the titles in the Danger Zone: Dieting and Eating Disorders series, provides clear and concise information about binge eating in five chapters that can be personally used by teenagers in order to understand and cope with this eating disorder. The introductory chapter defines binge eating and its causes. Additional chapters contain information on how binge eating affects the body and mind and treatment options. The last chapter, titled "Changing Your Relationship with Food and Yourself," is particularly valuable for teenage readers in order to begin a recovery program. The author includes a brief text about celebrities who are binge eaters. A glossary, suggested reading material, resources, and an index are included.

109. *Bulimia.* Watson, Stephanie. Series: Danger Zone: Dieting and Eating Disorders. New York: Rosen Publishing Group, 2007. 64 pp. ISBN: 1404219978. Grades 7–9.

This volume, one of the titles in the Danger Zone: Dieting and Eating Disorders series, provides clear and concise information about bulimia nervosa in five chapters that can be personally used by teenagers in order to understand and cope with this eating disorder. The introductory chapter defines bulimia nervosa and its causes. Additional chapters contain information on how bulimia affects the body and mind and treatment options. The last chapter, titled "Developing a Positive Body Image," is particularly valuable for teenage readers in order to begin a recovery program. The author includes brief text about celebrities who have bulimia. A glossary, suggested reading material, resources, and an index are included.

MENTAL ILLNESS

Fiction

110. *Brandon and the Bipolar Bear.* Anglada, Tracy; illustrated by Jennifer Taylor and Toby Ferguson. Victoria, BC: Trafford, 2004. 20 pp. ISBN: 1412039312. Grades 3–5.

Brandon does not understand why he feels the way he does. At times he gets so angry that he wants to explode like a volcano. Once when he explodes, he damages his new teddy bear. On this very day his mother takes him to see a new doctor, Dr. Samuel, who explains to Brandon that he has bipolar disorder and that with medication he will be able to control his feelings. This very simply easy-to-read text is a good story for younger readers who have experiences similar to Brandon's. Color drawings are included on each page.

111. *Wild Roses.* Caletti, Deb. New York: Simon Pulse, 2008. 296 pp. ISBN: 1416957820; ISBN: 9781416957829. Grades 9–12.

Seventeen-year-old Cassie Morgan lives near Seattle, Washington, with her mother and her stepfather of three years, the internationally renowned composer and musician, Dino Cavalli. As Dino prepares for his comeback concert, his behavior becomes more erratic and belligerent than usual. Cassie and her mother attribute his mood swings to his legendary status of being a child prodigy; however, as his concert approaches and he undertakes teaching Ian Waters, a gifted teenage violinist, Dino's behavior worsens. Cassie and Ian begin a romance that affects their parents, Ian's music progress, and Dino's secret. "With its profound observations and vivid, if occasionally profane, language, this multifaceted and emotionally devastating novel will stick with readers." *School Library Journal*

112. *Sometimes My Mommy Gets Angry.* Campbell, Bebe Moore; illustrated by E. B. Lewis. New York: G. P. Putnam's Sons, 2003. [27] pp. ISBN: 0399239723. Grades 1–3.

This realistic and sensitive story tells how Annie, a young girl, is challenged at home and at school due to the fact that her mother has a bipolar disorder. Annie never knows how her mother will act and is often embarrassed when her mother's disorder causes her mother to display uncontrollable behavior in front of Annie's friends. This sad, yet hopeful story shows how Annie copes at home with the support of her caring and beloved grandmother and her friends. This excellent story for young children can be read especially by those who may have friends and classmates who, like Annie, live in unsettling home situations. As the author states, "[this story will] address the fears and concerns of children who have a parent who suffers from mental illness." Beautiful color illustrations that are delicate and sensitive complement the text. "A skillful treatment of a troubling subject." *School Library Journal*

113. *Edward the "Crazy Man."* Day, Marie. Toronto, Ontario: Annick Press, 2002. [29] pp. ISBN: 1550377213. Grades 2–5.

Young Charlie is fascinated with Edward, a man who acts crazy and dresses in bizarre outfits. One day Edward saves Charlie's life as Charlie is crossing the busy city street. Never forgetting this incident, the adult Charlie encounters Edward on the street, now a homeless man. Not until Edward is hospitalized does Charlie have the opportunity to repay him for his past kindness. Color illustrations and easy reading text make this a touching story for even the youngest readers.

114. *Ceiling Stars.* Diersch, Sandra. Toronto, Ontario: Lorimer, 2004. 141 pp. ISBN: 1550288342; ISBN2: 1550288350. Grades 9–12.

Chris and Danielle have been best friends for a long time. However, when Chris notices that Danielle is acting differently, such as doing and saying strange things, she starts to wonder if substance abuse is involved. When Danielle starts skipping school and running away for days, Chris realizes that Danielle needs professional help. After Danielle is finally diagnosed as having a mental illness, she gets the help she needs due to Chris's intervention. Both girls hope that their friendship can survive in spite of this illness. "[A] good book for both middle school and high school as students will be able to identify with at least one of the characters." KLIATT

115. *Georgie.* Doyle, Malachy. New York: Bloomsbury Children's Books, 2001. 154 pp. ISBN: 1582347530. Grades 8–10.

Georgie, who is orphaned and mute, draws the reader into his unusual world by telling his story in the first person. Georgie's uncontrollable anger and violent interactions with most of the people in his life are the reasons why Georgie finds himself heading to a last resort facility. But the unusually perceptive and knowledgeable teacher, Tommo, and another fellow resident, Shannon, help Georgie realize that he can control his actions and learn how to resolve his personal issues regarding the horrific incident that sent Georgie into his violent, self-destructive world in the first place. This story is very easy to read and fast paced. "[O]n the whole this book is exceptionally well crafted, from its gripping opening to its hopeful conclusion." *School Library Journal*

116. *Helicopter Man.* Fensham, Elizabeth. New York: Bloomsbury, 2005. 159 pp. ISBN: 1582349819. Grades 7–9.

Twelve-year-old Pete Sinclair, who is unaware of the depth of his father's mental illness, has been living on the streets with his father. By telling his story in journal format, Pete gives the reader a firsthand account of his dealing with his father's schizophrenia, especially the delusions, the death of his mother a few years earlier, and his interactions with the upscale foster parents with whom he is living while his father is hospitalized. This insightful and very poignant story champions a son's loyalty to his father despite difficult times. "Once through the initial strangeness, students will find this a worthy and thoughtful look at mental illness and the strength of family bonds." *School Library Journal*

117. *King of the Pygmies.* Fuqua, Jonathon Scott. Cambridge, MA: Candlewick Press, 2005. 246 pp. ISBN: 0763614181. Grades 8–12.

Penrod, a 15-year-old, begins to hear voices, but is more concerned about Daisy, the new girl at school and their blossoming friendship and romance. His parents worry about the onset of schizophrenia and insist that Penrod receive medical attention so that he does not become like his alcoholic uncle, who also hears voices. Penrod's relationship with his older, slightly retarded brother keeps him grounded. The author states that his intention in this book is to address teenagers who might have mild schizophrenia, and for the reader to see the humanity of the individuals beset by it. Fuqua states that we tend to forget that the mentally ill have hopes, dreams, loves, and losses that completely mirror our own. "[T]he book will appeal to those who enjoy a quiet read." *School Library Journal*

118. *Invisible.* Hautman, Pete. New York: Simon & Schuster Books for Young Readers, 2005. 149 pp. ISBN: 0689868006. Grades 8–11.

Douglas, an introverted 17-year-old, narrates his struggle at being practically invisible to his fellow classmates. Everyone at school thinks that he is strange except Andy, his best friend. Andy, one of the most popular students at school, is always there for Douglas, especially after the tragedy that even Douglas has to accept. "With its excellent plot development and unforgettable, heartbreaking protagonist, this is a compelling novel of mental illness." *School Library Journal*

119. *My Bipolar, Roller Coaster, Feelings Book.* Hebert, Bryna; illustrated by Jessica Hannah and Matthew Hebert. Victoria, BC: Trafford, 2005. [27] pp. ISBN: 1412054257. Grades 2–4.

Robert tells the story of how having bipolar disorder affects his life. He is very honest and straight forth about his fears and what makes him mad. Robert also shares the important role that his family plays in helping him understand and control his feelings. Readers should appreciate Robert's honest narration of his interaction with his family and classmates, both in school situations and at play. Color illustrations drawn by younger kids are included.

120. *Kissing Doorknobs.* Hesser, Terry Spencer. New York: Bantam Doubleday Dell Books for Young Readers, 1998. 149 pp. ISBN: 0385323298. Grades 7–9.

Tara recounts her strange and uncontrollable feelings and actions as she spirals into an obsessive-compulsive disorder. Tara's mother becomes abusive. Her family does not understand her, neither do her friends. However, her friends do their best to accept her; but it is her younger sister Greta who supports her, even fights off the cruel bullies at school. After numerous trips to various doctors and the start of a relationship with a new friend, Tara finally discovers that she is not nuts and begins to get control of her life and actions. This is a very realistic telling of a young person's pain who does not understand what is happening to her. "The author's treatment of the subject is thorough and thoughtful . . . a great pick for reluctant readers." *School Library Journal*

121. *Almost Eden.* Horrocks, Anita. Plattsburgh, NY: Tundra Books of Northern New York, 2006. 284 pp. ISBN: 0887767427. Grades 5–8.

Elsie, who is 12 years old and the middle of three sisters, is having an awful summer in this story that takes place during the late 1960s. Her mother is in Eden, a low-level mental health facility located in a Mennonite Canadian community. Some of the problems that Elsie faces are her father's resistance to the Mennonite philosophy, her bossy older sister being in charge, and her younger sister getting Elsie into trouble. Elsie's journal-like conversations with God indicate her frustration with her family situation. Although she blames herself for her mother's latest stay in the facility, she is determined to get her mother back home. This is a very enjoyable read for the middle school age group, especially those readers who are challenged by older and younger sisters. "Both harsh and loving, the characters, seen through Elsie's eyes, are drawn with surprising complexity, and though the story includes two long adventures, its warmth and honesty about a brave girl who loses faith and then finds it again will hold young readers." *Booklist*

122. *Heck, Superhero.* Leavitt, Martine. Asheville, NC: Front Street, 2004. 144 pp.
ISBN: 1886910944. Grades 7–9.

Heck Berlioz is 13 years old and is accustomed to his mother's periodic disap-
pearances due to her fragile mental state. They are evicted from their apartment
building, forcing Heck to live on the streets as he tries to locate his mother. His
best friend Spence and his relationship with his eighth grade art teacher are his
only connections to some normalcy. An unexpected meeting with an 18-year-old
mentally disturbed street indigent creates a change in his life, hopefully for the
better. Middle school readers should enjoy this fast read story and appreciate
the resourcefulness of this likable young teen. "Credible characters are placed
in recognizable situations to create a poignant, fast-paced, and believable look
at homelessness, mental illness, and the way one boy copes with their impact."
School Library Journal

123. *A Dance for Three.* Plummer, Louise. New York: Delacorte Press, 2000.
230 pp. ISBN: 0385325118. Grades 9–12.

When 15-year-old Hannah becomes pregnant by an irresponsible boy from
school, she realizes that she has to grow up pretty fast. In facing reality, Hannah
convinces herself that she is mentally ill. Her stay in the mental health facility
is helpful—even in dealing with her mother, who has not been very functional
since her father's death several years earlier. This is a very realistic portrayal of
a young girl who faces an unplanned pregnancy at an early age. "In a crowded
genre, this story excels in character development, plot devices, and underlying
themes." *School Library Journal*

124. *Matthew Unstrung.* Seago, Kate. New York: Dial Books, 1998. 236 pp.
ISBN: 0803722303. Grades 9–12.

In the 1900s, Matthew is 17 years old and in college. He suffers a mental
breakdown trying to live up to his minister father's demanding high standards.
Only his older brother Zack, who has moved to a Colorado ranch, can understand
the toll and suffering that Matthew has endured from their father. With Zack's
determination to bring him back to reality, Matthew's love of popular music,
forbidden by his father, helps him on the road to mental health and the ability to
be his own person. This is an interesting story about one brother's love for the
other. Readers who like historical fiction should enjoy this story that is set during
the western expansion when the country experienced challenges of the separation
of church and state.

125. *Black-Eyed Suzie.* Shaw, Susan. Honesdale, PA: Boyds Mills Press, 2002.
167 pp. ISBN: 156397729X. Grades 8–10.

Suzie's uncle forces her parents, against their wishes, to admit 12-year-old Suzie to a mental hospital. While in the mental hospital, she neither eats nor talks. Even her older sister Deanna does not know how to help her. During her stay, Suzie meets Stella, a kind doctor, and several helpful staff members in whom she can trust. Some of the patients help Suzie resolve her inner conflict, especially one of the girls who is initially hostile toward her. Suzie's inner conflict is her mother's alcoholic-induced physical and emotional abusive behavior toward Suzie and her sister. Both her father and sister want to make excuses and cover up the mother's violent behavior. "Shaw's depiction of the intricate family dynamics that support an abusive situation is both realistic and sympathetic." *School Library Journal*

126. *The Turkey Prince.* Tooinsky, Izzi; illustrated by Edwina White. New York: Viking, 2001. [29] pp. ISBN: 0670888729. Grades 1–3.

This whimsical tale shows the extent of what an individual may do if he or she does not want to face life's challenges. A young prince, who does not want to rule his family's kingdom, becomes a turkey and lives under a table in the kitchen. Everyone in the kingdom tries to help. When a stranger arrives, also proclaiming himself a turkey, the prince encounters a sympathetic soul who, over time, provides a safe and caring environment that allows the prince to grow up and be the ruler of the kingdom. Color illustrations complement the text.

127. *Inside Out.* Trueman, Terry. New York: HarperTempest, 2003. 117 pp. ISBN: 0066239621. Grades 8–12.

Zach, a schizophrenic 16-year-old, is being held hostage by two teenage brothers after they bungle a robbery. As Zach tries to interact with the situation, the two brothers react differently to his schizophrenia. The older brother is understanding, but the younger brother is agitated and angered. This is an interesting narration told from inside Zach's unsettled mind. This realistic portrayal of Zach's functioning with the real world has an unfortunate ending. "Trueman sometimes captures moments of heartbreaking truth, and his swift, suspenseful plot will have particular appeal to reluctant readers." *Booklist*

128. *Like a Thorn.* Vidal, Clara; translated by Y. Maudet. New York: Delacorte Press, 2008. 119 pp. ISBN: 0385735642; ISBN: 9780385735643. Grades 7–9.

Mélie, a young adolescent girl, has always known that her mother is different—sometimes she is Rosy Mother and sometimes she is Dark Mother. As Mélie approaches puberty, her mother is more erratic and more often Dark Mother. Mélie responds to her mother's mental illness by developing her own mental illness, which is expressed in ritualistic behavior activities. No one is able to help Mélie, including her distant father and her affable grandmother. There may be hope for Mélie when she starts seeing a psychologist. "This tightly woven novel leaves the reader entranced." *Kirkus Reviews*

129. *So B. It.* Weeks, Sarah. New York: Laura Geringer Books, 2004. 245 pp. ISBN: 0066236223. Grades 6–8.

This is an interesting story of 12-year-old Heidi, who does not know about her background or the whereabouts of her father. Heidi's agoraphobic neighbor, Bernadette, is raising her as well as taking care of Heidi's mentally retarded mother. Unable to accept the fact that she does not know who she is or who her mother is or where they came from, Heidi travels across country to discover her mother's true identity as well as her own. This is a touching story of an extended family and a very realistic portrayal of the challenges and limitations a child experiences when a parent is mentally retarded. "This is lovely writing—real, touching, and pared cleanly down to the essentials." *Booklist*
2006 Dolly Gray Award for Children's Literature in Developmental Disabilities.

130. *Memories of Summer.* White, Ruth. Thorndike, ME: Thorndike Press, 2001. 165 pp. ISBN: 0374349452. Grades 7–11.

In the mid-1950s, Lyric is 13 years old and being raised by her older sister, Summer, after their mother died. Summer has always had some quirky notions. When their father moves the family to Michigan for employment, Summer's mental illness becomes increasingly disruptive for the family. This is a very inspiring story that teaches lessons about growing up without a mother, having a father who moves the family to find employment, being the new kid in school, and having a sister with unexplainable and uncontrollable behavior. This is a great story that many teenagers should find relevant. "A marvelous re-creation of time and place and a poignant story that has much to say about compassion." *School Library Journal*

131. *The True Colors of Caitlynne Jackson.* Williams, Carol Lynch. New York: Delacorte, 1997. 168 pp. ISBN: 0385322496. Grades 6–9.

Twelve-year-old Caity tries to be a perfect daughter for her physically and emotionally abusive mother. Her 11-year-old half sister Cara is relieved when their abusive mother abandons them for the summer. When two months have passed and there is still no sign of her mother, Caity seeks help from her grandmother. The sisters' instinct to survive provides inspiration to young readers who can identify with the sisters' situation. This realistic portrayal of domestic violence, disturbing at times for the reader, is unusual because the mother is the perpetrator of the abuse. "[S]tory is gracefully written and hard to put down." *Kirkus Reviews*

132. *The Illustrated Mum.* Wilson, Jacqueline. New York: Delacorte Press, 2005. 282 pp. ISBN: 0385902638. Grades 9–12.

Ten-year-old Dol, short for Dolphin, tells her family's story: Dol and her older sister Star were born to a manic-depressive mother and have different fathers. The sisters have raised themselves and have taken care of their mother, Marigold, who tries to resolve her issues in life by getting tattoos. When Star finally meets her father, she moves in with him. No longer able to control her mother, Dol watches helplessly as her mother is hospitalized. Dol finds her own father and begins visiting him and his family. However, Star returns to Dol when she realizes that her real family is Dol and her mother. "This isn't a fun read and the girls' future is only moderately hopeful, but it is an involving one on a subject not often portrayed in Children's Literature." *School Library Journal*

133. *Zane's Trace.* Wolf, Allan. Cambridge, MA: Candlewick Press, 2007. 177 pp. ISBN: 9780763628581. Grades 9–12.

Zane Guesswind, a 17-year-old from Baltimore, Maryland, is traveling to Zanesville, Ohio. Zane feels that the only way for him to handle his mother's suicide, which took place a few years earlier, his estranged father's death, his abusive grandfather who lived with them and whose death Zane feels he caused is to shoot himself at his mother's grave. Along the way Zane encounters a mysterious young girl and tries to resolve all of these issues. Zane's older sheriff deputy brother arrives in time to help Zachary. "This is a well told tale that will benefit all who read it." *Children's Literature*

Nonfiction

134. *Bipolar Disorder.* Abramovitz, Melissa. Series: Diseases and Disorders. San Diego, CA: Lucent Books, 2005. 112 pp. ISBN: 1590185897; ISBN2: 9781590185896. Grades 6–9.

This title in the Diseases and Disorders series provides comprehensive coverage for bipolar disorder, which is an increasingly common disorder. The two introductory chapters explain what bipolar disorder is and identify its causes. Additional topics explore the various treatment options and how individuals and family members cope with this disorder. The final chapter offers the most current research in the study of bipolar disorder and the future direction for those individuals diagnosed with bipolar disorder. The text is easy to read while providing all important concepts in manageable sections. Black and white photographs, graphics, text boxes, glossary, organizations, a section listing websites, and an index are included.

135. *Schizophrenia.* Abramovitz, Melissa. Series: Diseases and Disorders. San Diego, CA: Lucent Books, 2002. 112 pp. ISBN: 1560069082; ISBN2: 9781560069089. Grades 6–9.

This title in the Diseases and Disorders series provides comprehensive coverage about schizophrenia in six chapters. The introductory chapter contains background information beginning with a brief history of schizophrenia, which was tradition-ally considered a terrifying disease. The author defines schizophrenia and identi-fies its causes, such as genetics, family ties, stress, and prenatal viruses. Additional topics explore the various treatment options and how individuals and family members cope with this disorder. The final chapter offers the latest research in the study of schizophrenia and the future directions for individuals diagnosed with schizophrenia. The text is easy to read while providing all-important concepts in manageable sections. Black and white photographs, graphics, text boxes, glossary, organization information, a section listing websites, and an index are included.

136. *Mental Health Information for Teens: Health Tips about Mental Health and Mental Illness.* Bellenir, Karen, editor. Series: Teen Health. Detroit: Omnigraphics, 2006. 425 pp. ISBN: 0780808630; ISBN2: 9780780808638. Grades 9–12.

This updated edition volume, one of the titles in the Teen Health series, pro-vides excellent coverage on the topic of mental health for teenagers, one that is often hard to locate in print materials. Part I addresses mental health concerns, such as self-esteem, sadness, peer pressure, stress, and grief. Specific mental ill-nesses, such as seasonal affective disorder (SAD), bipolar disorder, panic disor-ders, phobias, and self-injury, are discussed in Part II. An overview of the various types of depression and suggestions for dealing with the depths of depression is also included in Part II. Part III examines teenage suicide, focusing on its effect on family and friends, and provides suggestions for its prevention. Part IV exam-ines the various treatment options and mental health resources for further read-ing. Text boxes throughout the book highlight essential facts, associations and organizations, and websites, and an index is included. "[A]n excellent resource." *School Library Journal*

137. *Wishing Wellness: A Workbook for Children of Parents with Mental Ill-ness.* Clarke, Lisa Anne; illustrated by Bonnie Matthews. Washington, DC: Magination Press, 2006. 127 pp. ISBN: 1591473136. Grades 2–4.

This unique resource provides valuable advice to young readers who face the challenges associated with having a mentally ill parent. Each chapter focuses on specific concerns that children experience and steps that can be taken to help. For example, chapter topics include what to do with one's feelings, building one's strengths, and developing support systems. Considering the sensitive nature of the topic, children should benefit by using this workbook with a counselor. The author states that the purpose of this book is to give children the best information about what is going on with their mentally ill parent and to make children feel better about that parent, and, most of all, feel good about themselves. An extensive dictionary containing mental illness words in Chapter 2, black and white illustrations, text boxes, and topic-specific forms, including exercises, are included.

138. *Bipolar Disorder, Depression, and Other Mood Disorders.* Demetriades, Helen A. Series: Diseases and People. Berkeley Heights, NJ: Enslow, 2002. 112 pp. ISBN: 0766018989. Grades 7–10.

This volume, one of the titles in the Diseases and People series, provides a good overview of mood disorders. The author begins by telling the story of Helen, a sixth grader who suffers from depression. The chapters that follow include topics such as explaining the types of mood disorders, symptoms and diagnoses, as well as treatment options. An interesting chapter covers the rarely discussed topic, "The History of Mood Disorders." The remaining topics cover mood disorders in our society and culture, as well as a look at the future in dealing with individuals who experience mood disorders. "Questions and Answers," "Mood Disorder Timeline," a glossary, an index, information about organizations, additional resources, Internet addresses, and black and white photographs and graphics are included.

139. *Nothing to Be Ashamed of: Growing Up with Mental Illness in Your Family.* Dinner, Sherry H. New York: Lothrop, Lee & Shepard Books, 1989. 212 pp. ISBN: 0688084826. Grades 5–10.

Dinner, a child psychologist, has written this book for those young teenagers who cope with a family member's mental illness. This older publication provides a unique perspective that is still appropriate and useful today. Firsthand scenarios, told in nonthreatening language, provide reassuring information that should help teenagers deal with the everyday challenges of having a mentally ill relative. Specific mental illnesses that are covered include schizophrenia, mood disorders, anxiety disorders, posttraumatic stress disorder, Alzheimer's disease, and eating disorders. Chapter 2, "Reactions to Living with a Mentally Ill Person," contains some of the most beneficial and valuable advice for the young teenager who feels that he or she may be the only one dealing with mental illness in one's family. The appendix provides information to help teenagers find support groups. An extensive glossary, additional reading material, and an index are included. "[T]his book should be purchased for its worthwhile and unique content." *School Library Journal*

140. *Good Mental Health.* Gray, Shirley Wimbish. Series: Living Well. Chanhassen, MN: Child's World, 2004. 32 pp. ISBN: 1592960820. Grades 3–5.

This resource, one of the titles in the Living Well series, encourages young readers to develop good, lifelong mental health skills. The helpful chapter topics told in straightforward text are filled with suggestions and guidelines that include relaxation tips, explanations of the functions of the brain, understanding of why individuals worry, and the different types of stress. The chapter titled "How Can You Develop Good Mental Health?" is especially beneficial. Color photographs, graphics, a glossary, mental health facts, a list of questions and answers about mental health, additional reading material, websites, and an index are included.

141. *Schizophrenia: Losing Touch with Reality.* Harmon, Daniel E. Series: Encyclopedia of Psychological Disorders. Philadelphia: Chelsea House, 2000. 93 pp. ISBN: 0791049531. Grades 9–12.

As one of the volumes in the Encyclopedia of Psychological Disorders series, this title provides a good, basic overview of the issues and challenges facing individuals who have schizophrenia. Chapter topics include an explanation of schizophrenia, its diagnosis, and the effects that individuals suffering from schizophrenia have on society. Additional chapter topics include the causes of schizophrenia as well as possible treatment options. By identifying several historical and famous individuals, such as the Russian ballet dancer Nijinsky, who have had schizophrenia and by recounting several recent headline stories from the news in which individuals who have schizophrenia have been involved, the author provides real faces to this mental illness. Appendices include a glossary, a list of national organizations that provide support, additional reading material, and black and white photographs. An index also is included.

142. *Youth with Bipolar Disorder: Achieving Stability.* Hunter, David and Phyllis Livingston. Series: Helping Youth with Mental, Physical, and Social Challenges. Philadelphia, PA: Mason Crest Publishers, 2008. 128 pp. ISBN: 1422201384; ISBN2: 9781422201381. Grades 8–12.

As part of the series titled Helping Youth with Mental, Physical, and Social Challenges, this book contains a story about Abigail Harper who has bipolar disorder. It discusses how the disorder impacts her life and her family's life in different ways. For example, her grades have slipped and her friendships are strained. In addition, information about the treatment of bipolar disorder is provided. A glossary, a list of books for additional information including websites, color photographs, and an index are included.

143. *Coping with Bipolar Disorder and Manic-Depressive Illness.* Jovinelly, Joann. Series: Coping. New York: Rosen Publishing Group, 2001. 92 pp. ISBN: 0823931935. Grades 7–9.

This work, one of the titles in the Coping series, provides an overview of the various types of mental illnesses. The first chapter discusses how to recognize mental illness and gives a historical overview of mental illness as well as identifying famous individuals who have had a mental illness. The rest of the chapters provide information regarding the benefits of modern drug therapies in treating mental illness and how bipolar disorder affects family and friends. The author uses realistic scenarios to illustrate the key concepts in each chapter. A glossary, a list of organizations including websites for the United States and Canada, additional reading material, and an index are included.

144. *Coping with Schizophrenia.* Kelly, Evelyn B. Series: Coping. New York: Rosen Publishing Group, 2001. 106 pp. ISBN: 0823928535. Grades 7–9.

The first chapter of this volume in the Coping series is titled, "What Is Schizophrenia?" Other chapter topics include suggestions for employing effective communication and for taking care of the individual who is diagnosed with schizophrenia. The chapter titled "The History of Mental Illness" is an excellent historical overview of mental illness for this age group. The author uses realistic scenarios to illustrate key concepts in each chapter and includes helpful and nonthreatening text and advice in order to explain what is happening to individuals with schizophrenia. A glossary, a list of support groups and organizations in the United States and Canada, additional reading material, and an index are included.

145. *Schizophrenia.* Landau, Elaine. Series: Life Balance. New York: Franklin Watts, 2004. 80 pp. ISBN: 0531122158. Grades 4–7.

This volume, one of the titles in the Life Balance series, provides excellent information and thorough coverage regarding the mental illness schizophrenia, which is often a challenging topic to explain to younger readers. Chapter topics include how to determine the cause of schizophrenia and how to understand schizophrenia, especially in those individuals who suffer from this mental illness. Additional chapter topics address how individuals cope and recover from schizophrenia. Real-life stories are used throughout this book in order to illustrate key concepts. A helpful glossary, additional reading material, and websites are included.

146. *Mental Illness.* Leigh, Vanora. Series: Talking Points. Austin, TX: Raintree Steck-Vaughn, 1999. 64 pp. ISBN: 0817253114. Grades 7–9.

This volume, one of the titles in the Talking Points series, contains color text boxes, color and black and white photographs in an easy-to-read and easy-to-follow format. The colorful format provides a nonthreatening work that younger readers can easily flip through. The following topics are discussed: anxiety, dementia, depression, eating disorders, personality disorders, schizophrenia, and addictions. The chapters on the causes of mental illness and family interactions should be very helpful for teenagers.

147. *Runaway Train: Youth with Emotional Disturbance.* Libal, Autumn. Series: Youth with Special Needs. Broomall, PA: Mason Crest, 2004. 127 pp. ISBN: 1590847326. Grades 7–10.

Libal tells the story of Sheila to illustrate a wide range of emotional experiences and challenges encountered during the teenage years in this title in the Youth with Special Needs series. The author places facts within a fictional framework in order to create a realistic scenario to illustrate a variety of emotions stemming from being abandoned by a mother or having a nonresponsive father. Other difficult issues covered are self-expression, friendship with an abused classmate who uses drugs, self-mutilation, time spent in a hospital's psychiatric unit, and genuine friendship. Each scenario has a follow-up section that contains symptoms, explanations, consequences, and possible resolutions. A glossary, additional reading material, websites, and an index are included. "Adolescents can use the information contained herein to understand the difference between normal teenage angst and problems requiring professional help." *School Library Journal*

148. *Youth with Juvenile Schizophrenia: The Search for Reality.* McIntosh, Kenneth and Phyllis Livingston. Series: Helping Youth with Mental, Physical, and Social Challenges. Philadelphia, PA: Mason Crest Publishers, 2008. 128 pp. ISBN: 1422201481; ISBN2: 9781422201480. Grades 8–12.

Part of the series titled Helping Youth with Mental, Physical, and Social Challenges, this book narrates the story about Josh Bruner who has schizophrenia and believes that a mysterious voice harasses him and that he has special powers. He is determined to obey the voices that he hears, which costs him everything. Important facts about schizophrenia are listed. A glossary, a list of books for additional information including websites, a bibliography, color photographs, and an index are included.

149. *Coping with Mental Illness.* Moe, Barbara A. Series: Coping. New York: Rosen Publishing Group, 2001. 138 pp. ISBN: 0823932052. Grades 7–9.

This title, one of the titles in the Coping series, provides a comprehensive look at mental illness. The first chapter provides an introduction to mental illness, including an interesting list titled "Debunking the Myths." The chapter titled "Getting Help" contains numerous suggestions and answers to questions that the reader can learn from. Other chapter topics include mood disorders and schizophrenia. The last chapter, "Hope for the Future," contains three detailed case studies that give the reader a sense of resolution and hope for overcoming mental illness. The author uses scenarios to illustrate key concepts throughout the text. A glossary, an extensive list of helpful organizations in the United States and Canada, additional reading material, websites, and an index are included.

150. *Coping with Social Anxiety.* Moehn, Heather. Series: Coping. New York: Rosen Publishing Group, 2001. 112 pp. ISBN: 0823933636. Grades 7–9.

This title in the Coping series addresses social anxiety as a topic worthy of discussion on its own. A wide variety of social anxieties are addressed: public speaking, taking tests, shopping, talking on the telephone, eating in public, and using public restrooms. The chapters are divided into manageable and understandable concepts, such as, ways to identify social anxiety, its causes, how life is affected by social anxiety, and how to cope when one has social anxiety. The author uses case studies to illustrate the specific social anxieties that are discussed and text boxes that contain quick quizzes for assessment tools, such as the Brief Social Phobia Scale (BSPS). A glossary, hotlines, support groups and organizations, websites, additional reading material, and an index are included.

151. *Bipolar Disorder.* Peacock, Judith. Series: Perspectives on Mental Health. Minnetonka, MN: Life Matters, 2000. 64 pp. ISBN: 073680434X. Grades 4–8.

This volume, one of the titles in the Perspectives on Mental Health series, uses bold colors throughout the book as welcoming visuals in order to deal with this challenging topic. Text boxes set in color provide an appealing way to highlight information, present case studies, and give "Points to Consider," which contents can be used by the reader alone or as discussion starters. This is a good, nonthreatening introduction to bipolar disorder. A glossary, an index, additional resources, and useful addresses and websites are included. "Colorful photos and graphics are used effectively. . . . Accessible to less-able readers, and interesting enough to be starting points for researchers." *School Library Journal*

152. *I Just Hope It's Lethal: Poems of Sadness, Madness and Joy.* Rosenberg, Liz and Deena November, editors. Boston: Graphia/Houghton Mifflin, 2005. 190 pp. ISBN: 0618564527. Grades 9–12.

This interesting and unique anthology is comprised of poems that deal with personal emotions, specifically darker emotions. The editors, poets themselves and whose own poems appear in this work, have selected poems that will "offer a better understanding of those people who know what it's like to never want to wake up in the morning." The ninety-two poems are divided into five sections: wide range of moods; crazy in love; world generated insanity; personal insanity; coming out of a bad period. The poems are international in scope. Poets range from the most widely read, such as Shakespeare and Poe, to lesser known ones including teenage writers and up-and-coming poets. Brief biographies of the poets as well as an index of titles and an index of "First Lines" are included. This is an excellent resource that teenagers can read alone or can be used in groups. "These raw, honest words from peers may speak most directly to teens." *Booklist*

153. *Coping When a Parent Is Mentally Ill.* Ross, Allison J. Series: Coping. New York: Rosen Publishing Group, 2001. 108 pp. ISBN: 0823933598. Grades 7–9.

This volume, one of the titles in the Coping series, is a useful and most welcome resource for young readers who, even at an early age, have to deal with life's challenges as they pertain to their own parents. This work covers numerous conditions such as depression, bipolar disorder, psychosis/schizophrenic, panic disorder, obsessive-compulsive disorder, substance abuse, and suicide. Although there are no visuals, the text is easy to read, and case studies are included for each topic. Useful chapters include "When to Get Help for Yourself" and "Helpful Coping Strategies." A glossary, a list of organizations including websites for the United States and Canada, additional reading materials, and an index are included.

154. *Mental Illness and Its Effect on School and Work Environments.* Shields, Charles J. Series: Encyclopedia of Psychological Disorders. Philadelphia, PA: Chelsea House Publishers, 2000. 101 pp. ISBN: 0791053180. Grades 9–12.

This volume, one of the titles in the Encyclopedia of Psychological Disorders series, provides a very clear explanation and history of mental illness and its treatment. The major impact of this work is placing mental illness in the context of school, work, and society. The sixth and the final chapter, "Recognizing Mental Illness and Finding Help," has excellent coverage including questions and answers and informal helpful lists. There are black and white photographs and the appendices include contact information for national organizations, a glossary, an index, and additional resources.

155. *Coping with Emotional Disorders.* Simpson, Carolyn. Series: Coping. New York: Rosen Publishing Group, 1991. 146 pp. ISBN: 0823912388. Grades 7–9.

The introductory section of this volume, one of the titles in the Coping series, provides helpful suggestions for teenagers who suffer from emotional disorders and for family members who want to understand these disorders. The two parts in this book provide suggestions for handling mental illness in the family. The first chapter in Part 2 includes a self-assessment tool for the reader to help determine if the reader has an emotional disorder. Various treatment options, such as outpatient therapy and hospitalization, are discussed. The causes of emotional disorders, a symptoms' checklist, and steps for getting treatment as well as scenarios that illustrate key concepts are included. A bibliography and an index complete this work.

156. *Schizophrenia.* Veague, Heather Barnett. Series: Psychological Disorders. New York: Chelsea House Publishers, 2007. 114 pp. ISBN: 9780791085448. Grades 7–9.

This title in the Psychological Disorders series examines the myths and misconceptions about schizophrenia. Chapter topics include a glimpse of the latest research on the causes of schizophrenia, its diagnosis, and treatment options. Additional chapters address the symptoms of schizophrenia as well as how both patients and family members are affected. The remaining chapters include information on how science is trying to identify multiple causes of schizophrenia and how effective the medication for treating this disorder is. Color photographs, graphics, and text boxes that contain facts about mood disorders, a glossary, additional reading material, websites, and an index are included.

157. *Coping with Compulsive Behavior.* Webb, Margot. Series: Coping. New York: Rosen Publishing Group, 1994. 107 pp. ISBN: 0823916049. Grades 7–9.

This slightly older volume, one of the titles in the Coping series, is still relevant because it contains valuable information regarding compulsive behavior. Each of the five chapters begins with questions for the reader, such as what is compulsive behavior and who is likely to be compulsive. Chapter topics include identifying the varying degrees of compulsion and how friends and family can provide help for the individual who displays compulsive behavior. The author includes case studies and narratives of individuals who have various compulsive behaviors, such as performing repetitive acts, out of control shopping, constant talking, maintaining rigid schedules, and gambling. Additional reading materials and an index are included. "This volume will be helpful in recognizing [compulsive behaviors] as well as providing information for reports." *School Library Journal*

MULTIPLE EMOTIONAL DISABILITIES

Nonfiction

158. *Healthy Teens: Facing the Challenges of Young Lives: A Practical Guide for Parents, Caregivers, Educators, and Health Professionals.* McCarthy, Alice R. Birmingham, MI: Bridge Communications, 2000. 266 pp. ISBN: 0962164550. Teens/Educators/Parents.

Now in its third edition, this guide continues to provide comprehensive coverage of the challenges facing teenagers today. Topics include psychological health, stress, depression, illnesses, suicide, and eating disorders. One chapter covers substance abuse from alcohol to the various drugs, and another chapter provides answers to questions pertaining to substance abuse. Each chapter contains a substantial listing of resources that include additional reading material, organizations, and websites. Appendices include school health programs, the Michigan Model for comprehensive school health education, school drug prevention guides, and what to expect when your adolescent is in trouble, such as interaction with police officers and potential incarceration. Black and white photographs, drawings, and an index are included. "This book is a good addition to all parenting collections." *Library Journal*

159. *Depression and Bipolar Disorder.* Thakkar, Vatsal. Series: Psychological Disorders. New York: Chelsea House Publishers, 2006. 100 pp. ISBN: 0791085422. Grades 7–9.

This title in the Psychological Disorders series examines the myths and misconceptions about depression and bipolar disorder. The introductory chapter provides a glimpse of mood disorders throughout history and attempts to explain what it means to be normal. The chapters that follow use case studies to illustrate the causes and symptoms of depressive disorders, bipolar spectrum disorders, and other mood disorders. The remaining chapters include the topics the relationship of mood disorders and suicide, risk factors, causes, and treatment options. The author identifies well-known individuals who have been diagnosed with mood disorders, such as Vincent van Gogh, Drew Carey, Elton John, to name a few. Color photographs, graphics, and text boxes that contain facts about mood disorders, a glossary, additional reading material, websites, and an index are included. "Because this title can be used for reports and for medical advice and because there are few books for this age group dealing with these subjects, it is a valuable addition to secondary school and public library collections." *School Library Journal*

Chapter 2

Learning

This chapter contains 190 entries: five are for Teens/Educators/Parents, forty are for high school level, eighty-four are for the middle school level, and sixty-one are for the elementary school grade level. The chapter is categorized into five sections: Attention-Deficit/Hyperactivity Disorder (AD/HD), Autism Spectrum Disorders, Down Syndrome, Dyslexia and Other Learning Disabilities, and Intellectual Disabilities. Each of these sections is divided into fiction and nonfiction entries. Variant spellings and abbreviations for several learning disabilities and disorders were encountered among many of the books reviewed, such as Asperger's syndrome versus Asperger syndrome, Down syndrome versus Down's syndrome, and attention-deficit/hyperactivity disorder versus AD/HD, ADD, or ADHD/ADD. In these cases, the spellings and abbreviations used by the authors in their respective books are used here.

ATTENTION-DEFICIT/HYPERACTIVITY DISORDER (AD/HD)

Fiction

160. *Rainy*. Deans, Sis Boulos. New York: Henry Holt, 2005. 199 pp. ISBN: 0805078312. Grades 4–6.

Written by the winner of the Maine Chapbook Award and also the recipient of a Lupine Honor Award, this story is about 10-year-old Rainy Tucker who has restless energy and gets into trouble. Rainy leaves her family for the first time to go to sleep-away camp in rural Maine and is not thrilled about spending time away from her family and her dog Max. She makes some friends at the camp, starts liking the camp, and even gets better at keeping track of her things. However, when she gets bad news from home, she starts having too many thoughts in her head and forgets the rules. "Offering more of a slice of life than a picture of personal growth through circumstances, the book has value in its fresh look into an alternate type of thought processing, making real both the experience itself and the related self-esteem issues that it brings." *School Library Journal*

161. *Mrs. Gorski, I Think I Have the Wiggle Fidgets.* Esham, Barbara; illustrated by Mike Gordon and Carl Gordon. Series: The Adventures of Everyday Geniuses. Perry Hall, MD: Mainstream Connections, 2008. 29 pp. ISBN: 1603364692; ISBN2: 9781603364690. Grades 2–4.

David Sheldon has a hard time paying attention in school. As David says, "I want to pay attention but it is just so hard when an exciting idea pops into my head." His teacher, Mrs. Gorski, is upset when David interrupts the class with distracting activities, such as rolling his pencil on his desk and standing on one foot during a fire drill. When Mrs. Gorski wants to meet with David's parents, David decides to brainstorm in order to find a way to cure the wiggle fidgets, which is what his father calls his restlessness. Young readers should enjoy how David develops a plan to manage his wiggle fidgets. The humorous color illustrations are wonderful and complement this award-winning text while maintaining young readers' interest in a topic that is rarely addressed in picture books.

162. *Otto Learns about His Medicine: A Story about Medication for Children with ADHD.* Galvin, Mathew; illustrated by Sandra Ferraro. Washington, DC: Magination Press, 2001. 32 pp. ISBN: 1557987718; ISBN2: 1557987726. Grades 3–5.

Using the easily grasped metaphor of a car whose engine runs too fast, this is a story about Otto, a high-octane young car who has trouble paying attention in school and is easily distracted. Otto and his parents visit a special mechanic named Dr. Beemer, who prescribes a medicine for Otto to help slow down Otto's racing motor and to control his hyperactive behavior. This third edition includes the latest advances in the understanding of ADHD. It includes "Notes to Parents," which discusses treatment approaches and current findings about medications, including their possible side effects.

163. *Joey Pigza Swallowed the Key.* Gantos, Jack. New York: HarperTrophy, 2000. 153 pp. ISBN: 0374336644; ISBN2: 0064408337. Grades 4–9.

Joey has trouble paying attention and cannot control his actions. He accidentally swallows a key while in school. Joey's mom, whom Joey had not seen since he was in kindergarten, returns to live with him. She is concerned about Joey's behavior and gets professional help. Joey takes medication for ADD, but these medications do not always work. He gets into more trouble and accidentally hurts another student. He is suspended from school for six weeks, during which time he tries to straighten out his life. At the end, the doctor replaces his medication with patches that help him keep calm. "There are plenty of Joeys in schools today, and it is good to have one of their stories told with such skill and sympathy." *VOYA*

164. *Joey Pigza Loses Control.* Gantos, Jack. New York: Farrar, Straus and Giroux, 2000. 195 pp. ISBN: 0374399891. Grades 4–9.

In this sequel to *Joey Pigza Swallowed the Key*, Joey goes to spend the summer with his father. His parents are divorced, and Joey has never really known his father. His father wants to make up for his past mistakes and wants Joey to be a baseball player. Joey has ADHD and is on medication that helps him calm down. It is obvious from his father's behavior that Joey inherited ADHD from his father, who decides that Joey's ADHD is not a disease and, therefore, does not need any medical treatment. He flushes Joey's medication down the toilet and, as a result, Joey feels out of control. This book is interesting and fun to read. "Joey is a young teen struggling to maintain control in an often out-of-control world, a struggle with which many teens will relate. Gantos's style of writing and the subject matter make this book a great middle school read-aloud." *VOYA* 2001 Newbery Honor Book.

165. *What Would Joey Do?* Gantos, Jack. New York: Farrar, Straus and Giroux, 2002. 229 pp. ISBN: 0060544031. Grades 4–9.

This is the third book in the Joey Pigza series. Joey, who has ADHD, deals with tense family situations due to the actions of his long-separated parents who get into fights. Joey lives with his alcoholic, trouble-filled mother and ailing grandmother who is dying of emphysema. His mother makes arrangement for him to be home schooled with a blind girl named Olivia. In spite of all the odds, Joey tries his best to make himself the best person he can. He realizes that he is able to be responsible and make his own choices in life. "[I]t's not just a funny story with nutty parents out of control, it's a poignant story of family, loss, lessons learned, and one boy's learning to make his way in the world with confidence and good cheer. This work easily stands by itself, but readers new to Joey Pigza will rush out to get the others, too. A must read." *Kirkus Reviews*

166. *I Am Not Joey Pigza.* Gantos, Jack. New York: Farrar, Straus and Giroux, 2007. 215 pp. ISBN: 0374399417; ISBN2: 9780374399412. Grades 4–9.

In this fourth title of the Joey Pigza series, just when Joey Pigza's unstable world finally seems to be under control, his good-for-nothing father returns into Joey's life. He has changed his name to Charles Heinz and apologizes for his past bad behavior. He thinks that by changing their names and helping him fix up the old diner he has bought that Joey and his mom will have a better life. Thus Joey faces several changes in his life: a new name, a new home, and a new family business, running the beat-up Beehive Diner. Joey realizes that he should forgive his dad for his past deeds, as his mom wants him to, and move forward by accepting the new family program. However, Joey believes that by doing so, he will lose sight of who he really is. "Gantos offers it all: outrageous schemes, funny scenes, strong voice, dramatic characters and profound reflections on identity, family and love. It stands well on its own, though anyone new to Joey's saga will want to read more. This is Gantos at his best, and that's saying a lot." *Kirkus Reviews*

167. *Parents Wanted.* Harrar, George; illustrated by Dan Murphy. Minneapolis: Milkweed Editions, 2001. 230 pp. ISBN: 1571316329; ISBN2: 1571316337. Grades 7–9.

A touching novel that explores self-acceptance and the power of a loving adopted family, this is a story about a 12-year-old Andrew who has ADD. His biological father has been in jail since Andrew was 10 years old, and his mother turns him over to the state because she thinks he is too hard to handle. After several years of being in foster homes, he is adopted by new parents, Jeff and Laurie, who are willing to give him a chance. Andy tests their patience by making bad decisions. He faces challenges of trusting his adopted parents and understanding the worth of being trusted. He realizes that he is a handful but knows that he desperately needs a caring family. The illustrations are quite amusing.

168. *Waiting for Mr. Goose.* Lears, Laurie; illustrated by Karen Ritz. Morton Grove, IL: Albert Whitman, 1999. [29] pp. ISBN: 0807586285. Grades 2–4.

This is a story about Stephen, who has trouble paying attention and staying still due to attention-deficit hyperactivity disorder (ADHD). He surprises himself and his mother when he demonstrates patience in catching and helping an injured goose. The watercolor illustrations are quite effective. The author has included a note for adults regarding children with ADHD who have difficulty in staying focused. "This is a simple, realistic story of overcoming one's limitations." *Children's Literature*

169. *Just Kids: Visiting a Class for Children with Special Needs.* Senisi, Ellen B. New York: Dutton Children's Books, 1998. 40 pp. ISBN: 0525456465. Grades 3–6.

Experiences of a second grader named Cindy who is assigned to spend part of each day in the classroom for students who have special needs are shared in this book. Cindy gets to know kids with a wide range of disabilities, such as epilepsy, Down syndrome, autism, ADHD, learning disabilities, and more. This book also introduces the readers to activities and learning techniques used in a special education classroom, such as speech lessons, physical therapy, art therapy, occupational therapy, and more. Color illustrations complement the text. "[C]lasses studying disabilities or schools hoping to increase awareness about the benefits of all types of special education will find this title useful." *School Library Journal*

170. *Trout and Me.* Shreve, Susan Richards. New York: Alfred A. Knopf, 2002. 136 pp. ISBN: 0375912193; ISBN2: 0375912199. Grades 5–9.

This humorous novel is about Ben who is diagnosed with ADD and often gets sent to the principal's office because things keep happening to him. Ben's troubles at school start getting worse after he starts associating with a new boy, named Trout, in his fifth grade class. Trout is also diagnosed with ADD. Both of them enjoy being bad and start troublemaking schemes of their own. Eventually, the school personnel and the parents of both boys get involved in order to help with the situation. It is up to Ben to come to his friend Trout's rescue and show everyone that Trout is not as bad as everyone thinks he is, but just a kid who is doing his best to do what is right. "A fast-paced, touching story told in the convincing and perceptive voice of the young protagonist." *School Library Journal*

171. *Eddie Enough.* Zimmett, Debbie; illustrated by Charlotte Murray Fremaux. Bethesda, MD: Woodbine House, 2001. [42] pp. ISBN: 1890627259. Grades 2–4.

This amusing story is about a third grader Eddie Minetti who talks nonstop, jumps down the stairs two at a time, bumps into people, and gets into trouble at school. Some incidents land him in the principal's office and earn him the new nickname "Eddie Enough." The school principal and the therapist help Eddie by diagnosing his ADD and providing him with treatment options. Eddie starts feeling better about himself and feels more like "Eddie Just Right." Black and white pencil drawings are included.

Nonfiction

172. *Attention Deficit Disorder.* Baldwin, Carol. Series: Health Matters. Chicago: Heinemann Library, 2003. 32 pp. ISBN: 1403402493. Grades 2–5.

This book, one of the titles in the Health Matters series, discusses the symptoms of attention deficit disorder (ADD), including types of ADD. Using very effective color illustrations, the author explains the causes of ADD. She also explains how ADD is diagnosed, and how ADD is treated using medicines, natural remedies, and other alternatives. This book should help children understand their classmates with ADD and ways they can help these children in various ways.

Success stories of individuals with ADD are shared. A glossary, an index, color photographs, and a list of additional sources on ADD are included.

173. *Ritalin: Its Use and Abuse.* Beal, Eileen. Series: The Drug Abuse Prevention Library. New York: Rosen Publishing Group, 1999. 64 pp. ISBN: 082392775X. Grades 5–10.

This book, part of the Drug Abuse Prevention Library series, is aimed at explaining Ritalin, a prescription drug for treating ADD and ADHD. The author explains the medical uses of Ritalin. In addition, the following topics are discussed: the problems that are encountered due to over prescribing Ritalin and its potential for abuse. The last chapter, "Knowing How to Say No," lists various helpful steps that can be taken to prevent such abuse. A glossary and a list of organizations and hotlines for help are included. "Parents, students, and educators may find the book helpful for addressing the potential pressure, social stigma, and recreational Ritalin abuse that may result from listening to uninformed classmates." *Booklist*

174. *Stuck on Fast Forward: Youth with Attention-Deficit/Hyperactivity Disorder.* Brinkerhoff, Shirley. Series: Youth with Special Needs. Broomall, PA: Mason Crest Publishers, 2004. 127 pp. ISBN: 159084727X. Grades 7–10.

This well-organized volume in the Youth with Special Needs series brings to life the challenges and triumphs experienced by Connor, who has attention-deficit/hyperactivity disorder, and by his family while dealing with his disorder. The text provides basic information regarding this condition, along with an awareness of some of the associated emotional impacts on affected children and their families. The author discusses how this controversial condition is diagnosed and offers treatment options. Strategies for teenagers and adults with ADHD at the end of the book should be quite helpful to the reader. Color photographs, an index, a glossary, and additional resources including some websites are included.

175. *Sparky's Excellent Misadventures: My A.D.D. Journal.* Carpenter, Phyllis and Marti Ford; illustrated by Peter Horjus. Washington, DC: Magination Press, 1999. [30] pp. ISBN: 1557986061. Grades 1–5.

Told in a first-person diary format, this is an autobiography of a schoolboy named Spencer Allen Douglass, known as "Sparky," who has ADD. In this very interesting journal, he writes about the frustrations, ups and downs, and triumphs of living with ADD. Humorous at times, this journal includes several valuable insights and ideas from a child's perspective that can be helpful to other children with ADD and ADHD. The illustrations complement the text.

176. *What Do You Mean I Have Attention Deficit Disorder?* Dwyer, Kathleen Marie; illustrated by Gregg A. Glory. New York: Walker, 1996. 40 pp. ISBN: 0802783929; ISBN2: 0802783937. Grades 3–6.

Like millions of children in the United States, 11-year-old Patrick is diagnosed with attention deficit disorder. This engaging book discusses many of the behavioral and educational problems faced by Patrick. Eventually, Patrick, along with his parents, meets his teachers who explain all the techniques for helping him focus and remember things. Black and white photographs, including "sources of help" are included. Teachers and families with children who have attention deficit disorder should benefit from this book. "While the writing is slightly stilted, this book will be a helpful resource for children with ADD, as well as for the adults who live and work with them." *School Library Journal*

177. *Attention Deficit Disorder.* Gold, Susan Dudley. Series: Health Watch. Berkeley Heights, NJ: Enslow Publishers, 2000. 48 pp. ISBN: 0766016579. Grades 5–8.

In this volume of the Health Watch series, Christopher who has attention-deficit hyperactivity disorder (ADHD), gets into trouble at school and frustrates his parents and teachers because of his inability to pay attention and complete various tasks. This book describes the causes, symptoms, diagnosis, various types of treatment of ADHD, and ways in which people live with ADHD. A glossary and a list of additional resources, organizations, newsletters, tapes and websites that deal with ADHD are included.

178. *Cory Stories: A Kid's Book about Living with ADHD.* Kraus, Jeanne; illustrated by Whitney Martin. Washington, DC: Magination Press, 2005. [27] pp. ISBN: 1591471486; ISBN2: 1591471540. Grades 2–5.

With the help of excellent illustrations provided by Martin, who has worked on many animated film projects, including several Walt Disney movies, this volume highlights numerous challenges that children with ADHD face. This book is intended to show children with ADHD that they are not alone in dealing with these challenges, and that they can overcome many of these challenges with help from others and with a broad range of skills they can learn. The author, an educational specialist, was inspired by one of her sons, who has ADHD, to write this book. "Note to Parents" at the end of the book includes some great tips for specific problem areas, such as social skills, school adjustments, and attention span.

179. *Attention Deficit Disorder.* Moragne, Wendy. Series: The Millbrook Medical Library. Brookfield, CT: Millbrook Press, 1996. 112 pp. ISBN: 1562946749; ISBN2: 9781562946746. Grades 5–9.

This valuable book in The Millbrook Medical Library series is for young people who have attention deficit disorder (ADD). The author explains the symptoms of attention-deficit hyperactivity disorder and outlines the various treatments, including medication, behavior management, counseling, and practical strategies for coping with this disorder. Eleven individuals with ADD offer their insights into how ADD has affected them, their daily activities, and their self-image. Black and white photographs, a glossary, an index, and a list of resources for more information are included. "[G]ives examples of young people who have developed positive feelings about themselves by pursuing the activities they enjoy." *School Library Journal*

180. *Coping with ADD/ADHD: (Attention Deficit Disorder/Attention Deficit Hyperactivity Disorder).* Morrison, Jaydene. Series: Coping. New York: Rosen Publishing Group, 2000. 106 pp. ISBN: 082393196X. Grades 7–9.

This revised volume in the Coping series examines the causes and symptoms of attention deficit disorder (ADD). In addition, the author provides detailed information regarding medication and techniques to help manage ADD as well as important tips in dealing with family members and friends. The appendix titled "Medical Management of Children with Attention Deficit Disorder: Commonly Asked Questions" should be very helpful to parents and teachers of children with ADD. A section titled "Where to Go for Help" and an index are included.

181. *Learning to Slow Down and Pay Attention: A Book for Kids about ADHD.* Nadeau, Kathleen G. and Ellen B. Dixon; illustrated by Beyl Charles. Washington, DC: Magination Press, 2004. 95 pp. ISBN: 1591471494; ISBN2: 1591471559. Grades 4–8.

This third expanded edition and easy-to-read book, illustrated with cartoons, is divided into four parts: "A Checklist about Me," "Things Other People Can Do to Help Me," "Things I Can Do to Help Myself," and "Special Projects with My Parents." In order to benefit the most, the book can be read by the parent along with his or her child, one section at a sitting, pausing to discuss various ideas and points whenever this seems useful. The third part in this book, which focuses on things that children can learn to do to help themselves, can be used repeatedly as a reference while the child builds attention-deficit hyperactivity disorder (ADHD) coping skills. Each section includes a fun activity page. This book allows the child with ADHD to look at the world from his or her point of view. Helpful websites, including additional reading material for parents and kids, are included.

182. *Help Is on the Way: A Child's Book about ADD.* Nemiroff, Marc A. and Jane Annunziata; illustrated by Margaret Scott. Washington, DC: Magination Press, 1998. 60 pp. ISBN: 1557985057. Grades K–4.

The purpose of this book is to help children 5 to 9 years old and their parents understand attention deficit disorder (ADD). The experience of having ADD is captured from the child's point of view. The illustrator, Margaret Scott, a prize-winning illustrator of children's books, has done an outstanding job. The last six pages are written specifically for parents and guardians to understand the symptoms and diagnosis of the ADD. These include some valuable suggestions regarding living with the ADD child, medication, and play as well as occupational therapy. "A positive message shines through." *School Library Journal*

183. *ADD and ADHD.* Peacock, Judith. Series: Perspectives on Mental Health. Mankato, MN: LifeMatters, 2002. 64 pp. ISBN: 0736810293. Grades 4–8.

This well-organized volume is one of the titles in the Perspectives on Mental Health series. The first chapter defines ADD and ADHD. The next couple of chapters discuss causes of ADHD, its diagnoses, and the treatment, which includes medication, behavior modification, counseling, and alternative therapies. The chapter "ADHD and School" explains legal rights for students with ADHD and the various school adaptations that can be made for learning disabilities. The last two chapters offer some helpful steps that can be followed by teens with ADHD to assume responsibility for managing ADHD. There is a short overview at the end of each chapter. Color photographs, a glossary, useful addresses, Internet sites, and an index are included.

184. *Attention-Deficit/Hyperactivity Disorder.* Peirce, Jeremy L. and Christine E. Collins. Series: Psychological Disorders. New York: Chelsea House Publishers, 2008. 118 pp. ISBN: 9780791085417. Grades 7–9.

This comprehensive volume in the Psychological Disorders series provides the most current information about attention-deficit/hyperactivity disorder (ADHD), an autistic spectrum disorder. ADHD is found in children and young adults. The introductory chapters address the different types of ADHD and the neurobiology of attention and ADHD. The following topics are covered: things that do not cause ADHD, disorders that mimic ADHD, and the role that genes and the environment play in ADHD. In addition, the following issues are discussed: medications, living with ADHD, and the future for individuals who have ADHD. Color photographs, graphics, and text boxes that contain facts about mood disorders, a glossary, additional reading material, websites, and an index are included.

185. *ADHD*. Pigache, Philippa. Series: Just the Facts. Chicago: Heinemann Library, 2004. 56 pp. ISBN: 1403451427. Grades 4–7.

The author provides the history, the symptoms, behaviors, and causes of attention-deficit hyperactivity disorder (ADHD) in this well-written book, which is one of the titles in the Just the Facts series. The author also discusses what it is like to have ADHD, its effect on one's daily life, and how various treatments can help keep ADHD under control. Pigache also presents new areas of scientific research. Additional resources listing some books and websites regarding ADHD are very helpful. A glossary, an index, and color photographs are included. "The well-organized information provides a good overview and a hopeful outlook." *School Library Journal*

186. *Only a Mother Could Love Him: My Life with and Triumph over ADD*. Polis, Benjamin. New York: Ballantine Books, 2004. 182 pp. ISBN: 034547189X; ISBN2: 0345471881. Grades 10–12.

Ben Polis, who has ADD/ADHD, attended six different schools, served over three thousand hours of detention, and drove his family into counseling. However, through great determination and the use of self-taught concentration techniques, Ben graduated from high school and also attended a university. In this book, Ben, at the age of 19, discusses his personal experiences in dealing with ADD/ADHD. In this inspirational book, Ben offers valuable advice to parents with children who have ADD/ADHD, including forms of discipline, surviving the daily homework struggle, medications, or seeking other methods of treatment. Older children between the ages of 14 to 16 with ADD/ADHD will benefit from this book.

187. *Adolescents and ADD: Gaining the Advantage*. Quinn, Patricia O. New York: Magination Press, 1995. 81 pp. ISBN: 0945354703. Grades 6–12.

Written by a developmental pediatrician who works extensively in the areas of ADD, learning disabilities, and mental retardation, this book is for adolescents who have ADD. The author provides information regarding scientific understanding of ADD. She offers adolescents with ADD advice in achieving success in and out of the classroom. She also offers tips on getting organized, on dating, on driving, and how to stand up for one's rights. The book includes a chapter in which students diagnosed with ADD tell personal stories about their experiences in coping with ADD. For additional reading, the book includes a list of other books on ADD. "The author is extremely positive when outlining the steps individuals with ADD may take in order to gain greater autonomy, and does an excellent job of putting the disorder in perspective." *School Library Journal*

188. *50 Activities and Games for Kids with ADHD*. Quinn, Patricia O. and Judith M. Stern, editors; illustrated by Kate Sternberg. Washington, DC: Magination Press, 2000. 94 pp. ISBN: 1591474833; ISBN2: 9781591474838. Grades 3–9.

This is an excellent resource for children with ADHD. A collection of games, puzzles, activities, and articles collected from the newsletter *Brakes* offers more than fifty ways for kids to handle the challenges of ADHD. This book is filled with useful information and practical exercises that will help children to understand ADHD better and offer helpful suggestions and solutions to everyday problems such as homework, getting along with others, and becoming better organized. Additional resources are included.

189. *Putting on the Brakes: Young People's Guide to Understanding Attention Deficit Hyperactivity Disorder*. Quinn, Patricia O. and Judith M. Stern. Washington, DC: Magination Press, 2001. 80 pp. ISBN: 1557987955. Grades 3–7.

This revised and expanded edition, written by a pediatrician and an educator, addresses the needs and questions of children with ADHD. Divided into two parts, the first part discusses the physical aspects of this condition. The second part includes the significant advances that have been made in the treatment and understanding of ADHD since the publication of the first edition ten years earlier. This book may be read by children alone or read aloud by a parent or a teacher. It has a companion activity book with the same title, which should be very helpful to put the children's understanding of ADHD into action. A glossary is provided to explain unfamiliar or difficult words. A list of additional resources and organizations is included as well. "The authors' suggestions are practical and clearly described. Children who have ADHD will gain self-confidence from the information presented here; anyone who knows someone who has it will be encouraged and reassured. A practical purchase for public and school libraries." *School Library Journal*

190. *The "Putting on the Brakes" Activity Book for Young People with ADHD*. Quinn, Patricia O. and Judith M. Stern; illustrated by Neil Russell. New York: Magination Press, 1993. 88 pp. ISBN: 0945354576; ISBN2: 9780945354574. Grades 3–7.

This activity book serves as a companion to the authors' book *Putting on the Brakes: Young People's Guide to Understanding Attention-Deficit Hyperactivity Disorder (ADHD)*. Using numerous ways to hold the interest of young readers with ADHD, this book allows children to put their understanding of ADHD into action. With the use of pictures, puzzles, and other methods, this book helps teach the reader to solve problems, develop skills, get organized, follow directions, study effectively, make friends, and find support. The structure of this book allows it to be used in a variety of ways. For example, some of the exercises can be done independently, while others can be done with a parent, grandparent, teacher, or a counselor. A glossary is provided so that the reader can look up a word if the child does not understand it. Black and white illustrations accompany the text. A list of additional resources is included.

191. *The "Best of Brakes" Activity Book for Kids with ADD and ADHD.* Quinn, Patricia O. and Judith M. Stern; illustrated by Kate Sternberg. Washington, DC: Magination Press, 2000. 94 pp. ISBN: 1557986614. Grades 3–7.

Information-packed feature articles, games, puzzles, and letters that were previously published in *Brakes*, the popular newsletter for kids with ADD and ADHD, are brought together in this book. The chapters offer helpful suggestions and solutions in five subject areas: school, sports and recreation, friends, feelings, and family. It is an excellent activity book written especially for kids with attention deficit disorder, with or without hyperactivity. The format is appealing and full of practical suggestions for solving problems and getting organized. Articles by counselors, other professionals, and teachers offer great ideas for young readers to learn about themselves and the challenges of ADD. Additional resources including books, board games, and organizational materials are also listed. This activity book can be used with the author's other book titled *Putting on the Brakes.*

192. *The A.D.D. Book for Kids.* Rotner, Shelley and Sheila Kelly. Brookfield, CT: Millbrook Press, 2000. [30] pp. ISBN: 0761317228. Grades K–1.

With the help of color photographs showing various activities performed by children with ADHD, the author does a very effective job of explaining what it is like to live with ADHD. The introductory pages, "Note for Parents and Teachers" by Sheila Kelly, define ADHD, list some basic statistics, and a brief history of ADHD. It should be a helpful book for very young children to understand the basics of ADHD.

193. *Sometimes I Drive My Mom Crazy, but I Know She's Crazy about Me: A Self-Esteem Book for ADHD Children.* Shapiro, Lawrence E.; illustrated by Parrotte. King of Prussia, PA: Center for Applied Psychology, 1993. 129 pp. ISBN: 1882732030. Grades 3–5.

Children who have ADHD are generally perceived as "problem" or "difficult" children, thus lowering their self-esteem. This is a heart-warming and an amusing story of a boy who has ADHD. With the help of his loved ones, he has developed a sense of self-worth by learning to deal with his problems. "Using Behavior

Charts" at the end of the book should be a very effective section for helping children with a variety of problems related to ADHD. This book, which has black and white illustrations, should help children with ADHD realize that they are not "weird" or "problem" kids, and that by learning to cope with their problems, with the help of their parents and teachers, they, too, can be successful.

194. *Attention Deficit Disorder.* Sheen, Barbara. Series: Diseases and Disorders. San Diego, CA: Lucent Books, 2001. 96 pp. ISBN: 1560068280. Grades 6–9.

This book, one of the titles in the Diseases and Disorders series, has six chapters. The first chapter looks at the history of attention deficit disorder (ADD). The rest of the book covers causes and diagnoses, treatment options, problems with certain solutions, and living with ADD. The last chapter discusses how experts believe that future research will lead to a better understanding of what causes ADD, leading to a more accurate diagnosis and treatment. Quotations from individuals who have ADD are included in the chapter titled "Problems with Few Solutions." An index, black and white photographs, a glossary, and a list of organizations and books including websites are included. "A solid choice for students with a personal interest in or research requests on the topic." *School Library Journal*

195. *The ADHD Update: Understanding Attention-Deficit/Hyperactivity Disorder.* Silverstein, Alvin, Virginia B. Silverstein, and Laura Silverstein Nunn. Series: Disease Update. Berkeley Heights, NJ: Enslow Publishers, 2008. 112 pp. ISBN: 0766028003; ISBN2: 9780766028005. Grades 4–6.

Atlanta Braves first baseman Adam LaRoches's struggles with ADHD are discussed at the beginning of the book. Information about the history of ADHD, what it is, its diagnosis and treatment, living with ADHD, and the future is provided. The two sections at the end, "Questions and Answer" and "ADHD Timeline," should be very useful. Color illustrations and photographs, a list of organizations, including websites, a glossary, and an index are included. "This book, which takes the mystique out of a condition affecting over two million children, will help kids who have ADHD feel a little better about themselves." *Children's Literature*

196. *Attention Deficit Disorder.* Silverstein, Alvin, Virginia Silverstein, and Laura Silverstein Nunn. Series: My Health. New York: Franklin Watts, 2001. 48 pp. ISBN: 0531117782; ISBN2: 0531139670. Grades 3–6.

This book, one of the titles in the My Health series, defines attention deficit disorder (ADD). Causes, diagnoses, and treatment of ADD are discussed in a very clear and informative way. The last section lists helpful steps those with ADD can take to help themselves listen better, remember things better, and get things done. Two activities—What's it like to have ADD? and Set your own goals—color photographs, a list of books on the subject, a glossary, and an index are included. "[T]his book would be best for adults working with ADD children to share in a positive manner." *School Library Journal*

197. *ADHD.* Trueit, Trudy Strain. Series: Life Balance. New York: Franklin Watts, 2004. 79 pp. ISBN: 0531122611. Grades 4–7.

One of the titles in the Life Balance series, this book discusses symptoms, causes, and methods of treatment of attention-deficit hyperactivity disorder (ADHD). A few individuals who have ADHD share their personal stories as well as the positive steps they have taken in order to cope with this disorder so that they can succeed in life. Additional online sites and organizations, resources, an index, and a glossary are included.

198. *Attention-Deficit/Hyperactivity Disorder.* Williams, Julie. Series: Diseases and People. Berkeley Heights, NJ: Enslow Publishers, 2001. 128 pp. ISBN: 076601598X. Grades 7–10.

This is one of the volumes in the Diseases and People series. Using real case studies, the author explains what attention-deficit hyperactivity disorder (ADHD) is and the various types of behaviors associated with ADHD. The history of ADHD beginning with the ancient Greeks to the present is traced. For example, the ancient Greeks believed that the bodily fluids, such as bile, determined a person's health and personality, which led to "restlessness syndrome" and "hyperkinetic reaction of childhood." Williams also presents profiles of people who have ADHD, the controversies that surround this condition, and the current research that is being conducted to help individuals with ADHD. A list of additional books, videos, Internet addresses, and an index are included.

199. *A Bird's-Eye View of Life with ADD and ADHD: Advice from Young Survivors! A Reference Book for Children and Teenagers.* Ziegler, Dendy, Chris A. Zeigler, and Alex Zeigler. Cedar Bluff, AL: Cherish the Children, 2003. 180 pp. ISBN: 0967991137. Grades 9–12.

This is an excellent resource for children with ADD and ADHD. A collection of games, puzzles, activities, and articles collected from the newsletter *Brakes* offers more than fifty ways for kids to handle the challenges of ADD and ADHD. This book is filled with useful information and practical exercises that will help children understand ADD and ADHD better and offer helpful suggestions and solutions to everyday problems such as homework, getting along with others, and becoming better organized. Additional resources are included. "The appendixes are chock-full of easy-to-understand information. . . . This is a pick-it-up, read-a-bit, and set-it-down kind of non-fiction, and the text is to the point and list filled. A very practical resource." *School Library Journal*

AUTISM SPECTRUM DISORDERS

Fiction

200. *Waiting for Benjamin: A Story about Autism.* Altman, Alexandra and Susan Keeter. Morton Grove, IL: Albert Whitman, 2008. [32] pp. ISBN: 0807573647; ISBN2: 9780807573648. Grades 2–4.

Alexander lives with his parents and his younger brother Benjamin who has autism. Alexander is frustrated because Benjamin is not able to play with him. At times he also feels embarrassed and gets jealous because Benjamin receives special attention from their parents and from Benjamin's special teachers. As Benjamin develops some interacting skills, Alexander learns to accept Benjamin the way he is. Written by a senior interventionist in an autism spectrum program, this is an excellent story that illustrates the emotional challenges faced by families, particularly siblings, of autistic children. "[T]his would be a good icebreaker to help siblings and other youngsters understand autism and express their own feelings more openly." *Children's Literature*

201. *Wild Orchid.* Brenna, Beverley A. Calgary: Red Deer Press, 2005. 156 pp. ISBN: 0889953309; ISBN2: 9780889953307. Grades 9–12.

Eighteen-year-old Taylor Jane Simon, who has Asperger's syndrome, has just graduated from high school. Taylor's mother wants to spend the summer with her new boyfriend, Danny, near a national park in Saskatchewan. When her mother encourages her to explore the park on her own, Taylor discovers that she is skilled at finding and identifying wild flowers. Taylor finds strength through her new friends and learns to accept her struggles so that she can face her future with confidence. "Nonetheless, Brenna has done a credible job of capturing the voice of a young woman on the brink of maturity; in some ways Taylor is incredibly similar to most teenage girls and in other ways she is exceedingly different." *School Library Journal*

202. *My Strange and Terrible Malady.* Bristow, Catherine. Shawnee Mission, KS: Autism Asperger Publishing, 2008, 143 pp. ISBN: 1934575194; ISBN2: 9781934575192. Grades 9–12.

Sixteen-year-old Ronnie Baker has just been diagnosed with Asperger's syndrome. Her weekly meetings with her life coach, Linda, help Ronnie understand that this disorder causes her to misread or exaggerate other people's signals. In addition, Ronnie becomes friends with Hannah, a new girl at school, who helps Ronnie change her misfit image. By reading this first person narrative, readers should gain a better understanding of individuals who have Asperger's syndrome. Readers who have Asperger's syndrome should identify with Ronnie's constant challenges at school, such as interacting with classmates and teachers, and at home, such as dealing with her mother, her brother, and her brother's new girl-friend.

203. *Al Capone Does My Shirts.* Choldenko, Gennifer. New York: G. P. Putnam's Sons, 2004. 228 pp. ISBN: 0399238611; ISBN2: 0142403709. Grades 5–8.

This story, which takes place in 1935, is about 12-year-old Moose Flanagan and his family who have just moved to Alcatraz Island. Moose and his autistic sister, Natalie, along with twenty-three other kids, live on the island because their fathers work as doctors, electricians, guards, or cooks for the prison. Moose has to adjust to the new school, including some of the kids, such as the danger-loving daughter of the warden, Piper Williams. Moose has to avoid getting caught up in one of Piper's countless schemes. In addition, Moose has to protect and watch out for his sister Natalie. It is a great read with some funny incidents. "With its unique setting and well-developed characters, this warm, engaging coming-of-age story has plenty of appeal, and Choldenko offers some fascinating historical background on Alcatraz Island in an afterword." *Booklist* 2005 Newbery Honor Book.

204. *The Very Ordered Existence of Merilee Marvelous.* Crowley, Suzanne Carl-isle. New York: Greenwillow Books, 2007. 380 pp. ISBN: 9780061231971. Grades 5–7.

Merilee is a 13-year-old girl who lives in Jumbo, Texas. Due to her Asperger's syndrome, Merilee's life is a very ordered existence, particularly keeping to a rigid daily schedule. When young Biswick, who has fetal alcohol syndrome, and his poet father move to town, Merilee's life changes drastically, but not always to Merilee's liking. Biswick becomes a part of Merilee's extended family and helps Merilee discover her ability to reach out to others, including her family members who have secrets. "Using one of Merilee's favorite words, this book is marvelous." *VOYA*

205. *The Flight of the Dove.* Day, Alexandra. New York: Farrar, Straus and Giroux, 2004. [28] pp. ISBN: 0374399522. Grades 3–5.

Four-year-old Betsy, an autistic girl, is withdrawn from everyone and does not speak except for making very primitive noises. One day she sees a dove, one of the animals at her preschool. Her love for the dove leads her to imitate its cooing and finally speaks her first word, "Mommy." It is a story that emphasizes the important role that animals can play in the comforting, balancing, and healing of humans. Color illustrations complement the text. "It is a beautiful book with a beautiful message." *Children's Literature*

206. *The London Eye Mystery*. Dowd, Siobhan. Oxford: David Fickling Books, 2008. 322 pp. ISBN: 0375849769; ISBN2: 9780375849763. Grades 5–8.

A young teenager Ted who has Asperger's syndrome and his older sister Kat cannot find their visiting cousin Salim after Salim takes a ride on an amusement park ride called the London Eye. Ted's parents, Aunt Gloria, including the police, discover that Ted's special cognitive skills, due to his Asperger's syndrome, are helpful in uncovering Salim's whereabouts. "The message, grippingly delivered, is that kids, even differently abled ones, are worth paying attention to." *Kirkus Reviews*

207. *My Brother Sammy*. Edwards, Becky; illustrated by David Armitage. Brookfield, CT: Millbrook Press, 1999. [24] pp. ISBN: 0761314172; ISBN2: 0761304398. Grades 1–3.

Accompanied by beautiful color illustrations, this story is about a young boy who is frustrated by his younger brother Sammy, who has autism. He describes some of the many feelings he has about Sammy. His mother always responds to him by describing Sammy as a "special" boy because of his special needs. Eventually, he accepts Sammy as a "special brother." "A good choice for sharing with children who have 'special' siblings and for discussions on feelings." *School Library Journal*
2002 Dolly Gray Award for Children's Literature in Developmental Disabilities.

208. *Looking after Louis*. Ely, Lesley; illustrated by Polly Dunbar. Morton Grove, IL: Albert Whitman, 2004. [26] pp. ISBN: 0807547468; ISBN2: 9780807547465. Grades K–1.

Louis, who has autism, is being taught in a regular class. The advantages of inclusion for both disabled children and their regular education classmates are highlighted in this story. With the help of a teacher's aide, who gives extra attention to him, Louis is able to watch, learn, and practice social skills with his peers, while his classmates try to understand Louis's world and to include him in theirs. The color illustrations are very effective and complement the text. "This [is an] upbeat look at mainstreaming." *School Library Journal*

209. *The Curious Incident of the Dog in the Night-time*. Haddon, Mark. New York: Doubleday, 2003. 226 pp. ISBN: 0385509456. Grades 8–12.

This is an interesting story about 15-year-old Christopher who is autistic. He is mathematically gifted and knows all the countries of the world and their capitals. He relates well to animals; however, he does not understand the emotional lives of others and cannot stand to be touched. He does not like the color yellow. While investigating the suspicious murder of a neighbor's dog, Christopher uncovers secret information about his mother. "The novel is being marketed to a YA audience, but strong language and adult situations make this a good title for sophisticated readers of all ages." *Library Journal*
2004 Dolly Gray Award for Children's Literature in Developmental Disabilities.

210. *Running on Dreams.* Heiman, Herb. Shawnee Mission, KS: Autism Asperger Publishing, 2007. 293 pp. ISBN: 1931282285; ISBN2: 9781931282284. Grades 8–10.

Justin, a 15-year-old boy who has autism, develops a friendship with Brad, one of the popular ninth graders at Pearblossom Middle School. Both boys experience typical teenage challenges, such as the first date, peer rejection, parental expectations, and group acceptance. By using different fonts to distinguish Justin's thoughts from Brad's, the author enables the reader to gain insight into both of their worlds. Teen readers, especially boys, should be able to identify with both Justin and Brad.

211. *All Cats Have Asperger Syndrome.* Hoopmann, Kathy. London: Jessica Kingsley Publishers, 2006. 65 pp. ISBN: 1843104814; ISBN2: 9781843104810. Grades 4–6.

This award-winning book introduces readers to the world of Asperger syndrome by using examples of behaviors and personality of a cat named Noah. Children with Asperger syndrome should be able to relate to this story and understand why they are different from other people. Color and delightful photographs of cats go very well with the captions.

212. *Blue Bottle Mystery: An Asperger Adventure.* Hoopmann, Kathy. London; Philadelphia: Jessica Kingsley Publishers, 2001. 96 pp. ISBN: 1853029785. Grades 3–6.

This is Hoopmann's first book in her series about two friends, Ben and Andy. Ben, a boy with Asperger syndrome, and his friend Andy find an old mysterious blue bottle in the school yard. They believe that the bottle belongs to a genie and begin to wish for certain things, which begin to come true. For example, Ben and his father win a lottery, Andy starts growing tall, which enables him to join the basketball team. Their forgotten wish comes true when their teacher finds happiness as a result of the relationship with Ben's father. "It's a gentle introduction to the challenges and unique qualities of people living with Asperger's and

a welcome read for families who have experienced it and similar conditions."
School Library Journal

213. *Of Mice and Aliens: An Asperger Adventure.* Hoopmann, Kathy. London;
    Philadelphia: Jessica Kingsley Publishers, 2001. 108 pp. ISBN: 184310007X.
    Grades 3–6.

This is the author's second book about two best friends, Ben and Andy, and
an alien, named Zeke. Ben has recently been diagnosed with Asperger syndrome
and is learning to cope with it. One day Ben and Andy discover Zeke in the
backyard of Ben's house, and they intend to help Zeke repair his ship, but they
are not sure if they should trust Zeke. Since Zeke does not know anything about
Earth's rules, it is up to Ben and Andy to help Zeke survive. Readers will enjoy
this humorous mystery that presents the interesting individuality of children with
Asperger syndrome.

214. *Lisa and the Lacemaker: An Asperger Adventure.* Hoopmann, Kathy.
    London; Philadelphia: Jessica Kingsley Publishers, 2002. 116 pp. ISBN:
    1843100711. Grades 3–6.

In the author's third book about Ben and Andy, their friend, Lisa, is introduced.
Lisa, who has Asperger syndrome, develops a deep friendship with her great aunt
Hannah as she learns from her how to make lace. While visiting her friend Ben,
Lisa discovers an abandoned hut with several rooms in Ben's backyard and is curi-
ous to explore these rooms. Lisa is surprised when Great Aunt Hannah reveals to
Lisa that at one time she worked as a servant girl in those very same rooms Lisa
has discovered. Written as a mystery but aimed at helping readers understand be-
havior of children with Asperger syndrome, this is an entertaining story.

215. *Haze.* Hoopmann, Kathy. London: Jessica Kingsley, 2003. 159 pp. ISBN:
    184310072X. Grades 9–12.

Seb is very knowledgeable regarding computer programming but has difficulties relating to people and adjusting to high school. Seb develops friendships
with Kristie, Madeline, and Jen, who try to help him cope with social situations
at school. The new computer teacher, Miss Adonia, in reality an Internet investi-
gator, is the first person to suggest that Seb has Asperger syndrome. Seb is soon
caught up in a web of computer fraud involving Miss Adonia and Madeline's
mysterious online chat buddy, Mr. Minty. With Seb's help, Mr. Minty resolves
Madeline's abusive relationship with her mother and solves the computer mystery. "The splintered narrative voice presents a solid Asperger's perspective but
offers a rounded view and a surprisingly smooth read. *Haze* is simply written and
accessible to readers of varying levels." *KLIATT*

216. *Joey and Sam.* Katz, Illana; illustrated by Fran Borowitz. Los Angeles: Real Life Storybooks, 1993. [38] pp. ISBN: 1882388003. Grades 1–2.

This is a heart-warming story about a family with an autistic child. Joey has a younger brother Sam, who is autistic. Joey is frustrated when Sam does not act normal like other brothers. However, when Sam and his special class perform at a school assembly, Joey feels very proud of his brother and lets him know that he loves him just the way he is. This book should help children and especially siblings be understanding and compassionate while playing with children who are not developing normally. Black and white illustrations are included.

217. *In His Shoes: A Short Journey through Autism.* Keating-Velasco, Joanna L. Shawnee Mission, KS: Autism Asperger Publishing, 2008. 147 pp. ISBN: 1934575267; ISBN2: 978193475260. Grades 6–8.

As 13-year-old Nick Hansen, who has autism, makes the transition to middle school, he faces various kinds of challenges such as new teachers, new friends, and a new environment. This well-organized and informative book should allow young readers to discover and respect the many sensory issues and challenges, to appreciate unique talents and gifts of children with autism, and to be able to put themselves "in their shoes." The readers will realize that in spite of Nick's challenges, especially communication, there are many similarities between Nick and themselves. The "Points to Ponder" at the end of each chapter is a valuable section for discussions. A glossary of terms, black and white illustrations, and a list of recommended books, DVDs, and websites for additional information are included.

218. *Ian's Walk: A Story about Autism.* Lears, Laurie; illustrated by Karen Ritz. Morton Grove, IL: Albert Whitman, 1998. [28] pp. ISBN: 0807534803; ISBN2: 0807534811. Grades 1–3.

Julie, her older sister Tara, and her younger brother Ian, who is autistic, go to the park. When Ian gets lost at the park, Julie realizes how much she cares for him. In order to find Ian, Julie must try to see the world through his eyes. This story teaches valuable lessons of responsibility, compassion, and tolerance of differences when it comes to siblings with disabilities such as autism. Color illustrations complement the text. "This story provides an insight into the world of autism and how it affects the healthy family members." *Children's Literature*
2000 Dolly Gray Award for Children's Literature in Developmental Disabilities.

219. *Rules.* Lord, Cynthia. New York: Scholastic Press, 2006. 200 pp. ISBN: 0439443822. Grades 4–7.

This is a story about a 12-year-old young girl named Catherine and her brother David who has autism. Their entire family revolves around David's disability. Catherine spends a lot of time with David, going over some of the basic rules in order to correct David's embarrassing behaviors. This novel, filled with warmth, takes a sensitive approach at feeling different and finding acceptance of a disability, beyond the rules. "A rewarding story that may well inspire readers to think about others' points of view." *Publishers Weekly* "A lovely, warm read, and a great discussion starter." *School Library Journal*
2007 Schneider Family Book Award in the Middle School category.
2007 Newbery Honor Book.

220. *Captain Tommy.* Messner, Abby Ward; illustrated by Kim Harris Belliveau. Arlington, TX: Future Horizons, 1996. [32] pp. ISBN: 1885477589. Grades 1–2.

With the help of color illustrations, the author tells the story of a young sensitive boy named Tommy, who after much reluctance agrees to play with a boy who is new and different from many of the other children at the camp. Initially, Tommy has a number of questions regarding John, who is autistic. However, with the help of his teacher, he is able to reach out to John and feels proud of making a new friend.

221. *The Speed of Dark.* Moon, Elizabeth. New York: Ballantine Books, 2004. 340 pp. ISBN: 0345447549; ISBN2: 0345447557. Grades 10–12.

Told through the eyes of Lou Arrendale, an autistic man living in the not-so-distant future, this is truly a moving and beautiful story. Lou has a steady job working with mathematical patterns with other autistic individuals. He is offered a chance to try a brand new experimental procedure that could cure him of autism. Lou must decide if he should submit to this procedure that might change the way he views the world. The writer has the unusual ability of making readers reevaluate the way they look at autism. The characters in the book are very believable. By the end of the novel, one feels like one knows Lou well and even loves him. Although the story is set in the future, it is far from being a fantasy. This is a well-recommended book. "Moon is effective at putting the reader inside Lou's mind, and it is both fascinating and painful to see the behavior and qualities of so-called normals through his eyes." *Booklist*

222. *Wishing on the Midnight Star: My Asperger Brother.* Ogaz, Nancy. London; New York: Jessica Kingsley Publishers, 2004. 144 pp. ISBN: 1843107570. Grades 5–8.

In this funny and adventurous heart-warming story, 13-year-old Alexander Stone is experiencing tough times. Some of his hardships are caused by the absence of his widowed mother due to her midwife duties, his desperate attempts to impress a beautiful girl, named, Brianna Santos, his attempts to deal with a threatening bully, and the challenges of helping his brother Nic who has Asperger syndrome. After undergoing a series of adventures, Alex appreciates Nic's exceptional qualities, and feels affection toward Nic. "[L]ibraries may find this a useful purchase for special-needs collections." *School Library Journal*

223. *Andy and His Yellow Frisbee.* Thompson, Mary. Bethesda, MD: Woodbine House, 1996. [20] pp. ISBN: 0933149832. Grades 1–4.

In this delightful story, Sarah, the new girl at school, is curious to know why Andy, an autistic boy, spends every recess by himself on the playground, spinning his yellow Frisbee. Andy's fascination for objects in motion, such as a Frisbee, is characteristic of his autism. Rosie, Andy's older sister who always watches out for him, is concerned about how her brother may react when Sarah tries to talk to him. Sarah thinks that she understands Andy in spite of the fact that he does not talk to her. Eventually, Rosie is relieved to find out that Andy does not need her protection. Using vivid watercolors, the story conveys a lesson of friendship, tolerance, and acceptance. "*Andy* is a book that will help youngsters see how those with special needs may be different but deserve tolerance and kindness just like all children do." *School Library Journal*

224. *Arnie and His School Tools: Simple Sensory Solutions That Build Success.* Veenendall, Jennifer. Shawnee Mission, KS: Autism Asperger Publishing, 2008. 47 pp. ISBN: 9781934575154. Grades 1–3.

In this delightful color picture book written by a school-based occupational therapist, Arnie, who has autism, has difficulty paying attention in class and doing his school work. With the help of physical movements, such as jumping, kicking, sweeping floors, and the use of basic school tools, such as chewy pencil toppers, fidgets, earplugs, headphones, and ball cushions, Arnie is able to keep his body calm, thus allowing him to feel more comfortable and learn better in school. Additional resources, definitions of sensory processing and sensory modulation disorder, suggested discussion questions, and lists of related books and websites are included at the end of the book.

225. *Adam's Alternative Sports Day: An Asperger Story.* Welton, Jude. London; Philadelphia: Jessica Kingsley Publishers, 2005. 112 pp. ISBN: 1843103001; ISBN2: 9781843103004. Grades 5–8.

Nine-year-old Adam has Asperger's syndrome. Each year the school has Sports Day, and Adam dreads it because he usually comes in last for the races and does not get chosen for the teams. Adam is delighted when his teacher, Mr.

Williams, announces that there will be an Alternative Sports Day that focuses on cognitive activities instead of the usual physical activities. This particular Sports Day includes quizzes, riddles to solve, and a treasure hunt—all the activities that Adam enjoys. He feels that he will at last have an opportunity to win one of the events. At the award ceremony, several cups are presented for special achievements. When Adam receives the Challenge Cup, he feels that this is definitely the best Sports Day ever. It is an interesting and enjoyable children's story that offers insights into how a child with Asperger's syndrome copes with many challenges in life. A short list of additional books on this subject is included.

Nonfiction

226. *Russell Is Extra Special: A Book about Autism for Children.* Amenta, Charles A. New York: Magination Press, 1992. [30] pp. ISBN: 0945354436; ISBN2: 0945354444. Grades 1–3.

The main objective of this book is to help children and families learn about autism in a simplified way. The first two pages, written specifically for parents of children with autism, explain some of the common characteristics of autistic children and what steps can be taken to help these children function better. The author discusses the daily life, habits, and likes and dislikes of an autistic boy named Russell Amenta and his family. The photographs of Russell should elicit greater sympathy for those individuals who may be different. A list of resources that supply further information, including organizations and periodicals, is included. "Regardless, and despite the fact that the black-and-white photographs are a bit grainy, the book is a good introduction to the subject, especially when Amenta tries to clarify some general notions about autism. The brief list of sources and other materials is also helpful." *School Library Journal*

227. *The Complete Guide to Asperger's Syndrome.* Attwood, Tony. London; Philadelphia: Jessica Kingsley Publishers, 2007. 397 pp. ISBN: 1843104954; ISBN2: 9781843104957. Teens/Educators/Parents.

Written by a clinical psychologist, this guide is based on the author's extensive clinical experience and from his correspondence with individuals with Asperger's syndrome. The book examines the following topics: causes of Asperger's syndrome, the diagnosis and its affect on the individual, theory of mind, the understanding and expression of emotions, social interaction, teasing, bullying and mental health issues, cognitive abilities, and life after school including careers. Frequently asked questions are addressed as well. It is a well-researched book that has a wealth of information regarding Asperger's syndrome. Illustrations and an index are included.

228. *Autism.* Baldwin, Carol. Series: Health Matters. Chicago: Heinemann Library, 2003. 32 pp. ISBN: 1403402507. Grades 2–5.

This volume in the Health Matters series defines autism, its causes, its symptoms, and its treatment. In addition, this book should help young readers understand the challenges that autistic classmates face at school and at home. The last chapter covers some of the success stories of individuals with autism. Color photographs complement the text; one exceptional photograph shows how the brain works differently than usual in a child with autism. A glossary, an index, and a list of additional resources on the subject are included.

229. *Congratulations! It's Asperger's Syndrome.* Birch, Jen. London; New York: Jessica Kingsley Publishers, 2003. 270 pp. ISBN: 1843101122. Grades 10–12.

Jen Birch, who is from New Zealand and the author of this very interesting book, was diagnosed with Asperger's syndrome at the age of 43. This is her story. She grew up knowing that something was different about her. Doctors and the psychiatric system were unable to help her. She attended a university lecture at the age of 43 when she learned the facts about Asperger's syndrome. During that time, she was officially diagnosed with Asperger's syndrome. This book has two parts: Part 1 discusses the chronology of her life; Part 2 discusses how her life changed for the better since the "revelation." Birch aims to use this knowledge to inform others about Asperger's syndrome and how, once its pros and cons are understood, the extent of one's potential can be fulfilled. In addition to a list of helpful resources on the subject, the author has also included a glossary and notes on the Maori language so that readers from New Zealand can understand the terms.

230. *My Friend with Autism.* Bishop, Beverly; illustrated by Craig Bishop. Arlington, TX: Future Horizons, 2002. 36 pp. ISBN: 1885477899. Grades 2–4.

Written and illustrated by the parents of an autistic child, this book explains what autism is and how the behavior of autistic children can be different from that of other children. "Notes for Adults" section provides adults with a detailed explanation of each page in the children's section of this thought-provoking book. In additional to a recommended reading list, "Ten Quick Strategies for Helping an Autistic Child" are listed, which should be very helpful for teachers and parents.

231. *The Hidden Child: Youth with Autism.* Bonnice, Sherry. Series: Youth with Special Needs. Broomall, PA: Mason Crest Publishers, 2004. 127 pp. ISBN: 1590847369; ISBN2: 9781590847367. Grades 7–10.

This book, one of the titles in the Youth with Special Needs series, describes how Livie and her family are impacted by her younger brother Tucker who has autism. Their story will help readers develop a better understanding of autism and a more in-depth awareness of how autism affects children, their families, and their friends. Other issues covered are the causes of autism, strategies families can use for coping with autism, and treatment options, including medical concerns. Color photographs, illustrations, graphics, additional reading material, organizations, a glossary, and an index are included. "Interspersed among the story are well-researched discussions on the history, diagnosis, kinds of treatment, and hope for the future for autistic children." *Children's Literature*

232. *Youth with Asperger's Syndrome: A Different Drummer.* Chastain, Zachary and Phyllis Livingston. Series: Helping Youth with Mental, Physical, and Social Challenges. Philadelphia: Mason Crest Publishers, 2008. 128 pp. ISBN: 1422201376; ISBN2: 9781422201374. Grades 8–12.

Part of the series titled Helping Youth with Mental, Physical, and Social Challenges, this book discusses the story about Duncan who has Asperger's syndrome. Different from other teenagers, Duncan does or says things that are improper and ends up in trouble without realizing the reason. One of the chapters covers very helpful information under these topics: who gets Asperger's syndrome, what causes Asperger's syndrome, and how it is treated. A glossary, a list of books for additional information, including websites, a bibliography, color photographs, and an index are included.

233. *The Social Success Workbook for Teens: Skill-Building Activities for Teens with Nonverbal Learning Disorder, Asperger's Disorder & Other Social-skill Problems.* Cooper, Barbara and Nancy Widdows. Oakland, CA: Instant Help Books/New Harbinger Publications, 2008. 132 pp. ISBN: 1572246146; ISBN2: 9781572246140. Grade 9–12.

This workbook contains forty activities for teens with Asperger's syndrome to help them understand and strengthen their social skills, particularly when it comes to getting along with others and building friendships in spite of facing challenges. The activities are arranged in order and build upon each other. Some of the activities sections include black and white illustrations for more clarification. Teenagers with Asperger's syndrome or with other social skill problems should benefit from this nicely organized and fun workbook.

234. *When My Autism Gets too Big: A Relaxation Book for Children with Autism Spectrum Disorders.* Dunn Buron, Kari. Shawnee Mission, KS: Autism Asperger Publishing, 2003. 34 pp. ISBN: 193128251X. Grades 1–4.

This personalized book is intended to assist children with autism spectrum disorders (ASD) understand the anxiety they experience and that they are not alone in dealing with this challenge. With the help of pencil illustrations, the author offers these children constructive strategies, such as relaxation and participation in special programs outside of the neighborhood schools. At the end of the book, the author includes a five-point scale to define different levels of stress, which allows children to label their own levels. At the beginning of the book, the author presents two very helpful pages of instructions to parents and teachers for using this book. This book is highly recommended.

235. *Taking Autism to School.* Edwards, Andreanna; illustrated by Tom Dineen. Series: Special Kids in School. Plainview, NY: JayJo Books, 2001. [30] pp. ISBN: 1891383132. Grades 1–3.

This is one of the titles from the Special Kids in School series. With the help of illustrations, the author tells the story about Sam, who is autistic. The author explains what autism is and how it affects children. She discusses how Sam's special teacher helps Sam by giving him extra help when he needs it. The author also explains how certain medicines can help children like Sam to feel better. "Let's Take the Autism Kids' Quiz," followed by "Ten Tips for Teachers" are very useful additions to the book. Additional resources on the subject are included.

236. *Autism.* Edwards, Michele Engel. Series: Diseases and Disorders. San Diego, CA: Lucent Books, 2001. 112 pp. ISBN: 156006829; ISBN2: 1560066954. Grades 6–9.

This is one of the titles in the Diseases and Disorders series. The author provides an easy-to-understand explanation of autism, its possible causes, and various treatments. Readers are offered information regarding options for autistic children such as schools for severe behavior problems, special friends program, and special education classes. The author also provides very helpful options for autistic adults, such as transitional programs, vocational training and college, adult education, employment opportunities, living arrangements, and rural life alternative. The last chapter, "The Autistic Savant and Asperger's Syndrome," discusses the main differences between these two disorders. The Epilogue discusses the current research findings and the focus on future research regarding autism. Detailed indexing, annotated bibliographies, and lists of organizations to contact for additional information are included.

237. *Making Sense of the Unfeasible: My Life Journey with Asperger Syndrome.* Fleisher, Marc. London; New York: Jessica Kingsley Publishers, 2003. 159 pp. ISBN: 1843101653. Grades 9–12.

The author was diagnosed with Asperger syndrome when he was 11 years old. He was considered to be mentally retarded, yet he graduated from college, and followed that with a postgraduate degree in mathematics. In this heart-warming, inspiring, and engaging story, Fleisher shares his life story from his childhood to the present day. Like many other individuals who have Asperger syndrome, he too had difficulties understanding what is socially acceptable and experienced difficulties in relationships. He discusses how he achieved success with the support of his family and services for individuals with Asperger syndrome. He shares ten key factors that helped him achieve many of his goals. He ends the book with appendices on the following topics: the art of joke telling; astronomy; and mathematics of unfeasibly large numbers.

238. *Autism.* Fredericks, Carrie, editor. Series: Perspectives on Diseases and Disorders. Detroit: Thomson Gale, 2008. 168 pp. ISBN: 0737738693; ISBN2: 9780737738698. Grades 10–12.

Part of the Perspectives on Diseases and Disorders series, this book provides helpful and clear information regarding autism. The introductory chapter covers an overview of autism, including signs and diagnoses, causes of autism and Asperger's syndrome, and treatment of autism. The second chapter discusses the controversial side of autism. Some personal experiences by individuals who are autistic are shared in the final chapter, "The Personal Side of Autism." A glossary, a chronology, indexes, and lists of organizations to contact for additional information are included.

239. *Mori's Story: A Book about a Boy with Autism.* Gartenberg, Zachary M.; illustrated by Jerry Gay. Minneapolis: Lerner Publications, 1998. 40 pp. ISBN: 0822525852. Grades 4–7.

Written by Zach, this is the story about his younger brother Mori who is 9 years old and is autistic. Mori starts acting in strange ways when he is 2 years old. He has difficulty relating to others and does not like changes in his routine. Zach discusses his home life, schooling, the foster home where Mori spends some time, and ways in which the whole family is affected due to Mori's condition. The last two pages provide information about autism. A glossary is included. Photographs by Jerry Gay, who has won numerous awards and recognition for his photography, complement the text.

240. *Caring for Myself: A Social Skills Storybook.* Gast, Christy and Jane Krug. London: Jessica Kingsley Publishers, 2008. 96 pp. ISBN: 1843108720; ISBN2: 9781843108726. Grades 2–4.

Excellent color photographs of young children provide the foundation for this book that was written for autistic children who need guidance in understanding everyday routines regarding their health and hygiene. The topics covered are washing hands, getting haircuts, taking baths, going to doctors, and brushing teeth. A list of related resources is included.

241. *Finding Out about Asperger's Syndrome, High-Functioning Autism, and PDD.* Gerland, Gunilla. London; Philadelphia: Jessica Kingsley Publishers, 2000. 46 pp. ISBN: 1853028401. Grades 4–7.

Gerland, who was diagnosed with Asperger's syndrome several years ago and works closely with the Swedish National Autism Society, has written this book from her own experience. This book should be helpful to all young people who need to understand what it is like to have Asperger's syndrome, pervasive developmental disorder (PDD), or autism. In addition to discussing the five senses, the author explains difficulties faced by individuals with disabilities, such as motor skills, eye contact, being in a group of people, facing changes, getting away from habits and routines, language, and thinking differently.

242. *Emergence: Labeled Autistic, a True Story.* Grandin, Temple and Margaret Scariano. New York: Warner Books, 2005. 188 pp. ISBN: 0446671827. Teens/Educators/Parents.

This is a fascinating biography written by a recovered autistic person. Temple Grandin longed for affection but feared human contact. Not able to experience reality like most other children, she was easily angered. In this astonishing true story, she explains how she went from being an autistic child to becoming a successful professional. She is an animal scientist who designed one-third of all the livestock-handling facilities in the United States. The last few pages in this book contain technical information, such as the causes of autism and its treatment, including medication, that will be helpful to parents, teachers, and other professionals who are treating a child or adult with autism. "This account will be significant reading for any professional or lay person interested in autism, and is also a moving story of the human hidden behind a distorting." *Library Journal*

243. *My Social Stories Book.* Gray, Carol and Abbie Leigh White, editors; illustrated by Sean McAndrew. London; Philadelphia: Jessica Kinglsey Publishers, 2002. 141 pp. ISBN: 1853029505. Grades 3–6.

Uniquely formatted, this book is a collection of social stories specifically for young children with autism spectrum disorders (ASD). The book is organized into three chapters: "Taking Care of Me," "Home," and "Going Places." Each chapter covers topics that are frequently encountered in early childhood. For instance, in the chapter "Taking Care of Me," the stories describe daily routines, such as taking medicine, brushing teeth, and taking a bath. Line drawings form a visual counterpart to the text. The book has a very helpful introduction that explains to parents and careers how to get the most out of this book.

244. *Asperger Syndrome: The Universe and Everything.* Hall, Kenneth. London; Philadelphia: Jessica Kingsley Publishers, 2001. 109 pp. ISBN: 1853029300. Grades 5–8.

Kenneth Hall, diagnosed with Asperger syndrome at the age of 10, describes some of his personal experiences in this inspirational book. Kenneth is also an exceptionally gifted boy who lives in Northern Ireland and is interested in mathematics, computers, and books of adventure stories. His mother, Brenda, is a member of the Parent's Education as Autism Therapists (PEAT) group, which allows parents to become familiar with and skilled in applied behaviour analysis (ABA). Brenda and Kenneth have devised an educational program over the past few years that has helped Kenneth become motivated to engage in many different areas of behavior. Kenneth feels that it is his mission to write this book to help others understand Asperger syndrome. This book reflects Kenneth's positive attitude to Asperger syndrome, which other children should find very inspiring. A list of useful addresses and websites is included.

245. *"Now You Know Me Think More": A Journey with Autism Using Facilitated Communication Techniques.* Hundal, Ppinder and Pauline Lukey. London; New York: Jessica Kingsley Publishers, 2003. 64 pp. ISBN: 1843101440. Grades 6–9.

The two authors of this book first met when Ppinder was 8 years old. Pauline Lukey is a qualified nurse and caregiver and has worked with autistic children for numerous years. At first, Ppinder could not communicate except using nonverbal ways. This is the story of their communication journey and how their ability to communicate developed along the way through the use of facilitated communication techniques. In the beginning, Ppinder uses sign language to communicate, but later on, she moves on to assisted typing followed by her current desire to learn to read and write. This book demonstrates the remarkable effects of facilitated communication. The book includes some illustrations and a list of excellent organizations in the United Kingdom, Europe, the United States, Australia, and New Zealand.

246. *Freaks, Geeks and Asperger Syndrome: A User Guide to Adolescence.* Jackson, Luke. London; Philadelphia: Jessica Kingsley Publishers, 2002. 217 pp. ISBN: 1843100983. Grades 7–12.

Thirteen-year-old Luke, who has Asperger syndrome, writes this book drawn from his own experiences and information from his teenage brother and sisters. His style of writing this book is unique in that he writes as though he were having a conversation with the reader. In this delightful, enlightening, honest, and witty book, Luke adopts a very positive attitude. He writes, "I have what some people would call a disability but I call a gift." He discusses topics such as fascinations, sensory perception, diet, sleep, teenage language, problems with socializing at school, homework, dealing with bullies, the dos and don'ts of dating, and an explanation of idioms that are particularly confusing for those with Asperger syndrome. The book includes an index and lists some very useful addresses and websites pertaining to Asperger syndrome. It is an excellent book that is very informative, pleasant to read, and inspirational, particularly for teenagers.

247. *Autism.* Landau, Elaine. New York: Franklin Watts, 2001. 128 pp. ISBN: 0531117804. Grades 8–12.

Written by an award-winning author, this very important resource provides a history of autism, from its first identification in 1943. The signs of autism, various treatments, and the most important advances in drugs and therapy are discussed. Using personal stories, Landau also discusses the 10 percent of the autistic people who possess some truly extraordinary abilities. These individuals, known as "savants," have skills that range from memorizing pages of the telephone book in seconds to exceptional musical or artistic abilities. Suggestions for further reading and contact information for organizations and an index are included.

248. *I Am Utterly Unique: Celebrating the Strengths of Children with Asperger's Syndrome and High Functioning Autism.* Larson, Elaine Marie; illustrated by Vivian Strand. Shawnee Mission, KS: Autism Asperger Publishing, 2006. [52] pp. ISBN: 1931282897; ISBN: 9781931282895. Grades K–2.

Using the letters A to Z, this delightful book presents an understanding of the unique qualities and attributes of children with Asperger's syndrome and high functioning autism. Color illustrations are inviting and complement the text.

249. *Autism.* Lennard-Brown, Sarah. Series: Health Issues. Chicago: Raintree, 2004. 64 pp. ISBN: 073986422X. Grades 6–9.

The author, who spent many years working as a nurse, counselor, and health educator, gives an in-depth introduction to autism in this volume of the Health Issues series. She discusses how autism affects the way a person experiences and interacts with the rest of the world and how the world may appear to people with autism. The causes of autism, including therapies for autism and strategies designed to make everyday life easier, are explained in a clear manner. A glossary, resources listing some websites, and an index are included. Color photographs are very effective.

250. *More Than Little Professors: Children with Asperger's Syndrome: In Their own Words.* Mann, Lisa Barrett and Brenda Smith Myles. Shawnee Mission, KS: Autism Asperger Publishing, 2008. 206 pp. ISBN: 1934575259; ISBN2: 9781934575253. Grades 3–8.

This is a very unique book in that the information provided about how children feel about themselves, others, and the world is directly from the children with Asperger's syndrome. The children share their experiences and important insights. The book is a collection of stories, poems, and artwork by more than sixty children from toddlers through teens. The introductory chapter provides an overview of Asperger's syndrome. Each of the rest of the chapters starts with a quotation from a famous person who has had some of the characteristics of Asperger's syndrome, followed by children's writings. An index is included.

251. *Dear Charlie: A Grandfather's Love Letter: A Guide to Your Life with Autism.* Martin, Earle P. Arlington, TX: Future Horizons, 1999. 104 pp. ISBN: 1885477619. Grades 4–8.

This thought-provoking book starts as a personal message for Charlie from his grandfather. Earle, Charlie's grandfather, answers the questions regarding autism that Charlie may have in case Earle is not around to answer the questions personally. This contribution should help parents, family members, and others affected by autism understand this condition. The last chapter, titled "I Think I Can," should be most inspiring to autistic children.

252. *Out of Silence: An Autistic Boy's Journey into Language and Communication.* Martin, Russell. New York: Penguin Books, 1995. 300 pp. ISBN: 0140247017. Grades 10–12.

Martin writes this story about his nephew Ian Drummond, who is diagnosed as autistic at a preschool age. The book discusses the family's hope for a cure, the emotional and financial struggles undergone by the parents, and Ian's older sister's distress at the situation. Martin approaches autism as a primarily linguistic problem, not an emotional or mental problem as usually defined. He also claims that autism is caused when children are vaccinated. However, this theory is unsupported. He gives an interesting account of the history of language acquisition and examines its various theories. It is an interesting read to find out how Ian fared over the years developmentally.

253. *Asperger Syndrome, Adolescence, and Identity: Looking beyond the Label.*
Molloy, Harvey and Latika Vasil. London; New York: Jessica Kingsley
Publishers, 2004. 173 pp. ISBN: 1843101262. Teens/Educators/Parents.

This highly recommended book is based on interviews with six adolescents diagnosed with Asperger syndrome. These teenagers talk about their experiences at
school, their relationships with friends and peers, their home lives, their interests,
and how Asperger syndrome has impacted and shaped their growing identities.
During the course of the authors' discussions with these teenagers and their families, many important themes and issues from the stories were raised. The authors
focus on the following six key themes: diagnosis as a sense-making narrative,
labeling and identity, socializing and making friends, the dilemma of schooling,
family life, and rages and the blues. This book strikes a balance between teenagers telling their own stories and authors reflecting on the significance of these
stories. An index and an appendix, which explains the research process used by
the authors, are included. Parents, professionals, and people with Asperger syndrome should benefit a great deal from this book.

254. *All about My Brother: An Eight-Year-Old Sister's Introduction of Her
Brother Who Has Autism.* Peralta, Sarah. Shawnee Mission, KS: Autism
Asperger Publishing, 2002. 27 pp. ISBN: 1931282110. Grades 2–4.

This is a heartwarming book written and illustrated by 8-year-old Sarah about
her brother Evan, who has autism. Sarah gives insight into the sibling relationship that only a child would know. Her writing style is appropriate for younger
children. The bright and playful illustrations are interesting, unique, and funny. A
"must read" book for families and siblings of children who have autism.

255. *Coping with Asperger Syndrome.* Rosaler, Maxine. Series: Coping. New York:
Rosen Publishing Group, 2004. 112 pp. ISBN: 0823944824. Grades 7–9.

This easy to understand book, one of the titles in the Coping series, provides
information about Asperger syndrome, the different stages of Asperger syndrome,
common misconceptions, needs of people with Asperger syndrome, coping with
Asperger syndrome at school, and working with parents of children with this
syndrome. "Where to Go for Help" in the United States and in Canada is a helpful
resource. A list of websites related to the subject of this book as well as a bibliography and a glossary are included. "[I]t is one of the first overviews to present
what is known in a manner that is accessible to younger readers." *Booklist*

256. *Coping When a Brother or Sister Is Autistic.* Rosenberg, Marsha Sarah.
Series: Coping. New York: Rosen Publishing Group, 2001. 138 pp. ISBN:
0823931943. Grades 7–9.

What is autism? What causes autism? How is autism diagnosed and assessed? These are some of the questions addressed in this book, which is part of the Coping series. The author seeks to help the siblings of individuals who have been diagnosed with autism understand and realize that they are not alone in the joys and challenges of growing up with siblings who have autism. The special bond between brothers and sisters, disabled or not, is lifelong, and this special and unique relationship can foster and encourage the positive growth of an entire family. The book offers some very important positive nuggets to siblings of individuals with autism. A glossary, an index, a list of additional resources and websites, and addresses of organizations are included.

257. *Everything You Need to Know When a Brother or Sister Is Autistic.* Rosenberg, Marsha Sarah. Series: The Need to Know Library. New York: Rosen Publishing Group, 2002. 64 pp. ISBN: 0823931234. Grades 5–8.

This story, part of the Need to Know Library series, is about Jacob and his brother Noel, who is five years younger than Jacob and autistic. When Jacob tries to talk to him, it is almost as if Noel does not hear him or ignores him. Noel does not like to be held or cuddled and has never made a single friend and likes it best when he is just left alone. Jacob feels embarrassed by the way Noel acts and is too ashamed to have friends over to his house. This book discusses what autism is, how it is diagnosed and treated, and the various ways in which siblings of autistic children can find support. A glossary and a list of helpful websites are included.

258. *Asperger Download: A Guide to Help Teenage Males with Asperger Syndrome Trouble-shoot Life's Challenges.* Santomauro, J. and Damian Santomauro. Shawnee Mission, KS: Autism Asperger Publishing, 2007. 109 pp. ISBN: 193457502X; ISBN: 9781934575024. Grades 11–12.

Damian was 5 years old when he was diagnosed with Asperger syndrome. He graduated from high school and is currently pursuing his bachelor's degree. Damian and his mother, Josie, have written this book specifically for teenager boys who are between the ages of 11 and 17 and have Asperger syndrome. Damian provides advice and knowledge based on his personal real-life experiences, while Josie reveals her perspective from her role as a mother, caring nurturer, a coach, and a leader. The topics are listed by categories in alphabetical order from A to Z and are that that can be identified with by teenage boys, such as acne, alcohol, dating, gossip, money, parties, and much more.

259. *Asperger's, Huh? A Child's Perspective.* Schnurr, Rosina G.; illustrated by John Strachan. Ottawa, Canada: Anisor, 2002. 52 pp. ISBN: 0968447309. Grades 2–5.

Written by a clinical psychologist and illustrated by a cartoonist, this is a unique book in that it is written and illustrated from the perspective of a child with Asperger's syndrome. Using stories and incidents, the author discusses the common characteristics of any child with Asperger's syndrome. This book truly gives an insightful view into the world of a child with Asperger's syndrome.

260. *I Love My Brother: A Preschooler's View of Living with a Brother Who Has Autism.* Sullivan, Connor. Stratham, NJ: Phat Art 4, 2001. [20] pp. ISBN: 0970658117. Grades 1–2.

Connor Sullivan, who is 4 and a half years old, talks about being a brother to his 2-and-a-half-year-old younger brother Sean, who has autism. With the help of beautiful color illustrations, Connor offers insights about himself, his brother Sean, and his parents. He describes Sean's special needs, his daily activities, including eating, playing, and getting help from therapists. It is a great book for helping young children understand their autistic siblings, including other children who are autistic.

261. *Talking to Angels.* Watson, Esther. San Diego, CA: Harcourt Brace, 1996. [29] pp. ISBN: 0152010777. Grades K–1.

A child tells the story about her sister, Christa, who is autistic. Christa sees the world in a different way compared to most children. She is not able to explain as to how she sees the world differently. With the exception of very few people, most will not even try to understand the reason behind Christa's different way of thinking. One of these people is Christa's sister, the narrator of the story. The color illustrations are done in mixed media on drawing paper. "[T]he pictures are moving, dynamic, and expressive, reflecting how Christa might see the world. This artistic, loving tribute to a child who is sensitive and joyful despite her disability truly helps dispel some misunderstandings about autism." *School Library Journal* "A sensitive and loving look at the world of an autistic child through the eyes of her sister." *Children's Literature*

262. *Can I Tell You about Asperger Syndrome? A Guide for Friends and Family.* Welton, Jude. London; New York: Jessica Kingsley Publishers, 2004. 48 pp. ISBN: 1843102064. Teens/Educators/Parents.

Adam, who has Asperger syndrome, helps children learn about Asperger syndrome from his perspective. He explains what Asperger syndrome is and what it feels like to have this condition, including the difficulties faced by a child with Asperger syndrome. The last chapter in the book discusses how teachers and other classmates can help children with Asperger syndrome by understanding their differences and appreciating their talents. This book, containing simple but effective illustrations, should be quite helpful to teachers and parents and family members of children with Asperger syndrome. Useful resources, including books, websites, and organizations, are listed at the end of the book.

263. *Taking Care of Myself: A Hygiene, Puberty and Personal Curriculum for Young People with Autism.* Wrobel, Mary J. with contributions by Patricia Rielly. Arlington, TX: Future Horizons, 2003. 246 pp. ISBN: 1885477945. Grades 3–12.

The main purpose of this book is to teach students with autism and other disabilities, without confusion, the necessary information and skills necessary to learn to live safe and healthy lives as independently as possible. The book is divided into seven units: Hygiene, Health, Modesty, Growth and Development, Menstruation, Touching and Personal Safety, and Masturbation. Although students from the ages of 5 to adult can benefit from this book, some of the activities in this book would not be appropriate for younger students, particularly instructions for puberty. The information is written using simple, concrete vocabulary aimed at students who are cognitively low; however, it can be used by higher functioning students as well. A few references and resources including some websites are included.

DOWN SYNDROME

Fiction

264. *The Hangashore.* Butler, Geoff. Plattsburgh, NY: Tundra Books, 1998. [27] pp. ISBN: 0887764444. Grades 4–6.

In this story, which takes place in a small Newfoundland fishing village at the end of World War II, Magistrate Mercer who arrives from England refuses to give up his front-row pew to accommodate a service honoring local soldiers. As a result, he makes many townspeople angry, but they remain silent, except the minister's 16-year-old son John, a boy with Down syndrome. He calls the magistrate a "hangashore," a term used in Newfoundland for "an unlucky person deserving pity," which angers the magistrate who threatens to institutionalize John. While fishing one day, the magistrate's life is at risk due to a fishing accident, and it is John who saves his life. This incident changes the magistrate's mind about the boy and the rest of the community. The full-page color oil paintings complement the text.
2007 IBBY Outstanding Book for Young People with Disabilities.

265. *Big Brother Dustin.* Carter, Alden R.; illustrated by Dan Young and Carol Carter. Morton Grove, IL: Albert Whitman, 1997. [30] pp. ISBN: 0807507156. Grades 1–2.

Beautifully illustrated with color photographs, this book is about Dustin, a boy with Down syndrome. He is very excited to hear from his parents the wonderful news that they are going to have a new baby girl. Dustin helps his parents and grandparents get ready for the birth of his baby sister. He also chooses the perfect name for her—MaryAnn. He enjoys helping his mom take care of MaryAnn. This story should be very valuable to siblings of children with Down syndrome. "The book is crisply organized with an easy-to-read text and an appealing snapshot album at the end with pictures of Dustin and MaryAnn as she begins to grow. A welcome addition." *School Library Journal*

266. *Be Good to Eddie Lee.* Fleming, Virginia M.; illustrated by Floyd Cooper. New York: Philomel Books, 1993. [28] pp. ISBN: 0399219935. Grades 2–4.

In this touching story, the author paints an accurate picture of the attitudes children may have toward those who are different. Christy considers Eddie Lee, a boy with Down syndrome, a pest and a mistake of God. Her mother says that she has to be good to Eddie Lee because he is lonesome and different. Christy's friend, JimBud shows no tolerance for Eddie Lee. Eddie Lee follows Christy and JimBud into the woods and shares several special discoveries. The oil wash illustrations complement the text. Though targeted for young children, this story can teach children of all ages to be more considerate and sensitive to individuals different from themselves. "This successful collaboration is a rarity for its potential to entertain, educate and encourage deeper consideration for others." *Publishers Weekly*

267. *Welcome to the Great Mysterious.* Landvik, Lorna. New York: Ballantine Books, 2000. 324 pp. ISBN: 0345438817. Grades 10–12.

This is a story of Tony-winning Broadway actress Geneva Jordan and her twin sister Ann and Ann's 13-year-old son Rich, who has Down syndrome. While Ann and her husband go on a vacation to Italy, Geneva journeys to Minnesota to babysit her nephew Rich. Not being used to kids, especially those with special needs, Geneva finds it very difficult at first to deal with Rich until she learns his ways. Geneva's next door neighbor Barbara has a disabled son Conrad who has cerebral palsy. Both Conrad and Rich become very close friends. Geneva finds the true meaning of life in an old trunk where she discovers a childhood memory book, *The Great Mysterious.* This book, a collection of thoughts and feelings, was created by Geneva and Ann while they were growing up. Well written, this book explores relationships, the love between twin sisters and between two disabled teenagers, and demonstrates the meaning of unconditional love. "While the plot extends few surprises, Landvik's unpretentious story admirably captures the ups and downs of a small town from the humorous perspective of a big-city star." *Publishers Weekly*

268. *A Small White Scar.* Nuzum, K. A. New York: Joanna Cotler Books, 2006. 180 pp. ISBN: 006075639X; ISBN: 9780060756390. Grades 5–8.

This story, which takes place on a ranch in Colorado in 1940, is about 15-year-old Will and his twin brother Denny who has Down syndrome. They share internal and external scars through several tragic incidents, which included witnessing the drowning death of their mother seven years earlier. In this coming-of-age book, Will tries to be on his own and runs away to compete in a rodeo, thus separating himself from Denny. Finally, both brothers, through persistence, discover their own identities without losing each other. Readers will enjoy the vivid picture of western cattle country and the rodeo experience. "A thoughtful, perceptive story, beautifully told." *School Library Journal* "It's a quick and engaging read that will appeal to reluctant readers and adventure fans alike." *KLIATT*
2008 Dolly Gray Award for Children's Literature in Developmental Disabilities.

269. *Veronica's First Year.* Rheingrover, Jean Sasso; illustrated by Kay Life. Morton Grove, IL: Albert Whitman, 1996. |22| pp. ISBN: 0807584746. Grades 1–2.

Nine-year-old Nathan welcomes his newly born baby sister Veronica, who has Down syndrome. With the help of his parents, Nathan adds new pictures to Veronica's baby album during her first year. Nathan eagerly looks forward to the day when Veronica will be able to ride Nathan's tricycle. It is a book that promotes care by an older brother for his younger sister with Down syndrome. Includes color illustrations. The last page "Note to Parents" suggests some helpful steps that can be followed by parents of children with Down syndrome. "A final 'Note to Parents' defines this congenital disorder with suggestions for dealing with both child and family in a positive manner. Useful for a limited audience." *School Library Journal*

270. *Russ and the Apple Tree Surprise.* Rickert, Janet Elizabeth; illustrated by Pete McGahan. Series: A Day with Russ. Bethesda, MD: Woodbine House, 1999. |26| pp. ISBN: 189062716X. Grades K–1.

Five-year-old Russ, who has Down syndrome, is sad because he wants a swing set in his backyard, but all he has in his backyard is a big apple tree. One day, Russ's grandparents come over to visit him. He helps his grandfather pick apples from the apple tree in their backyard and helps his mother and grandmother make a pie. Later on, Russ's grandfather invites him into the backyard and surprises him with a swing set. This is the first book in the series A Day with Russ. Color photographs complement the text.

271. *Russ and the Firehouse.* Rickert, Janet Elizabeth; illustrated by Pete McGahan. Series: A Day with Russ. Bethesda, MD: Woodbine House, 2000. [28] pp. ISBN: 1890627178. Grades K–2.

This is the second book in the Day with Russ series. Beautifully photographed in color, this is a story about 5-year-old Russ, who has Down syndrome. He visits his uncle Jerry at the firehouse where Jerry works as a fireman. Russ spends the day at the firehouse and helps with the daily chores at the firehouse.

272. *Russ and the Almost Perfect Day.* Rickert, Janet Elizabeth; illustrated by Pete McGahan. Series: A Day with Russ. Bethesda, MD: Woodbine House, 2000. [26] pp. ISBN: 1890627186. Grades K–1.

Russ, a student with Down syndrome, is having a great day right from the start watching his favorite TV show, receiving an invitation to a birthday party, and playing with hula hoops. While walking to school with his friend Kevin, Russ finds a five-dollar bill. Russ wants to spend that money to buy ice cream for his friend Kevin and himself. He realizes that the money belongs to a classmate. Russ and Kevin hand over the five-dollar bill to the classmate who had lost it. This is the third book in the children's series A Day with Russ. Color photographs complement the text. "It is heartening to see a special-needs child so positively integrated into a school setting." *School Library Journal*

273. *We'll Paint the Octopus Red.* Stuve-Bodeen, Stephanie; illustrated by Pam DeVito. Bethesda, MD: Woodbine House, 1998. [26] pp. ISBN: 1890627062. Grades K–1.

Six-year-old Emma discusses with her father all the things she will be able to do when the new baby arrives. After the birth of Isaac, Emma's father tells Emma that Isaac will not be able to do all the things they had discussed because Isaac was born with Down syndrome. Emma visits Isaac in the hospital and whispers in his ear, "I'll show you how to paint the octopus, Isaac, and I think we'll paint it red." Includes color photographs and two pages of questions and answers about Down syndrome, which should be very helpful. "[T]his is a thoughtful, focused book that will be of enormous help to families with Down syndrome children." *Booklist*

274. *The Best Worst Brother.* Stuve-Bodeen, Stephanie; illustrated by Charlotte Fremaux. Bethesda, MD: Woodbine House, 2005. [26] pp. ISBN: 1890627682. Grades 1–3.

Written by an award-winning author of several picture books, this sequel to *We'll Paint the Octopus Red* is a story about Emma who is frustrated with her younger 3-year-old brother Isaac, who has Down syndrome. She tries to be patient and communicate with Isaac, using sign language. Color illustrations complement the text. The last three pages of the book, which include some very helpful questions and answers about sign language, are more appropriate for grade levels three to five. "The text is simple but the message could be shared with a fairly wide audience." *School Library Journal*

275. *My Friend Isabelle.* Woloson, Eliza; illustrated by Bryan Gough. Bethesda, MD: Woodbine House, 2003. [28] pp. ISBN: 189062750X; ISBN2: 9781890627508. Grades K–1.

Charlie and Isabelle are good friends. Both of them have interests that are similar. For example, each of them likes to read, dance, draw, and play at the park. However, they are also different from each other because Isabelle has Down syndrome. This book teaches young children that friendships are special in spite of their differences, and that differences can make the world more interesting. "This book is perfect for building awareness and acceptance of Down syndrome." *Children's Literature*

Nonfiction

276. *Everything You Need to Know about Down Syndrome.* Bowman-Kruhm, Mary. Series: The Need to Know Library. New York: Rosen Publishing Group, 2003. 64 pp. ISBN: 0823937674. Grades 5–8.

This volume, one of the titles in the Need to Know Library series, discusses the causes of Down syndrome and some of the challenges faced by people with this condition. It also examines the medical treatment, including ways in which people with Down syndrome can improve their skills in coping with life and how family and friends can help them grow into valuable members of the community. In addition to illustrations, a glossary, additional resources, an index, and a very helpful section "Where to Go for Help" are included.

277. *Down Syndrome.* Brill, Marlene Targ. Series: Health Alert. New York: Marshall Cavendish Benchmark, 2007. 64 pp. ISBN: 0761422072; ISBN2: 9780761422075. Grades 4–7.

This volume, one of the titles in the Health Alert series, contains four chapters. The first chapter discusses what it is like to have Down syndrome. The second chapter defines Down syndrome, its symptoms, and causes. Chapter 3 explores the history of this condition, followed by the final chapter explaining what it is like to live with a family member who has Down syndrome, myths and facts, and how special education can help individuals who have Down syndrome. A glossary, a list of helpful organizations, and additional reading material are included. "If you do not know what Down Syndrome is then this book will be an excellent starting place. The textbook look may be a turn off, but the writing is engaging and the information easily understood." *Children's Literature*

278. *Living with Down Syndrome*. Bryan, Jenny. Series: Living With. Austin, TX: Raintree Steck-Vaughn, 1999. 32 pp. ISBN: 081725577X. Grades 3–6.

This inspiring book, part of the Living With series, provides useful information regarding the causes, symptoms, and treatment of Down syndrome. It discusses how the four individuals, Stacey, Richie, Maria, and Jack, who have Down syndrome, are affected by this condition, and how they have learned to accomplish things independently. Color photographs, a glossary, an index, and useful addresses and organizations to contact for support are included.

279. *Our Brother Has Down's Syndrome: An Introduction for Children*. Cairo, Shelley, Jasmine Cairo, and Tara Cairo; illustrated by Irene McNeil; designed by Helmut W. Weyerstrahs. Toronto: Annick Press, 1985. [21] pp. ISBN: 0920303307; ISBN2: 0920303315. Grades 1–2.

Tara and Jasmine discuss what it is like for them to be around their brother Jai, who has Down's syndrome. They begin their story by explaining the cause of Down's syndrome. Using color illustrations, Jai's daily activities, including help given to him in special ways, are discussed. They conclude by these remarks, "Jai may be a little different (we all have different things about us), but mostly he's just like the rest of us."

280. *1, 2, 3 for You and Me*. Girnis, Margaret; illustrated by Shirley Leaman Green. Morton Grove, IL: Albert Whitman, 2001. [28] pp. ISBN: 080756107X. Grades K–1.

With the help of beautiful color photographs, the author shows children with Down syndrome performing various activities involving objects that correspond to numbers one through twenty. For example, one bird, two butterflies, three bananas, four dogs, and so forth. Children are thus familiarized with numbers as well as names of simple objects. "Although the book will be most useful as an introduction to the concept, it also clearly makes the point that children with Down's syndrome enjoy the same playthings and activities as other youngsters." *School Library Journal*

281. *ABC for You and Me*. Girnis, Margaret; illustrated by Shirley Leaman Green. Morton Grove, IL: Albert Whitman, 2000. 30 pp. ISBN: 0807501018. Grades K–1.

Using beautiful color photographs, this book shows children with Down syndrome involved in activities with various objects corresponding to the letters of the English alphabet. "This is a terrific concept book for preschoolers with the added bonus of exposing them to a group of children not usually seen in picture books." *School Library Journal*

282. *Down Syndrome.* Girod, Christina M. Series: Diseases and Disorders. San Diego, CA: Lucent Books, 2001. 96 pp. ISBN: 1560068248. Grades 6–9.

This volume, one of the titles in the Diseases and Disorders series, explores Down syndrome and its history in Chapter 1. The second chapter discusses various types of developments with Down syndrome: motor development, cognitive development, social development, and language development. The next chapter examines the types of screening tests used for identifying fetuses that are likely to be carrying the disorder. Chapter 4 presents programs available that enhance the overall development of children with Down syndrome such as early intervention, special education, and community integration. Chapters 5 and 6 discuss ways to help prepare individuals with Down syndrome to live as independent citizens by acquiring the necessary skills. The final chapter, "Current Trends: Looking toward the Future," discusses research that is being done on this subject. Detailed indexes, annotated bibliographies, and lists of organizations to contact for additional information are included. "Overall, the information . . . is more thorough and accessible than that in many books. Well-done and intuitively organized." *School Library Journal*

283. *Taking Down Syndrome to School.* Glatzer, Jenna; illustrated by Tom Dineen. Series: Special Kids in School. Plainview, NY: JayJo Books, 2002. [30] pp. ISBN: 1891383191.Grades 1–3.

In this book, which is part of the Special Kids in School series, Nick, who has Down syndrome, tells his story. He discusses characteristics that are common in children with Down syndrome. "Down Syndrome Kids' Quiz" and "Ten Tips for Teachers" at the end of the book should be very helpful in understanding facts about Down syndrome and dealing with various conditions associated with Down syndrome. Bright color illustrations accompany the text. Additional resources are included.

284. *Let's Talk about Down Syndrome.* Gordon, Melanie Apel. Series: Let's Talk Library. New York: PowerKids Press, 1999. 24 pp. ISBN: 0823951979. Grades 1–4.

Part of the Let's Talk Library series, this book explains the causes of Down syndrome and its effect on the children who have this condition. Steps that can be taken by these children with the help of physical, occupational, and speech therapists to lead happy lives are discussed. Color photographs, an index, and a glossary are included.

285. *My Sister Is Special.* Jansen, Larry; illustrated by Robert Pepper. Cincinnati, OH: Standard Publishing Company, 1998. [23] pp. ISBN: 0784707979. Grades 1–2.

Nathan explains that God made everyone different and special, including his sister Rachel. She is different and special because she has Down syndrome. The last page contains "Advice for Parents and Teachers," a good resource for families and classmates of children with Down syndrome. Bright color illustrations complement the text.

286. *Count Us In: Growing Up with Down Syndrome.* Kingsley, Jason and Mitchell Levitz. New York: Harcourt Brace, 1994. 182 pp. ISBN: 0151504474; ISBN2: 015622660X. Grades 9–12.

The introductory part of this moving book is written by the mothers of Mitchell and Jason (the authors) when the authors, as newborn babies, were diagnosed with Down syndrome. The rest of the book is written by Mitchell and Jason, who in their own words share their own experiences, which cover a broad spectrum of topics, including their families, marriage, sex, employment, ambitions, and education. This book is unique in that it is written straight from the source and not from an outsider's perspective. Written in a dialogue format, the mission of the book is to educate and enlighten people about what it is like to be a teenager with Down syndrome. "Hearing about Down syndrome directly from these young men has a good deal more impact than reading any guide from a professional or even a parent. Their comments are eye-opening and heartening." *Booklist*

287. *My Name Is Not Slow: Youth with Mental Retardation.* Libal, Autumn. Series: Youth with Special Needs. Broomall, PA: Mason Crest Publishers, 2004. 127 pp. ISBN: 1590847318; ISBN2: 159084727X. Grades 7–10.

This volume is part of the series Youth with Special Needs. Mr. Brown looks at his newly born daughter Penelope, who looks very frail in the incubator. He is told by the doctors that Penelope has Down syndrome. This is the story of Penelope, her growth and development. She and her family face challenges due to her medical condition, the ignorance of others, and Penelope's mixed feelings such as love, loss, disappointment, and hope. It is a great resource that provides basic information to help young readers understand Down syndrome, mental retardation, and the impact of these conditions on children, their families, and peers. Includes a glossary and a list of helpful websites and additional books on the topic.

288. *Down Syndrome.* Margulies, Phillip. Series: Genetic Diseases and Disorders. New York: Rosen Publishing Group, 2007. 64 pp. ISBN: 1404206957; ISBN2: 9781404206953. Grades 8–10.

This volume is part of the Genetic Diseases and Disorders series. It covers five chapters in addition to the introductory chapter. The first chapter discusses the history of Down syndrome. Chapter 2 provides information regarding the genetic basis of Down syndrome. Chapter 3 discusses the impact of Down syndrome on individuals, for example, other medical complications, special needs, and so forth. Chapter 4 explains how various types of tests are used to determine the probability that a mother is carrying a fetus with Down syndrome. The final chapter is focused on genetic research and the future of Down syndrome. A very useful "Timeline," a glossary, websites of organizations dealing with Down syndrome, and a list of books for additional information on the subject are included.

289. *I Can, Can You?* Pitzer, Marjorie W. Bethesda, MD: Woodbine House, 2004. [13] pp. ISBN: 1890627577; ISBN2: 9781890627577. Grades K–1.

Complemented by beautiful color photographs, this book explains various simple activities performed by very young children who have Down syndrome. Activities such as "pat-a-cake," playing with blocks, taking a bath, going down a slide, learning sign language, drawing, smiling, and playing with ball are presented. "This book would be a great book for a family who has a child with Down syndrome, but any family with infants or toddlers would like this book as well. Infants and toddlers would enjoy seeing the pictures of other children playing like they do." *Children's Literature*
2007 IBBY Outstanding Book for Young People with Disabilities.

290. *Luke Has Down's Syndrome.* Powell, Jillian. Series: Like Me, Like You. Langhorne, PA: Chelsea Clubhouse, 2004. 29 pp. ISBN: 0791081834. Grades 2–4.

Part of the Like Me, Like You series, this book describes a day in the life of Luke who has Down's syndrome. It discusses how Luke copes with day-to-day situations, including learning to read, Makaton signing, and his weekly activities at cub scout meetings. Color photographs, a glossary, an index, and resources for additional information are included.

291. *Down Syndrome.* Routh, Kristina. Series: Just the Facts. Chicago: Heine-
     mann Library, 2004. 36 pp. ISBN: 1403451451. Grades 7–9.

This volume is part of the Just the Facts series. It explains why some individuals
are born with Down syndrome. The author discusses three types of Down syndrome, including characteristics of Down syndrome, some of the popular myths and
misconceptions about this condition, and what it is like to have Down syndrome.
Some medical conditions common in people with Down syndrome are explained
in an easy-to-understand way. Prenatal testing, which includes screening tests to
find out how likely it is that the baby has Down syndrome, and the diagnostic tests
to determine whether the baby is affected, is also explained. In addition to the importance of early intervention program of activities, exercise, and physical therapy
specifically designed for the first years of life of a baby with Down syndrome, the
author also discusses how support from friends, family, and professionals can be
very helpful. New areas of scientific research are also discussed. A glossary, a list
of additional books, and organizations for additional information are listed. "[W]ell
written and substantive without being overly technical." *School Library Journal*

292. *Down's Syndrome.* Royston, Angela. Series: What's It Like? Chicago:
     Heinemann Library, 2005. 32 pp. ISBN: 1403458510. Grades 2–4.

This work, one of the titles in the What's It Like? series, introduces Down's
syndrome to young children. Conditions and disabilities that may affect individuals with the Down's syndrome and their families are discussed. Some of the
topics covered are learning, moving, speaking, reading and writing, seeing and
hearing, having fun, working, and living on one's own. A glossary, color photographs, an index, and additional resources for more information are provided.

293. *Down Syndrome.* Tocci, Salvatore. New York: Franklin Watts, 2000. 144
     pp. ISBN: 0531115895. Grades 10–12.

After providing a simple explanation of the genetic causes of Down syndrome,
the author focuses on the various stages of life, from infancy through adulthood, of
an individual with Down syndrome. Solutions to help these individuals cope with
these challenges are suggested by the author. A special emphasis is given to family
issues, such as accepting a baby with Down syndrome; overcoming emotions of anger, grief, and guilt; handling sibling jealousy; and dealing with hurtful comments
by friends and relatives. Some of the myths and truths regarding this syndrome are
discussed as well. An exciting, though controversial, endeavor, known as the Human Genome Project, may provide a method to correct genetic defects responsible
for Down syndrome. A glossary and a list of resources are provided for additional
information. "[H]ighly recommended . . . would be of great benefit to children with
family members, classmates, and neighbors with Down Syndrome." *VOYA*

DYSLEXIA AND OTHER LEARNING DISABILITIES

Fiction

294. *If You're Smart, How Come You Can't Spell Mississippi?* Esham, Barbara; illustrated by Mike Gordon and Carl Gordon. Series: The Adventures of Everyday Geniuses. Perry Hall, MD: Mainstream Connections, 2008. 29 pp. ISBN: 160336448X; ISBN2: 9781603364485. Grades 2–3.

Katie is a third grader at Westover Elementary School. When 8-year-old Katie asks her father, who is an attorney, to help her with her spelling homework, Katie is surprised to learn that her father has dyslexia. After talking with her father and visiting the library in order to read about dyslexia, Katie learns that a lot of people who have trouble with reading and writing have become great actors, artists, athletes, presidents, doctors, lawyers, writers, scientists, entrepreneurs, inventors, even teachers. When Katie realizes that one of her classmates has dyslexia, Katie is more accepting of him. The color illustrations should maintain young readers' interest in this topic, which is rarely addressed in picture books, and delightfully complement this award-winning text.

295. *Last to Finish: A Story about the Smartest Boy in Math Class.* Esham, Barbara; illustrated by Mike Gordon and Carl Gordon. Series: Adventures of Everyday Geniuses. Perry Hall, MD: Mainstream Connections, 2008. 29 pp. ISBN: 1603364560; ISBN2: 9781603364560. Grades 2–3.

Max, a third grader at Perryville Elementary School, has trouble completing his math tests when Mrs. Topel, his teacher, uses a timer. Max's heart pounds, his hands sweat, and his mind freezes. Some of his classmates make fun of Max, which causes him tremendous embarrassment. During a meeting with his teacher and principal, Max and his parents learn that Max processes math concepts on a different level, which is more advanced than his fellow third graders. The color illustrations in this award-winning text are delightful and should maintain young readers' interest in this topic that is rarely addressed in picture books.

296. *Stacey Coolidge's Fancy-Smancy Cursive Handwriting.* Esham, Barbara; illustrated by Mike Gordon and Carl Gordon. Series: Adventures of Everyday Geniuses. Ocean City, MD: Mainstream Connections, 2008. [32] pp. ISBN: 1603364625; ISBN2: 9781603364621. Grades 2–3.

Carolyn has been eagerly waiting to be in second grade so that she will be able to play with Frederick, the class guinea pig. She likes her teacher and her classmates until she has to learn cursive handwriting. Carolyn practices and practices, but unlike her classmate Stacey, who seems to be perfect at everything, cursive handwriting is extremely difficult for her. When her teacher Mrs. Thompson tells Carolyn that cursive handwriting is just a tool for learning, and that Carolyn will have to find another tool to work with, Carolyn discovers that she can be proud of her creative ideas and imagination. The delightful color illustrations complement the text and should maintain young readers' interest in this topic, which is rarely addressed in picture books. A note to parents and teachers and information regarding the Mainstream Connections website, which provides additional resources for parents and teachers, are included. "Given the pressure to introduce cursive writing to younger students, this picture book will resonate with a growing number of children." *Booklist*

297. *One Little Girl.* Fassler, Joan; illustrated by M. Jane Smyth. New York: Behavioral Publications, 1969. [24] pp. ISBN: 0877050082. Grades 2–4.

Although this story was published forty years ago, it is still unique and very valuable in addressing what youngsters feel like when they are labeled "slow." Laurie is called slow by all the grown-ups around her. When her parents take Laurie to a doctor for an examination, the doctor's diagnosis is most favorable, especially for Laurie. The doctor tells Laurie and her parents that "Laurie is slow at some things, and a little bit fast at other things." But the doctor's most important advice is that Laurie seems quite happy to be herself and that Laurie and her parents need to accept who she is. This is a great message for younger readers about acceptance. Black and white drawings with green highlights are included.

298. *The Don't-Give-Up Kid and Learning Differences.* Gehret, Jeanne; illustrated by Sandra Ann Depauw. Fairport, NY: Verbal Images Press, 1996. 38 pp. ISBN: 1884281109; ISBN2: 188428115X. Grades 2–4.

After Alex becomes aware of his different learning style, he gets help from a specialized teacher to find a personalized way to learn. He discovers that his hero Thomas Edison had also faced similar problems. Like Thomas Edison, he keeps on trying new solutions until he succeeds at his dream to create things that no one has ever thought of. Written by an award-winning writer, this book includes spirited illustrations, a bibliography for talking to kids about learning differences, and a very useful "Parent Resource Guide."

299. *Lily and the Mixed-Up Letters.* Hodge, Deborah; illustrated by France Brassard. Toronto, Ontario: Tundra Books, 2007. [29] pp. ISBN: 0887767575; ISBN2: 9780887767579. Grades 3–5.

Lily loved school when she was in kindergarten, but now she is in second grade, and school is not fun for her any more. Whenever she tries reading, the letters jump around and get all mixed up. When each of the children in her class is asked by the teacher to read in front of the class, Lily realizes that she must

tell her mother about her reading problems. With hard work and help from Lily's mother, her teacher, and her friend Grace, Lily surprises everyone including herself on Parent's Day by reading a whole page from a book in front of the class. This is an uplifting story for any child who lacks confidence. Color illustrations complement the text. "Heart-warming encouragement for the child with reading problems, this book also shows Lily as a talented artist who can help Grace with her art work. Brassard's sympathetic, naturalistic scenes convincingly depict Lily's world at home and in school." *Children's Literature*
2007 IBBY Outstanding Book for Young People with Disabilities.

300. *Two-Minute Drill.* Lupica, Mike. New York: Philomel Books, 2007. 180 pp. ISBN: 0399247157; ISBN2: 09780399247156. Grades 6–9.

The new kid at school, Scott Parry is a very smart kid who struggles with football but is a good kicker. Only Chris Conlan, Scott's friend, knows about Scott's talent of being a good kicker. Chris, who is the star quarterback, has a secret of his own. He has dyslexia and is afraid that he will be kicked off the team if this secret gets out. These two friends team up to help each other in football as well as at school and prove that the will to succeed is more important than raw talent. "Though simply written and predictable, this brisk story of friendship and football will be a huge hit with the target audience." *Kirkus Reviews*

301. *A Mango-Shaped Space: A Novel.* Mass, Wendy. New York: Little, Brown, 2003. 220 pp. ISBN: 0316523887. Grades 7–12.

This is an intriguing story about a 13-year-old girl named Mia who happens to see colors for all letters, words, sounds, and smells. She has a rare condition called synesthesia. She keeps this a secret until she becomes overwhelmed by school, her relationships with friends, and the loss of a cat named Mango whom she loved very much. Some comprehensive websites at the end of the book should be very helpful for additional information regarding synesthesia. "Mia's voice is believable and her description of the vivid world she experiences, filled with slashes, blurs, and streaks of color, is fascinating." *School Library Journal*
2004 Schneider Family Book Award in the Middle School category.

302. *Sparks.* McNamee, Graham. New York: Wendy Lamb Books, 2002. 119 pp. ISBN: 0385729774. Grades 4–6.

Todd spent fourth grade in the special needs class and became best friends with Eva. Now in a regular fifth-grade class, Todd is being challenged by both the school work and his classmates who call him names. Eva still wants to be friends but does not understand that Todd is struggling due to his association with special needs students. Todd's new teacher Mr. Blaylock helps him to gain confidence.

This is an excellent story that illustrates the frustrations faced by students who have learning disabilities. "McNamee crafts a warm and humorous story about a boy's struggle to overcome his learning difficulties and his own self-doubt. McNamee . . . succeeds in making Todd an endearing and believable character. This sweet story sparkles with wit and warmth." *Kirkus Reviews*

303. *The Alphabet War: A Story about Dyslexia.* Robb, Diane Burton; illustrated by Gail Piazza. Morton Grove, IL: Albert Whitman, 2004. [30] pp. ISBN: 0807503029. Grades 2–4.

Adam, who has dyslexia, finds out that reading is a great struggle for him. He is frustrated because, in spite of trying very hard, learning to read and spell becomes a real war. At the end of first grade, Adam's parents hire a special tutor during the summer to help him learn reading. With expert help, hard work, and self-confidence, Adam wins the Alphabet War. Includes color illustrations and "A Note for Parents and Teachers." "It is a good selection for children to read or have read to them, and it is useful for adults who have to deal with these problems." *Children's Literature*

304. *Holy Enchilada!* Winkler, Henry and Lin Oliver. Series: Hank Zipzer, the World's Greatest Underachiever. New York: Grossett & Dunlap, 2004. 158 pp. ISBN: 0448433532; ISBN2: 0448435543. Grades 4–7.

This is part of the Hank Zipzer, the World's Greatest Underachiever series. Hank Zipzer and his family host a Japanese student, Yoshi. In honor of Yoshi and his father, everyone in Hank's class is assigned by Ms. Adolph to bring in a dish from another country to celebrate the multicultural day. Ms. Adolf piles lots of food on her plate, including some enchiladas. After a few bites, her face turns red because of the super-spicy dish of enchiladas that she had tried. Ms. Adolf thinks that someone in the class is playing a mean joke on her. She punishes the entire class with no recess until the person responsible for playing this joke comes forward. Hank who had prepared the enchiladas, realizes that because of his trouble with numbers due to dyslexia, he might have used three cups of peppers instead of one-third cup, thus making the dish very spicy.

305. *The Life of Me: Enter at Your Own Risk.* Winkler, Henry and Lin Oliver. Series: Hank Zipzer, the World's Greatest Underachiever. New York: Grosset & Dunlap, 2008. [64] pp. ISBN: 0448443767; ISBN2: 9780448443768. Grades 4–7.

In this story, part of the Hank Zipzer, the World's Greatest Underachiever series, fifth-grader Hank finds himself in a dilemma. He must decide whether he should attend the after-school class of tae kwon do with his friends or attend the reading improvement program taught by his favorite teacher, where he could spend time with Zoe, the new girl he likes. Hank decides to go out with Zoe, but first he needs to stand up against the school bully, who happens to be Zoe's cousin.

306. *Ms. McCaw Learns to Draw.* Zemach, Kaethe. New York: Arthur A. Levine Books, 2008. [28] pp. ISBN: 0439829143; ISBN2: 9780439829144. Grades 1–3.

Dudley Ellington, who is not very good at learning, spends most of his day bored and is not very attentive in the classroom. His favorite teacher Ms. McCaw is always patient with him and works with Dudley until he learns the lesson. The class is surprised when Ms. McCaw becomes frustrated because she cannot draw a face on the chalkboard. Finally it is Dudley who helps Ms. McCaw to draw. The lively color illustrations complement the text. "Because the text is simple and straightforward, the book is a good choice to read aloud, especially with a marker and whiteboard nearby. The pen and watercolor illustrations are expressive and full of energy." *School Library Journal*

Nonfiction

307. *My Thirteenth Winter: A Memoir.* Abeel, Samantha. New York: Orchard Books, 2003. 203 pp. ISBN: 0439339049. Grades 9–12.

This is an inspiring autobiography about courage and strength. In this memoir, Samantha describes how her life was affected due to dyscalculia, a learning disability that affected her capacity to learn skills based on sequential processing, such as math, spelling, and grammar. She suffers anxiety attacks as she struggles with junior high school pressures. In spite of the fact that signs of a learning disability were there, she was not diagnosed until she was 13 years old. The struggle to overcome these challenges teaches her to be creative, persistence, and to reach out for help. It is a well-written book that delivers profound insights about what it means to have a learning disability. The author's book of poetry titled *Reach for the Moon* won 1994 Margot Marek Award. "Her inspiring memoir should make teachers proud of their profession, remind families what unconditional love can do, and help people know that learning disabilities are common and nothing to be ashamed of." *Children's Literature* "Educational and beautifully written, perfectly demonstrating how learning disabilities can coexist with real talent." *Kirkus Reviews*
2005 Schneider Family Book Award in the Teen category.

308. *Why Can't I Learn Like Everyone Else: Youth with Learning Disabilities.* Brinkerhoff, Shirley. Series: Youth with Special Needs. Broomall, PA: Mason Crest Publishers, 2004. 127 pp. ISBN: 159084730X; ISBN2: 159084727X. Grades 7–10.

Part of the Youth with Special Needs series, this book provides information regarding the most common learning disabilities. Charlie Begay, a Navajo boy from New Mexico, is one of those individuals who discovers that he cannot read the way the other students do because of his learning disability. Diagnosis of these conditions and the type of help available to those who have learning disabilities are explained in a clear understandable way. Color photographs, a glossary, an index, and additional resources on this subject are included. "The series is appropriate for pre-service teachers, in-service teachers, and students from late elementary through adolescence and would be a valuable addition to every school library." *VOYA*

309. *If I Can Do It, So Can You: Triumph over Dyslexia.* Bursak, George J. [s.l.]: G. J. Bursak, 1999. 47 pp. Grades 7–12.

This is a biography of George Bursak who, as a boy, struggled with dyslexia. Over the years, his determination and creativity lead to a rewarding family life and successful career. This inspirational story shows that there is no limit to the creative spirit. Some examples of his accomplishments are winning awards for his ceramics, which evoke pottery styles from throughout the world, and revolutionizing the packaging industry by inventing machines that automatically form and fill disposable sterile packets of medications for the health care industry. As a result, he has received recognition and awards for his innovative products. Includes black and white photographs and illustrations.

310. *Dyslexia.* Clark, Arda Darakjian. Series: Diseases and Disorders. Detroit: Thomson/Gale, 2005. 112 pp. ISBN: 1590180402; ISBN2: 9781590180402. Grades 6–9.

This book, one of the titles in the Diseases and Disorders series, defines dyslexia and how to identify and treat this condition. The last chapter provides information that can be used to help individuals live and cope with dyslexia. Primary and secondary quotations, annotated bibliographies, detailed indexes, and lists of organizations to contact for additional information are included.

311. *Coping with a Learning Disability.* Clayton, Lawrence. Series: Coping. New York: Rosen Publishing Group, 1999. 122 pp. ISBN: 082392887X. Grades 7–9.

Young readers and parents will find information, encouragement, and help from this revised edition, which is part of the Coping series. Topics covered in this book are types of learning disabilities; personal, family, and friends' responses to learning disabilities; peer issues; testing and evaluation; dealing with classroom teachers; special education; finding professional help outside the school; and building self-esteem. Examples of some of the celebrities who were successful in spite of having a learning disability will give young readers with a learning disability hope and a positive message that they are not alone and that they too can succeed in life. Includes a helpful glossary, an index, and additional resources and websites.

312. *A World Upside Down and Backwards: Reading and Learning Disorders.* Connelly, Elizabeth Russell. Series: Encyclopedia of Psychological Disorders. Philadelphia: Chelsea House Publishers, 1999. 95 pp. ISBN: 0791048942. Grades 9–12.

One of the titles in the Encyclopedia of Psychological Disorders series, this volume addresses questions regarding learning disorders. The first chapter provides an overview of learning disorders, highlighting the features of reading, mathematics, and writing disorders. By using examples of General George Patton and Walt Disney, it helps readers understand how individuals with learning disorders can achieve success. The second chapter traces the history of learning disorders. Chapter 3 examines the criteria for diagnosing these disorders and describes how the disorders and their possible complications can affect the day-to-day lives of individuals with learning disabilities. Chapter 4 discusses the impact of learning disorders on the society. The last two chapters cover the causes of these disorders and methods typically used to treat the behavioral and emotional stress associated with them. A glossary of key terms and an appendix with information on organizations and agencies that can help people who are diagnosed with these disorders are included.

313. *Coping with Dyslexia.* Donnelly, Karen. Series: Coping. New York: Rosen Publishing Group, 2000. 121 pp. ISBN: 0823928500. Grades 7–9.

In this book, which is part of the Coping series, the author defines characteristics of dyslexia, common difficulties associated with dyslexia, and coping with this condition. Assistive technology, which can be used as one of the learning tools, is discussed. Strategies for learning and for preparing for college or a career should be helpful to individuals who have dyslexia and for the adults who work with them. The last chapter gives brief biographies of some famous and successful dyslexics such as Nolan Ryan, Woodrow Wilson, Tom Cruise, and Cher. A glossary, an index, and a list of additional resources and organizations are included.

314. *My Friend Has Dyslexia.* Edwards, Nicola. Series: My Friend Has. North Mankato, MN: Chrysalis Education, 2005. 32 pp. ISBN: 1593891679; ISBN2: 9781593891671. Grades 4–7.

This volume is part of the My Friend Has series. Beautifully illustrated with color photographs, this is a story about Rachel and her good friend Bella, who is dyslexic. Rachel spends time with Bella doing some fun things like visiting Bella's grandmother, sleeping overnight, and so forth. The author explains, in a very simplified way, the symptoms of dyslexia, how Bella deals with dyslexia, and how Bella's dyslexia affects her friend Rachel. One of the chapters lists names of some famous and successful dyslexics. "Questions People Ask," a glossary of terms related to dyslexia, and a list of useful organizations are included.

315. *The Survival Guide for Kids with LD: Learning Differences.* Fisher, Gary L. and Rhoda Woods Cummings; illustrated by Jackie Urbanovic. Minneapolis: Free Spirit Publishing, 2002. 102 pp. ISBN: 157542119. Grades 5–9.

This revised updated edition answers many questions about learning disabilities (LD), such as: Why do kids with LD have trouble learning? What can kids with LD do about this condition? Are kids with LD stupid? Why do kids with LD have a hard time in school? How can kids with LD set goals and plan for the future? Well organized and easy to understand, this book has excellent tips for kids with LD. It includes very helpful resources for parents and teachers, a list of educational software, multimedia companies, organizations, cartoon photographs, and an index. "The clearly written, factual material will help those with LD and those who live or work with them to understand the complexities of this disability." *School Library Journal*

316. *Everything You Need to Know about Dyslexia.* Goldish, Meish. Series: The Need to Know Library. New York: Rosen Publishing Group, 2001. 64 pp. ISBN: 0823934624. Grades 5–8.

This title in the Need to Know Library series offers a wealth of information regarding dyslexia. The first chapter discusses characteristics and daily activities of Caleb, who has dyslexia. The next three chapters explain the causes and symptoms of dyslexia and how to overcome this disability and how to become a good reader and writer, with the help of professionals, public agencies, and special schools. One of the chapters, "The Gift of Dyslexia," discusses famous people with dyslexia and related learning problems who have led very successful lives. A glossary of terms and a list of organizations, "Where to Go for Help" in the United States and Canada, are also included.

317. *Let's Talk about Dyslexia.* Gordon, Melanie Apel. Series: Let's Talk Library. New York: PowerKids Press, 1999. 24 pp. ISBN: 1568382758; ISBN2: 0823951995. Grades 1–4.

The author explains that dyslexia is not an illness but a learning disability that causes difficulties with reading, writing, and math in this title, which is part of the Let's Talk Library series. Gordon reiterates that most dyslexics are just as smart as other people, and that they can be whatever they want to be. It is a misconception that they are not intelligent. Famous people are listed, such as Tom Cruise, Albert Einstein, and Thomas Edison, as examples of individuals who have been very successful in spite of being dyslexic. The author suggests that children who are having trouble with reading, writing, or math need to get help from their parents and teachers. An index, a glossary, and color photographs are included.

318. *Learning Disabilities.* Gunton, Sharon. Series: Social Issues First Hand. Detroit: Greenhaven Press, 2008. 122 pp. ISBN: 0737738405; ISBN: 9780737738407. Grades 9–12.

In this title of the Social Issues First Hand series, the author presents a collection of personal narratives related to learning disabilities such as in the following chapters: living with learning disabilities; learning disabilities in family life; learning disabilities in the clinic; learning disabilities in the classroom as well as at the workplace. A bibliography, a list of organizations to contact, including an annotated table of contents, and an index are included.

319. *Living with Learning Disabilities: A Guide for Students.* Hall, David E. Series: Living With. Minneapolis: Lerner Publications, 1993. 64 pp. ISBN: 0822500361. Grades 3–6.

Written by a pediatrician, this book, part of the Living With series, explains various learning disabilities such as attention deficit disorder, fine motor problems, and visual information. The author offers positive advice on adjusting attitude, coping with learning disabilities, and selecting the appropriate medical treatments. A glossary, an index, and a list of additional resources and organizations are included. "A book that answers some important questions without overwhelming readers in detail or sugar-coating the facts." *Booklist*

320. *Let's Talk about Needing Extra Help at School.* Kent, Susan. Series: Let's Talk Library. New York: PowerKids Press, 2000. 24 pp. ISBN: 0823954226; ISBN2: 9780823954223. Grades 1–4.

Part of the Let's Talk Library series, this book discusses some of the reasons why children with learning disabilities may need extra help in school and how they can get that help. Color photographs, a glossary, and an index are included.

321. *Dyslexia.* Landau, Elaine. Series: Life Balance. New York: Franklin Watts, 2004. 79 pp. ISBN: 0531122174; ISBN2: 9780531122174. Grades 4–7.

This volume, one of the titles in the Life Balance series, defines dyslexia, how it is diagnosed, and explains the way dyslexics are affected. Real-life situations and various educational techniques to help individuals with dyslexia cope with this condition are presented. A glossary, an index, and additional resources, including online sites and organizations, are included. "While several fictional titles have featured dyslexic characters, this is unique in its presentation of the topic for this age level, and deserves consideration." *School Library Journal*

322. *Learning Disabilities Information for Teens.* Lawton, Sandra Augustyn, editor. Series: Teen Health. Detroit: Omnigraphics, 2006. 400 pp. ISBN: 0780807960. Teens/Educators/Parents.

Various kinds of learning disabilities and their common signs, causes, and diagnostic procedures are described in this well-organized book, one of the titles in the Teen Health series. Information regarding academic issues, such as study habits, homework, and facts about laws designed to protect the rights of people with learning disabilities, is also given. This book is divided into eight parts, and each part is subdivided further into chapters. Parts focus on broad areas of interest, and chapters are devoted to single topics within a part. The last part contains a list of resources (articles, organizations, websites) that can help teenagers find information on learning disabilities and other related topics. Includes an index. Although some of the resources are intended for all audiences, the majority of these are written specifically for teenagers. A highly recommended book for teenagers, parents, special education teachers, and librarians.

323. *Keeping a Head in School: A Student's Book about Learning Abilities and Learning Disorders.* Levine, Melvin D. Cambridge, MA: Educators Publishing Service, 1990. 297 pp. ISBN: 0838820697. Grades 9–12.

The main purpose of this book is to prevent misunderstandings about learning disorders. This work reflects the author's two decades of work evaluating children with learning disabilities. The first chapter deals with some basic concepts related to learning disorders. Chapters 2 through 5 discuss specific developmental functions such as attention, language, and memory. Chapter 6 reviews the four basic skills areas: reading, spelling, writing, and math. Chapter 7 deals specifically with social skills because many students with learning disorders experience social stress in school. Chapter 8, which contains a series of questions students have regarding learning disorders, is a very useful because at times the students with learning disabilities are either too embarrassed to ask questions or they may have difficulty wording their questions. The final chapter relates to the future and it lists possible actions that a student can take to minimize the long-range effects of learning disorders. Simple black and white illustrations are very helpful for additional clarification of the ideas presented in this book. This book is well organized and easy to understand. "Important Words and Phrases" at the end of the book should be very helpful to the reader.

324. *Dyslexia.* Moragne, Wendy. Series: The Millbrook Medical Library. Brookfield, CT: Millbrook Press, 1997. 96 pp. ISBN: 9780761302063. Grades 5–9.

Nine young teenagers offer their insights into how having dyslexia has affected their self-image, their daily activities, particularly in school, and their relationships with family and friends in this volume, which is part of the Millbrook Medical Library series. The author clearly explains the signs and symptoms of dyslexia, presents various treatment options, and discusses the many challenges faced every day by individuals with dyslexia. Black and white photographs, a glossary, an index, and a list of some resources for additional information are included. This should be a useful book for teenagers who have dyslexia and for people in their lives. "Short paragraphs and sentences, although containing a great deal of information, make this book a valuable research tool for students." *VOYA*

325. *Taking Dyslexia to School.* Moynihan, Lauren E.; illustrated by Tom Dineen. Series: Special Kids in School. Plainview, NY: JayJo Books, 2002. [27] pp. ISBN: 1891383175; ISBN2: 9781891383175. Grades 1–3.

Part of the Special Kids in School series, this is the story about Matt, who is dyslexic. He has a lot of trouble with reading, spelling, and math. With the help of his parents and a special teacher, Mr. Davis, Matt starts doing better in school. "Let's Take the Dyslexia Kids' Quiz" at the end of the book has ten basic informative questions and answers regarding dyslexia. "Ten Tips for Teachers" provides additional information. A list of five organizations as additional resources is also included. Children should enjoy the color illustrations accompanying the text.

326. *Copy This! Lessons from a Hyperactive Dyslexic Who Turned a Bright Idea into One of America's Best Companies.* Orfalea, Paul and Ann Marsh. New York: Workman Publishing Company, 2005. 225 pp. ISBN: 0761137777. Grades 10–12.

The founder of Kinko's, Paul Orfalea, who has ADHD and dyslexia, opened up his first copy shop while he was still a student in college. He got the idea for the business while working on a term paper with fellow college mates. Most people consider ADHD and dyslexia weaknesses. In this book, Orfalea describes how he overcame the challenges of dyslexia and hyperactivity and gives advice and suggestions on life and business success. His story reveals his biggest failures and his biggest successes. He feels that his dyslexia was a critical ingredient in his success. He shares a very important message in this book—life success comes to people even when scholarly success passes by due to learning differences. This is a highly recommended book. "Written with wit and style, this book offers much to inspire readers with obstacles to overcome or who march to a different drummer." *School Library Journal*

327. *Learning Disabilities: The Ultimate Teen Guide.* Paquette, Penny Hutchins and Cheryl Gerson Tuttle. Series: It Happened to Me. Lanham, MD: Scarecrow Press, 2006. 301 pp. ISBN: 0810856433. Grades 7–12.

In this very well-organized guide, part of the It Happened to Me series, written exclusively for teens and young adults dealing with a wide variety of learning disabilities, the authors present an overview of learning disabilities and brain structure in the first two chapters. The next few chapters focus on specific disabilities, including ADHD, dyscalculia, dysgraphia, and dyslexia. Each of the chapters discusses how it feels to have each of the various learning disabilities, their symptoms, their causes, and coping strategies. Resources, including websites, are given. The chapter "Your Test Report" provides a sample of test results with explanation and definitions. Another chapter, "The IEP (Individualized Education Plan)," discusses proactive student participation. The final chapters explain transition from high school to life after high school, including higher education and career choices, vocational or trade programs, military service, and volunteer opportunities. Throughout the book, profiles, success stories, and quotes are presented. "Well organized, up-to-date, and practical, this title is a necessary addition for media centers and special-education collections and will certainly be useful for any student who has a learning disability." *School Library Journal*

328. *Straight Talk about Learning Disabilities.* Porterfield, Kay Marie. New York: Facts on File, 1999. 148 pp. ISBN: 0816038651. Grades 8–12.

Gary, Wanda, and Nathan all have something in common with one another. They also share an important similarity with George Washington, Thomas Edison, and Cher. They are all bright individuals; however, they all have a learning disability (LD). Using these three fictional case studies, Porterfield explains various kinds of learning disabilities, their symptoms, their emotional impact, methods of their diagnosis, and available treatments. "Learning to Live with LD" is a helpful chapter that discusses steps that can be taken for goal setting and getting along with others. The last chapter, "Rising to the LD Challenge," is an inspiring chapter that emphasizes that successful people such as Walt Disney, Tom Cruise,

Stevie Wonder, Winston Churchill, among many others, made big contributions to the world, and they turned their challenges of learning disabilities into assets. Organizations, including resources on the Internet, that offer help for children and adults who struggle with learning disabilities are listed. "The author's own experience with a learning disability is poignantly described in the preface, adding resonance to her subject. Her talent for organizing information has produced an accessible book, but more than that, one that offers reassurance." *Booklist*

329. *Dyslexia: Understanding Reading Problems.* Savage, John F. New York: J. Messner, 1985. 90 pp. ISBN: 0671542893. Grades 4–8.

The definition of dyslexia, its causes, the problems caused in and out of school for those who have dyslexia, and how these children can learn to read are discussed in this book. Individual stories of students who have dyslexia are shared as well. One of the chapters is about the Public Law 94-142, which explains the educational rights for children with special needs. A list of the organizations pertaining to dyslexia and an index are included.

330. *Dyslexia.* Silverstein, Alvin, Virginia Silverstein, and Laura Silverstein Nunn. Series: My Health. New York: F. Watts, 2001. 48 pp. ISBN: 0531118622; ISBN2: 9780531118627. Grades 3–6.

The introductory chapter in this volume of the My Health series discusses reading problems, followed by an explanation of dyslexia and the parts of the brain involved in reading and speaking. The last two chapters explain how dyslexia is diagnosed and how dyslexics can learn ways to improve their language skills by getting proper help and following the recommended suggestions. Color photographs, a glossary, an index, and additional titles of books and names of helpful organizations and online sites are included.

331. *Dyslexia.* Wiltshire, Paula. Series: Health Issues. Austin, TX: Raintree Steck-Vaughn, 2002. 64 pp. ISBN: 0739852213. Grades 6–9.

The introductory part of this volume, one of the titles in the Health Issues series, defines dyslexia, including myths and truths about dyslexia. With the help of clear illustrations, the author explains in the first chapter, titled "The Dyslexic Brain," the role played by the left and right hemispheres in the human brain. Chapter 2 looks at the signs to watch for if someone thinks he or she may be dyslexic and how to go about being assessed. Chapter 3 explains how dyslexia affects reading and writing both at school and in everyday life. Chapter 4 discusses how other subject areas can be affected by dyslexia, such as foreign languages, math, music, and organizational skills. The last chapter, "Techniques for Success," lists some excellent steps that can be taken to face the challenges of taking examinations in school. This chapter also includes short biographies of some of the famous and successful individuals who have dyslexia. Some of the ways in which family members and friends can support individuals with dyslexia are also suggested throughout the book. A glossary, books, and websites about dyslexia are included in this highly recommended book. "This book will be helpful to children afflicted with this condition who are trying to understand themselves as well as to students doing research." *School Library Journal*

INTELLECTUAL DISABILITIES

Fiction

332. *The Babbs Switch Story.* Beard, Darleen Bailey. New York: Farrar, Straus and Giroux, 2002. 165 pp. ISBN: 0374304750. Grades 6–9.

In this story, which takes place in 1924, Ruth Ann Tillman, a 12-year-old girl, lives on a farm in Babbs Switch, Oklahoma, with her parents and her intellectually disabled sister Daphne. Ruth loves to sing, but her parents do not allow her to perform on the schoolhouse stage during the Christmas Tree Celebration because of their embarrassment over an almost tragic incident with a neighbor's baby involving Daphne. During the annual Celebration, a horrendous fire breaks out, and Daphne and the neighbor's baby disappear. When Daphne and the baby are eventually found, Ruth realizes how much her sister means to her. The entire town considers Daphne a hero since she rescued the very baby she had "nearly killed" earlier. This story is loosely based on an actual tragic fire incident in 1924 in Babbs Switch, Oklahoma, which killed thirty-five people. "However, the story deals more with Ruth Ann's personal dilemmas than the historical tragedy. It is a quick read, packed with period detail." *School Library Journal*

333. *My Friend Jacob.* Clifton, Lucille; illustrated by Thomas DiGrazia. New York: Dutton, 1980. [32] pp. ISBN: 0525354875. Grades 1–3.

Narrated by a young boy named Sam, this is a story about Jacob, who is mentally slower. Sam considers Jacob his best friend in spite of the fact that he is older than Sam. He helps Jacob to learn several things, such as knocking instead of barging into a house. Although this is an older publication, it offers a unique and positive perspective on relationships, particularly for younger readers who are in similar situations. Black and white illustrations are included.

334. *Ben, King of the River.* Gifaldi, David; illustrated by Layne Johnson. Morton Grove, IL: Albert Whitman, 2001. [30] pp. ISBN: 0807506354. Grades 3–5.

Beautifully illustrated, this story discusses Chad's experiences of emotions during the camping trip that he makes with his parents and his 5-year-old mentally disabled brother Ben. The last page in this book is a "note" contributed by the author's 13-year-old nephew Josh Keys, who writes his personal experiences about what it is like living with a disabled sibling. The book lists tips for living with a disabled brother or sister, which should be helpful for understanding and dealing with a sibling's disability. The author also includes a website that offers information regarding "sibling support." "Kids with a disabled relative or friend will strongly relate to this, but the story can also be used to increase awareness and sensitivity among a wider audience." *Booklist*

335. *Keeping Up with Roo.* Glenn, Sharlee Mullins; illustrated by Dan Andreasen. New York: G. P. Putnam's Sons, 2004. [32] pp. ISBN: 0399234302. Grades 2–4.

Gracie has a very special bond with her aunt Roo, who is mentally disabled. It seems like they would be best friends forever; however, the relationship between them changes when Gracie starts school and gets new friends and takes piano lessons. Gracie does not want to play with Roo anymore and is embarrassed to introduce Roo to her friend Sarah. But later on, Gracie changes her attitude and shares her aunt Roo with Sarah. Watercolor illustrations complement the text. "All youngsters will benefit by reading this book. It is an especially good one for anyone who knows a mentally challenged adult." *Children's Literature*
2006 Dolly Gray Award for Children's Literature in Developmental Disabilities.

336. *The Silent Boy.* Lowery, Lois. Boston: Houghton Mifflin, 2003. 178 pp. ISBN: 0618282319. Grades 5–8.

This is an excellent story told in flashback. Katy is the 8-year-old daughter of a doctor in a small New England town during the 1910s. Katy enjoys accompanying her father on his house calls because she wants to be a doctor when she grows up. Katy befriends Jacob, the 13-year-old brother of her family's new house-helper Peggy. Jacob, who is "touched in the head" and loves animals, starts hanging around Katy's barn. Katy's life and outlook changes when Jacob is found responsible for the death of a newborn. "Lowry still manages to create an appealing character in the curious, unusually compassionate girl, layering her story with questions about how families shape lives and the misunderstandings that can lead to heartbreak." *Booklist*

337. *A Corner of the Universe.* Martin, Ann M. New York: Scholastic Press, 2002. 189 pp. ISBN: 0439388805. Grades 5–8.

In this story, which takes place in 1960, Hattie Owen, a 12-year-old, begins her summer vacation in the sleepy town of Millerton. Hattie helps her parents run their boarding house and stays out of the way of her overbearing, wealthy grandmother who lives in Millerton's upscale neighborhood. When her mother's 21-year-old mentally challenged brother returns home, Hattie quickly becomes a kindred spirit with Uncle Adam, someone she never knew. Hattie also becomes friends with Leila, a girl her own age, whose family owns the carnival that has recently arrived in town. Hattie tries to share the excitement of the carnival with her Uncle Adam, but devastating circumstances ensue. Hattie is hopeful that her family can resolve their conflicts after another unfortunate tragedy. "Readers will relate to Hattie's fear of being as 'different' as Adam, and will admire her willingness to befriend an outcast. Hearts will go out to both Hattie and Adam as they step outside the confines of their familiar world to meet some painful challenges." *Publishers Weekly*
2003 Newbery Honor Book.

338. *Me and Rupert Goody.* O'Connor, Barbara. Thorndike, ME: Thorndike Press, 2000. 133 pp. ISBN: 0374448043. Grades 5–7.

Jennalee Helton is 11 years old and has a good life. To get away from her large, boisterous family, she spends her free time helping her friend Uncle Beau at his General Store. Her daily routine and her relationship with Uncle Beau are disrupted when Rupert B. Goody arrives, claiming to be Uncle Beau's son. Rupert is mentally slow. Jennalee is challenged in accepting Rupert and the fact that he is not going away. O'Connor's first-person narration, written in the dialect of the communities situated in North Carolina's Smoky Mountains, lends authenticity in this enjoyable story. Readers should enjoy Jennalee's road to self-discovery. "An absorbing story people with carefully drawn and memorable characters." *School Library Journal*
2002 Dolly Gray Award for Children's Literature in Developmental Disabilities.

339. *Thank You, Mr. Falker.* Polacco, Patricia. New York: Philomel Books, 1998. [36] pp. ISBN: 0399231668. Grades 3–5.

Trisha is excited at the thought of starting school and learning to read. But right from the very beginning, when she tries to read, all the letters and numbers just get jumbled up. Her classmates call her "dummy" and she starts to feel dumb. However, in the fifth grade, she has a new teacher, Mr. Falker, who sets out to help Trisha understand and overcome her problem and prove to herself that she can and will read. "This is a story close to author Patricia Polacco's heart. It is her personal song of thanks and praise to teachers like Mr. Falker, who quietly but surely change the lives of the children they teach" (from book jacket). Color illustrations by the author are included. "Nonetheless, it is a moving tribute and really brings home the message that teachers can and do make a difference in their students' lives." *Children's Literature*

340. *Way to Go, Alex!* Pulver, Robin; illustrated by Elizabeth Wolf. Morton Grove, IL: Albert Whitman, 1999. [30] pp. ISBN: 0807515833. Grades 2–4.

Carly's relationship with her older brother Alex, who has mental retardation, is narrated in this book. The family's experiences with Special Olympics, an organization founded by Eunice Kennedy Shriver in 1968, allow Alex to focus on his abilities and not his disabilities. Alex trains for and competes in the Special Olympics. Water-color illustrations accompany the text. A note from the Special Olympics is included.

341. *Clay.* Rodowsky, Colby F. New York: Farrar, Straus and Giroux, 2001. 165 pp. ISBN: 0374313385. Grades 5–8.

Elsie, an 11-year-old, and her intellectually disabled brother Tommy have been kidnapped by their noncustodial mother. Their mother, who is emotionally disturbed, has changed their birth names from Linda and Timmy to Elsie and Tommy, respectively, and does not allow them to talk to anyone or attend school. When Tommy becomes seriously ill, Elsie finds the courage to seek help and reveal her true identity. Elsie and Tommy are reunited with their father, and their mother gets the medical help that she needs. "A moving and realistic story for readers who can recognize the power of Clay's narrative and not be frightened by it." *School Library Journal*

342. *What's Wrong with Timmy?* Shriver, Maria; illustrated by Sandra Speidel. Boston: Little, Brown, 2001. [48] pp. ISBN: 0316233374. Grades K–5.

When 8-year-old Kate meets Timmy, the 8-year-old son of her mother's friend, Kate immediately notices that Timmy is different from her in many ways, such as he takes longer to learn and cannot walk or run well. After Kate's mother explains to her that Timmy "loves his family, he wants friends, he goes to school, and he dreams about what he wants to be when he grows up," in spite of the fact that he has special needs, Kate quickly learns to accept Timmy the way he is. "The book reads well, though, and would be a good introduction for youngsters welcoming a disabled child into their school or neighborhood." *School Library Journal*

343. *Tru Confessions.* Tashjian, Janet. New York: Scholastic, 1999. 167 pp. ISBN: 0590960474. Grades 4–8.

Trudy Walker's twin brother Eddie suffered asphyxia, the loss of oxygen, at birth. Twelve-year-old Tru, as she is known to her friends, keeps an electronic diary in which she writes all her thoughts, hopes, and dreams. One of her dreams is to find a cure for Eddie. This insightful story about the feelings of a sibling, whose life continues to be dominated by a disabled brother, is very poignant and provides a good read for young readers experiencing the same situation. "The story is a good mix of well-handled subject matter and reader appeal." *Booklist* 2000 Dolly Gray Award for Children's Literature in Developmental Disabilities.

Nonfiction

344. *Mental Retardation.* Abramovitz, Melissa. Series: Diseases and Disorders. Detroit: Lucent Books, 2007. 104 pp. ISBN: 9781590184127. Grades 6–9.

This title in the Diseases and Disorders series provides comprehensive coverage regarding mental retardation. The introductory chapters explain what mental retardation is and identifies its causes. Additional chapters explore prevention possibilities, remediation strategies, and various treatment options available to individuals faced with mental retardation. The chapter titled "Living with Mental Retardation" provides families with positive suggestions for dealing with family members who are intellectually disabled. The final chapter offers a glimpse of what the future holds for intellectually disabled individuals and their family members. The text is easy to read while providing important concepts in manageable sections. Black and white photographs, graphics, and text boxes, glossary, organizations, a section listing websites, and an index are included.

345. *The Treasure on Gold Street.* Byrd, Lee Merrill; translated by Sharon Franco; illustrated by Antonio Castro. El Paso, TX: Cinco Puntos Press, 2003. 37 pp. ISBN: 093831775X. Grades 1–3.

This story, based on real people from the author's life, is about Hannah and her best friend Isabel, an intellectually disabled adult, who lives with her mother and enjoys playing childhood games in the neighborhood with Hannah. On Isabel's birthday, all the neighbors come to celebrate her birthday. Hannah's mother shows how special her friend is by baking a birthday cake for Isabel. The neighbors acknowledge Isabel as their neighborhood treasure. Color illustrations complement the bilingual English and Spanish text.

346. *Don't Forget Tom.* Larsen, Hanne. New York: Crowell, 1978. [25] pp. ISBN: 0381900606. Grades 3–5.

Accompanied by color photographs, this story is about a mentally disabled 6-year-old boy named Tom who faces daily struggles and frustrations. Although this is an older publication, it is a good representation of how special education teachers and family members provide intervention in order to help children with mental disabilities.

347. *Author: A True Story.* Lester, Helen. Boston: Houghton Mifflin, 1997. 32 pp. ISBN: 0395827442. Grades 2–4.

By sharing her struggles as a child and later as a successful author, Helen Lester, author of several popular books for children, demonstrates in this book that challenges are all part of the process of authoring a book. She uses her unique ability to laugh at her own mistakes and shares an interesting personal story of the disappointments and successes of a writer's life. It is an inspirational story for other young writers. Includes color illustrations. "Lester's clever writing and the slapstick humor of the story make this a funny, funny picture book." *Booklist.*

348. *Leslie's Story: A Book about a Girl with Mental Retardation.* McNey, Martha. Minneapolis: Lerner Publications, 1996. 32 pp. ISBN: 0822525763. Grades 2–4.

This is a story about a 12-year-old girl named Leslie who had meningitis when she was a baby. As a result of the meningitis, she becomes mentally retarded. Through the eyes of this 12-year-old, the author describes the home life, school life, and special interests of Leslie. The last page provides information about mental retardation in general. Addresses of some helpful associations related to mental retardation, a glossary, and black and white photographs are included. "The first-person narratives give an all-around view of the special and mundane aspects of their worlds and conclude with information about the condition under discussion." *School Library Journal*

349. *Disorders First Diagnosed in Childhood.* Partner, Daniel. Series: The Encyclopedia of Psychological Disorders. Philadelphia: Chelsea House Publishers, 2001. 103 pp. ISBN: 0791053121. Grades 9–12.

This volume, one of the titles in the Encyclopedia of Psychological Disorders series, examines several of the most important conditions that affect the human mind: mental retardation, pervasive developmental disorders including autism, tic disorders, such as Tourette's disorder, and communication disorders. Written specifically for young adults to better understand mind-affecting disorders, this well-organized and well-documented book provides up-to-date information on the history of, causes and effects of, and treatment and therapies for problems affecting the human mind. For additional help, a list of related organizations and a very helpful glossary are included. "[W]ell-organized and succinctly written . . . well documented." *School Library Journal*

Chapter 3

Physical

This chapter encompasses 181 fiction and nonfiction entries pertaining to various physical disabilities. There are seventeen entries for high school, fifty-two for middle school, and 111 for elementary school grade levels. The 181 entries are further subdivided under the following sections: Blindness and Visual Impairments, Deafness and Hearing Impairments, Sign Language, Mobility Impairments, and Multiple Physical Disabilities. The research revealed a scarcity of materials regarding physical disabilities specifically for the high school grade level compared to the elementary and middle school grade levels. Also, no fiction titles were found that pertained exclusively to sign language within the scope established for this project.

BLINDNESS AND VISUAL IMPAIRMENTS

Fiction

350. *Teacher's Pet.* Anderson, Laurie Halse. Series: American Girl Wild at Heart. Middleton, WI: Pleasant Company Publications, 2001. 128 pp. ISBN: 1584850558. Grades 4–6.

In this story, part of the American Girl Wild at Heart series, 12-year-old Maggie MacKenzie begins middle school and discovers that it is more challenging than she ever thought. Maggie helps her new biology teacher, who is blind, learn to care for his new guide dog Scout. This is a good story to teach children to understand how blind individuals function on a daily basis. Illustrations are included. "This is an easy-read with a typical plotline, but also highly enjoyable, perhaps because the characters are likable and easy to relate to." *Children's Literature*

351. *The Double Digit Club.* Bauer, Marion Dane. New York: Holiday House, 2004. 116 pp. ISBN: 0823418057. Grades 4–6.

Sarah and Paige are 9-year-old best friends looking forward to summer vacation. When Paige turns 10 and is invited to join the silly Double-Digit Club, open only to girls over 10 years old, Sarah feels the loss of her best friend and begins spending more time with her elderly blind neighbor Miss Berglund. When Sarah takes Miss B's antique porcelain doll, in an attempt to be popular, and damages it, she learns a valuable lesson about trust and honesty. Paige realizes that the Club is not as enjoyable as she thought it would be and that her friendship with Sarah has permanently changed.

352. *Hello, Goodbye, I Love You: The Story of Aloha, a Guide Dog for the Blind.* Bauer Mueller, Pamela. St. Simons Island, GA: Piñata Publishing, 2003. 160 pp. ISBN: 0968509738; ISBN: 9780968509739. Grades 3–7.

The author weaves a wonderful tale based on the true-life story of Aloha, a young lab puppy who was bred to be a guide dog. Eleven-year-old Diego is raising Aloha who is eventually given to Miss Kimberly Louise, a woman who lost her sight in a car accident. Readers will learn how guide dogs are raised and trained. In addition, they will also learn about the mixed emotions experienced by the young boy who raises a guide dog, in spite of the fact that he cannot keep the dog. A Braille version of this book is also available. "This book does an excellent job of explaining the process of training guide-dog puppies, a topic that will fascinate many children." *School Library Journal*

353. *Aloha Crossing.* Bauer Mueller, Pamela. St. Simons Island, GA: Piñata Publishing, 2008. 176 pp. ISBN: 9780968509791. Grades 5–7.

In this sequel, a year has passed since Kimberly Louise, who lost her sight in a car accident, was given a yellow lab guide dog named Aloha. Kimberly Louise and Aloha are crossing a busy street in the beginning of the story. As Aloha is alerted to a speeding car, she pushes Kimberly Louise to safety. Kimberly Louise invites Diego, now 13 years old, to spend summer vacation with her and Aloha. Diego enjoys going places with Kimberly Louise and Aloha, including his visit to the Okefenokee Swamp with Kimberly Louise's neighbors. During a hurricane, Aloha gets loose, surviving the terrible storm with the help of a kind stranger. Meanwhile, Diego administers first aid to Kimberly Louise after she is bitten by a rattlesnake. Finally, Aloha is returned safely to Kimberly Louise. A list of resources for additional information about schools for guide dogs in the United States, Canada, and Ireland is included.

354. *Things Not Seen.* Clements, Andrew. New York: Philomel Books, 2002. 251 pp. ISBN: 0399236260. Grades 8–12.

Bobby Phillips, an average 15-year-old boy, wakes up one winter morning and for no rhyme or reason, cannot see his reflection in the mirror. He is not blind and is not dreaming, but is simply invisible. Bobby meets a blind girl named Alicia in whom he confides his secret regarding his invisibility. Can Bobby, his parents, and Alicia find out what caused his condition and reverse it? Meanwhile, the school officials, including the local police, believe that his disappearance is a result of foul play, maybe murder. The possibility of his parents being imprisoned makes Bobby even more determined to find out what happened to him and how to be visible again. With the help of Alicia, Bobby figures out a solution to his problem. "A readable, thought-provoking tour de force, alive with stimulating ideas, hard choices, and young people discovering bright possibilities ahead." *Kirkus Reviews*
2004 Schneider Family Book Award in the Teen category.

355. *Granny Torrelli Makes Soup.* Creech, Sharon and Christopher Raschka. New York: Joanna Cotler Books, 2003. 141 pp. ISBN: 0060292911. Grades 5–9.

This is a touching story about 12-year-old Rosie, her loving Italian grandmother, and Rosie's new friend Bailey, who is blind. Rosie enjoys making delicious dishes with Granny Torrelli and listening to Granny Torrelli share her interesting stories about her childhood. Rosie learns valuable lessons about growing up and relationships from Granny and Bailey. "Teachers and librarians who are focusing on children with disabilities can use this as an insightful tool, as Bailey's blindness is faced head-on." *School Library Journal*

356. *Brian's Bird.* Davis, Patricia A.; illustrated by Layne Johnson. Morton Grove, IL: Albert Whitman, 2000. [32] pp. ISBN: 0807508810. Grades K–3.

For his eighth birthday, Brian, a young blind boy, receives a parakeet, whom he names Scratchy. One day, Brian's older brother Kevin accidentally leaves the house door open and Scratchy flies outside to a nearby tree. By working together, they manage to get Scratchy safely back home. Illustrations in bright colors complement the text. "The deceptively simple story credibly introduces several themes: sibling rivalry, dealing with a disability, and the loss of a pet." *Booklist*

357. *Luna and the Big Blur.* Day, Shirley; illustrated by Don Morris. New York: Magination Press, 1995. [29] pp. ISBN: 0945354665. Grades 2–4.

Young Luna is the only one in her family who has to wear glasses and she hates it. Determined to be like others, she decides not to wear her glasses one day. The reader discovers along with Luna, in mostly humorous ways, the importance of wearing glasses. Pastel watercolor illustrations complement this wonderfully written text.

358. *Mirror, Mirror on the Wall: The Diary of Bess Brennan.* Denenberg, Barry. Series: Dear America. New York: Scholastic, 2002. 139 pp. ISBN: 0439194466. Grades 4–8.

This title in the Dear America series is a believable but fictional story set in the 1930s about a young girl who loses her eyesight in an accident and is determined to make her way in society as a normal individual. Bess, who always kept a diary, continues to record her daily thoughts and actions with the help of her twin sister. Bess attends the Perkins School for the Blind in Boston and meets other girls coping with varying degrees of sight loss. Reading about how her family and friends adjust to Bess's blindness is equally interesting.

359. *The Million Dollar Putt.* Gutman, Dan. New York: Hyperion Books for Children, 2006. 169 pp. ISBN: 0786836415. Grades 5–8.

Bogie is a well-adjusted 13-year-old blind boy who is very popular both at school and with his neighbors. With the help of Birdie, Bogie's new neighbor, Bogie learns that he is a naturally gifted golfer. Birdie helps Bogie discover the entire truth about his mother's death and why his father never seemed to appreciate the sport. "This novel's appeal is enhanced by humorous, lively dialogue." *School Library Journal*

360. *The Window.* Ingold, Jeanette. New York: Harcourt Brace, 1996. 181 pp. ISBN: 0152012656. Grades 9–12.

Mandy is 15 years old and alone after a car accident has killed her mother and blinded her. Mandy is sent to a farm in northern Texas to live with relatives she has never met. Mandy must adjust to a new life, a new school, and new friends, as well as learn about her mother's and her grandmother's lives. By discovering her family's past through the ghosts of the old family farm, Mandy is able to accept herself as she is and move forward to develop her life. "[T]he knowledge she gains through her journeys into the past allows her to see her own life more clearly and to adjust to her new circumstances more easily." *School Library Journal*

361. *Safe at Second.* Johnson, Scott. New York: Philomel Books, 1999. 245 pp. ISBN: 0399233652. Grades 8–12.

Older readers who are interested in sports will enjoy and be moved by this story of two high school friends. Paulie, the not-so-popular, not-so-smart friend, who sits on the bench, is best friends with Todd, the school's most popular star baseball player. When Todd loses an eye in a sports injury, both Todd and Paulie discover themselves in new roles and discover the strengths of their friendship. "An outstanding novel." *School Library Journal*

362. *Mandy Sue Day.* Karim, Roberta; illustrated by Karen Ritz. New York: Clarion Books, 1994. 32 pp. ISBN: 0395661552. Grades 2–4.

A young girl, Mandy Sue, enjoys a wonderful autumn day on a farm spending time with the horses. Mandy Sue enjoys doing all the things that young girls typically do and enjoy. Not until the story's end does the reader discover that Mandy Sue is blind. Karim's touching text and Ritz's muted watercolor illustrations create this exceptional story about self-esteem and self-assurance both for visually impaired and not impaired young readers. "What the pictures communicate so clearly is the extent of the world Mandy Sue knows and what a day full of fun she has." *Booklist*

363. *Apt. 3.* Keats, Ezra Jack. New York: Macmillan, 1971. [38] pp. ISBN: 0021790426. Grades K–3.

One rainy day, two brothers, Sam and Ben, who live in an urban neighborhood, hear interesting and mysterious sounds of a harmonica. Sam wonders who is playing this sad music. Sam's inquisitive search leads him to Apt. 3 where he discovers the source of the music, which happens to be a blind musician. Sam develops a friendship with this blind musician. Subtle color illustrations complement the text. "Two boys discover the miracle of music and the miracle of compassion in themselves." *Publishers Weekly*

364. *Mary Ingalls on Her Own.* Kimmel, Elizabeth Cody. Series: Little House. New York: HarperCollins, 2008. 180 pp. ISBN: 006009055; ISBN: 9780060009052. Grades 4–7.

Readers who enjoy the Little House books should enjoy Kimmel's story of Mary Ingalls. Having lost her sight to scarlet fever, 16-year-old Mary begins attending the Iowa College for the Blind in 1881. Mary must leave Pa, Ma, and her beloved sisters, especially Laura, as she learns how to be independent. Mary's new roommates, Blanche and Hannah, help her adjust to her new surroundings and college living. The Afterword contains a brief historical accounting of Mary Ingalls until her death. "Loyal fans and new readers will appreciate this addition to the 'Little House' series." *Children's Literature*

365. *The Storyteller's Beads.* Kurtz, Jane. San Diego: Gulliver Books/Harcourt Brace, 1998. 154 pp. ISBN: 0152010742. Grades 5–8.

This beautiful and touching story, set during the harsh and tragic political trauma of mid-1980 Ethiopia, is about Sahey and Rahel, two teenage girls from different ethnic groups and religions, one Christian and one Jewish, who are forced to leave their homes. Both girls are challenged by their traditional prejudices and by the physically demanding trek across the harsh environment; the girls discover their similarities and develop a new friendship. This story is for older readers who understand the ravages of hostile political conditions as well as geographical and historical settings. Different ethnic words included throughout the text lend an authentic feel to the story. "This ultimately heartening novel is a solid addition to the growing body of middle-grade books for a multicultural world." *School Library Journal*

366. *The Sound of Colors: A Journey of the Imagination.* Liao, Jimmy; translated by Sarah L. Thomson. New York: Little, Brown, 2006. [80] pp. ISBN: 0316939927. Grades 2–5.

This is the translation of a Chinese story about a young girl who lost her sight. She travels on various subways in her journey and tries to remember what the different places and things she is passing by look like. The fantastic illustrations explore the young girl's memory and what she currently is seeing in her mind. This is a wonderful story for young children to start thinking what it means to be blind. "Children might imagine what it would be like to be sightless, but the story will inspire them to use their own senses with more clarity as they look at their own surroundings, even the most familiar ones." *School Library Journal*

367. *Gentle's Holler.* Madden, Kerry. New York: Viking, 2005. 237 pp. ISBN: 0670059722. Grades 9–12.

This moving story, set in the 1960s, tells of 12-year-old Olivia Hyatt Weems, known as Livy Two, and her family who live in a North Carolina holler. Livy Two, named after her deceased sister Olivia, assumes most of the responsibility of taking care of her eight siblings, particularly her little sister Gentle, who was born blind. Although the family experiences hunger and poverty, the loving parents keep the family together during the rough times. There are humorous moments, particularly when Livy Two tries to make the family's pet, a dachshund, into a seeing-eye dog for Gentle. "Taken individually, these characters are very human, but together they form a strong unit that will help readers understand what it means to be a family." *Booklist*

368. *Knots on a Counting Rope.* Martin, Bill and John Archambault; illustrated by Ted Rand. New York: Holt, 1989. [32] pp. ISBN: 0805005714. Grades 2–4.

This perennial favorite is about a young Navaho boy, blind since birth, who listens to his grandfather recount the story of the young boy's birth, his very first horse, and an amazing race in which he does not win, but at least competes in and finishes. The young boy's family and Navaho traditions are showcased in this tale since they provide the encouragement and love for the young boy who learns that in spite of his blindness, he does have a rich and fulfilling life ahead. The illustrations of soft, dark colors evoke a nighttime atmosphere. "Parents and grandparents should share this book, and then their own stories, with children." *School Library Journal*

369. *Jennifer Jean, the Cross-Eyed Queen.* Naylor, Phyllis Reynolds; illustrated by Karen Ritz. Minneapolis: Carolrhoda Books, 1994. [27] pp. ISBN: 0876147910. Grades K–3.

Jennifer Jean, a young girl with beautiful green eyes, is teased by her friends because she squints due to her crossed eyes. Her friends call her "Jennifer Jean, cross-eyed queen." Her doctor gives her an eye-patch and a pair of sparkling green glasses. With the help of special eye exercises, she no longer needs to wear the patch. By the time she attends kindergarten, Jennifer Jean has perfectly straight eyes. This is an excellent story for young readers with physical challenges who can learn from Jennifer Jean's example to be self-confident. Bright watercolor illustrations capture the young reader's attention. "In addition to its obvious bibliotherapeutic uses, this book should appeal to young readers and listeners who like a strong heroine." *School Library Journal*

370. *Keep Your Ear on the Ball.* Petrillo, Genevieve. Gardiner, ME: Tilbury House, 2007. [31] pp. ISBN: 0884482960; ISBN: 9780884482963. Grades 2–4.

When Ms. Madison introduces the new boy Davey to the class, his classmates are surprised to learn that he is blind. Davey is very self-sufficient and kindly refuses any of his classmates' attempts to help him. When Davey realizes that playing kickball is challenging, he accepts his classmates' help. The expressive, soft, watercolor illustrations complement the text. "Based on an actual occurrence, this book will aid children in understanding some of the attributes of being blind." *Children's Literature*

371. *Portraits of Little Women: Jo Makes a Friend.* Pfeffer, Susan Beth. Series: Portraits of Little Women. New York: Delacorte Press, 1998. 99 pp. ISBN: 0385325819. Grades 4–6.

Pfeffer uses the characters from Louisa May Alcott's famous novel in her books in the Portraits of Little Women series. Ten-year-old, exuberant Jo March's aunt introduces Jo to Pauline Wheeler, a frightened blind girl. Dependent entirely on her governess, Pauline spends most of her day alone in her room. Jo and Pauline have nothing in common until they are caught in a snow squall, which changes their lives. Illustrations are included. Young readers will enjoy this book written by the award-winning author.

372. *The Blind Hunter.* Rodanas, Kristina. New York: M. Cavendish, 2003. [28] pp. ISBN: 0761451323. Grades 2–4.

Wise and kind Chirobo enjoys telling stories to the children in his African village. Being blind does not prevent him from doing anything until one day a stranger stops in the village while on his way to go hunting. When Chirobo joins him and is more successful in the hunt, the stranger tries to cheat the blind Chirobo. Chirobo teaches the stranger a lesson about human nature. The beautiful color illustrations depict the scenic countryside. "A thoughtful and satisfying book." *School Library Journal*

373. *Sarah's Sleepover.* Rodriguez, Bobbie; illustrated by Mark Graham. New York: Viking, 2000. [29] pp. ISBN: 0670877506. Grades 2–4.

During a weekend visit and sleepover, Sarah, a young blind girl, and her five cousins are trying to decide what games to play when the lights go out. With the adults away visiting neighbors, the girls are frightened until Sarah shows them how to remain calm and even have fun in the dark. Graham has depicted Sarah's facial expressions most exceptionally in his color illustrations.

374. *From Charlie's Point of View.* Scrimger, Richard. New York: Dutton's Children's Books, 2005. 278 pp. ISBN: 0525473742. Grades 7–10.

Charlie, blind since birth, and his friends, Bernadette and Lewis, are in the seventh grade. When Charlie's father is arrested for a robbery that he did not commit, Charlie and his friends are determined to find the real culprit. Along the way, Charlie and his friends deal with the typical situations that many middle school students experience, such as the class bully and strange neighbors. This story illustrates for young teenagers that disabled individuals are not limited by their disabilities. "With a fast-paced plot, witty dialogue, and compelling characters, this mystery is riveting all the way to its exciting and surprising conclusion." *School Library Journal*
2007 IBBY Outstanding Book for Young People with Disabilities.

375. *Rainbow Joe and Me.* Strom, Maria Diaz. New York: Lee & Low Books, 1999. [29] pp. ISBN: 1880000938. Grades 1–3.

This text, written and beautifully illustrated by Strom, is about a young Eloise, who loves to paint bright and bold colors, and her neighbor Rainbow Joe. Joe is blind but still talks to Eloise about the wonderful colors that he can see. Rainbow Joe surprises both Eloise and her mother one day when he plays his saxophone for them, which unleashes the colors in his mind. This very upbeat story, a feast of colors for the young reader's eyes, forces the young reader to go beyond the ability to see. "This exploration of sensory differences and similarities is enlightening and enchanting." *Kirkus Reviews*

Nonfiction

376. *Do You Remember the Color Blue? And Other Questions Kids Ask about Blindness.* Alexander, Sally Hobart. New York: Viking, 2000. 78 pp. ISBN: 0670880434. Grades 8–12.

This is a very straightforward book about the author, Sally, who started losing her sight as a young adult in her twenties. She tells the reader about the early signs of her condition and what steps she took to find out what was happening and the treatments she tried. Sally's honest writings detail her acceptance of her visual loss and how she moved forward with her life, including getting married and having children as well as having a successful career as a writer and a speaker, particularly in schools. The thirteen chapters are based on questions that Sally has been asked by children during her many visits to schools. Such questions include: How did you become blind? Is it hard being a blind parent? Do people treat you differently? Black and white personal photographs of Sally and her family and friends, items, such as helpful tools, as well as Braille resources are included. "A witty, wise, inspiring book." *Kirkus Reviews*

377. *Vision without Sight: Human Capabilities.* Brocker, Susan. Series: Shockwave. New York: Children's Press, 2008. 36 pp. ISBN: 0531177696; ISBN: 9780531177693. Grades 5–7.

This color-illustrated book, part of the Shockwave series, explains how we see and how blind individuals were treated in the past. Some of the famous people who were blind are listed. One of the sections discusses various ways of seeing, such as with touch, with technology, with guide dogs, with sound, and with music. The last chapter, "Vision for the Future," explains how researchers, using satellite navigation systems, are creating aids for people who are blind. A glossary of terms related to blindness, a list of books including websites for additional information, and an index are included.

378. *Seeing Things My Way.* Carter, Alden R. Morton Grove, IL: A. Whitman, 1998. [32] pp. ISBN: 0807572969. Grades 1–3.

Second-grader Amanda is visually impaired due to a tumor. But Amanda does not allow her loss of sight to stop her from having fun with her friends or doing everyday activities at home and school. Young readers learn which aids, such as magnifiers and guide dogs, help visually impaired individuals. Color illustrations complement this text. "The text evokes compassion and empathy by presenting real people living normally despite their impairments." *School Library Journal*

379. *Brave Norman: A True Story.* Clements, Andrew; illustrated by Ellen Beier. New York: Simon & Schuster Books for Young Readers, 2001. 32 pp. ISBN: 0689829140. Grades PreK–1.

This beginning-to-read book is about Norman, a blind golden retriever, who saves a girl from drowning in the ocean. As a result, Norman becomes a local celebrity, and, with the love of his family, thrives in spite of the fact that he is visually impaired. Watercolor illustrations complement the text. "Children will be charmed by this lovable pooch and his ability to overcome his obstacles and help others." *School Library Journal*

380. *All about Braille: Reading by Touch.* Jeffrey, Laura S. Berkeley Heights, NJ: Enslow Publishers, 2004. 48 pp. ISBN: 076602184X. Grades 4–6.

This is a good introduction to Braille basics. The first chapter provides a brief history of Helen Keller. Other chapters cover specific topics, such as finger reading, which is an excellent introduction to Braille; communicating; and getting around. Chapter 5 discusses some famous individuals who, although blind, lead productive and fascinating lives. Other sections include a "Timeline," "Words to Know," and a resource section, including books and Internet addresses. There is an index and color photos and graphics.

381. *Blindness.* Landau, Elaine. Series: Understanding Illness. New York: Twenty-First Century Books, 1994. 64 pp. ISBN: 0805029923. Grades 5–8.

This volume, one of the titles in the Understanding Illness series, contains good information for this age level. Chapter topics include being blind, causes of blindness, how to prevent blindness, and separating the truth about being blind from the myths. Color photographs and graphics, a glossary, additional reading resources, organizations, websites, and an index are included.

382. *Looking Out for Sarah.* Lang, Glenna.Watertown, MA: Talewinds, 2003. [29] pp. ISBN: 0881066478. Grades 2–4.

Perry, a black Labrador retriever, and his visually impaired owner spend their days traveling to various locations in order to illustrate how important guide dogs are and what services they provide for blind individuals. This story follows Perry and his owner through a typical day, showing how they work together at home and how they travel to schools to entertain and inform the students about guide dogs. Color illustrations keep the reader focused on Perry and his duties

and responsibilities. Not only is this an enjoyable story, it is also valuable in informing young readers about guide dogs and seeing-eye dog etiquette, such as what to do and what not to do while they are working with their blind owners. "This informative and easy-to-read book is a good addition to most collections." *School Library Journal*
2004 Schneider Family Book Award in the Young Children category.

383. *Being Blind.* O'Neill, Linda. Series: Imagine. Vero Beach, FL: Rourke Press, 2001. 32 pp. ISBN: 1571033769. Grades 2–4.

This volume, one of the titles in the Imagine series, is a good introduction to the issues and challenges facing individuals who are blind. Using an interactive approach, the narrator begins the book by asking the reader to close his or her eyes and imagine, hence the title of the series. One-page chapters, such as "Hearing," "Touch," "The Braille System," "Guide Dogs," and "Games and Gadgets," as well several real-person profiles, give the reader an overview of this disability. Color photographs, a glossary, additional reading resources, websites, and an index are included.

384. *Seeing.* Pryor, Kimberley Jane. Series: The Senses. Philadelphia: Chelsea Clubhouse Books, 2003. 32 pp. ISBN: 0791075559. Grades 2–4.

One of the titles in the Senses series, this book is an excellent resource for the beginner reader about the sense of seeing, written in very simple text. This information is divided into manageable chapters and contains the following topics: eyesight, a message to your brain, all kinds of sights, wearing glasses, blindness, and protecting one's eyes. Color photographs, graphics, text boxes, a glossary, and a brief list of websites are included. The colorful layout will keep younger readers interested in the topic.

385. *Private and Confidential: A Story about Braille.* Ripley, Marion; illustrated by Colin Backhouse. New York: Dial Books for Young Readers, 2003. [32] pp. ISBN: 0803729006. Grades 3–5.

Young Laura enjoys writing to Malcolm, her new pen pal who lives in Australia. When Laura does not receive a letter from Malcolm for three weeks, Laura learns from Malcolm's sister that due to his poor eyesight, he is in the hospital recovering from an eye operation. In order to continue her correspondence with her new friend, Laura starts typing out her letters in Braille. The readers will enjoy translating Malcolm's letter, written in Braille, with the help of the Braille alphabet card included in the text. Color illustrations complement the text. "Useful as an introduction to Braille, this is best suited for classroom use and larger collections." *Booklist*

386. *Blindness.* Royston, Angela. Series: What's It Like. Chicago: Heinemann Library, 2005. 32 pp. ISBN: 1403458499. Grades 2–4.

This volume, one of the titles in the What's It Like series, is an excellent introductory resource for the beginning reader. Two-page chapters include: "What Is Blindness?" "Causes of Blindness," "Living with Blindness," "Guide Dogs," "Crossing the Road," "Reading, Working and Enjoying Life." Each page has a large color photograph or graphic. Very up-to-date language, color photographs, and graphics make this a very inviting and nonthreatening resource for the youngest of readers. A list of additional resources, a glossary, and an index are included.

387. *Some Kids Are Blind.* Schaefer, Lola M. Series: Understanding Differences. Mankova, MN: Capstone Press, 2008. 24 pp. ISBN: 1429617748; ISBN: 9781429617741. Grades PreK–2.

This revised and updated title in the Understanding Differences series portrays blind children in everyday activities. In addition, the reader should learn how an individual feels to live with blindness. The color photographs and text illustrate how blind children use Braille and participate in various activities. A glossary, a brief list of additional reading titles, Internet sites, and an index are included. "[W]ill help young children understand at an early age to appreciate differences rather than ridicule those who are different." *Multicultural Review*

388. *Coping with Vision Disorders.* Stanley, Debbie. Series: Coping. New York: Rosen Publishing Group, 2001. 106 pp. ISBN: 0823931986. Grades 7–9.

This title in the Coping series provides a good overview of all vision disorders. Nearsightedness, farsightedness, astigmatism, and strabismus are just some of the disorders discussed. The chapters on treatment options are most helpful, particularly for teenagers who feel pressured to correct any physical faults. Young readers will greatly benefit from the advice offered in the chapter that discusses emotional issues for individuals with severe vision disorders. The author uses realistic scenarios to illustrate key concepts. A glossary, organizations in the United States and Canada, websites, additional reading material, and an index are included.

389. *Living with Blindness.* Westcott, Patsy. Series: Living With. Auston, TX: Raintree Steck-Vaughn, 2000. 32 pp. ISBN: 0817257411. Grades 3–6.

This is one of the titles in the Living With series that provides inspiring and useful information regarding individuals who are blind. Color photographs depict Mathar, Lucy, and Katie, who are blind, in various situations and show how they adapt to everyday activities, such as Lucy going shopping. The two-page chapter format covers a wide variety of topics including what blindness is, how blind individuals cope with everyday life, and possible cures for blindness. Color photographs, a glossary, useful addresses and organizations that provide support for blind individuals, and an index are included.

DEAFNESS AND HEARING IMPAIRMENTS

Fiction

390. *Handtalk Zoo.* Ancona, George and Mary Beth Miller. Series: Handtalk. New York: Four Winds Press, 1989. [28] pp. ISBN: 0027008010. Grades 1–3.

Mary Beth and a group of her friends visit the local zoo in this title of the Handtalk series. Her young and multiethnic friends use fingerspelling and sign language to communicate with each other while teaching the reader the various names of the zoo animals. The color photographs and story, first published twenty years ago, are still enjoyable for today's young readers. As with the other titles in this series, this is a wonderful visual experience showing how individuals in the deaf community communicate with one another. "[A] creative and exuberant manner." *School Library Journal*

391. *Read My Lips.* Brown, Teri. New York: Simon Pulse, 2008. 238 pp. ISBN: 1416958681; ISBN: 9781416958680. Grades 9–12.

Sixteen-year-old Serena is the new girl in school. When the popular girls, who are members of a secret sorority, discover that Serena, who is deaf, can read lips, they use her ability to uncover secrets of both the students and teachers. Serena is faced with numerous challenges: pleasing her helicopter parents; trying to keep up with the popular girls; and dealing with her feelings toward Miller, the school rebel who happens to be living with Serena's aunt since the death of his mother. When one of the popular girls turns against her, Serena's secrets come out with surprising results. "It is unique to see a deaf main character, which makes this book a great addition to any library collection." *KLIATT*

392. *Handtalk Birthday.* Charlip, Remy, Mary Beth Miller, and George Ancona. Series: Handtalk. New York: Four Winds Press, 1987. [44] pp. ISBN: 0027180808. Grades 1–3.

This is one of the titles in the Handtalk series in which Mary Beth's friends help her celebrate her birthday by throwing her a surprise birthday party. Mary

Beth and her friends use fingerspelling and sign language as they experience all the fun activities associated with a birthday party. Although this title is an older book, the lively and humorous color photographs depicting Mary Beth and her friends celebrating her birthday can still be shared with and enjoyed by young readers today. As with the other titles in this series, this is a wonderful visual experience showing how individuals in the deaf community communicate with one another. "This creative original story is an exciting way to share the joy of signing with children." *School Library Journal*

393. *Herbie Hears the Horn: The Journey of a Young Deaf Child from Silence to Sound.* Chorost, Susan; illustrated by Steven Parton. Washington, DC: Alexander Graham Bell Association for the Deaf and Hard of Hearing, 2001. 32 pp. ISBN: 0882002120. Grades 1–3.

This is a unique story told in verse about Herbie whose parents do not realize that Herbie has hearing loss. As time passes and Herbie does not react to sounds, his parents take him to the audiologist who fits Herbie with hearing aids, allowing him to hear for the first time. A parent/teacher guide section provides suggestions for sharing this story with children. Also included is a detailed drawing of the anatomy of the ear, definitions used in the story, such as parts of a hearing aid, activities to do with children that pertain to hearing loss, an excellent timeframe of "Average Speech and Hearing Behavior for Your Child's Age Level," a list of national organization and associations, and color drawings.

394. *Spike the Special Puppy.* Dale, Jenny; illustrated by Frank Rodgers. New York: Aladdin Paperbacks, 1999. 60 pp. ISBN: 0689842996. Grades 3–5.

This is a charming story about Karen's new puppy Spike. Karen absolutely adores Spike, but she does not know what to do with him because Spike does not listen to her or any member of the family. Karen and her family love Spike, but his behavior is terrible, even dangerous at times. Finally the family realizes that there is something very special about Spike—Spike cannot hear. Spike's veterinarian suggests that Spike attend special training classes. This unique story reveals what a family does when they discover that their beloved pet has a disability.

395. *Of Sound Mind.* Ferris, Jean. New York; Farrar, Straus and Giroux, 2001. 215 pp. ISBN: 0374355800. Grades 8–12.

This is an interesting and insightful story of Theo, the only hearing son in a deaf family. The challenges and frustrations are demanding, but his family's total reliance on him is becoming almost unbearable. When he meets Ivy, whose father is deaf and suffers serious health conditions, Theo is forced into a new way of seeing things.

396. *Down in the Boondocks.* Gage, William; illustrated by Glen Rounds. Series: Greenwillow Read-alone. New York: Greenwillow Books, 1977. 32 pp. ISBN: 0440417457. Grades 2–3.

One of the Greenwillow read-alone titles, this is a humorous tale of a thief who tries to steal from an old, deaf farmer. The farmer's deafness creates numerous silly and humorous activities involving the farmer, his wife, the farm animals, and the thief. Although this is an older publication, the black and white illustrations and story are humorous without offending deaf individuals.

397. *A Screaming Kind of Day.* Gilmore, Rachna; illustrated by Gordon Sauve. Markham, Ontario: Fitzhenry & Whiteside, 1999. 38 pp. ISBN: 155041514X. Grades 2–4.

A young deaf girl, Scully, wakes up one day feeling that the day will be full of challenges. She fights with her brother Leo the entire day until a rain shower entices her to venture outside, even though she knows her hearing aids could be damaged. She disobeys her mother's orders and goes outside to enjoy the rain. When her mother grounds her for the rest of the day, Scully plays inside the house. Includes color illustrations with very expressive faces. "Rachna Gilmore, a talented author, magically captures a child's over brimming love of life and irrepressible spirit of mischief and rebellion." *Children's Literature*

398. *Lester's Dog.* Hesse, Karen; illustrated by Nancy Carpenter. New York: Crown, 1993. [32] pp. ISBN: 0517583577. Grades 2–4.

A young boy's neighborhood and its interesting residents provide the backdrop for this tale of overcoming the fear of a neighbor's dog that bit him when he was 6 years old. His good friend Corey, who cannot hear, helps him overcome his fear by standing up to the dog. The importance of Corey's role and his not talking in the story provides a silent strength that helps the young boy overcome his fears. Color illustrations provide excellent action scenarios that complement the story. This story is a nice slice of Americana that showcases the value of friendship, regardless of a disability. "This unassuming tale shimmers with wisdom and persuasive intelligence." *Publishers Weekly*

399. *Silent Lotus.* Lee, Jeanne M. New York: Farrar, Straus and Giroux. 1994. [28] pp. ISBN: 0374466467. Grades K–3.

This is a wonderful fairy-tale–like story of Lotus, who, despite being born deaf and unable to speak, grows into an exceptionally expressive girl. Her parents, knowing that Lotus is very lonely because the other children avoid her, ask the king and queen to let Lotus stay in the palace and learn how to dance the tales of the gods and kings. Lotus becomes the most famous dancer in the entire Khmer Kingdom. The full-page color illustrations are exceptionally expressive and beautiful. This is a good resource for diversity and cultural studies. "Libraries serving Cambodian populations will want to consider this offering." *School Library Journal*

400. *T4: A Novel in Verse.* LeZotte, Ann Clare. Boston: Houghton Mifflin, 2008. 105 pp. ISBN: 0547046847; ISBN: 9780547046846. Grades 6–12.

Thirteen-year-old Paula Becker is deaf and lives an idyllic life with her family in a German village. In order to avoid being sent to Tiergartenstrasse 4, the Nazi headquarters for eliminating individuals with disabilities, Paula is sent into hiding with others who are considered undesirables. At the end of World War II, Paula returns to her family and learns to appreciate how devastating war is. "Even though this is a short and quick read, this novel will have a lasting effect on readers, giving insight into an often-forgotten aspect of the horrors of the Third Reich. The unique writing style makes this a good choice for reluctant as well as proficient readers." *School Library Journal*

401. *Elana's Ears, or, How I Became the Best Big Sister in the World.* Lowell, Gloria Roth; illustrated by Karen Stormer Brooks. Washington, DC: Magination Press, 2000. 29 pp. ISBN: 1557987025. Grades 1–4.

This delightful story, based on actual individuals, is told in the first person by Lacey, an only dog. One day his parents bring home a baby girl named Elana. Lacey is quite jealous until she realizes that Elana cannot hear and needs Lacey's help. The story can be read on its own or used as a discussion starter for what happens when a new baby is brought home. The text is quite humorous and enjoyable, particularly Lacey's personal observations. For example, Lacey says, "Did you know that some hotels don't allow dogs? What nerve." The section, "A Note to Parents about Babies and Older Children" is written by well-known psychologist Jane Annunziata. The color illustrations are also humorous and equally delightful for young and older readers.

402. *Silent Observer.* MacKinnon, Christy. Washington, DC: Kendall Green Publication, 1994. 42 pp. ISBN: 156368022X. Grades 2–4.

This is the story of Christy, a young deaf girl who lives in a farming community in Nova Scotia during the late 1890s and early 1900s. Christy tells, in her own words and by her own illustrations, what life is like for her. Her story is full of humorous anecdotes, including stories of her family dealing with the death of her mother during childbirth and the arrival of her new stepmother, who becomes wonderfully understanding and supportive of Christy. The color illustrations are expressive and a perfect complement to the text. This story provides the reader with a unique look into the past and how some individuals coped with having a disability over 100 years ago. "[T]he book may be useful to teachers presenting units on nineteenth-century life or on deafness." *Booklist*

403. *Deaf Child Crossing.* Matlin, Marlee. New York: Simon & Schuster Books for Young Readers, 2002. 200 pp. ISBN: 0689822081. Grades 4–6.

Two new friends struggle with their limitations of hearing and friendship—Megan, who is deaf, independent, outgoing, and sometimes stubborn, meets her new neighbor, Cindy, who is shy, quiet, and eager to learn how to sign. Megan gets very upset when Cindy tries to help her too much. When Megan meets another deaf girl at camp, Cindy is left out. The realistic portrayal of a young deaf girl who resents others treating her differently stands equally well with a young girl who wants to help a new best friend. "Indeed, the story's greatest strength is in demonstrating that the two protagonists' main differences have nothing to do with hearing or the lack of it." *School Library Journal*

404. *Can You Feel the Thunder?* McElfresh, Lynn E. New York: Atheneum Books for Young Readers, 1999. 144 pp. ISBN: 068982324X. Grades 4–7.

In this story, 13-year-old Mic Parson is convinced that all his neighbors on Bixby Court are weird. Mic considers his older sister Stephanie, who is deaf and blind, the weirdest of them all. Mic experiences all the usual anxieties that middle school students face, in addition to being embarrassed by Stephanie's actions due to her disability. This is a very good story for those young readers who have to cope with having a disabled sibling. "A warm look at that awkward time of leaving childhood behind that will strike a chord with many readers." *School Library Journal*

405. *Handtalk School.* Miller, Mary Beth and George Ancona. Series: Handtalk. New York: Four Winds Press, 1991. [29] pp. ISBN: 0027009122. Grades 1–3.

This story in the Handtalk series is about Jen who lives in a residential facility in a school for deaf children. Jen, her classmates, a very diverse group of students, and their teachers fingerspell and use sign language as they prepare for the annual Thanksgiving play at school. Although this book is an older title, the manner in which the topic and individuals are depicted in color photographs makes this a book that can be used and enjoyed by younger readers today. As with the other titles in this series, this is a wonderful visual experience showing how individuals in the deaf community communicate with one another. Miller and Ancona are successful in demystifying deaf individuals and any of the challenges that may appear with deaf children. "[A]n excellent addition." *Kirkus Reviews*

406. *Moses Goes to School.* Millman, Isaac. New York: Frances Foster Books/ Farrar, Straus and Giroux, 2000. [30] pp. ISBN: 0374350698. Grades 2–4.

This is a story about a young deaf boy, Moses, and his first day at his new school for the deaf. He discovers that his classmates are welcoming and his teacher is supportive. Moses learns what his classmates and his teacher already know that although he is deaf, his world has no limits. Millman creates not only a wonderful story but also a learning text about the deaf community and their use of sign language to communicate. The color illustrations, both detailed and informational, depict Moses and his classmates using American Sign Language (ASL) in everyday activities, particularly those activities that students typically experience at school. "This is another great contribution to children's education about disabilities that also succeeds as effective storytelling in its own right." *School Library Journal*

407. *Moses Goes to a Concert.* Millman, Isaac. New York: A Sunburst Book/ Farrar, Straus and Giroux, 2002. [38] pp. ISBN: 0374453667. Grades 2–4.

This is the second story about Moses, a young deaf boy. Moses and his classmates attend a concert and meet the orchestra's extraordinary percussionist who is also deaf. Millman creates not only a wonderful story but also a learning text about the deaf community and their use of sign language to communicate. The color Illustrations, both detailed and informational, depict Moses and his classmates using American Sign Language (ASL) in everyday activities, particularly those activities the students encounter while attending a concert. This is an excellent book and highly recommended. "The power of Millmans' book comes from the simple fact that he levels the playing field." *Kirkus Reviews*

408. *Moses Goes to the Circus.* Millman, Isaac. New York: Farrar, Straus and Giroux, 2003. [30] pp. ISBN: 0374350647. Grades 2–4.

In this third book, Moses, a young deaf boy, and his family go to the Big Apple Circus to see a special show called Circus of the Senses. During the show, the sounds and the spoken words are translated for Moses and others who are deaf by American Sign Language (ASL) interpreters. Millman creates not only a wonderful story but also a learning text about the deaf community and their use of sign language for communicating. The color illustrations, both detailed and informational, depict Moses and his family while attending the circus. This is an excellent book and highly recommended. "Seeing these pictures emphasizes how truly wonderful sign language is for the deaf. This book would be very useful to help children understand the world of the deaf." *Children's Literature*

409. *Moses Sees a Play.* Millman, Isaac. New York: Farrar, Straus and Giroux, 2004. [30] pp. ISBN: 0374350663. Grades 2–4.

In this fourth book, Moses, a young deaf boy, his classmates, and their teacher, Mr. Samuels, enjoy an in-school visit from the Little Theatre of the Deaf, who perform *Cinderella*. When another class joins them, Moses meets Manuel, who recently arrived in the United States and does not speak English. Moses and Manuel become friends in spite of their language differences. Millman creates not only a wonderful story but also a learning text about the deaf community and their use of sign language to communicate. The color illustrations, both detailed and informational, depict Moses and his classmates using American Sign Language (ASL) in everyday activities. "A book that's as pleasurable to read as it is informative." *Booklist*
2007 IBBY Outstanding Book for Young People with Disabilities.

410. *Amelia Lends a Hand.* Moss, Marissa. Middleton, WI: American Girl/ Pleasant Company Publications, 2002. [33] pp. ISBN: 1584855398. Grades 3–6.

In this title of Moss's Amelia stories, Amelia's summer is not going to be the quiet and peaceful one that she is looking forward to. She has to attend the family reunion, deal with her grouchy older sister, discover that she has asthma, and get to know the new young neighbor, a boy who happens to be deaf. Amelia's statement about Enzo is a great message to all readers: "I can't let his being deaf get in the way of being friends." Following what Amelia does and has to learn to be able to communicate with Enzo is admirable. The text and the illustrations are written in the form of a journal.

411. *A Place for Grace.* Okimoto, Jean Davies; illustrated by Doug Keith. Seattle: Sasquatch Books, 1993. [29] pp. ISBN: 09123650. Grades 1–4.

Grace's dream is crushed when she learns that she is too small to be a seeing-eye dog. After saving a little boy from a car accident, Charlie spots her and knows that she would be wonderful as a hearing-ear dog. But Grace has trouble distinguishing some of the sounds in school. Charlie will not give up on her and continues to help Grace pass the necessary tests. This heart-warming tale of the underdog and the deaf young man who will not give up on her is a good tale read aloud or individually. The colorful illustrations are a wonderful complement to the text. "[A] valuable lesson in the rewards of hard work and persistence." *School Library Journal*

412. *Singing Hands.* Ray, Delia. New York: Clarion Books, 2006. 248 pp. ISBN: 0618657622; ISBN2: 9780618657629. Grades 8–12.

This is the story of Gussie, a young teenager and one of three hearing daughters of a minister and his wife, who are both deaf. Gussie gives the reader an interesting and rare glimpse of the everyday challenges that her deaf parents face at home, in her father's church, and with the people who live in their hometown. Ray based this story on the childhood stories of her mother who was a hearing child of deaf parents. This very enjoyable and humorous story takes place in the South during the late 1940s. It excellently portrays the challenges and the intense emotions that a family experiences when the parents are deaf. "While not strictly autobiographical, Ray effectively presents an inside look at deaf culture, with sympathy and imagination." *Children's Literature*

413. *Hurt Go Happy.* Riorby, Ginny. New York: Tom Doherty Associates, 2006. 267 pp. ISBN: 0765353040; ISBN2: 9780765353047. Grades 6–9.

This carefully crafted, multifaceted novel is about the coming of age of 13-year-old Joey Willis. Joey, who has been deaf since the age of 6, has been strangely forbidden by her mother to learn sign language. Joey meets her elderly neighbor Dr. Charles Mansell and his chimpanzee Sukari, who Dr. Mansell has taught American Sign Language. With the help of Sukari, Joey secretly learns to communicate using sign language. As a result of being able to communicate, she begins to makes new friends at school which makes her very happy. "This unusual and emotional story will intrigue animal lovers and those looking for a gripping family drama. The characters are well crafted. . . . The novel is beautifully written and believable." *VOYA*
2008 Schneider Family Book Award in the Teen category.

414. *River of Hands: Deaf Heritage Stories.* by Bonner, Symara Nichola (et al.); illustrations by Faim Poirier (et al.). Toronto: Second Story Press, 2000. 47 pp. ISBN: 1896764363. Grades 5–8.

This unique collection of four stories about kids in the deaf community is written by deaf kids between the ages of 12 and 17. Five illustrators contribute their talents to this work and they, too, are deaf. The stories are at times whimsical, such as the story of two boys who decide to go fishing in the toilet bowl. However, the stories do illustrate the concerns and special challenges faced by those who have hearing loss. The humor and off-beat activities illustrate that there are no limits to authors and artists who are deaf. The four-page afterword explains the history of the Canadian Deaf Heritage Project.

415. *The Deaf Musicians.* Seeger, Pete and Paul Dubois Jacobs; illustrated by R. Gregory Christie. New York: G. P. Putnam's Sons, 2006. [32] pp. ISBN: 039924316X. Grades K–3.

After Lee, a jazz pianist, loses his hearing and is asked to leave the band, he discovers a new way to communicate with his music at a local school for the deaf. Lee forms a new friendship with his sign language teacher Max, who plays the sax. While riding on the subway, Lee and Max sign about all the songs they love. Rose, a bass player, joins in and the three of them form a little sign language band. Night after night, they perform for audiences in the subway. This story, written by living music legend Pete Seeger and renowned poet Paul DuBois Jacobs, emphasizes the human ability to compensate for loss through creative acts. "Both uplifting and inclusive, it is a celebration of music and resilience." *School Library Journal*
2007 Schneider Family Book Award in the Young Children category.

416. *The Boys of San Joaquin.* Smith, D. J. New York: Atheneum Books for Young Readers, 2005. 231 pp. ISBN: 0689876068; ISBN2: 978689876066. Grades 6–9.

Twelve-year-old Paolo's narrative of his family and friends in the 1950s takes the reader to a small town in California, where neighbors know one another and one another's business. Paolo and his friends, including Paolo's deaf cousin Billy, stumble onto a mystery that they try to solve together. This enjoyable story shows how Paolo's sisters and brothers learn to sign in order to communicate with Billy. "Middle-school readers should enjoy this engaging, frequently funny coming-of-age story." *Booklist*

417. *Kami and the Yaks.* Stryer, Andrea Stenn; illustrated by Bert Dodson. Palo Alto, CA: Bay Otter Press, 2007. |48| pp. ISBN: 0977896102; ISBN2: 9780977896103. Grades 1–4.

Kami is a young Sherpa boy who lives in the rugged Himalayas of Nepal. Since Kami is deaf and unable to speak, he has taught the family's yaks, the sole source of the family's livelihood, to obey his shrill whistle. One day the yaks could not be found, and Kami sets out to find them. One of the young yaks has injured its leg on the steep mountainside. Together Kami, his father, and brother rescue the young yak. Kami's family, particularly his father, is very proud of Kami. "Readers will find inspiration in his abilities, his resourcefulness, and his courage. . . . This story opens the doors to new worlds and gives readers a character to admire." *School Library Journal*
2008 Schneider Family Book Award in the Young Children category.

418. *Dad, Jackie, and Me.* Uhlberg, Myron; illustrated by Colin Bootman. Atlanta: Peachtree, 2005. [30] pp. ISBN: 1561453293. Grades 2–4.

This is a story from Uhlberg's childhood about the heyday of the Brooklyn Dodgers, when in 1947, a young boy and his deaf father witness a young Jackie Robinson breaking the color barrier in baseball. The young boy's father learns

about baseball from his son and the son learns about prejudices, both about his father's disability and about Jackie Robinson's race. Colorful illustrations complement the text. "Use this title for classroom discussions focusing on labor history, handicaps, or moral values." *School Library Journal*
2006 Schneider Family Book Award in the Young Children category.
2007 IBBY Outstanding Book for Young People with Disabilities.

419. *The Printer.* Uhlberg, Myron; illustrated by Henri Sorensen. Atlanta: Peachtree, 2003. [29] pp. ISBN: 1561452211. Grades 2–4.

Based on the author's childhood, a young boy tells how his deaf father, working as a printer at a large metropolitan newspaper, saved his co-workers from a devastating fire. This very loving story reveals how much the boy loves his father in spite of his father's disability. Color illustrations complement this text. "[W]ill appreciate the story's insightful treatment of deafness as viewed through the eyes of a child." *School Library Journal*

420. *Jamie's Tiger.* Wahl, Jan; illustrated by Tomie DePaola. New York: Harcourt Brace Jovanovich, 1978. [48] pp. ISBN: 0152395008. Grades 1–3.

This older publication continues to be a useful source regarding a young child's experience with hearing loss and his subsequent interactions with his family and friends. Jamie is frightened due to losing his hearing after being sick with German measles. With the love of his parents and caring health providers and educators, Jamie learns how to sign and lip read. Soon his friends realize that not only is he still their old friend, but they learn how to sign words in order to have a secret code. This is a rather light approach to a youngster trying to cope with being deaf; however, the positive attitude of everyone involved presents a good lesson, as the author writes, "*Jamie's Tiger* was written for the hearing child as well as the hearing-impaired child, in order to help create a better understanding and friendship between the two." Pencil drawings in earth tones colors complement the text.

Nonfiction

421. *My Sister's Silent World.* Arthur, Catherine; illustrated by Nathan Talbot. Chicago: Children's Press, 1979. 30 pp. ISBN: 0516020226. Grades 1–3.

This interesting story is told by the sister of Heather, a young deaf girl who is celebrating her eighth birthday by going to the zoo. Full page color photographs show Heather in realistic situations, such as watching the animals and signing with her sister. Heather's sister also discusses some of the challenges that Heather faces because she is deaf, such as other children not being able to understand her. This is an enjoyable, upbeat story for young readers.

422. *I'm Deaf and It's Okay.* Aseltine, Lorraine, Evelyn Mueller, and Nancy Tait; illustrated by Helen Cogancherry. Niles, IL: Whitman, 1986. [40] pp. ISBN: 0807534722. Grades 2–4.

This slightly older title provides a personal glimpse into the feelings of a young boy who is struggling with being deaf. By using first-person narrative, his feelings are very identifiable as he tells about his frustrations with his classmates, jealousy with his sister, and various social challenges. He does not think his future holds any promise until he meets an older boy in high school who is also deaf. The brown and gray illustrations are soft and gentle against the sometimes very sad text. There are two pages of the young boy signing a dozen words. All three authors have extensive experience with deaf education.

423. *Hearing Loss.* Baldwin, Carol. Series: Health Matters. Chicago: Heinemann Library, 2003. 32 pp. ISBN: 1403402515. Grades 2–5.

This title in the Health Matters series discusses hearing loss and will help children understand their friends and classmates who have a hearing loss. In addition, it provides suggestions on how they can help their deaf classmates. The introductory chapter topics include what is a hearing loss and what causes hearing loss. The topics covered in the next three chapters are excellent topics for classroom discussion, such as identifying classmates with hearing loss, helping a deaf classmate, and visiting a friend who has a hearing loss. Young readers will enjoy the chapter titled "Learning More about Hearing Loss" because it contains an introduction to sign language and information about hearing-ear dogs. Color photographs, graphics, text boxes, a glossary, additional reading material, and an index are included.

424. *What Is the Sign for Friend?* Greenberg, Judith E.; photographs by Gayle Rothschild. New York: Watts, 1985. 30 pp. ISBN: 0531049396. Grades 1–3.

Young readers will enjoy this book that shows Shane, a young deaf boy, conducting his everyday activities at home and at school. Shane's positive interactions with his classmates at school, his friends at play, and his family members at home demonstrate that Shane is not limited by his hearing loss. The photographs are black and white.

425. *Living with Deafness.* Haugthon, Emma. Series: Living With. Austin, TX: Raintree Steck-Vaughn, 2000. 32 pp. ISBN: 081725742X. Grades 3–6.

This is one of the titles in the Living With series that provides inspiring and useful information about individuals who are deaf. Color photographs of Tom,

Gita, Alison, and Alfred depict how these four deaf individuals have adapted to everyday situations. The two-page chapter format covers a wide variety of issues regarding deafness, including growing up with deafness and society's attitude toward the deaf. Color photographs, a glossary, useful addresses and support organizations, and an index are included.

426. *Can You Hear a Rainbow? The Story of a Deaf Boy Named Chris.* Heelan, Jamee Riggio; illustrated by Nicola Simmonds. Series: The Rehabilitation Institute of Chicago Learning Book. Atlanta: Peachtree Publishers, 2002. [29] pp. ISBN: 1561452688. Grades 2–4.

In this title, which is part of the Rehabilitation Institute of Chicago Learning Book series, 10-year-old Chris tells his story about being deaf. Chris tells about the things that he misses and does not experience, such as hearing the sound of rain hitting his window. He also tells about his everyday activities, such as using his sense of smell to tell when dinner is ready, signing with his dog, playing with his friends, and going to school. Chris tells the reader that he has friends who can hear and those who cannot. The interesting illustrations are actually collages, part photographs and part color drawings. "Although the material is covered isn't new, it is accurate and worth repeating, and the format is appealing." *School Library Journal*

427. *Deafness.* Landau, Elaine. Series: Understanding Illness. New York: Twenty-First Century Books, 1994. 64 pp. ISBN: 0805029931. Grades 5–8.

This title in the Understanding Illness series contains good information about deafness for the middle school reader. Chapter topics include varying degrees of deafness, causes, accepting a hearing loss, achievements of deaf individuals, and the importance of the deaf community. All known causes and effects of deafness are explained in light of the most recent scientific information and modern technical advances. The actual case histories that are used emphasize how individuals cope with conditions for which there may be no cure or easy answers. Role models and numerous old wives' tales are destroyed, and stigmas attached with being deaf are confronted and discussed. Color photographs, graphics, a glossary, additional reading material, organizations that help individuals with hearing loss, and an index are included.

428. *My Friend Is Deaf.* Levene, Anna. Mankato, MN: Smart Apple Media, 2003. 32 pp. ISBN: 1932333274. Grades 2–4.

In telling a wonderful story about her friendship with Daniel, Amy shares some of the challenges that Daniel and others who have hearing loss have to encounter.

Some of the topics that Amy discusses are the different kinds of deafness, hearing aids, and how deaf students function at school. There are two interesting chapters that provide a glimpse of what it is like to be at the home of Amy's deaf friends. "Questions People Ask," color photographs, color graphics, text boxes containing interesting information, a glossary, a list of organizations, and an index are included.

429. *The Ocean Inside: Youth Who Are Deaf and Hard of Hearing.* Libal, Autumn. Series: Youth with Special Needs. Broomall, PA: Mason Crest Publishers, 2004. 127 pp. ISBN: 1590847296. Grades 7–10.

This volume, one of the titles in the Youth with Special Needs series, provides information about deafness. Fictional scenarios using individuals illustrate the book's variety of topics about deafness, such as feeling alone, breaking the silence, and bumps in the road. Text boxes scattered throughout this work showcase famous deaf individuals such as Helen Keller and Beethoven. Color photographs, a glossary, an index, and additional resources on this subject are included. The Youth with Special Needs series provides a unique forum for demystifying a wide variety of childhood medical and developmental disabilities.

430. *A Button in Her Ear.* Litchfield, Ada Bassett; illustrated by Eleanor Mill. Chicago: Whitman, 1976. [32] pp. ISBN: 0807509876. Grades 2–4.

This older title is still a good book because of the positive attitude of the main character. Young Angela's experience with hearing loss and her interactions with her friends are very typical. Some of her friends accept her, but one friend makes fun. After her visits to a health professional, Angela is fitted with a hearing aid. Angela's teacher gives the whole class an important lesson that Angela's hearing aid is as neat as people wearing glasses. The text includes both color and black and white illustrations. The nonthreatening scenarios portray real challenges; for example, Angela mishears words. This is a good story that demystifies this disability for both the hearing and nonhearing reader.

431. *Being Deaf.* O'Neill, Linda. Series: Imagine. Vero Beach, FL: Rourke Press, 2001. 32 pp. ISBN: 1571033777. Grades 2–4.

This volume, one of the titles in the Imagine series, is a very good introduction to the issues and challenges facing individuals who are deaf. Using an interactive approach, the narrator begins the book by asking the reader to imagine that a friend wants to tell him or her a secret he or she cannot hear. Hence the title of the series. One-page chapters, for example, "Causes of Hearing Loss," "Speech Reading," "Hearing Aids," and "Sign Language We All Use," as well as several real-person profiles give the reader an overview of this disability. Color photographs and graphics, a glossary, additional reading resources, websites, and an index are included.

432. *Jordan Has a Hearing Loss.* Powell, Jillian. Series: Like Me, Like You. Langhorne, PA: Chelsea Clubhouse, 2004. 29 pp. ISBN: 0791081796. Grades 2–4.

This first-person narrative is one of the volumes in the Like Me, Like You series in which Jordan shares his personal experiences and interactions with family and friends at home and at school. In this easy-to-read text full of color photographs, Jordan's everyday activities show that Jordan is not limited by his disability. Jordan tells the reader about the importance of his hearing aids and how others with hearing loss use sign language and lip reading. Excellent color photographs, a glossary, additional reading material, organizations, and an index are included.

433. *Hearing.* Pryor, Kimberley Jane. Series: The Senses. Philadelphia: Chelsea Clubhouse Books, 2003. 32 pp. ISBN: 0791075540. Grades 2–4.

This title in the Senses series is an excellent introductory source for elementary school children regarding the topic of hearing. Chapter topics include how the ear works, sound waves, how information is delivered to the brain, hearing dangers, types of deafness, and protecting one's ears. Each page has either a color graphic of the human anatomy or photograph of multicultured individuals in everyday activities that accompany the text, making this an exceptionally helpful resource. Color photographs, graphics, a glossary, and an index are included. This excellent title is highly recommended as are the other titles in this series.

434. *Deafness.* Royston, Angela. Series: What's It Like? Chicago: Heinemann Library, 2005. 32 pp. ISBN: 1403458529. Grades 2–4.

This title in the What's It Like? series contains thirteen, two-page chapters, such as "What Is Deafness?" "Why Are People Deaf?" "Living with Deafness," and "Lip Reading." Each page contains a full page, or half page, color photograph that depict deaf individuals performing everyday activities. Informative text boxes are placed throughout the chapters. The author explains that some illnesses can cause deafness and that sign language allows a deaf person to communicate. The chapter titled "Using Sign Language" shows a young girl signing the phrase thank you and a young boy signing the word cat. Color illustrations, graphics, a brief glossary, additional reading material, and an index are included. This is an excellent book.

435. *Some Kids Are Deaf.* Schaefer, Lola M. Series: Understanding Differences. Mankova, MN: Capstone Press, 2008. 24 pp. ISBN: 1429617756; ISBN: 9781429608114. Grades PreK–2.

This revised and updated title in the series Understanding Differences provides young readers excellent photographs and text portraying children who are deaf. In addition, the reader should learn how an individual feels to live with deafness. Children are depicted using tools for hearing and sign language. A glossary, a brief list of additional resources, Internet sites, and an index are included. "[W]ill help young children understand at an early age to appreciate differences rather than ridicule those who are different." *Multicultural Review*

436. *Deafness.* Sheen, Barbara. Series: Diseases and Disorders. Detroit: Lucent Books, 2006. 112 pp. ISBN: 1590184084. Grades 6–9.

This volume, one of the titles in the Diseases and Disorders series, provides comprehensive coverage of deafness. The introductory chapters provide an excellent message that the lack of knowledge leads to problems. The remaining five chapters cover the following topics: various types of deafness, diagnosis, treatment, ways to communicate, living with deafness, and what the future holds for deaf individuals. The text is easy to read while providing all important concepts in manageable sections. Black and white photographs, graphics, text boxes, a glossary, additional reading material, and an index are included. "Highly Recommended." *Library Media Connection*

437. *Anna's Silent World.* Wolf, Bernard. Philadelphia: Lippincott, 1977. 48 pp. ISBN: 0397317395. Grades 1–3.

The acclaimed photographer Bernard Wolf provides us with a glimpse of a young girl and her daily activities as she copes with her hearing loss. Anna is shown at home, at school including her sessions with the professionals at the New York League for the Hard of Hearing, and at ballet classes. This is an older title and probably not as attractive with the black and white photographs; however, it does give the young reader a realistic portrayal of a young deaf girl and her interactions throughout her world.

SIGN LANGUAGE

Nonfiction

438. *My First Book of Sign.* Baker, Pamela J.; illustrated by Patricia Bellan Gillen. Washington, DC: Kendall Green Publications, Gallaudet University Press, 1986. 76 pp. ISBN: 0930323203. Grades PreK–3.

Baker's text is an excellent resource for the primary school student who wants to learn how to sign basic words. The book lists 150 words with their sign descriptions, including nouns and verbs, that are arranged alphabetically.

Color illustrations depicting young, diverse children signing the word make a wonderful visual and engaging text for both the hearing impaired and hearing reader. Baker also includes an encouraging "A Letter to Parents" as well as "How to Use This Book." An index is included.

439. *Little Red Riding Hood: Told in Signed English.* Bornstein, Harry and Karen L. Saulnier; illustrated by Bradley O. Pomeroy. Washington, DC: Kendall Green Publications, Gallaudet University Press, 1990. [43] pp. ISBN: 0930323637. Grades K–3.

This is an excellent telling of "Little Red Riding Hood" in signed text. Each page contains color illustrations, the corresponding text, and signline drawings of the narrator. Mother, Little Red Riding Hood, and even the wolf himself are shown signing text. Bold, color illustrations are most attractive. This is a good text for the hearing impaired and the nonimpaired reader. Some of the black lettering text is difficult to read against the color illustrations. The author states that this title "makes a well-known folktale accessible to hard-of-hearing children in a new and inviting way."

440. *Nursery Rhymes from Mother Goose: Told in Signed English.* Bornstein, Harry; illustrated by Patricia Peters; signline drawings by Linda C. Tom. Washington, DC: Kendall Green Publications, Gallaudet University Press, 1992. 41 pp. ISBN: 0930323998. Grades K–4.

This is Bornstein's excellent updated edition of *Nursery Rhymes Told in Signed English.* The fourteen nursery rhymes in this version include "Humpty Dumpty," "Old Mother Hubbard," and "Twinkle, Twinkle, Little Star." Each page shows Mother Goose herself signing the text of each nursery rhyme, accompanied by the corresponding text and signline drawings. The bold, color illustrations complement the text, which presents an exceptional visual experience for both hearing and hearing-impaired readers. The author states that it "makes well-known nursery rhymes accessible to hard-of-hearing children in a new and inviting way."

441. *Sesame Street Sign Language ABC with Linda Bove.* Bove, Linda; illustrated by Tom Cooke; photographs by Anita and Steve Shevett. New York: Random House, 1985. [32] pp. ISBN: 0394875168. Grades K–2.

This is one of Linda Bove's well-written, well-illustrated, and enjoyable books for younger readers about sign language. Linda's pleasing and approachable personality comes through as she signs the letters of the alphabet as well as whole sentences. The Sesame Street characters make this text entertaining and most nonthreatening for even the youngest reader. This is a good companion work to Linda's *Sesame Street Sign Language Fun.*

442. *My Signing Book of Numbers.* Gillen, Patricia Bellan. Washington, DC: Kendall Green Publications, 1988. 59 pp. ISBN: 0930323378. Grades PreK–3.

This is an excellent resource about signing numbers for slightly older elementary school children. The numbers zero to one million are depicted in interesting and pleasing groupings. In addition, each number has a corresponding number of items, for example, the number four has four clowns, the number twenty has twenty ladybugs, and the number one thousand has one thousand little fern leaves. The color illustrations depicting young, diverse children signing each number make it a wonderful visual and engaging text for both the hearing impaired and hearing reader. Gillen includes a helpful section for adults titled "All About Signing Numbers."

443. *All Day Long: Teaching Your Baby to Sign.* Heller, Lora. Series: Baby Fingers. New York: Sterling Publishing Company, 2008. |21| pp. ISBN: 1402753950; ISBN:9781402753954. Grades PreK–1.

This board book contains twenty-one everyday words that both preschoolers and adults can learn in order to identify needs throughout the day and prepare the youngest children for necessary activities, such as taking a bath, eating, and so forth. Additional words included are book, toy, bed, park, ball, and others. Each page contains a full-page color photograph of a child signing the word or concept, including written instructions for signing the depicted word or action. Young children will enjoy seeing children their own age signing.

444. *Sign Language for Kids: A Fun & Easy Guide to American Sign Language.* Heller, Lora. New York: Sterling Publishing, 2004. 95 pp. ISBN: 1402706723; ISBN:9781402706721. Grades 3–6.

This title is an excellent resource for young readers who want to learn American Sign Language (ASL). Color photographs depict six young models signing the basic vocabulary for ASL. Each photograph contains text explaining the signing movement. The introductory section includes a brief history of ASL as well as several websites containing additional information for kids and parents. Each of the twenty sections begins with a paragraph that provides instructions and tips for signing. The ASL vocabulary is divided into the following categories: alphabet and numbers, school, colors, favorite foods, musical instruments, clothing, holidays and religions, and much more. The concluding sections contain practical words, linking words, making sentences guidelines, and an index. "This book is a helpful adjunct for anyone (not just kids) who wants to learn sign language." *Children's Literature*

445. *American Sign Language.* Kent, Deborah. New York: Watts Library, 2003. 63 pp. ISBN: 0531166627. Grades 3–5.

This is a very good introductory resource for American Sign Language (ASL). The chapters are divided into manageable topics, such as "Language for the Eyes," "A Living Language," and "Keys to Communication." A basic history of ASL as will as a well-rounded description of what is happening today in schools and society for those with a hearing loss are included. A timeline about ASL, a glossary, resources including organizations and online sites, and color and black and white photographs are included.

446. *The Night before Christmas in Signed English.* Moore, Clement Clarke; illustrated by Ralph R. Miller, Sr. Washington, DC: Gallaudet College Press, 1973. 56 pp. ISBN: 0913580155. Grades K–3.

This charming telling of Moore's classic Christmas poem is a visual delight for hearing and nonhearing readers. Each page contains a full color illustration, the corresponding text, and signline drawings of the narrator, Pa, with Saint Nick signing the verse. The author states in the opening letter to parents and teachers that "everything needed to make this poem meaningful to the deaf child is contained in this text."

447. *The Handmade Alphabet.* Rankin, Laura. New York: Puffin Pied Piper, 1996. [29] pp. ISBN: 0590462393. Grades 1–4.

In Rankin's first signing book, the beautiful pastel color drawings reflect her message as stated in this work's introduction: "that this introduction to the alphabet begin to open the world of sign communication to all who see this book." On each page Rankin has drawn a hand that is holding an object that begins with the letter of the alphabet that is being signed in American Sign Language. For example, for the letter "T" the hand is signing the letter surrounded by thimbles and thread. "An excellent introduction." *Kirkus Reviews*

448. *The Handmade Counting Book.* Rankin, Laura. New York: Dial Books, 1998. [32] pp. ISBN: 0803723113. Grades K–2.

Rankin creates another wonderful visual experience for young readers who want to learn how to sign the numbers one to one hundred in American Sign Language. Each number is signed by a delicately drawn child's hand, while the appropriate numbers of toys or nature items are depicted. For example: the number two has two hand puppets, the number seven has seven boats, and the number one hundred is depicted by one hundred animals embarking Noah's ark. The soft, color illustrations present a wonderful resource for those who want to learn to sign or for those readers who just want to enjoy the pictures. "Visually, the book is a delight, with charming pictures to pore over." *School Library Journal*

449. *Sesame Street Sign Language Fun with Linda Bove.* New York: Random House, 1980. [65] pp. ISBN: 039484212X. Grades 2–4.

This older title is still a favorite with elementary children for introducing sign language. The Sesame Street Muppets are shown doing normal, routine activities at home and at school, playing with friends, and visiting neighbors. Bove signs a complete sentence under each two-page scene. There are also pages of signing words, such as "Action Words," "People in the Neighborhood," "Utensils," and "Food." The color illustrations and the popular Muppets make this an excellent book.

450. *Animal Signs: A First Book of Sign Language.* Slier, Debby. Washington, DC: Kendall Green Publications, 1995. [14] pp. ISBN: 0563680491. Grades PreK–2.

This board book is a follow-up to Slier's *Word Signs.* This work contains fourteen animal words that even the youngest child would need to know, such as dog, cat, and bird. Each page is a full-page color photograph of the animal being depicted. In a smaller text box on the page there is a signed drawing of a youngster signing or just the hands. This is a very good basic text for both the hearing impaired and hearing youngster who wants to learn a few basic words.

451. *Word Signs: A First Book of Sign Language.* Slier, Debby. Washington, DC: Kendall Green Publications, 1995. [12] pp. ISBN: 1563680483. Grades PreK–2.

This board book contains fourteen everyday words that even the youngest child can learn, such as flower, shoes, crackers, and baby. Each page contains a full-page color photograph of the item being depicted and a text box in which the item is being signed. This is a good text for the hearing and nonhearing young reader. The color photographs provide visual encouragement for learning to sign words.

452. *A Book of Colors.* Votry, Kim and Curt Waller. Washington, DC: Gallaudet University Press, 2003. 15 pp. ISBN: 1563681471. Grades PreK–2.

This board book contains fourteen words about colors that even the youngest child needs to know, such as color, red, yellow, brown, and rainbow. Each page is a full-page colorful illustration of a young boy signing the word. In a smaller text box in a corner, there is a signline drawing of the boy and a helpful tip for signing (e.g., open and close fingers). This is a very good basic text for both the hearing impaired and hearing youngster for learning a few basic words.

453. *Baby's First Signs.* Votry, Kim and Curt Waller. Washington, DC: Gallaudet University Press, 2001. 14 pp. ISBN: 1563681145. Grades PreK–2.

This board book contains fourteen everyday words that even the youngest child needs to know, such as bath, socks, daddy, and milk. Each page is a full-page color illustration of a young boy involved in the word being depicted. For example, for the word bird, the young boy is sitting in a tree and a bird is on a branch. In a smaller text box in the lower corner, there is a signline drawing of the boy and a helpful tip for signing (e.g., open and close fingers). This is a very good basic text for both the hearing impaired and hearing child to learn a few basic words. "The bright, simple illustrations outlined in black will be appealing to preschoolers." *School Library Journal*

454. *More Baby's First Signs.* Votry, Kim and Curt Waller. Washington, DC: Gallaudet University Press, 2001. 14 pp. ISBN: 1563681153. Grades PreK–2.

This board book is a follow-up to Votry's *Baby's First Signs.* The text contains fourteen everyday words that younger children can learn, such as ball, water, blanket, and baby. Each page is a full-page color illustration of a young boy expressing the word being depicted. For example, for the word tree, the young boy is standing next to a tree. In a smaller text box in the lower corner, there is a signline drawing of the boy and a helpful tip for signing, such as twist hand back and forth. This is a very good text for both the hearing impaired and hearing youngster who wants to learn a few basic words in sign language.

455. *Out for a Walk.* Votry, Kim and Curt Waller. Washington, DC: Gallaudet University Press, 2003. [12] pp. ISBN: 1563681463. Grades PreK–2.

This board book contains fourteen words describing the experiences when one goes outside for a walk. These are basic words that even the youngest child can learn, such as outside, walk, dog, hear, touch, and friend. Each page is a full-page color illustration of a young boy signing the word. In a smaller text box in a corner, there is a signline drawing of the same boy and a helpful tip for signing (e.g., open and close fingers). This is a very good basic text for both the hearing impaired and hearing youngster to learn a few basic words.

456. *More Simple Signs.* Wheeler, Cindy. New York: Viking, 1998. [28] pp. ISBN: 0670874779. Grades 1–3.

As Wheeler's follow-up book to *Simple Signs*, this text contains thirty practical words that both the hearing impaired and nonhearing impaired child can learn for everyday conversation. Words such as sun, house, yes, no, red, fish, and thank you are included. Each page has a word and its color illustration. On the same page is a signline drawing of the word and a hint for signing. For example, for the word thank you, a youngster is shown eating a dish of ice cream and under the signline drawing is the hint: like blowing a kiss.

457. *Simple Signs.* Wheeler, Cindy. New York: Viking, 1995. [28] pp. ISBN: 0606118462. Grades 1–3.

The author, who learned sign language at the same time as her hearing-impaired son, includes twenty-nine American Sign Language movements of everyday words, phrases, and concepts, such as hello, ball, car, eat, and finished. Each page contains a color illustration, the printed word, and the corresponding signline drawing. In addition there is a hint that will help the reader learn how to sign the specific word. For example, for the word eat, a young boy is shown eating a cookie and under the signline drawing is hint: like putting food in your mouth. The color illustrations are visually pleasing, making this a good text for both the nonhearing and hearing children. The author states in the introductory section that this book "is a loving tribute to the language that let me communicate with my son."

MOBILITY IMPAIRMENTS

Fiction

458. *Sosu's Call.* Asare, Meshack. La Jolla, CA: Kane/Miller Books, 2002. 37 pp. ISBN: 1929132212. Grades 1–4.

Sosu, a young African boy who lives in a fishing village in Ghana, is unable to walk and is shunned by most of the villagers who consider Sosu bad luck. One day a sea storm threatens the lives in the village, and Sosu, with the help of his dog Fusa, manages to reach the village drum to warn everyone of the impending danger. The villagers are so grateful that they give Sosu a wheelchair. Sosu is no longer considered by the villagers to be bad luck. Pastel watercolor illustrations evoke the beauty of this African fishing village. "[T]his story of overcoming a serious physical challenge and achieving acceptance may offer hope and inspiration to young readers." *School Library Journal*
2001 first prize IBBY Outstanding Book for Young People with Disabilities.

459. *Tiger's Fall.* Bang, Molly. New York: Henry Holt, 2001. 110 pp. ISBN: 0805066896. Grades 4–7.

Lupe lives in a rural village in Mexico. Her family calls 11-year-old Lupe, Tiger, because she is full of energy and somewhat wild. When her cousin visits from the city, Lupe climbs a tree, falls, and becomes paralyzed. Readers discover what Lupe has to do in order to cope with her disability, especially medical treatments that she has to undergo. "The disabled and those who love them will appreciate the truth of Lupe's anger and depression and her struggle to find her own kindness and courage." *Booklist*

460. *Arthur's Room.* Bend, Cynthia Davidson. Edna, MN: Beaver's Pond Press, 2002. 193 pp. ISBN: 1931646341. Grades 10–12.

This story takes place in St. Paul, Minnesota, in 1929. Arthur Dean, a 7-year-old boy, is confined to his room due to his cerebral palsy. Arthur's sister Phyllis is also confined, not physically, but mentally by their domineering mother. Arthur shares his experiences with the reader regarding his challenges of learning to control his body, recognizing his romantic urges, and understanding his life, which exists only within the four walls of his room. Phyllis helps her brother as best she can, considering his limitations. Not until Arthur takes control of his life does Phyllis discover the beauty of living.

461. *My Pal, Victor/Mi Amigo, Victor.* Bertrand, Diane Gonzales; translated by Eida de la Vega; illustrated by Robert Sweetland. Green Bay, WI: Raven Tree Press, 2004. 32 pp. ISBN: 0972019294. Grades K–4.

This wonderful story of two friends is told in a unique format, both the English and the Spanish text are included on the same page. Dominic and Victor are best friends who do everything together and go everywhere together. Not until the very end of the story does the reader learn that one of the friends uses a wheelchair. Dominic, the narrator of the story, who is the nondisabled friend, provides a humorous message at the end of the story by saying, "But, the most important thing about my pal, Victor, is that he likes me just the way I am." Very detailed color illustrations complement this bilingual text beautifully.

2005 Schneider Family Book Award in the Young Children category.

462. *Wheel Wizards.* Christopher, Matt. Boston: Little, Brown, 2000.120 pp. ISBN: 0316136115. Grades 4–8.

A car accident confines 12-year-old Seth to a wheelchair. He believes that he cannot play basketball any longer and as a result becomes frustrated with his family, his friends at school, and his therapist. Seth thinks that his life is meaningless, until he meets Danny, a high school student and star player in the wheelchair basketball league. Drawing inspiration from Danny's example, Seth resolves his bitterness with everyone and sees a future for himself. Seth's feelings and dialogue with the other characters in the story are very realistic.

463. *With the Wind.* Damrell, Liz; illustrated by Stephen Marchesi. New York: Orchard Books, 1991. [26] pp. ISBN: 0531058824. Grades 1–3.

A young boy rides a horse and experiences a sense of freedom and power. The beautiful color illustrations exquisitely express the almost dreamlike quality of the boy's sensations. Not until the very end does the reader discover that the young boy uses a wheelchair. "Successfully portrayed is the essence of riding, which frees the child from the confinement of a wheelchair." *School Library Journal*

464. *Sammy Wakes His Dad.* Emmons, Chip; illustrated by Shirley Venit Anger. New York: Star Bright Books, 2002. [13] pp. ISBN: 1887734872. Grades 2–4.

Sammy goes fishing every morning and does all the things just the way his father taught him. Sammy misses doing all the things he used to do with his father, who has been in a wheelchair since an accident. When he tells his father that he misses him, his father examines his own life and decides to rejoin his son in doing everyday activities and move forward with his life. This positive story is an excellent example of how a parent can learn from a child. Beautiful watercolor illustrations complement the text. "A good choice on a topic not often covered for this age group." *School Library Journal*

465. *Seal Surfer.* Foreman, Michael. San Diego: Harcourt Brace, 1997. [30] pp. ISBN: 0152013997. Grades 4–6.

Young Ben's use of crutches and a wheelchair does not prevent him from surfing with a special surfboard. One day, Ben and his grandfather witness the birth of a seal pup. Ben and the seal form a special friendship that is tested when Ben gets into trouble in rough seas and the young seal saves him. Watercolor illustrations reflect the depths of the sea, which provides a wonderful background for this story.

466. *Bluish.* Hamilton, Virginia. New York: Blue Sky Press, 1999. 127 pp. ISBN: 0590288792. Grades 5–8.

Dreenie is 10 years old and coping with a brainy younger sister and a brand new school. She tries to become friends with her classmate Natalie, who uses a wheelchair. The students call Natalie Bluish due to her skin color affected by chemotherapy treatments for leukemia. This is an interesting story in which the main character, herself an outsider, is drawn to another outsider. Their friendship grows out of their understanding of each other's peripheral status at school and in society. "Many readers will be caught by the jumpy, edgy story of sorrow and hope, of kids trying to be friends." *Booklist*

467. *Grandma Drives a Motor Bed.* Hamm, Diane Johnston; illustrated by Charles Robinson. Niles, IL: A. Whitman, 1987. [32] pp. ISBN: 0807530255. Grades K–3.

Josh's grandmother has lost the use of her legs and is almost entirely confined to a hospital bed in her home. When Josh visits his grandmother, he finds out about the special care that she has to have, such as throw-away diapers that she has to wear. The book is a good introduction for younger readers regarding aging. Color illustrations complement the text. "Gentle understanding and steadfast love fill this brief story, which is as useful for children who don't have aging relatives as for those who do." *School Library Journal*

468. *The Storm.* Harshman, Marc; illustrated by Mark Mohr. New York: Cobblehill Books/Dutton. 1995. [30] pp. ISBN: 0525651500. Grades 1–3.

Jonathan, confined to a wheelchair since his accident, strives to remain as independent and self-sufficient as he can. One day, when Jonathan is alone at the farm, a tornado approaches. Jonathan knows that he has to protect the farm animals. This wonderful story illustrates the resourcefulness of those in wheelchairs, and how that they can be heroes in the face of danger. Watercolor illustrations complement the text. "It's a knowing book that will speak to all children about self-image and hard-won success." *Booklist*

469. *Grandma's Wheelchair.* Henriod, Lorraine; illustrated by Christa Chevalier. Chicago: Albert Whitman, 1981. [32] pp. ISBN: 0807530352. Grades PreK–2.

Four-year-old Thomas visits his grandmother while his mother rests during her pregnancy. His grandmother, whose legs are paralyzed, reads to Thomas and encourages him to participate in a number of chores around the house with her. While outside, his grandmother's wheelchair breaks down, and Thomas helps her by locating a second wheelchair in the garage. Younger readers learn that they, like Thomas, can help others who are in need. Color illustrations are included.

470. *Featherless.* Herrera, Juan Felipe; illustrated by Ernesto Cuevas, Jr. San Francisco: Children's Book Press. 2004. 30 pp. ISBN: 0892391952. Grades 1–3.

This powerful story, told both in English and in Spanish, demonstrates the determination and courage shown by Tomasito, who was born with spina bifida and is confined to a wheelchair. One day, Tomasito's father gives him a pet bird. At first the little bird, who is lame and featherless, disturbs him. At his new school, Tomasito's new friend Marlena treats him the same way as she treats other friends. When Tomasito is selected to play on his school's soccer team, he realizes that his bird, like him, is only as limited as he wants to be. As Tomasito tells his pet bird, "There's more than one way to fly!" This excellent story provides encouragement to readers who have disabilities. The bright and bold color illustrations are exceptional. "An encouraging story, especially for Latino children with disabilities, who may recognize themselves and find their own ways to fly." *Booklist*

471. *Accidents of Nature.* Johnson, Harriet McBryde. New York: Holt, 2006. 229 pp. ISBN: 0805076344. Grades 10–12.

During her first vacation at Camp Courage, away from her family, 17-year-old Jean, who has cerebral palsy, shares a cabin with Sara, herself in a wheelchair. Jean always prided herself on being normal in spite of the fact that she has cerebral palsy. Jean starts wondering about her role in the world among able-bodied individuals. This novel explores the relationship between caregivers and people with disabilities. "This book is smart and honest, funny and eye-opening." *School Library Journal*

472. *Stoner & Spaz.* Koertge, Ron. Cambridge, MA: Candlewick Press, 2004. 169 pp. ISBN: 0763621501. Grades 7–12.

This is a story about 16-year-old Ben Bancroft who has cerebral palsy, no parents, and an overprotective grandmother. This loner spends most of his time at the local theater, the Rialto Theatre. One evening, Colleen Minou, a drugged-up, tattooed social outcast, sits next to Ben in the Rialto. Despite their differences, Ben and Colleen become friends and challenge each other to change their ways. After meeting a new neighbor who made a short documentary film, Ben develops an interest of his own and makes his own documentary titled "High School, Confidential." "Listeners will find this story riveting. The concerns of real teens come through in vivid dialogue and film-shot narratives." *School Library Journal*

473. *Jungle School.* Laird, Elizabeth and Roz Davison; illustrated by David Sim. Series: Green Bananas. New York: Crabtree Publishing Company, 2006. 48 pp. ISBN: 0778710262. Grades 1–3.

In this beginning reader of the Green Bananas titles, Jani the monkey is the new girl in school. Her classmates become her new friends because they treat her as an individual, not as someone in a wheelchair. Color illustrations depict Jani at school playing with her new classmates. This is an excellent story that depicts disabled students in everyday school situations. "Each title includes some descriptive words that may help young readers develop a larger vocabulary when the books are read aloud." *School Library Journal*

474. *Nathan's Wish*. Lears, Laurie; illustrated by Stacey Schuett. Morton Grove, IL: Albert Whitman, 2005. [30] pp. ISBN: 0807571016; ISBN2: 9780807571019. Grades 1–3.

Young Nathan uses a wheelchair because he has cerebral palsy. He lives next door to Miss Sandy, a raptor rehabilitator, who rescues birds of prey, such as eagles, hawks, and owls. Miss Sandy's latest charge is Fire, an owl with a broken wing. When Fire is not able to fly again, Nathan suggests that Fire care for orphaned baby owls. Nathan learns from Fire that he can have a meaningful life in spite of his physical limitations. Color illustrations complement the text.
2007 IBBY Outstanding Book for Young People with Disabilities.

475. *A Very Special Critter*. Mayer, Gina and Mercer Mayer. New York: Golden Book, 1992. [23] pp. ISBN: 0307627632. Grades PreK–2.

One of Mercer Mayer's wonderful works for the younger reader in which the new critter at school is in a wheelchair. Initially scared, the new critter learns that his new classmates welcome him as just another classmate who sometimes does things differently. This story contains realistic dialogue and scenes that depict challenges faced by critters in a wheelchair. Includes delightful color illustrations.

476. *Rolling Along with Goldilocks and the Three Bears*. Meyers, Cindy; illustrated by Carol Morgan. Bethesda, MD: Woodbine House, 1999. [26] pp. ISBN: 1890627127. Grades 1–4.

The author, a physical therapist assistant, has adapted the classic fairy tale of "Goldilocks and the Three Bears" into this interesting version. In this story, when Goldilocks visits the home of the three bears, she discovers that Baby Bear is in a wheelchair. She learns how Baby Bear does normal activities around the house as well as the special things that he needs to do as a disabled individual. Realistic, everyday activities, such as going to physical therapy, are depicted. Detailed color illustrations contribute in making this an enjoyable interpretation of the classic tale. Not only is this an excellent story that depicts disability, but this book could be used in the classroom for creative writing exercises. "An attractive, informative offering." *Booklist*

477. *Petey*. Mikaelsen, Ben. New York: Hyperion Books for Children, 1998. 280 pp. ISBN: 0786823763. Grades 8–12.

Based on a true story, in the 1920s, a young boy at the age of 2 who has cerebral palsy is misdiagnosed as an idiot and placed in an insane asylum. This touching story follows Petey's lifelong experience with staff and fellow patients. Well into his sixties, Petey is befriended by another misfit, teenage Trevor. This story provides the older reader with a realistic background of the time and what patients experienced in various care facilities. "Give this book to anyone who has ever shouted 'retard' at another. Give it to any student who 'has' to do community service. Give it to anyone who needs a good book to read." *School Library Journal*

478. *Zoom!* Munsch, Robert N.; illustrated by Michael Martchenko. New York: Scholastic, 2003. 30 pp. ISBN: 0439187745. Grades 2–4.

This fun book shows daredevil Lauretta trying out a new wheelchair, a super-duper, ninety-two speed, black, silver, and red dirt-bike wheelchair. Lauretta gets into humorous situations, such as getting a speeding ticket. But she saves the day when she rushes her brother to the hospital after he cuts his finger. This is a lighthearted look at the role and importance of a wheelchair and how young Lauretta adapts to its use within society's limitations. The bright and bold color illustrations are enjoyable. "An amusing story with a positive message about young people with disabilities." *School Library Journal*
2007 IBBY Outstanding Book for Young People with Disabilities.

479. *My Grampy Can't Walk.* Oelschlager, Vanita; illustrated by Robin Hegan and Kristin Blackwood. Akron, OH: Vanita Books, 2008. [36] pp. ISBN: 9780980016208. Grades 1–3.

This excellent story demonstrates that although Grampy uses a wheelchair, he can still play and have fun with his grandchildren in everyday activities, such as exploring the park. Grampy is based on the author's own husband who has multiple sclerosis (MS) and uses a wheelchair. This uplifting and positive story told by one of Grampy's grandchildren gives young readers an understanding regarding the limitations and abilities of individuals in wheelchairs. As Grampy says, "life's great even from a wheelchair." Bright, bold color illustrations beautifully complement the text.

480. *Six Innings: A Game in the Life.* Preiller, James. New York: Feiwel and Friends, 2008. 147 pp. ISBN: 0312367635; ISBN: 9780312367633. Grades 5–8.

Sam Reiser has always enjoyed playing on baseball teams. Due to cancer, the almost 13-year-old is now confined to a wheelchair and can only be the announcer, instead of a player. Readers who enjoy baseball will be able to identify with the various team players and will learn how personal situations can impact their playing. This story also illustrates how one boy adapts to his physical limitations both at home and in his participation in the game that he always enjoyed. "A tale of baseball, friendship, growth, and coming to terms with hardships, this fast read will grasp any reader who enjoys sports." *School Library Journal*

481. *The Balancing Girl.* Rabe, Berniece; illustrated by Lillian Hoban. New York: Dutton, 1981. 32 pp. ISBN: 0525261605. Grades K–2.

Margaret, though she has limited use of her legs, is not at all limited in imagination and action. While she has made a hobby of balancing things on top of each other, she has not been able to impress one of her classmates. Some of her projects have met with "accidents" and others have been overtly attacked. Margaret gets to shine when one of her balancing projects makes the most money at the school fair through the sale of tickets to a drawing. The winner is Margaret's nemesis, Tommy. Margaret is assertive, active, and thoughtful. The portrayal is limited to school and interactions within the classroom setting. It is not clear what the other students are doing when Margaret is off creating her own space. The teacher might have to be explained since she defuses confrontations rather than guides the class through negative interactions to learning experiences.

482. *Small Steps.* Sachar, Louis. New York: Delacorte Press, 2006. 257 pp. ISBN: 0385733143; ISBN2: 0385903332. Grades 5–8.

In this sequel to Sachar's novel *Holes*, 16-year-old Theodore "Armpit" Johnson tries to turn his life around in Austin, Texas, after being released from Camp Green Lake, a juvenile detention center. Everyone expects the worst from Armpit except his 10-year-old disabled neighbor Ginny. Armpit and Ginny become best friends and support each other. Just when Armpit seems to be on the right track, X-Ray, Armpit's buddy from Camp Green Lake, shows up and comes up with a scheme to get rich quick. This scheme leads to Armpit's chance meeting with a pop-star, Kaira DeLeon, and as a result, his life spins out of control. "Like *Holes*, *Small Steps* is a story of redemption, of the triumph of the human spirit, of self-sacrifice, and of doing the right thing." *School Library Journal*
2007 Schneider Family Book Award in the Teen category.

483. *All Kinds of Friends, Even Green!* Senisi, Ellen B. Bethesda, MD: Woodbine House, 2002. [27] pp. ISBN: 1890627356; ISBN2: 9781890627355. Grades 1–4.

When Moses has an assignment in class to write about a friend, he decides to write about Zaki, his neighbor's pet iguana. Zaki, like Moses, is disabled. Moses identifies with Zaki's adaptability and his courage. This is a good story by itself and also a good discussion starter about how a disability does not have to limit a person or an animal. Full-page color photographs of Moses, his classmates, family and friends, along with the text written in various fonts and sizes make this an appealing work. "The message of acceptance, coupled with a matter-of-fact portrayal of a disabled youngster, makes this a good choice for most collections." *School Library Journal*

484. *Best Friend on Wheels.* Shirley, Debra and Judy Stead. Morton Grove, IL: Albert Whitman, 2008. [30] pp. ISBN: 0807588687; ISBN:9780807588680. Grades K–3.

When a young girl is asked to show the new girl Sarah around school, she hesitates because Sarah is in a wheelchair. Both girls soon discover that they share many interests, such as rock collecting, sleepovers, scrapbook making, dancing, and much more. The power and importance of friendship is demonstrated through the use of rhyming text and vibrant color illustrations. "This is an excellent addition that will work for groups as well as individual reading." *School Library Journal*

485. *Harry Sue.* Stauffacher, Sue. New York: Alfred A. Knopf, 2005. 288 pp. ISBN: 0375832742. Grades 5–8.

Harry Sue has had a lifetime of hardships, including having been tossed out of a seven-story building at the age of 5 by her father and having no contact with her mother, who is imprisoned after being caught selling drugs. Now at the age of 11, she is sent to live with her paternal grandmother who runs a home day care center. Harry Sue tries to resolve some of her personal issues, with the help of her quadriplegic friend Christopher, while trying to protect the day care center's youngsters from her grandmother's neglectful ways. Harry Sue's love of reading, her desire to find her mother, and her willingness to help Christopher fulfill his potential make this an interesting read. A glossary of Conglish, prison language, is included to help readers understand the text, since Harry Sue and Christopher use prison slang throughout the text. "This is a riveting story, dramatically and well told, with characters whom readers won't soon forget." *School Library Journal*

486. *Helping Sophia.* Suen, Anastasia and Jeffrey Ebbeier. Edina, MN: Magic Wagon, 2008. 32 pp. ISBN: 1602700303; ISBN: 9781602700307. Grades 2–3.

One day Miss K announces to her third-grade class that their classmate Sophia, who uses a wheelchair, needs help since her helper Mrs. Lopez is unavailable. When all of Sophie's classmates want to help, Sophie has a hard time deciding who should help her. As her classmates take turns helping her, they discover that pushing a wheelchair is much harder than it appears. This book with bold and expressive color illustrations is a good starter story for discussing how children interact with others who use a wheelchair.

487. *Cruise Control.* Trueman, Terry. New York: HarperTempest, 2004. 149 pp. ISBN: 0066239613. Grades 9–12.

High school senior, star athlete, and honors student Paul has a violent and volatile temperament. His father, a recent Pulitzer Prize winner, left the family because Shawn, Paul's younger brother, was born severely developmentally disabled. Shawn's care is left to Paul's mother, his sister, and Paul himself. Paul tries to resolve his own hostility, and also improve his relationship with both Shawn and his father. This is a very identifiable story for those readers who find themselves in truly no-win family situations and need to resolve life and future challenges. This is a companion book to Trueman's *Stuck in Neutral.* "Trueman does a passionately convincing job portraying a boy who feels trapped and suffocated by responsibilities he never asked to shoulder." *Booklist*

488. *Stuck in Neutral.* Trueman, Terry. New York: HarperCollins, 2000. 114 pp. ISBN: 0060285184. Grades 9–12.

Shawn McDaniel, a 14-year-old, has cerebral palsy and cannot walk or talk. Shawn, who lives with his mother, a brother, and a sister, is in constant fear that his father may kill him, because Shawn's father believes that Shawn's life is meaningless. However, Shawn, in spite of his physical limitations, is still happy to be alive. This book offers a moving story of a disabled person who is the hero of his own story. This is a companion book to Trueman's *Cruise Control.* "Readers must draw their own conclusions as his father's dilemma is left unresolved. This story is bound to spark much lively discussion." *School Library Journal* "Trueman has a son with CP, and has obviously drawn in part from that experience, both for the story's events and for the issues he raises involving the social and emotional costs of caring for the physically helpless." *Booklist* 2001 Michael L. Printz Honor Book.

489. *The Barn at Gun Lake.* Tuitel, Johnnie and Sharon Lamson. Series: The Gun Lake Adventure. Clovis, CA: Cedar Tree Publishing, 1997. 103 pp. ISBN: 0965807509. Grades 4–7.

In this first story of the Gun Lake Adventure series, the reader meets Johnnie Jacobson who was born with cerebral palsy and has just moved with his family from California to Michigan. Johnnie's likable personality enables him to make friends easily. The fact that Johnnie uses a wheelchair does not limit his fun or keep him from completing the initiation rite that he needs to do in order to become a member of his new friends' club. When Johnnie finds a compact disk case, Johnnie and his friends stumble on a mystery that they can solve together.

490. *Mystery Explosion.* Tuitel, Johnnie and Sharon Lamson. Series: The Gun Lake Adventure. Norton Shores, MI: Cedar Tree Publishing, 1998. 121 pp. ISBN: 0965807517. Grades 4–7.

In the second book of the Gun Lake Adventure series, Johnnie Jacobson and his friends from Gun Lake try to solve the mystery of an exploding race car.

491. *Discovery on Blackbird Island.* Tuitel, Johnnie and Sharon Lamson. Series: The Gun Lake Adventure. Norton Shores, MI: Cedar Tree Publishing, 2000. 108 pp. ISBN: 0965807525. Grades 4–7.

In the third book of the Gun Lake Adventure series, Johnnie Jacobson and his friends from Gun Lake are enjoying the end of their summer vacation on Blackbird Island. The group discovers a puppy and a kitten on the island supposedly inhabited only by birds. Now the friends need to uncover the mysterious appearance of these animals and the connection with a local animal shelter.

492. *Searching the Noonday Trail.* Tuitel, Johnnie and Sharon Lamson. Series: The Gun Lake Adventure. Norton Shores, MI: Cedar Tree Publishing, 2000. 106 pp. ISBN: 0965807533. Grades 4–7.

In the fourth book of the Gun Lake Adventure series, Johnnie Jacobson starts the new year at school with hopes of playing on the football team. During a field trip to the local museum with his classmates and his Gun Lake friends, Johnnie becomes involved with a new mystery: who placed the missing Native American necklace in his backpack?

493. *Adventure in the Bear Tooth Mountains.* Tuitel, Johnnie and Sharon Lamson. Series: The Gun Lake Adventure. Grand Rapids, MI: Cedar Tree Publishing, 2003. 137 pp. ISBN: 0965807541. Grades 4–7.

In the fifth book of the Gun Lake Adventure series, Johnnie Jacobson and three of his friends' families from Gun Lake spend Christmas vacation at a ski lodge in Montana. Their vacation becomes an adventure of a lifetime when Johnnie learns to ski; but when he joins his friends exploring the mountains full of wild animals, a stranger appears.

494. *The Light in Bradford Manor.* Tuitel, Johnnie and Sharon Lamson. Series: The Gun Lake Adventure. Norton Shores, MI: Cedar Tree Publishing, 2004. 130 pp. ISBN: 096580755X. Grades 4–7.

In the sixth book of the Gun Lake Adventure series, Johnnie Jacobson and his friends are spending two weeks at Camp Riley, a facility in Indiana that accommodates teenagers with disabilities. When they learn about the legendary ghost of Bradford Manor, an old house near the camp, and see strange lights after midnight, Johnnie and his friends decide to investigate.

495. *Tibby Tried It.* Useman, Sharon and Ernie Useman; illustrated by Cary Pillo. Washington, DC: Magination Press, 1999. 44 pp. ISBN: 1557985588. Grades 1–3.

Tibby Tree Swallow cannot fly because he was born with a crooked wing. When the other birds do not play with him, his mother gives him a special cloth that gives him courage and strength to make new friends with the other animals. Tibby uses his new courage to face dangers, such as rescuing a baby robin from Meany the Cat. All of his friends, including the other birds that used to laugh at him, now know that Tibby is not limited by his disability. Soft, pastel color illustrations are warm and delightful. This is a wonderful discussion starter for how to adapt to a disability.

496. *Susan Laughs.* Willis, Jeanne; illustrated by Tony Ross. New York: Henry Holt, 2000. [26] pp. ISBN: 0805065016. Grades PreK–2.

This story, told in verse, is about Susan who does everything one expects a child to do: Susan dances, rides, swims, and plays hide-and-seek. Not until the very last page does the reader discover that Susan uses a wheelchair. The last line in this story, "just like me, just like you," reveals Susan's powerful message that her disability does not define who she is or what her limitations are. The author uses rhyming phrases and color illustrations to present a positive representation of a disabled child. "This book works for sharing one-on-one, for smaller story times, and for classroom use." *School Library Journal*

497. *Dear Santa, Please Come to the 19th Floor.* Yin; illustrated by Chris Soentpiet. New York: Philomel Books, 2002. [38] pp. ISBN: 0399236368. Grades 1–3.

Two good friends, Willy and Carlos, live in an apartment building in a rough, urban neighborhood. Carlos had an accident that has left him paralyzed. As Christmas approaches, both friends wish that Santa will visit them. Santa does make a very unusual visit to their apartment building on Christmas Eve. This is a unique glimpse of a Hispanic family dealing with a child's disability and a touching story about friendship that survives a challenging environment. The urban description is at times a little stark and rough to the nonurban reader. Color illustrations add depth to the story. "This is a powerful, poignant book about dignity and hope in the midst of poverty and despair." *School Library Journal*

498. *Reaching for Sun.* Zimmer, Tracie Vaughn. New York: Bloomsbury Children's Books, 2007. 181 pp. ISBN: 1599900378. Grades 5–8.

Josie Wyatt, a seventh grader born with cerebral palsy, tells her story in verse about living with her single mother, who attends college, and her grandmother, who tends the last few acres of the once larger farm where her family has lived for four generations. Josie becomes friends with her new neighbor Jordan, who sees beyond Josie's disability. "More sophisticated readers will find added enjoyment as they begin to appreciate the poetic structure and imagery. Readers of all levels will enjoy spending time with Josie and may gain an increased awareness of what it's like to live with a disability." *School Library Journal*
2008 Schneider Family Book Award in the Middle School category.

Nonfiction

499. *Knockin' on Wood: Starring Peg Leg Bates.* Barasch, Lynne. New York: Lee & Low Books, 2004. [29] pp. ISBN: 1584301708. Grades 2–5.

This is a wonderfully told story based on the life of Clayton Peg Leg Bates, one of the twentieth century's legendary tap dancers. As a young boy, Clayton loses his leg in a factory accident and must face the world disabled. Another challenge that Clayton faces is being African American during a time of bigotry and segregation. He does not let society's prejudices stop him as he makes his way to the top in the entertainment world by dancing for all groups, including queens and kings. Not only is this a great story about someone adapting to a disability, but is also a great story about society's expectations and limitations for certain ethnic groups. Soft, pastel watercolor illustrations are an excellent match for the sensitive text. "This book about a remarkable black man and his triumph over adversity would be an excellent addition to any elementary school library." *Children's Literature*

500. *Cerebral Palsy.* Bjorklund, Ruth. Series: Health Alert. New York: Marshall Cavendish Benchmark, 2007. 64 pp. ISBN: 0761422099; ISBN2: 9780761422099. Grades 4–7.

This volume, one of the titles in the Health Alert series, provides a good introduction to cerebral palsy. The first two chapters are "What Is It Like to Have

Cerebral Palsy?" and "What Is Cerebral Palsy?" The chapter titled "The History of Cerebral Palsy" is an excellent overview, and the chapter titled "Living with Cerebral Palsy" covers treatment options, assistive aids and technologies, medications, as well as insight into the daily challenges for those with cerebral palsy. Color photographs, graphics and text boxes, black and white photographs, a glossary, additional reading resources, an extensive listing of organizations, websites, and an index are included.

501. *Kids on Wheels: A Young Person's Guide to Wheelchair Lifestyle.* Dobbs, Jean. Horsham, PA: No Limits Communications, 2004. 150 pp. ISBN: 0971284237. Grades 3–12.

This is a companion volume to *Kids on Wheels: A Guide to Wheelchair Lifestyle for Parents, Teachers, & Professionals.* It is a comprehensive resource for young people who use wheelchairs. This guide helps in building self-esteem by providing suggestions for meeting people and making friends, learning about adaptive sports and recreation, obtaining service animals, participating in the arts, and much more. The guidelines in this exceptional book should encourage children of all ages to realize their potential. A valuable section lists fiction and nonfiction titles appropriate for readers from the third grade through high school. Color and black and white illustrations and bibliographic references are included.

502. *We Can Do It!* Dwight, Laura. New York: Star Bright Books, 1997. [34] pp. ISBN: 1887734341. Grades K–1.

In spite of being an older edition, this volume is unique in that the author discusses how children with multiple disabilities, such as spina bifida, Down syndrome, cerebral palsy, and blindness, manage to function with the help of family members and teachers. Color photographs help readers to distinguish various disabilities. The glossary and resources at the end of the book are very helpful for additional information.

503. *Breaking Down Barriers: Youth with Physical Challenges.* Esherick, Joan. Series: Youth with Special Needs. Broomall, PA: Mason Crest Publishers, 2004. 127 pp. ISBN: 1590847377. Grades 7–10.

This volume, one of the titles in the Youth with Special Needs series, provides information regarding the most common physical disabilities: cerebral palsy, amputation, spinal cord injury, spina bifida, and muscular dystrophy. Different scenarios that use real individuals to explain the topics make this enjoyable for all young readers, particularly those who are disabled. Color photographs and graphics, a glossary, a list of organizations including websites, additional reading material, and an index are included.

504. *Coping with Cerebral Palsy.* Gilman, Laura Anne. Series: Coping. New York: Rosen Publishing Group, 2001. 92 pp. ISBN: 0823931501. Grades 7–9.

This volume, one of the titles in the Coping series, is a quick guide to cerebral palsy. The chapters provide teenagers information that will enable them to make choices for themselves in everyday situations. Encouraging suggestions are provided throughout the chapters as well as realistic scenarios that will help the reader become more social and active at home and at school. A glossary, a list of organizations including websites, additional reading material, and an index are included. This is a good starter book for cerebral palsy.

505. *Rolling Along: The Story of Taylor and His Wheelchair.* Heelan, Jamee Riggio; illustrated by Nicola Simmonds. Series: A Rehabilitation Institute of Chicago Learning Book. Atlanta: Peachtree Publishers, 2000. [30] pp. ISBN: 156145219X. Grades PreK–3.

This is another one of the wonderful Rehabilitation Institute of Chicago Learning Book titles. Taylor writes in first-person narrative and discusses his personal experiences of being born with cerebral palsy. Taylor describes all the different people in his life who help him: his best friend, his twin brother Tyler, and his helpful therapist Kathryn. Taylor also addresses the challenges he faces at school because he uses a wheelchair. Taylor reveals his message of encouragement for both disabled and nondisabled young readers in the following quote: "My wheelchair helps me go more places on my own and do more of the things I want to do. Now nothing can stop me." The interesting illustrations are collages of photographs and color drawings.

506. *Dancing Wheels.* McMahon, Patricia; photographs by John Godt. Boston: Houghton Mifflin, 2000. 48 pp. ISBN: 0395888891. Grades 3–6.

This is a wonderfully uplifting and inspiring story of a woman born with spina bifida and whose parents taught her "not to think of what she couldn't do but of what she could do." Mary established Dancing Wheels, a dance troupe that showcases wheelchair dancing. She also created a children's dance troupe. This book tells the story of the children and adults who make this troupe a success, whether they use wheelchairs or do not use wheelchairs. The color photographs throughout the text relay a most positive message. "This outstanding volume presents unique content in a lively, attractive format on a much-needed subject." *School Library Journal*

507. *Imagine Being Paralyzed.* O'Neill, Linda. Series: Imagine. Vero Beach, FL: Rourke Book, 2001. 32 pp. ISBN: 1571033785. Grades 2–4.

This volume, one of the titles in the Imagine series, is a good, up-to-date introduction. One- to two-page chapters include the following: "The Message Center," "Illnesses and Injuries," "Getting Around Sports," and "Helping Others." Real people, young and old, are depicted in everyday situations. There is a chapter about the late actor and disabilities activist Christopher Reeve. Color photographs and graphics, a glossary, additional reading resources, websites, and an index are included. From the author's introduction: "This series of books is meant to enlighten and give children an awareness and sensitivity to those people who might not be just like them."

508. *Living with Cerebral Palsy.* Pimm, Paul. Series: Living With. Austin, TX: Raintree Steck-Vaughn, 2000. 32 pp. ISBN: 0817257446. Grades 3–6.

This is one of the titles in the Living With series that provides inspiring and useful information about individuals who have cerebral palsy. Katie, Jenny, Paul, and Simon, who have cerebral palsy, show how they have adapted to everyday situations and life in general. The two-page chapter format covers a wide variety of issues, including why cerebral palsy happens, treatment options, and what the future holds for individuals who have cerebral palsy. Color photographs, a glossary, useful addresses and support organizations, and an index are included.

509. *Sam Uses a Wheelchair.* Powell, Jillian. Series: Like Me, Like You. Langhorne, PA: Chelsea Clubhouse, 2004. 29 pp. ISBN: 079108180X. Grades 2–4.

This is the story of Sam, one of the titles in the Like Me, Like You series. Sam, who uses a wheelchair, discusses her interactions with her family and friends at home and at school. Sam performs wheelchair racing as well as other sports and activities. This is a very positive representation in easy-to-read language that shows what Sam can do, not what she cannot do. Excellent color photographs, a glossary, additional reading materials, a list of organizations, and an index are included.

510. *Extraordinary Friends.* Rogers, Fred; photographs by Jim Judkis. Series: Let's Talk about It. New York: Putnam, 2000. [32] pp. ISBN: 0698118618. Grades 1–3.

In this photo book, part of the Let's Talk about It series, Rogers discusses the concerns and questions children may have regarding children with special needs. This book dispels the fear, the curiosity, and the surprise that nondisabled children experience when they meet a disabled individual. Young readers are reassured that their feelings are normal, and that, by getting to know disabled individuals, they can overcome these feelings. Rogers offers some suggestions that enable younger readers to become friends with "extraordinary friends." The bright color photographs complement the text. "The well-known Rogers states simply that all people want to love and be loved and that people are alike even if they don't 'walk or talk or learn the same way you do.'" *Booklist*

511. *Using a Wheelchair.* Royston, Angela. Series: What's It Like? Chicago: Heinemann Library, 2005. 32 pp. ISBN: 1403458537. Grades 2–4.

This volume in the What's It Like? series is about children who use wheel-chairs. The topics covered in the thirteen two-page chapters involve questions and concerns such as: why do some people use wheelchairs and how do people in wheelchairs get around. Additional topics include what everyday life is like for those in wheelchairs and how individuals in wheelchairs participate in sports and activities at school and work. The text is accompanied by color photographs that show individuals in wheelchairs doing normal activities, both functional and fun. The author also provides suggestions and tips for readers to learn when they encounter individuals in wheelchairs, such as not to lean on a wheelchair or not to hang on to it. This is a good resource for younger readers. A glossary, additional reading material, and an index are included.

512. *Some Kids Use Wheelchairs.* Schaefer, Lola M. Series: Understanding Differences. Mankova, MN: Capstone Press, 2008. 24 pp. ISBN: 1429608129; ISBN: 9781429608121. Grades PreK–2.

This revised and updated title in the Understanding Differences series provides exceptional color photographs and text about children who use wheelchairs. In addition, the reader should learn how an individual feels to live with mobility impairment. The three sections cover why kids use wheelchairs, how kids remain active, and how they interact with others in everyday life. A glossary, a brief list of additional resources, Internet sites, and an index are included. "[W]ill help young children understand at an early age to appreciate differences rather than ridicule those who are different." *Multicultural Review*

513. *Some Kids Wear Leg Braces.* Schaefer, Lola M. Series: Understanding Differences. Mankova, MN: Capstone Press, 2008. 24 pp. ISBN: 1429608137; ISBN: 9781429608138. Grades PreK–2.

This revised and updated title in the series Understanding Differences provides younger readers with exceptional realistic portrayals of children who wear leg braces. In addition, the reader should learn how it feels to live with wearing leg braces. Using color photographs, children are shown doing everyday activities at home and at play. A glossary, a brief list of print resources, Internet sites, and index are included. "[W]ill help young children understand at an early age to appreciate differences rather than ridicule those who are different." *Multicultural Review*

514. *Don't Call Me Special: A First Look at Disability.* Thomas, Pat; illustrated by Lesley Harker. New York: Barron's, 2002. 29 pp. ISBN: 0764121189. Grades K–2.

This title, written by a therapist, is an excellent introduction to the concept of disability for the youngest readers. Disabled children engaged in everyday activities at home and at school illustrate that some people who seem different from us are in fact really the same. A one-page guide "How to Use This Book" provides suggestions for activities and background information for the educator in addressing the concept. A glossary, additional reading resources, and organizations are included.

MULTIPLE PHYSICAL DISABILITIES

Fiction

515. *My Heart Glow: Alice Cogswell, Thomas Gallaudet, and the Birth of American Sign Language.* McCully, Emily Arnold. New York: Hyperion Books for Young Children, 2008. [40] pp. ISBN: 142310028X; ISBN: 9781423100287. Grades 2–5.

Based on historical figures, the author tells the story of Alice Cogswell, a deaf and mute girl who lives next door to the family of Thomas Gallaudet. When Gallaudet notices young Alice's inquisitive and intelligent nature, he is determined to teach Alice how to read. With the assistance of Alice's father, Gallaudet travels to Europe in order to learn the best methods for teaching individuals who are deaf and mute. Gallaudet returns with Laurent Clerc, and together they establish a school for the deaf and the American Sign Language. Soft, watercolor illustrations complement the text. "This is a book that has been sorely needed for some time, and McCully pulls it off with panache." *School Library Journal*

516. *Little Tree: A Story for Children with Serious Medical Problems.* Mills, Joyce C.; illustrated by Brian Sebern. Washington, DC: Magination Press, 2003. 31 pp. ISBN: 1591470412. Grades PreK–2.

This is the second edition of a wonderful story about a little tree who is disabled during a terrible storm when several of his branches fall off. His good friend Amanda the squirrel remains faithful and helps the little tree understand that even though he has changed on the outside, he is still the same on the inside. Bold, vibrant color illustrations complement the exceptional text. The author's essay, "The Roots and the Power of Little Tree," provides parents with the necessary background in order to discuss the topic of being disabled. "Magic Happy Breath: A Relaxation Exercise for Children" and an article, "When Children Have Serious Medical Problems," are included.

517. *Becoming Naomi Leon.* Ryan, Pam Munoz. New York: Scholastic Press, 2004. 246 pp. ISBN: 0439269695. Grades 4–8.

Naomi Soledad Leon Outlaw, an 11-year-old, and her disabled younger brother Owen live with their great-grandmother Gram in a trailer park full of loving neighbors. After a seven-year absence, their irresponsible substance abusing mother returns with her new boyfriend. When she wants Naomi to live with them, Naomi embarks on a personal journey to discover her own identity, which means traveling to Mexico to locate her long lost father. This is a great story for younger readers who have to deal with distant parents, mixed ethnic backgrounds, and finding their identities in society. "Characterization is excellent and listeners will be happy that Naomi finds confidence, love, and security." *School Library Journal*
2005 Schneider Family Book Award in the Middle School category.
2006 Pura Belpré Honor Book.

518. *Sea Crow.* Stewart, Shannon; illustrated by Liz Milkau. Victoria, BC: Orca Book Publishers, 2004. [32] pp. ISBN: 1551432889. Grades 2–4.

Young Jessica's family moves to a house near the sea. Jessica is afraid to reveal that she has an artificial leg. Her younger brother Miles is afraid of certain things, such as the unpacked boxes and goblins and spiders. With the help of Alicia, her new friend, Jessica builds a sea crow to ward away all the frightening things in her new environment. This is an interesting story in which young Jessica creates her own weapon for combating her fear. Pastel color illustrations complement the text.

Nonfiction

519. *A Picture Book of Helen Keller.* Adler, David A.; illustrated by John and Alexandra Wallner. Series: Picture Book Biography. New York: Holiday House, 1990. [30] pp. ISBN: 0823408183. Grades 1–3.

One of the titles in the Picture Book Biography series, this is an excellent resource and introduction to the life of Helen Keller for the younger reader. Adler covers Helen's birth, her challenging childhood until meeting Anne Sullivan, and her adulthood until her death in 1968. The illustrations are colorful and will keep the young reader's attention. The faces are quite expressive as are the actions depicted in the illustrations. "It is interesting enough to awaken children's interest in learning more about Keller." *School Library Journal*

520. *Helen Keller.* Adler, David A.; illustrated by John Wallner. Series: A Holiday House Reader. New York: Holiday House, 2003. 32 pp. ISBN: 0823416062. Grades 2–3.

Using their highly acclaimed *Picture Book of Helen Keller* as a basis for this work, Adler and Wallner have written this wonderful book about Helen Keller in the Holiday House Reader series. Helen's biography has been divided into four chapters: "Illness," "From Darkness into Light," "That Living Word," and "Hope and Love." The beautiful, full-page color illustrations throughout the book will appeal to younger readers who have enjoyed Adler's and Wallner's *Picture Book of Helen Keller*. "The elemental narrative is truly inspiring because it is told without rhetoric or direct message, and Wallner's lively, colorful pictures show the brave child and her bond with her amazing mentor, who helped Keller, reach out to people all over the world." *Booklist*

521. *She Touched the World.* Alexander, Sally Hobart. New York: Clarion Books, 2008. 100 pp. ISBN: 0618852999; ISBN: 9780618852994. Grades 5–7.

At the age of 2, Laura, who was born in 1829, contracted scarlet fever, which left her deaf and blind. Imprisoned in her own body, Laura's parents send her to the New England Institution for the Education of the Blind, the first school for blind children in America. Laura blossomed at this school, which would eventually become the Perkins School for the Blind. By the time Laura was 12 years old, she was world famous, had traveled throughout the country meeting celebrities, and generated support for the education of disabled individuals. After visiting Laura in 1842, Charles Dickens devoted a chapter to her in his *American Notes*. Forty years later, Kate Keller read this book and was inspired to seek help for her daughter, Helen Keller. The abundant black and white illustrations and photographs of Laura, her surroundings, as well as artifacts used in teaching blind students provide an excellent visual complement to the text. Source notes, a bibliography, a list of websites, and an index are included. "Illustrated with period photos and prints, and supported by extensive notes and resource lists, this will be a valuable and long-overdue addition to library shelves." *Kirkus Reviews*

522. *We Go in a Circle.* Anderson, Peggy Perry. Boston: Houghton Mifflin, 2004. 32 pp. ISBN: 0618447563. Grades PreK–2.

This picture book tells the story of a racehorse that can no longer race because of an injury but is enlisted in a program where a variety of children with different disabilities participate in guided horseback riding. The subtext seems to be that regardless of your abilities, there is a shared need to feel important and to help others feel important. Information about hippotherapy is explained. Vivid watercolor illustrations complement the text. "Unique in its topic, this gentle story is useful for story times on horses and disabilities." *School Library Journal*

523. *The World at Her Fingertips: The Story of Helen Keller.* Dash, Joan. New York: Scholastic Press, 2001. 235 pp. ISBN: 0590907158. Grades 5–8.

This straightforward narration of Helen Keller's remarkable life is aimed for the middle school student. The important role that Anne Sullivan, Helen's teacher, who became celebrated in her own right, played in helping Helen develop her potential is addressed. All major events in Helen's life, as well as all of the famous individuals who knew Helen, are included in this informative text. Notable individuals who knew Helen are Alexander Graham Bell, Mark Twain, and John F. Kennedy. Black and white photographs are included. "The volume is detailed and engaging, and extensive use of Keller's own words lends authenticity." *VOYA*

524. *Helen Keller.* Garrett, Leslie. New York: DK Publishing, 2004. 127 pp. ISBN: 0756603390. Grades 5–9.

This DK (Dorling Kindersley) biography, written specifically for the reluctant middle school reader, divides Helen's biography into eighteen manageable chapters, beginning with "A Remarkable Life," through "Opening Her Mind," and finally, "A Life Well Lived." The visuals that complement the text make this an enjoyable title. Photographs, illustrations, text boxes, graphics, visual timeline, bibliography, additional reading material, websites, and an index are included. "[H]ighly readable, worthwhile overview for young people that introduce[s] both personal and wider background and historical issues." *Booklist*

525. *The Story of Helen Keller.* Koestler-Grack, Rachel A. Philadelphia: Chelsea Clubhouse, 2004. 32 pp. ISBN: 0791073157. Grades 4–6.

This excellent overview of the life of Helen Keller explores Helen's life, from her birth to her adult life. Color text boxes and photographs enhance the text and provide a visual dimension of Helen and those individuals who made up the sphere of her extended family and friends. Each page includes Helen's quotations, a sign language chart, information about organizations for the blind, and events during Helen's lifetime. A brief biography of Helen, photographs and brief biographies of notable women during Helen's lifetime, a glossary, additional reading material, and websites are included. This is an exceptional resource. "[C]arefully researched, presenting good and respectful coverage." *School Library Journal*

526. *Helen Keller.* Lawlor, Laurie. New York: Holiday House, 2001. 168 pp. ISBN: 0823415880. Grades 5–8.

This is a captivating story of Helen Keller's life and the lives of those individuals who helped her reach her potential and to succeed. The author provides the reader with a real glimpse of Helen as well as her family, her teacher, and the famous historical individuals whom she knew, such as Alexander Graham Bell. The reader will enjoy the historical photographs that not only complement the text but also give visual depth to Helen and her sphere of friends. A chronology of Helen's life, additional reading material, films, and an index are included. "Lawlor looks with affection and honesty at the whole woman." *Booklist*

527. *Coping with Being Physically Challenged.* Ratto, Linda Lee. Series: Coping. New York: Rosen Publishing Group, 1991. 103 pp. ISBN: 0823913449. Grades 7–9.

This volume is one of the titles in the Coping series. The author includes several topics that are not typically perceived as physical challenges, such as the grief process and self-worth. Throughout this work, there are different scenarios, describing individuals with challenges. Helpful advice, such as how to feel good about oneself and adapting to everyday frustrations, is found in the chapters "Life Is a Challenge—for Everyone" and "Ways to Face Each Day—with Happiness." An in-depth glossary, extensive additional resources, and an index are included.

528. *Teens with Disabilities.* Stewart, Gail. Series: The Other America. San Diego, CA: Lucent Books, 2001. 96 pp. ISBN: 1560068159. Grades 8–12.

As one of the books in the Other America series, this title profiles four teenagers who tell their own stories about their struggles as individuals with disabilities. The first teenager has muscular dystrophy, another teenager has cerebral palsy, one teenager needs to wear leg braces, and the fourth teenager has multiple, congenital health problems. The teenagers reveal very personal information about the everyday challenges they experience and encounter due to their disabilities. In addition, the experiences they share with both family members and friends reveal how these relationships have enabled them to live successful and fulfilling lives. Black and white photographs of the actual teenagers, suggestions for getting involved, additional reading material, and an index are included. The reader will enjoy the epilogue, which provides updated information on the profiled teenagers. "A useful and approachable book for research or general reading." *School Library Journal*

529. *Helen Keller.* Sullivan, George. New York: Scholastic Reference, 2000. 128 pp. ISBN: 0439147514. Grades 4–8.

This is a very good overview of Helen Keller's life that uses Helen's own words, both from print sources and interviews, to tell her story. By using quotes from friends, family, and those who knew her, the author has made Helen come to life. As stated in the book, she is a symbol of hope and courage for people in every country of the world. A chronology of Helen's life, bibliography, additional reading material, organizations, and an index are included. "[W]ell written, fast moving, and highly readable, squeezed into a small format that should appeal to many students." *School Library Journal*

530. *Physical Disabilities: The Ultimate Teen Guide.* Thornton, Denise. Series: It Happened to Me. Lanham, MD: Scarecrow Press, 2007. 162 pp. ISBN: 0810853000; ISBN2: 9780810853003. Grades 9–12.

This excellent title in the It Happened to Me series provides exceptional information about the challenges that young teenagers who have physical disabilities face in life's everyday situations. The author addresses the fact that many of these situations are indeed situations that all teenagers face, both physically disabled teenagers and nondisabled teenagers. Chapter topics include how the physically disabled teenager functions in high school, what tools and technologies are available, and how the physically disabled teenager can become involved in sports and recreational activities. Additional issues that are explored are how to express oneself, how to handle relationships, and how to declare one's independence. The chapter titled "Advocacy" contains a comprehensive overview of noteworthy historical facts regarding disabled individuals and the ten laws that have historically defined the rights of the disabled. Black and white photographs, text boxes that showcase disabled individuals and their accomplishments, and an index are included.

Chapter 4

Multiple Disabilities

In this chapter, there are five fiction and nonfiction entries: two are for the high school, two are for the middle school, and one is for the elementary school grade levels. These entries contain disorders and disabilities that fall into more than one of the following categories: emotional, learning, and physical.

FICTION

531. *Be Quiet, Marina.* DeBear, Kirsten; illustrated by Laura Dwight. New York: Star Bright Books, 2001. [28] pp. ISBN: 1887734791. Grades 1–2.

Marina, a noisy little girl who was born with cerebral palsy, and Moira, a quiet little girl with Down syndrome, play together because they enjoy many of the same activities. However, at times Moira gets frustrated with Marina because she is loud and impatient. Eventually they become best friends. This story teaches children that in spite of difficulties and differences, they can all get along. The black and white photographs complement the text. A list of helpful organizations dealing with Down syndrome and cerebral palsy in various countries is included.

NONFICTION

532. *Oh, Brother! Growing Up with a Special Needs Sibling.* Hale, Natalie; illustrated by Kate Sternberg. Washington, DC: Magination Press, 2004. 48 pp. ISBN: 1591470617. Grades 4–7.

Rebecca, known as Becca, is 11 years old and is often frustrated with her 13-year-old brother Jonathan, who is different. He breaks things in her room and he talks and acts differently from other children. Becca is upset when other children make fun of him, as well as the fact that her parents spend most of their time and attention on him. This title realistically addresses the challenges that siblings and parents of kids with special needs experience. Becca's scenarios provide excellent starting points for discussion. Black and white drawings are included. As the author writes, "It's a true story . . . Becca has coped with all of the problems and worries. Doesn't sugar coat the feelings and struggles that she faces every day."

533. *The Sibling Slam Book: What It's Really Like to Have a Brother or Sister with Special Needs.* Meyer, Donald, editor. Bethesda, MD: Woodbine House, 2005. 152 pp. ISBN: 1890627526. Grades 7–12.

The slam book, which resembles a spiral notebook, was a popular format in the mid-1960s. In this slam book, the editor has gathered the feelings, writings, and reflections of eighty young teenagers, ranging in age from 13 to 19, based on fifty-four questions. Each of these originally asked questions comprises a section title under which the teenagers' responses are listed as the answers. Some section titles include "What Do You Want People to Know about Your Sib," "Does Your Sib Ever Frustrate You," and "Has Something Ever Happened to Your Sib That Scared You." These writings, some of which may be too honest for younger readers, reveal identifiable concerns experienced by brothers and sisters of siblings who have a variety of emotional, learning, and physical disabilities and disorders. The slam book format remains an appealing venue in which teenagers can express concerns and feelings. The black and white photographs include the first name only of the contributing teenager. "Highly recommended for all middle, high school, and public libraries." *School Library Journal*

534. *Views from Our Shoes: Growing Up with a Brother or Sister with Special Needs.* Meyer, Donald, editor; illustrated by Cary Pillo. Bethesda, MD: Woodbine House, 1997. 113 pp. ISBN: 0933149980. Grades 2–6.

This is a wonderful collection of forty-five essays by siblings, ages 4 to 18, who tell, in their own words, what it is like to have a brother or sister with special needs. These very personal stories and reflections reveal their honest feelings about the good and bad situations during family and social situations. These stories illustrate that they often feel neglected and embarrassed. Many of these writings also reveal how the siblings protect their special brother or sister against the prejudices and ignorance of others. The appendix contains a glossary of medical terms, informative advice for siblings, an extensive list of support organizations, websites, and an index. Black and white drawings accompany over half of the essays. "As such, this book would be useful for schools that have special-ed programs or a number of mainstreamed students." *School Library Journal*

535. *Embracing the Sky: Poems beyond Disability.* Romkema, Craig. London: Jessica Kingsley, 2002. 80 pp. ISBN: 1843107287. Grades 7–12.

This collection of poems is written by Craig Romkema, who has autism and cerebral palsy. He shares his life experiences and offers insights into his life beyond his disabilities. The reader will discover, through his poems, Romkema's hopes, fears, and aspirations. His last poem, a short manifesto, is a very good reflection on Romkema's life as a whole.

Chapter 5

General Reference Resources

In this chapter the reader will find twenty-eight resources for traditional reference materials, such as annotated bibliographies, dictionaries, encyclopedias, and additional resources relevant for research. These offer extensive information regarding various disorders and disabilities covered in this book.

GENERAL

536. *Encyclopedia of Disability.* Albrecht, Gary L., editor. Thousand Oaks, CA: Sage Publications, 2006. 5 volumes. ISBN: 0761925651.

This five-volume comprehensive set is designed to bring up-to-date information about the many faces of disability, covering a wide variety of topics, places, and conditions. The thousand entries regarding disabilities are listed alphabetically in the first four volumes: Volume 1: A–D; Volume 2: E–I; Volume 3: J–R; Volume 4: S–X. The entries range from half a page to several pages in length, and include cross-references. Also included are websites that refer to government documents and data that provide rich resources to examine how disability is measured and treated on an international level. Volume 5 contains primary source documents dealing with disabilities, such as historical accounts, scripture references, and stories from Asian and African cultures. Excerpts from literature that contain disability issues are included. Volume 5 is the only volume that contains black and white photographs and illustrations. A chronology from 1500 B.C.E. to the present and a section titled "Searching for and Evaluating Websites" conclude this volume. "The only really comprehensive resource on disability; this is an important foundation for disability collections in any academic, public, or high school library." *Library Journal*

537. *Outstanding Books for Young People with Disabilities 2009.* Boiesen, Heidi Cortner. Baerum Municipality, Norway: IBBY Documentation Centre of Books for Disabled Young People, Haug School and Resource Centre, 2009. [39] pp.

This is the current volume of the annotated catalog started in 1997 by the International Board on Books for Young People (IBBY), a nonprofit organization that represents an international network of people who are committed to bringing books and children together. The books included in this volume were published in 2004. In addition, one outstanding title that was published in 1998 has also been included. For nominations, the IBBY national sections considered books that met one or more of the specified categories, such as books produced specifically for young people with special needs; picture books containing sign language illustrations, pictograms, tactile pictures, or easy-to-read books for young people with mental disabilities; books that portrayed young people with disabilities that not only focused on their disabilities and the difference it makes to their lives, but also stressed similarities between them and the world at large. IBBY's intent is to promote understanding, knowledge, and acceptance of inclusion of young people with disabilities in society and to encourage the publication and promotion of new books in this field. Due to the prestige of IBBY, books included in the 2007 volume of this title have been identified in Appendix A.

538. *The Gale Encyclopedia of Mental Health.* Fundukian, Laurie J. and Jeffrey Wilson, editors. Detroit: Thomson Gale, 2008. 2 volumes. ISBN: 1414429878; ISBN2: 9781414429878.

This updated, two-volume set provides detailed coverage of approximately 150 specific disorders recognized by the American Psychiatry Association, as classified in the *Diagnostic and Statistical Manual of Mental Disorders*, text revision (DSM-IV-TR). While providing comprehensive and useful explanations, this encyclopedia uses simple language for lay persons to understand. Over 450 entries regarding mental health topics are listed alphabetically in two volumes: Volume 1: A–L (examples: ADHD, anorexia, grief, juvenile bipolar, learning disabilities, etc.), and Volume 2: M–Z (examples: schizophrenia, stress, etc.). All entries begin with a definition, followed by sections that include descriptions, causes and symptoms, demographics, diagnosis, treatments, prognosis, prevention, and resources containing books, periodicals, organizations, and some websites. Each entry contains a text box highlighting key terms, which should help readers understand the contents. Black and white and color photographs and graphics are included. The second volume contains an extensive glossary and an index. Highly recommended resource.

539. *Encyclopedia of Special Education: A Reference for the Education of Children, Adolescents, and Adults with Disabilities and Other Exceptional*

Individuals. Reynolds, Cecil R. and Elaine Fletcher-Janzen. Hoboken, NJ: Wiley, 2007. 3 volumes. ISBN: 0471678023; ISBN2: 9780471678021.

This updated third edition, containing three volumes, is an essential reference tool for professionals working in special education. Others who help in formulating the policies and education of the disabled and the gifted, such as educators, lawyers, physicians, psychologists, social workers, and school board members, will find this to be an indispensable resource. More than 2,000 entries are listed alphabetically in three volumes: Volume 1: A–D; Volume 2: E–O; Volume 3: P–Z. Entry topics include biographies and contributions of key figures in the field; educational and psychological tests; techniques of intervention and service delivery; descriptions of handicapping conditions; a directory of related services; and information on legal issues related to special education. Entries contain additional reading material and see references. Black and white photographs are included. "This critical reference includes entries addressing the full gamut of special-education research. . . . This is a valuable resource for parents, professionals, and other laypeople with an interest in the education of youths with special needs." *Library Journal*

540. *Voices from the Margins: An Annotated Bibliography of Fiction on Disabilities and Differences for Young People.* Ward, Marilyn. Westport, CT: Greenwood Press, 2002. 154 pp. ISBN: 0313317984.

Ward identifies two hundred fiction books that feature characters with disabilities and differences that teachers, librarians, and other professionals can use with children and young people in order to broaden their awareness and understanding of disabilities. The titles, published between 1990 and 2001, include picture books, middle-grade chapter books, and young adult novels that cover contemporary realistic fiction, historical fiction, mysteries, fantasies, and poetry. This book is divided into five sections: annotated bibliography, title index, author index, age-level index, and an index listing ninety subject headings. The criteria used for the selection of these books were accuracy of information, literary quality, realistic and believable portrayal of people, settings that are integral to the action and characters, reasonable story resolution, and audience/age level and genre. The alphabetical listing of titles contains complete bibliographic citation and a substantial summary. Subject terms are included at the end of each entry.

EMOTIONAL

Depression

541. *The Encyclopedia of Depression.* Rosesch, Roberta. Series: Facts on File Library of Health and Living. New York: Facts on File, 2001. 278 pp. ISBN: 0816040478.

As one of the titles in the Facts on File Library of Health and Living series, this second revised and updated edition is an excellent resource for professionals and parents. More than 550 entries are arranged alphabetically, with the length of entry varying from two to three sentences to several pages. Certain terms that are defined elsewhere in this encyclopedia are capitalized and listed at the end of some of the entries. Cross-references are used to refer the reader from unused to preferred terms. Entries cover a wide range of depression-related topics such as holiday depression, stress, and unipolar disorder. Various drug types, geographic locations, as well as important individuals are also included. The appendices include "World Health Organization Studies," "Central Monoamine Systems," "Chemical and Trade Names of Psychiatric Drugs," as well as "Sources of Information," which includes a comprehensive listing of U.S. national associations, institutes, organizations and government agencies, Canadian resources, and journals. A bibliography and index complete this work. "An excellent resource for high school libraries." *School Library Journal*

Depression-Related Disorders

542. *The Encyclopedia of Phobias, Fears, and Anxieties.* Doctor, Ronald M., Ada P. Kahn, and Christine A. Adamec. Series: Facts on File Library of Health and Living. New York: Facts on File, 2008. 572 pp. ISBN: 0816075581; ISBN: 9780816075584.

As one of the titles in the Facts on File Library of Health and Living series, this third revised edition is an excellent resource for professionals and parents. More than 2,000 entries are arranged alphabetically, with the length of entry varying from two or three sentences to several pages. Certain terms that are defined elsewhere in this encyclopedia are capitalized and listed at the end of some of the entries. Cross-references are used to refer the reader from unused to preferred terms. Entries cover a wide range of topics such as phobia types, anxiety disorders, fear factors, medications, treatments, and so forth. A historical overview of phobias is provided in the introductory chapter. Resources including organizations and contact information, a bibliography, and an index complete this work.

543. *The Encyclopedia of Stress and Stress-Related Diseases.* Kahn, Ada P. Series: Facts on File Library of Health and Living. New York: Facts on File, 2006. 438 pp. ISBN: 0816059373; ISBN2: 9780816059379.

Part of the Facts on File Library of Health and Living series, this second edition is the most current information on stress and stress-related diseases. It includes more than eight hundred entries that address the different types of stress, possible causes, how stress impacts an individual's health, how to cope, and much more. Entries are arranged alphabetically, with the length of entry varying from two or three sentences to several pages. Certain terms that are defined elsewhere in this encyclopedia are capitalized and listed at the end of some of the entries. Cross-references are used to refer the reader from unused to preferred terms. Entries cover a wide range of stress and stress-related topics such as airplanes, burnout, family, headaches, loneliness, puberty, and support groups. An index and a glossary are included. It is a well-recommended encyclopedia as a reference guide for parents, teachers, and professionals.

Eating Disorders

544. *The Encyclopedia of Obesity and Eating Disorders.* Cassell, Dana K. and David H. Gleaves. Series: Facts on File Library of Health and Living. New York: Facts on File, 2006. 362 pp. ISBN: 0816061971.

This third updated edition in the Facts on File Library of Health and Living series is an excellent resource for professionals and parents. Entries are arranged alphabetically with entry length varying from two or three sentences to several pages. Certain terms that are defined elsewhere in this encyclopedia are capitalized and listed at the end of some of the entries. Cross-references are used to refer the reader from unused to preferred terms. The eight-page "Introduction: A History of Obesity and Eating Disorders" is an excellent overview. More than 450 entries cover a wide range of topics related to obesity and eating disorders, such as anorexia nervosa, body fat, religion and obesity, and suicide. Seven appendices list the following: a chronology that documents historical events; tables reflecting physical dimensions, food qualities, and DSM-IV criteria; sources of information and obesity and eating disorder treatment centers; websites; and audiovisual materials. A bibliography and index complete the book. "[T]he encyclopedia is recommended for high-school, undergraduate, and public libraries." *Booklist*

Mental Illness

545. *The Encyclopedia of Mental Health.* Kahn, Ada P. and Jan Fawcett. Series: Facts on File Library of Health and Living. New York: Facts on File, 2008. 508 pp. ISBN: 0816064547; ISBN2: 9780816064540.

Part of the Facts on File Library of Health and Living series, this revised and updated third edition provides an overview of mental health topics. Entries are arranged alphabetically, with the length of entry varying from two or three sentences to several pages. Certain terms that are defined elsewhere in this encyclopedia are capitalized and listed at the end of some of the entries. Cross-references are used to refer the reader from unused to preferred terms. It includes over 2,000 entries on topics such as adoption, depression, domestic violence, environmental hazards, holistic medicine, performance anxiety, and more related to mental health. An extensive bibliography organized according to various topics, a seventeen-page list of various resources including organizations and websites, and an index are included. It is a well-recommended encyclopedia as a reference guide for parents, teachers. and professionals. "Highly recommended for all libraries." *Library Journal*

546. *The Encyclopedia of Schizophrenia and Other Psychotic Disorders.* Noll, Richard. Series: Facts on File Library of Health and Living. New York: Facts on File, 2007. 409 pp. ISBN: 0816064059.

This third updated edition in the Facts on File Library of Health and Living series is an excellent resource for professionals and parents. Entries are arranged alphabetically, with entry length varying from two or three sentences to several pages. Certain terms that are defined elsewhere in this encyclopedia are capitalized and listed at the end of some of the entries. Cross-references are used to refer the reader from unused to preferred terms. A twelve-page history of madness, psychosis, and schizophrenia is included. More than six hundred entries cover a wide range of topics related to schizophrenia and other psychotic disorders, such as affective disorders, bleeding, electroshock therapy, and prognosis. Geographic locations are included such as Italy and Hotel-Dieu, as well as individuals, such as Manfred Bleuler and Sigmund Freud. Many contain additional resources at the end of the entry. Appendices include "North American Diagnostic Criteria for Schizophrenia," "European Diagnostic Criteria for Schizophrenia," "Sources of Information Concerning Schizophrenia," and a directory of organizations and professional affiliations. "[T]he language is clear, making this volume equally suitable for use by patients, scholars, and general readers." *Booklist*

LEARNING

Attention-Deficit/Hyperactivity Disorder (AD/HD)

547. *Therapist's Guide to Learning and Attention Disorders.* Fine, Aubrey H. and Ronald Kotkin, editors. San Diego, CA: Academic Press, 2003. 579 pp. ISBN: 0122564308.

This is a comprehensive and practical guide to understand attention and learning disorders. The first four chapters in this book present an overview of the neuropsychology of these disorders and the assessment by both traditional and innovative ways. The rest of the eleven chapters discuss practical educational interventions in a therapy setting and school, as well as behavioral interventions for home management. The guide also provides information on how attention and learning disorders affect lives and impact social behavior, emotions, and cognition. Medication management, including career and educational transitions by the therapists, is also discussed. Appendices with practical forms, illustrations, and rating scales are well organized and can be incorporated into practice. Additional references and an index are included.

548. *Attention Deficit Disorder and Learning Disabilities: Realities, Myths, and Controversial Treatments.* Ingersoll, Barbara D. and Sam Goldstein. New York: Doubleday, 1993. 246 pp. ISBN: 0385469314.

This comprehensive book defines attention-deficit hyperactivity disorder (ADHD) and learning disabilities and discusses the causes, symptoms, and diagnoses of these conditions. The authors explore and critique the various treatments from stimulant medications to sugar-free diets, from electromyographic (EMG) feedback, to vitamin supplements. In addition to an index, the book includes a list of information sources and support groups for parents, recommended texts, and videos for parents.

Autism Spectrum Disorders

549. *Autism Spectrum Disorders from A to Z: Assessment Diagnosis & More!* Doyle, Barbara T. and Emily Doyle Iland. Arlington, TX: Future Horizons, 2004. 462 pp. ISBN: 1932565078.

This valuable source is aimed at helping parents, educators, and teachers learn about the subject of autism spectrum disorders (ASD). Organized into ten chapters, the book provides information and essential ideas and concepts regarding the following topics: understanding ASD; considerations in the diagnosis of ASD; assessment and diagnosis; types of assessments and what they measure; differences in opinion and diagnosis; supporting the family of a person with ASD; sharing information about people with ASD; and causes and cures. Each of the chapters has a brief summary of the contents covered in the chapter as well as the sources used. A list of helpful organizations and contacts, websites, and an index are provided.

550. *The Incredible 5-Point Scale: Assisting Students with Autism Spectrum Disorders in Understanding Social Interactions and Controlling Their Emotional Responses.* Dunn Buron, Kari and Mitzi Curtis. Shawnee Mission, KS: Autism Asperger Publishing, 2003. 73 pp. ISBN: 1931282528.

The main objective of this book is to illustrate how to utilize a simple five-point scale to support a program for teaching social understanding to students with Asperger syndrome and autism. Written by two autism resource specialists, this book will help parents, teachers, and principals understand the behavior of students with Asperger syndrome and autism. It will also help students with this condition to self-manage their behavior. Highly recommended.

551. *The Autism Sourcebook: Everything You Need to Know about Diagnosis, Treatment, Coping, and Healing.* Exkorn, Karen Siff. New York: Reagan Books, 2005. 416 pp. ISBN: 0060799889.

This comprehensive guidebook focuses on children under the age of 12 who have been diagnosed with autism. It is divided into four main parts: 1. Diagnosis. 2. Treatment. 3. Coping. 4. Healing. Each part is further divided into sections that include questions and answers based on questions most frequently asked by parents of children diagnosed with autism. Well organized, it is written in user-friendly language. At the end of the book there is a recommended reading list, a glossary, a resource guide, descriptions of current treatments, and a list of national and international autism organizations.

552. *This Is Asperger Syndrome.* Gagnon, Elisa and Brenda Smith Myles; illustrated by Sachi Tahara. Shawnee Mission, KS: Autism Asperger Publishing, 1999. 20 pp. ISBN: 0967251419.

This is a wonderful educational resource that can be used in a classroom since it helps develop an understanding and awareness for children with Asperger syndrome and their peers. It is a great tool for helping students with Asperger syndrome learn about some of the characteristics they do not understand about themselves. It can also be a helpful resource for family members of children with Asperger syndrome. "Notes on Asperger Syndrome" on the last page summarize common characteristics of an individual with Asperger syndrome. Includes black and white cartoon drawings.

553. *The Autism Encyclopedia.* Neisworth, John T. and Pamela S. Wolfe, editors. Baltimore: Paul H. Brookes Publishing, 2005. 306 pp. ISBN: 1557667950; ISBN2: 1557666717.

Contributed by more than one hundred autism experts from various disciplines, this comprehensive encyclopedia provides definitions and descriptions of terms related to the study and treatment of autism and other pervasive development disorders. Cross-references for abbreviations appear throughout the encyclopedia, which lead the reader to the spelled-out term. In many instances, one or more related terms of interest are listed at the end of the entry as a cross-reference. Selected screening, assessment, and instructional materials are listed separately in Appendix A. Appendix B lists government, professional, and advocacy organizations. It is a nicely organized and valuable resource for teachers, parents, and professionals.

554. *An Asperger Dictionary of Everyday Expressions.* Stuart-Hamilton, Ian. London: New York: Jessica Kinglsey Publishers, 2004. 240 pp. ISBN: 1843101521.

This dictionary is put together particularly for people with Asperger's syndrome and other autism spectrum disorders who generally have difficulty interpreting everyday phrases that must be interpreted symbolically rather than literally. It provides definitions of the common everyday phrases that are mostly used among British English speakers. However, there are a considerable number of common American English phrases as well as some Australian phrases. In the interest of keeping this dictionary rather small, it does not include historical phrases, contemporary slang, and single ambiguous words. A detailed guide to using the dictionary is provided.

555. *The Encyclopedia of Autism Spectrum Disorders.* Turkington, Carol and Ruth Anan. Series: Facts on File Library of Health and Living. New York: Facts on File, 2007. 324 pp. ISBN: 0816060029; ISBN2: 9780816060023.

Part of the Facts on File Library of Health and Living series, this title provides the most current information on autism spectrum disorders. It includes more than three hundred entries that address different types of autism, treatments, social impact, possible causes, and much more. Entries are arranged alphabetically, with the length of entry varying from two or three sentences to several pages. Certain terms that are defined elsewhere in this encyclopedia are capitalized and listed at the end of some of the entries. Cross-references are used to refer the reader from unused to preferred terms. It includes topics in three key areas: autism spectrum disorders, legal discussion of relevant topics, and school-related issues. The six appendices list many new organizations, websites, state autism organizations, autism resources by state, collaborative programs of excellence in autism, and clinical trials for autistic disorder. An index and a glossary are included. It is a well-recommended encyclopedia as a reference guide for parents, teachers, and professionals. "[T]his one provides useful information written in an accessible style." *Booklist*

Down Syndrome

556. *Down Syndrome: A Resource Handbook.* Tingey, Carol, editor. Austin, TX: Pro-ed, 1991. 209 pp. ISBN: 0890793115.

This book is divided into four parts. The first part discusses the basic medical issues of Down syndrome, physical characteristics, chromosome analysis, treatment approaches, and medical considerations. The second part covers a triad of family concerns, including family counseling. The third part explains the importance of gross motor and speech and language development in individuals with Down syndrome. The last part discusses the transition into school and from school into adult life for individuals with Down syndrome. Black and white photographs and an index are included. This should be a useful tool for teachers and parents of children with Down syndrome.

Dyslexia and Other Learning Disabilities

557. *Learning Disabilities.* Knox, Jean McBee. Series: Encyclopedia of Health, Psychological Disorders and Their Treatment. New York: Chelsea House, 1989. 100 pp. ISBN: 0791000494; ISBN2: 0791005291.

Part of the Encyclopedia of Health, Psychological Disorders and Their Treatment series, this volume explains learning disabilities, such as dyslexia, dyscalculia, and related ailments. Possible causes, symptoms, and current treatments are discussed. The book also chronicles the growing knowledge researchers have recently amassed about these disabilities, including programs and treatments that are now available to learning-disabled individuals. In addition to black and white photographs, an index, and a glossary, this book also includes a list of associations and organizations that can provide information on learning disabilities and facilities and programs that treat the learning disabled.

558. *The Encyclopedia of Learning Disabilities.* Turkington, Carol and Joseph R. Harris. Series: Facts on File Library of Health and Living. New York: Facts on File, 2006. 304 pp. ISBN: 0816063990; ISBN2: 08160644008.

Part of the Facts on File Library of Health and Living series, this revised and updated second edition includes the most current information on learning disabilities. Entries are arranged alphabetically, with the length of entry varying from two or three sentences to several pages. Certain terms that are defined elsewhere in this encyclopedia are capitalized and listed at the end of some of the entries. Cross-references are used to refer the reader from unused to preferred terms. It includes approximately 1,000 entries on key terms, legislation, drugs, diagnostic tests, and much more related to learning disabilities. The entries range from basic terms to highly technical, from the matter-of-fact to the controversial. The six appendices include many new organizations, government sources of health, assistive technology resources, hotlines, commercial technology resources, and books of interest to people with learning disabilities. A glossary is included as well as the detailed index, which includes key words, names, legislation, court cases, standardized tests, and drugs. It is a well-recommended encyclopedia as a reference guide for parents, teachers, and professionals. "[T]his edition offers a wealth of information useful to teachers, health-care providers, and parents as they seek to communicate and learn about particular developmental and learning problems." *Booklist*

PHYSICAL

Blindness and Visual Impairments

559. *The Encyclopedia of Blindness and Vision Impairment.* Sardegna, Jill, Susan Shelly, Allan Richard Rutzen, and Scott M. Steidl. Series: Facts on

File Library of Health and Living. New York: Facts on File, 2002. 333 pp. ISBN: 0816042802.

As one of the titles in the Facts on File Library of Health and Living series, this second updated volume is an excellent resource for professionals and parents. Entries are arranged alphabetically, with the length of entry varying from two or three sentences to several pages. Certain terms that are defined elsewhere in this encyclopedia are capitalized and listed at the end of some of the entries. Cross-references are used to refer the reader from unused to preferred terms. More than five hundred entries cover a wide range of blindness and vision impairment topics such as bifocals, cataracts, eye drops, and venous occlusion. Geographic locations as well as important individuals are also included. The twelve excellent appendices list disability databases, dog-guide schools, federal agencies, national organizations, schools, radio reading services, and rehabilitation services (by state). A bibliography and an index complete this book. "[I]ts coverage and convenience make *The Encyclopedia of Blindness and Vision Impairment* unique." *Booklist*

Deafness and Hearing Impairments

560. *The Encyclopedia of Deafness and Hearing Disorders.* Turkington, Carol and Allen E. Sussman. Series: Facts on File Library of Health and Living. New York: Facts on File, 2004. 294 pp. ISBN: 0816056153.

As one of the titles in the Facts on File Library of Health and Living, this second revised and updated edition with over six hundred entries is an excellent resource for professionals and parents. Entries are arranged alphabetically, with the length of entry varying from two or three sentences to several pages. Certain terms that are defined elsewhere in this encyclopedia are capitalized and listed at the end of some of the entries. Cross-references are used to refer the reader from unused to preferred terms. Entries cover a wide range of deafness and hearing loss topics such as digital hearing aids, hearing-ear dogs, and tuning forks. Geographic locations as well as important individuals are also included. Fourteen excellent appendices list statewide services, devices for people with hearing loss, health care delivery and special services, performance groups, a list of periodicals, summer camps for deaf and hard-of-hearing children, where to learn communication skills, as well as print sources, a bibliography, and an index. "[P]rovides solid, easily digested, dependable information." *Booklist*

Sign Language

561. *The American Sign Language Phrase Book.* Fant, Louie J., Barbara Bernstein Fant, and Betty G. Miller. Dubuque, IA: McGraw-Hill Contemporary Learning, 2008. 384 pp. ISBN: 0071497137; ISBN: 9780071497138.

The third edition of this popular title, which is written to make communication with deaf individuals easier by illustrating frequently used phrases, is an indispensable guide. This resource provides the necessary graphics for teaching those who want to converse with deaf individuals. The first two chapters provide instructions for using the book and explain the major components of American Sign Language (ASL). The remaining sixteen chapters are divided into categories that reflect everyday life, such as greetings, getting acquainted, health, weather, family, school, food and drink, clothing, sports, travel, animals and colors, civics, religion, technology and numbers including time, dates, and money. A dictionary/ index and an appendix that explains the manual alphabet, which allows individuals to fingerspell English words, are included.

562. *Number Signs for Everyone: Numbering in American Sign Language.* Mac-Dougall, Cinnie. San Diego, CA: Dawn Sign Press, 2008. 95 pp. with DVD. ISBN: 1581210574; ISBN: 9781581210576.

This valuable resource provides over 1,000 illustrations of number signs that are used in American Sign Language. The introductory chapter explains how to read the illustrations and demonstrates the four basic parameters used in every sign: handshape, palm orientation, location, and movement. In addition, the importance of movements when signing is explained because this is the most difficult element to show in sign illustration. The first chapter illustrates numbers. The next three chapters illustrate signs for money, finances, and measurements. Signs for time units and the relation of physical space to time are provided in the next three chapters. Chapters 8 and 9 illustrate numbers used in age and sports. The remaining chapters provide signs for location concepts, personal numbers, and scientific numbers. A ninety-minute DVD with voice-over English subtitles containing signs that coincide with the topics in the book is included.

563. *The Gallaudet Dictionary of American Sign Language.* Valli, Clayton, editor; illustrated by Peggy Swartzel Lott, Daniel Renner, and Rob Hills. Washington, DC: Gallaudet University Press, 2005. 558 pp. with DVD. ISBN: 1563682826.

This comprehensive dictionary of American Sign Language (ASL) can be used by those who are learning to sign as well as advanced signers and hearing-impaired individuals. This volume's extensive introduction contains a history of the American deaf community and an explanation of ASL as a language. Classifiers that enable signers to express whole phrases with a single sign are illustrated in a section because of their important and wide use in ASL. The alphabetical list contains more than 3,000 black-lined ASL sign illustrations, including synonyms. A complete index of English synonyms for every sign enables users to cross-reference words and signs. A fully searchable DVD is included that has native ASL signers demonstrate how to form each of the over 3,000 signs. The user can slow the action as well as make the action a full screen image. This extraordinary volume is highly recommended for all libraries.

Chapter 6

Educators/Parents/Professionals Resources

This chapter contains 107 resources for educators, parents, and professionals, which have been put together by practicing clinicians, certified therapists, and researchers who have extensive experience and are specialized in the fields of various disabilities. These invaluable resources provide educators a wide range of practical intervention strategies to promote learning, social development, communication, and appropriate behavior in the classroom. In addition, some of the resources offer parents and family members outstanding suggestions and guidelines in recognizing, understanding, and coping with their children who have various disorders and disabilities.

GENERAL

564. *Disability Studies in Education.* New York: Peter Lang, 2005–2008. 5 volumes. Volume 1: *Reading Resistance: Discourses of Exclusion in Desegregation and Inclusion Debates.* Ferri, Beth A. and David J. Connor, editors. ISBN: 9780820474281. Volume 2: *Vital Questions Facing Disability Studies in Education.* Danforth, Scot and Susan L. Gable. ISBN: 9780820478340. Volume 3: *Disability Studies in Education: Readings in Theory and Method.* Gable, Susan L. ISBN: 9780820455495. Volume 4: *Creating the Continuum: A History of Specialized Support for People with Intellectual Disabilities and the Future of Inclusive Reform.* Ferguson, Phillip M. and Dianne L. Ferguson. ISBN: 9780820486123. Volume 5: *Urban Narratives: Portraits in Progress, Life at the Intersections of Learning Disability, Race, & Social Class.* Connor, David J. ISBN: 9780820488042. Level: Educators/Professionals.

These five volumes in the Disability Studies in Education series provide innovative research that challenges the traditional ways of thinking about individuals with disabilities and their educational experiences in classrooms. Each volume, written by researchers and educators, contains the most current research related to disability studies. Some of the topics covered are reading resistance in inclusive education, segregation in education, labeling, accessible information technology in education, internationalization and the impact of disability studies, critical analysis of public school programs for students with emotional and behavioral disorders, the family and the continuum, the future of inclusive services, normalizing practices of schooling, stereotypes and degrees of self-inscription, and the politics of empowerment, such as awareness and choices. These books should benefit educators and professionals who are new to the field of disability studies as well as current practitioners. Bibliographic references and an index are included in each volume.

565. *Health Problems in the Classroom, 6–12: An A–Z Reference Guide for Educators.* Huffman, Dolores M., Karen Lee Fontaine, and Bernadette K. Price. Thousand Oaks, CA: Corwin Press, 2003. 456 pp. ISBN: 0761945636. Level: Educators/Professionals.

This exceptional volume, the companion book to *Health Problems in the Classroom PreK–6*, is an indispensable resource for educators in today's inclusive classroom. The authors state that the classroom teacher needs to respond to classroom emergencies, recognize potential health problems, and provide support to their students with chronic illnesses or disabilities that teachers are likely to encounter in their classrooms. The information in this easy-to-use book is concise and practical. Each entry provides a description, primary group affected, signs and symptoms, classroom guidelines, attendance guidelines, medications, communication, and resource website. Part I addresses health issues in the classroom such as illnesses, injuries, disabilities, family and community concerns, stigma and self-esteem. Part II is an A–Z listing of health problems that include anxiety disorders, Asperger's disorder, attention deficit/hyperactivity disorder, autism, bipolar disorder, cerebral palsy, depression, Down syndrome, eating disorders (anorexia and bulimia), hearing loss, schizophrenia, vision problems, and many more. Part III contains eleven health policies and procedures: hand washing, bleeding, care of casts, care of tracheostomy, tube feedings, medical emergencies, pets in the classrooms, testicular self-examination, skin cancer prevention, immunizations, and EpiPen. A bibliography and index are included.

566. *Health Problems in the Classroom, PreK–6: An A–Z Reference Guide for Educators.* Huffman, Dolores M., Karen Lee Fontaine, and Bernadette K. Price. Thousand Oaks, CA: Corwin Press, 2003. 372 pp. ISBN: 0761945776. Level: Educators/Professionals.

This exceptional volume, the companion book to *Health Problems in the Classroom 6–12*, is an indispensable resource for educators in today's inclusive classroom. The authors state that the classroom teacher needs to respond to classroom emergencies, recognize potential health problems, and provide support to their students with chronic illnesses or disabilities that teachers are likely to encounter in their classrooms. The information in this easy-to-use book is concise and practical. Each entry provides a description, primary group affected, signs and symptoms, classroom guidelines, attendance guidelines, medications, communication, and resource website. Part I addresses health issues in the classroom such as illnesses, injuries, disabilities, family and community concerns, stigma, and self-esteem. Part II is an A–Z listing of health problems that include anxiety disorders, Asperger's disorder, attention deficit/hyperactivity disorder, autism, bipolar disorder, cerebral palsy, depression, Down syndrome, eating disorder (anorexia), hearing loss, schizophrenia, vision problems, and many more. Part III contains nine health policies and procedures: hand washing, care of minor cuts, care of casts, care of tracheostomy, tube feedings, medical emergencies, pets in the classrooms, immunizations, and EpiPen. A bibliography and index are included.

567. *Helping Kids with Special Needs: Resources for Parenting and Teaching Children with Emotional and Neurological Disorders.* Nekola, Julie. Wayzata, MN: Nekola Books, 2001. 296 pp. ISBN: 0970679106. Level: Educators/Parents.

This resource explains emotional and neurological disorders in children. Disorders covered are anxiety, attention deficit disorder, autism, bipolar, cerebral palsy, depression, Down syndrome, eating disorders, learning disorders, mental retardation, schizophrenia, and others. The author discusses information regarding symptoms, potential causes, and types of treatments for each of these disorders. There are 2,700 references to additional sources such as organizations, books, websites, videos, periodicals, and vendors. In addition, this resource identifies two hundred references to books written for children. A glossary with 250 related terms, an additional section on resources for teachers and siblings, and an index are included.

568. *Exceptional Teaching: A Comprehensive Guide for Including Students with Disabilities.* Pierson, Jim. Cincinnati, OH: Standard Publishing, 2002. 240 pp. ISBN: 0784712557. Level: Educators/Professionals.

Compiled by the founder and director of a Christian foundation for the disabled, this resource provides exhaustive coverage of physical, learning, and emotional disabilities. Each of the first sixteen chapters provides a detailed definition of a disability, including lists of categories, characteristics, helpful information, causes, and exceptional teaching tips. One of the features of this resource is that it contains multiple disability issues that are often overlooked in other guides, such as deaf-blind, severe and multiple disabilities, students who are functionally delayed, and students with developmental delays. In spite of the fact that this resource has some text in the chapters referencing Christian education and two chapters that specifically address providing Christian education and ministering to families, it does not distract from the overall value of the comprehensive nature of disability coverage. A resource section listing national disability organizations and ministry resources and an index are included.

EMOTIONAL

Depression

569. *Understanding Teenage Depression: A Guide to Diagnosis, Treatment and Management.* Empfield, Maureen and Nicholas Bakalar. New York: H. Holt, 2001. 250 pp. ISBN: 0805067612. Level: Educators/Parents.

Empfield, a psychiatrist who has extensive experience with teenagers, has compiled this helpful and in-depth guide that examines depression among teenagers. Using her own clinical experience and the latest scientific findings, Empfield provides educators and parents with the necessary information in order to understand how depression develops, how depression can be diagnosed, and what treatment options are available. First-person accounts from teenagers who themselves have suffered from depression are used to illustrate chapter topics and key concepts. Chapter topics include identifying the various types of depression, depression diagnoses, depression, and which teenagers are at risk. Additional topics covered are concerns about suicide and various treatment options, including therapy, medication, and hospitalization. Parents can peruse the chapter titled "Legal and Ethical Concerns" in order to understand the concepts of consent and confidentiality, particularly as these concepts apply to treatment options. An extensive list of resources, organizations, support groups, and an index are included. "An invaluable resource for teens, parents, teachers, and others affected by a growing epidemic." *Booklist*

570. *Depression Sourcebook : Basic Consumer Health Information about Unipolar Depression, Bipolar Disorder, Dysthymia, Seasonal Affective Disorder, Postpartum Depression, and Other Depressive Disorders, Including Facts about Populations at Special Risk, Coexisting Medical Conditions, Symptoms, Treatment Options, and Suicide Prevention; along with Statistical Data, a Glossary of Related Terms, and a Directory of Resources for Additional Help and Information.* Judd, Sandra J., editor. Series: Health

Reference. Detroit: Omnigraphics, 2008. 673 pp. ISBN: 0780810031; ISBN: 9780780810037. Level: Educators/Professionals.

This second edition of this title from the Health Reference series is divided into seven parts that cover broad topics regarding depression. Each part is further divided into multiple chapters that are devoted to specific topics pertaining to depression. Part I provides a comprehensive introduction to depression, the various types of depression, and chapters devoted to specific age ranges and gender issues. The following four parts cover medical concerns, risk factors, causes, symptoms, and treatment options, including pharmacological treatments. Part VI is devoted to suicide. The final part contains a glossary, a directory of resources for information about depression and its treatment, and a list of mental health hotlines including contact information. An index is included.

571. *Helping Students Overcome Depression and Anxiety: A Practical Guide.* Merell, Kenneth W. Series: The Guilford Practical Intervention in the Schools. New York: Guilford Press, 2008. 265 pp. ISBN: 1593856482; ISBN: 9781593856489. Level: Educators/Professionals.

This updated edition in the Guilford Practical Intervention in the Schools series, written by a professor of school psychology, provides practical, everyday guidelines for counselors, psychologists, social workers, mental health specialists, and special education consultants who work with depressed students. Teachers and support staff should also benefit from this resource, which focuses on helping students, specifically in school settings. The introductory section includes an index of intervention programs and general intervention strategies and a list of specific treatment techniques for depression and anxiety. The first two chapters explain the different ways depression and anxiety are developed and internalized. The third chapter contains guidelines for assessment and intervention, and the fourth chapter explores social and emotional learning. The next four chapters provide information regarding comprehensive intervention programs and strategies for individuals suffering from depression. Chapters 9 and 10 focus on treatment options for those experiencing anxiety disorders. The final chapter provides referral guidelines for mental health counseling, including medications and alternative treatments. An appendix containing twenty-six reproducible worksheets, an extensive list of references, an author index, and subject index complete the book.

Depression-Related Disorders

572. *If Your Adolescent Has an Anxiety Disorder: An Essential Resource for Parents.* Foa, Edna B. and Linda Wasmer Andrews. Series: Adolescent Mental Health Initiative. New York: Oxford University Press, 2006. 227 pp. ISBN: 9780195181517. Level: Parents.

This resource, one of the titles in the Adolescent Mental Health Initiative series, is a comprehensive guide for parents whose teenagers may be afflicted with an anxiety disorder. The introductory section provides instructions for using the book. The next section defines anxiety disorders by exploring the causes for anxiety disorders; the seven types of anxiety disorders; the psychology, biology, and genetics of anxiety; the benefits of seeking help; and the adverse consequences of ignoring anxiety disorders. The following four sections address social anxiety disorder, generalized anxiety disorder, obsessive-compulsive disorder, and posttraumatic stress disorder. Each section defines the specific disorder, lists causes and contributors, identifies signs and symptoms, and offers diagnosis and treatment options. Section 7 covers treatment options and recovery strategies such as choosing an appropriate therapist and taking medications. Parents will also find suggestions for dealing with insurance concerns and for helping their teenagers with school issues. The final section offers parents advice for obtaining the necessary services for their teenagers and for dispelling myths about anxiety disorders. Case studies illustrate key concepts. An appendix contains diagnostic criteria. A glossary, extensive additional reading material, organizations, a bibliography and an index are included. This excellent title is highly recommended. "An essential addition to public, middle, and high school libraries." *Library Journal*

Eating Disorders

573. *Take Charge of Your Child's Eating Disorder: A Physician's Step-by-Step Guide to Defeating Anorexia and Bulimia.* Carlton, Pamela. New York: Marlowe & Company, 2007. 226 pp. ISBN: 1569242631; ISBN2: 9781569242636. Level: Parents.

This is a very up-to-date resource for today's parents who need assistance in being pro-active with a child who has an eating disorder. This comprehensive text is divided into five manageable parts: Part 1 covers background information; Part 2 covers proven methods to help with a child's social and medical concerns; Part 3 covers treatment options; Part 4 covers what to do at home and at school; Part 5 covers practical financial concerns that parents may have to face. Two of the most valuable chapters that parents can appreciate and use are "Why My Child? What Did I Do Wrong?" and "Accepting the Truth and Moving Forward." The appendices contain excellent information: Internet resources, additional reading material, information about getting insurance assistance, and resources that physicians can consult. "An empowering guide for parents who know or suspect their child has an eating disorder." *Kirkus Reviews*

574. *The Parent's Guide to Childhood Eating Disorders.* Herrin, Marcia. New York: Henry Holt, 2002. 324 pp. ISBN: 0805066497. Level: Parents.

This comprehensive resource written by a renowned clinician in the area of eating disorders provides parents with essential information to help their children cope with and overcome eating disorders. The information is divided into three parts: "Identifying an Eating Disorder," "Taking Action," and "Healthy Eating Guide." Each part is subdivided into manageable sections that cover a wide variety of topics regarding eating disorders such as who's at risk, boys at risk, parental discussions, avoiding parent traps, developing a food plan, and reaching out for professional help. The author provides guidelines and activities that have been proven to produce successful results. In addition, sound and solid advice based on proven case studies, including the author's personal account of her own battle with anorexia during her teenage years, is provided. Appendices include "Diagnosing Eating Disorders" and "Body Weight Assessments." Additional reading material, a list of American and Canadian support and advocacy organizations, websites, residential and hospital programs listed by state (United States) and by province (Canada), and an index are included. "An excellent guide to children's eating disorders." *Library Journal*

575. *Boys Get Anorexia Too: Coping with Male Eating Disorders.* Langley, Jenny. London; Thousand Oaks, CA: Paul Chapman Publishing, 2006. 178 pp. ISBN: 1412920213. Level: Parents.

This excellent resource for parents, written by an author from her personal experience with her own son's eating disorder, covers a rarely explored or discussed topic: boys can develop eating disorders too. Part 1 has thirteen detailed chapters covering topics such as triggers for boys and what to look for, the effects on the family and treatment options, and other eating disorders that boys may develop. A suggested suggesting reading list and a list of useful British organizations conclude Part 1. In Part 2, Joe, the author's son, narrates how he developed anorexia, how it affected his relationships with his family and friends, and how his treatment was a success. Joe also tells of the not-so-successful times during his recovery. This exceptional work that reveals the taboo nature and almost shameful aspect associated with boys having an eating disorder fulfills Joe's hope that "If one other family benefits from reading this book it will have been well worthwhile." "Any parent or carer concerned about a boy who may be developing or has already developed an eating disorder will find this book useful and supportive even when it is talking about the most difficult problems that affect sufferers and their families." *Signpost*

576. *Treating Bulimia in Adolescents: A Family-Based Approach.* LeGrange, Daniel and James Lock. New York: Guilford Press, 2007. 260 pp. ISBN: 1593854145; ISBN2: 9781593854140. Level: Educators/Parents.

The authors of this volume have a combined total of over thirty years of professional experience in the field of child psychiatry and are currently involved in treating bulimic adolescents and their families. Although they compiled the information in this text for clinicians who work with families and teenagers experiencing eating disorders, particularly bulimia, this book provides teachers and parents with the information they need in order to work with their bulimic teenagers in overcoming this disorder. Suggestions for treatment options, as well as some insight into the reasons why teenagers develop eating disorders, will empower adults who usually feel helpless when confronting this situation. This is a companion text to the authors' 2005 work titled *Help Your Teenager Beat an Eating Disorder.*

577. *Help Your Teenager Beat an Eating Disorder.* Lock, James and Daniel LeGrange. New York: Guilford Press, 2005. 296 pp. ISBN: 1572309083. Level: Parents.

Detailed scenarios throughout this book present realistic challenges for parents to evaluate and respond to their child's eating disorder. This in-depth text is divided into three parts: "Getting Started," "Understanding Eating Disorders," and "Making Treatment Work." The very first chapter sets the tone for the entire book by telling parents about the importance and urgency of acting immediately once an eating disorder is suspected. The chapter titled "Don't Waste Time on 'Why?'" is most helpful to parents. Signs, warnings, symptoms, and options for treatment as well as good explanations, definitions, insights into behavior, and the value of family involvement in recovery are covered very thoroughly by the authors, who are two practicing psychologists. An excellent extensive list of resources of diagnosis and treatment options is provided with contact information for facilities not only in the United States, but also in Canada, the United Kingdom, and Australia. Additional reading material and an index complete the work. "The book of high quality and would be of help to any family facing this difficult situation." *Doody's Review*

578. *I'm Like So Fat! Helping Your Teen Make Healthy Choices about Eating and Exercise in a Weight-Obsessed World.* Neumark-Sztainer, Dianne. New York: Guilford Press, 2005. 317 pp. ISBN: 1572309806. Level: Parents.

Written by a public health professor who investigates for Project EAT (Eating Among Teens), this resource provides excellent background information and guidelines for parents. Each chapter begins with a question, such as "How Can We Protect Our Teens When Society Pushes Fat but Promotes Thin?" The sections that follow attempt to answer those specific questions. Interactive activities, dialogue, and suggestions are found in every chapter. End sections include resources for parents and teenagers, both print and online, a bibliography, and an index. "In this thorough and sensible book, Neumark-Sztainer (epidemiology, Univ. of Minnesota) shows parents how to help their teens make wise food choices—now and in the future." *Library Journal*

579. *Just a Little Too Thin: How to Pull Your Child Back from the Brink of an Eating Disorder.* Strober, Michael A. and Meg Schneider. Cambridge, MA: DaCapo Lifelong, 2005. 235 pp. ISBN: 0738210188. Level: Parents.

This resource provides background information for parents whose children have eating disorders. The authors use brief, realistic scenarios throughout the chapters to illustrate specific concerns associated with eating disorders. The chapter topics explore important factors that may contribute to the development of eating disorders in teenagers, such as the media factor, which promotes the idea that only very thin women are beautiful. Additional topics include the role the family plays in a child developing an eating disorder and the emotional undercurrent present in both the child and the family as a whole. The authors use a straightforward approach in presenting the information that parents need to know and what signs to look for in their children in order to help their children overcome an eating disorder and possibly prevent children from initially developing a disorder. The appendix contains BMI (body mass index) charts. Additional reading material and an index are included.

580. *If Your Adolescent Has an Eating Disorder: An Essential Resource for Parents.* Walsh, Timothy and V. L. Cameron. Series: Adolescent Mental Health Initiative. Oxford: Oxford University Press, 2005. 182 pp. ISBN: 0195181530. Level: Parents.

Written by a medical expert in the field of eating disorders, this resource provides a comprehensive guide for parents that will reassure them that they can help their teenagers overcome and possibly prevent developing an eating disorder. The introductory chapters of Section 1 provide an overview of eating disorders. Section 2 details specific eating disorders, such as anorexia, its conditions, and factors. Section 3 provides parents with essential information that enables them to evaluate treatment options for their teenagers. Section 4 illustrates what activities a teenager with eating disorders experiences on a daily basis. Section 5 presents suggestions that may enable parents to prevent their teens from developing eating disorders. The final section offers advice for all individuals who want to prevent and help teenagers who have eating disorders. This excellent title, both very readable and nonjudgmental, uses actual case stories to illustrate the topics. A glossary, extensive additional reading material, organizations, a bibliography, and an index are included. "The case stories that are woven through the book wonderfully illuminate the realities of eating disorders while effectively embracing the reader with support and the reality that their family is not alone." *National Eating Disorders Association*

Mental Illness

581. *If Your Adolescent Has Schizophrenia: An Essential Resource for Parents.* Gur, Raquel E. and Ann Braden Johnson. Series: Adolescent Mental Health Initiative. New York: Oxford University Press, 2006. 163 pp. ISBN: 0195182111. Level: Parents.

This resource, one of the titles in the Adolescent Mental Health Initiative series, is a comprehensive guide for parents regarding schizophrenia, a disorder that afflicts almost 2.2 million individuals. The information in this guide should enable parents to identify warning signs in their teenagers so that appropriate, meaningful, and timely medical support can be undertaken. The introductory chapters define schizophrenia and list signs and symptoms, causes and diagnosis, and other related problems. Section 3 focuses on getting the right treatment for teenagers. Topics in this section include medication, behavioral and psychological therapies, hospitalization, outpatient therapy, and health care system details. Section 4 contains topics and issues that pertain to everyday life, such as dealing with feelings, dealing with the stigma of mental illness, handling family dynamics, and finding patient and family support. Section 5 explores various current findings that suggest methods of preventing schizophrenia as well as the many challenges associated with this disorder. The final section offers parents advice for obtaining the necessary services for their teenagers and for educating others about schizophrenia. Appendices contain diagnostic criteria for schizophrenia and assertive community treatment (ACT) and supported employment programs. A glossary, extensive additional reading material, organizations, a bibliography, and an index are included. "Unique and invaluable, concise, accurate, informative, and instructive." National Institute of Mental Health (NIMH)

Multiple Emotional Disabilities

582. *If Your Adolescent Has Depression or Bipolar Disorder: An Essential Resource for Parents.* Evans, Dwight L. and Linda Wasmer Andrews. Series: Adolescent Mental Health Initiative. New York: Oxford University Press, 2005. 197 pp. ISBN: 019518209X. Level: Parents.

Evans, who is a medical expert in the field of mood disorders, has written this comprehensive guide along with Andrews, one of the titles in the Adolescent Mental Health Initiative series. This resource will help parents understand their teenagers with depression or bipolar disorder. The introductory sections define mental illness, particularly depression and bipolar disorder, and identify characteristics, causes, and risk factors. Section 3 addresses treatment options, including medications, therapy, parental role in the treatment process, mental health professionals and services, and hospitalization. Section 4 focuses on the day-to-day living situations and struggles faced by teenagers and family members. Suggestions for helping teenagers at home and at school, as well as support systems for parents, are included. Section 5 provides information that should empower parents to reduce risks and recognize those red flags that indicate potential personal harm for teenagers with mood disorders. The final section offers advice for all individuals who want to help teenagers live productive and healthy lives. This excellent title is very readable and nonjudgmental. A glossary, extensive additional reading material, organizations, a bibliography, websites, and an index are included. "Evans and Andrews act as Sherpas through the thickets of adolescent depression and bipolar disorder, guides who point out the warning signs and who offer support and advice for the depressed or the wild emotional ride of a bipolar teenager." *Kirkus Reviews*

LEARNING

Attention-Deficit Hyperactivity Disorder (AD/HD)

583. *A Parent's Guide to Attention Deficit Disorders.* Bain, Lisa J. New York: Dell Publishing, 1991. 216 pp. ISBN: 0440506395. Level: Parents.

Written by a science and medical writer who works with doctors at the Children's Hospital of Philadelphia, this guide discusses causes of attention-deficit disorder (ADD), its diagnosis, treatment, therapy, and taking care of social and emotional needs of an individual with ADD. It draws on the expertise of pediatricians, neurologists, child psychologists, and social workers at the hospital and its affiliates. This book should help parents understand their children with ADD. It includes a list of support groups and organizations specializing in ADD that can help parents find the appropriate treatment and support. "As a parent resource, Bain's book is especially thorough and well balanced in its approach, and a superb value." *Library Journal*

584. *Attention-Deficit/Hyperactivity Disorder: A Practical Guide for Teachers.* Cooper, Paul and Katherine Bilton. Series: Resource Materials for Teachers. London: David Fulton, 2002. 106 pp. ISBN: 1853467316; ISBN2: 9781853467318. Level: Educators/Professionals.

This second revised title, part of the Resource Materials for Teachers series, is a well-organized guide for teachers dealing with students with attention-deficit/ hyperactivity disorder (AD/HD), a condition that affects approximately one in every twenty-five children. Divided into six chapters, this book discusses the following topics: the nature of AD/HD; the assessment of AD/HD; approaching AD/HD from the teacher's perspective; interventions that can be used by teachers to help children with AD/HD; the role of medication in the treatment of AD/HD; and special issues and concerns related to AD/HD. In addition, three appendices at the end of the book cover diagnostic criteria, glossary of AD/HD-related terms, and a list of relevant addresses and resources. A list of references and an index are included.

585. *Educating Children with AD/HD: A Teacher's Manual.* Cooper, Paul and Fintan J. O'Regan. London; New York: Routledge/Falmer, 2001. 116 pp. ISBN: 0415213878. Level: Educators/Professionals.

The authors have written this comprehensive guide based on their experience of working on a daily basis with children with attention-deficit/hyperactivity disorder (AD/HD). The guide is divided into three parts. Part 1 deals with understanding AD/HD in terms of its origins and the biological, psychological, and social influences on its development. Part 2 covers some of the basic principles and practices related to effective intervention, including specific educational interventions and behavior management techniques. Part 3 illustrates, using case studies, examples of the many different ways in which AD/HD manifests itself in the classroom situation and gives suggestions for school-based interventions. This book includes two appendices. The first appendix presents the diagnostic criteria for AD/HD, while the second appendix presents information regarding hyperkinetic disorder. Additional references for more information are included. It is a useful teaching manual for teachers and other educational professionals.

586. *Maybe You Know My Kid: A Parents' Guide to Identifying Understanding, and Helping Your Child with Attention-Deficit Hyperactivity Disorder.* Fowler, Mary Cahill. Secaucus, NJ: Carol Publishing Group, 1999. 265 pp. ISBN: 1559724900. Level: Parents.

In this very well-researched third edition of her book, the author has created a very useful guide for parents just like her whose children have attention-deficit hyperactivity disorder (ADHD). Chapters are organized according to age level, from infancy through adulthood. Each chapter describes the patterns and characteristics of ADHD at a specific stage of child development and, where possible, outlines the recommended management approaches. Samples of behavior management charts at the end of the book should be very helpful. Includes an index and a list of national organizations for information, support, and advocacy. This highly recommended book offers outstanding guidelines in recognizing, understanding, and helping children with ADHD.

587. *Attention Deficit Hyperactivity Disorder: Questions & Answers for Parents.* Greenberg, Gregory S. Champaign, IL: Research Press, 1991. 133 pp. ISBN: 0878223223. Level: Parents.

Written by two clinical child psychologists, this book uses a questions and answers format. Chapters 1 and 2 cover questions about the problems most often observed in children with attention-deficit hyperactivity disorder (ADHD) and effective available treatments. Chapters 3 through 8 answer questions concerning the particular behavioral techniques found useful in helping children with ADHD. Chapter 9 deals with questions that help teenagers with ADHD. Chapter 10 answers parents' concerns about their children's behavior at school. The last chapter summarizes the techniques parents can use in troubleshooting if further problems arise. An index and additional resources are included.

588. *100 Ideas for Supporting Pupils with ADHD.* Kewley, Geoff D. London: Continuum International Publishing, 2008. 150 pp. ISBN: 08226496601; ISBN2: 9780826496607. Level: Educators.

Divided into thirteen sections, this well-organized book covers the following topics pertaining to attention-deficit hyperactivity disorder (ADHD): preparing to teach the child with ADHD; lesson planning; classroom environment; behavioral challenges; strategies for helping with organization; specific learning difficulties; handwriting problems; enhancing self-esteem and social skills; medication; gifted children with ADHD; parents and colleagues; and transitions from primary school to higher education. A list of recommended reading and websites is included in the appendix for additional information.

589. *ADHD: Living without Brakes.* Kutscher, Martin L. London: Jessica Kingsley Publishers, 2008. 189 pp. ISBN: 1843108739; ISBN2: 9781843108733. Level: Educators/Parents.

Written by a pediatric neurologist, this well-organized book describes the spectrum of attention-deficit hyperactivity disorder (ADHD), the symptoms, and common difficulties faced by parents of children with ADHD. The author focuses on four rules pertaining to the solutions: 1. positive approach which can improve attitude; 2. importance of keeping calm in order to be able to solve problems logically; 3. keeping organized particularly when it comes to the child's school life; and 4. repeating rules 1, 2, and 3. The role of medication for treating ADHD is also discussed. The book offers helpful information and advice for parents and professionals who are attempting to keep up with children who are "living without brakes." The three appendices list a behavioral checklist, a childhood index of executive functions (ChIEF), books and Internet resources for additional information, references, and black and white illustrations and an index are included.

590. *Teaching Young Children with ADHD: Successful Strategies and Practical Interventions for PreK–3.* Lougy, Richard A., Silvia L. DeRuvo, and

David Rosenthal. Thousand Oaks, CA: Corwin Press, 2007. 188 pp. ISBN: 1412941598; ISBN2: 1412941601. Level: Educators/Professionals.

The authors provide an understanding of attention-deficit hyperactivity disorder (ADHD), with detailed descriptions of how it manifests in preschool and the primary grades, in this well-written, well-researched, and comprehensive book. It is an excellent tool for teachers who face the intense time demands of working with children with ADHD and addresses challenges of these children's educational needs. The authors also provide classroom strategies, information regarding medication, and suggestions for communicating effectively. Three resources are included: Resource A recognizes ADHD in preschool and primary grades; Resource B lists disorders sometimes associated with ADHD; and Resource C discusses childhood conditions that can mimic ADHD in young children. Some illustrations, bibliographical references, and an index are included.

591. *Attention Deficit Disorder Sourcebook: Basic Consumer Health Information about Attention Deficit/Hyperactivity Disorder in Children and Adults.* Mathews, Dawn D., editor. Series: Health Reference. Detroit: Omnigraphics, 2002. 470 pp. ISBN: 0780806247. Level: Educators/Professionals.

This volume, one of the titles in the Health Reference series, is divided into six parts that focus on broad areas of attention-deficit hyperactivity disorder (ADHD). Each part is further divided into chapters that are devoted to single topics within a part. The first three parts provide an overview of ADHD, symptoms, diagnosis, causes of ADHD, and various treatments, including medication therapy, behavior therapy, and tips about creating an individualized education program (IEP). Part 4 discusses ADHD facts for specific populations, such as gifted children, teenagers, and college students. Part 5 provides advice for adults in improving social skills, maintaining close relationships, and finding an ADHD-friendly job. The final part contains a glossary of related terms, a list of support groups, Internet resources, and suggested additional reading.

592. *Academic Success Strategies for Adolescents with Learning Disabilities and ADHD.* Minskoff, Esther H. and David Allsopp. Baltimore: Paul H. Brookes, 2003. 330 pp. ISBN: 1557666253. Level: Educators/Professionals.

This strategy-filled book is for teachers of students with mild disabilities, from middle school to post–high school. The following eight critical areas are discussed: reading, writing, mathematics, advanced thinking, organization, test taking, study skills, and notetaking. Using an assessment component, educators can work one-on-one with students to evaluate each student's learning style, strengths, and weaknesses. The next step for educators is to help these students improve their performance by following the strategies listed in each of the areas as needed. Includes a very unique and helpful website "Learning Toolbox" that expands on the book's strategies with sections specially tailored for students, teachers, and parents. (http://coe.jmu.edu/Learningtoolbox/)

593. *ADHD in the Young Child: A Guide for Parents and Teachers of Young Children with ADHD.* Reimers, Cathy L. and Bruce A. Brunger. Plantation, FL: Specialty Press, 2006. 202 pp. ISBN: 1886941327; ISBN2: 9781886941328. Level: Educators/Parents.

Written specifically for parents and teachers, this interactive book provides practical solutions to common problems related to attention-deficit hyperactivity disorder (ADHD). It has over seventy-five cartoon illustrations and hands-on activities, which children should find motivating. Parents and teachers should be able to engage young children with ADHD in discussing their proper and improper behaviors. The ten chapters address the following topics: understanding ADHD in the preschool child; building self-esteem and improving social skills; communication with the child with ADHD; effective techniques to manage behavior; typical problems and remedies situations that occur at home and at school; assessment and treatment of ADHD; and the parent/teacher survival guide. Support services for parents, suggested readings and videos, helpful charts, lists, and guidelines, and fun stuff for kids are covered in the four appendices, which should be very helpful. This book has a companion book titled *Buzz & Pixie Activity Coloring Book.*

594. *Teaching Teens with ADD and ADHD: A Quick Reference Guide for Teachers and Parents.* Zeigler Dendy, Chris A. Bethesda, MD: Woodbine House, 2000. 352 pp. ISBN: 1890627208. Level: Educators/Parents.

Containing seventy-five, easy-to-implement summaries on key strategies for teaching students with attention-deficit disorder/attention-deficit hyperactivity disorder (ADD/ADHD), this book covers the following topics: what every teacher must know about ADD, assigning effective homework, reasons for school failure and intervention strategies, individualized education plans (IEP), troubleshooting tips, maximizing medication effectiveness at school, tips for mastering math, strategies for behavior management, and common learning problems. Blank checklists and forms are included, which can be used for parent-teacher partnerships and communication. Illustrations are included. Zeigler's 2006 book titled *Teenagers with ADD and ADHD* can be used as a companion book.

595. *Teenagers with ADD and ADHD: A Guide for Parents and Professionals.* Zeigler Dendy, Chris A. Bethesda, MD: Woodbine House, 2006. 415 pp. ISBN: 1890627313; ISBN2: 9781890627317. Level: Educators/Parents.

Written specifically for parents and professionals, this updated and expanded second edition, a companion to *Teaching Teens with ADD and ADHD: A Quick Reference Guide for Teachers and Parents*, looks at the key issues for teenagers with attention-deficit disorder (ADD) or attention-deficit/hyperactivity disorder (ADHD), such as academics, dating, driving, socializing, and greater independence. The author has written this guide using her experience not only as a former teacher, school psychologist, mental health counselor, and administrator, but also as a mother of two sons who struggled to cope with this disorder. She shares her insight on numerous critical topics, from understanding the diagnosis to treatment options, and from behavioral and academic issues to parent involvement and self-advocacy. A chapter on medications provides details on specific drugs, including many new ones, and what research shows about their effectiveness in improving attention, impulse control, and distractibility. Zeigler also advises parents on their role in working with schools to find strategies for academic success. Other parents and professionals who have lived with ADD or ADHD give their insight through their personal experiences. A thoroughly researched and well-organized guide. "[A] valuable resource to which parents will refer even as their teens enter adulthood; highly recommended for all public libraries." *Library Journal*

Autism Spectrum Disorders

596. *Self-Help Skills for People with Autism: A Systematic Teaching Approach.*
Anderson, Stephen R. et al. Series: Topics in Autism. Bethesda, MD: Woodbine House, 2007. 187 pp. ISBN: 9781890627416. Level: Educators/ Parents.

A systematic approach that can be used by parents and educators to teach basic self-care skills for children, ages 24 months to early teens, is the focus of this very useful book, which is part of the Topics in Autism series. The authors emphasize the importance of devoting extra time and effort to teach self-help skills to these autistic children rather than have them dependent on others forever. The process for teaching these skills is explained in detail using the following steps: the specification of the target skills to be taught, task analysis, a systematic approach to instruction, monitoring progress by collecting and analyzing data, and modifying the approach as needed to achieve the target goal. Finally, a chapter is devoted to teaching the four important skills: dressing, personal hygiene, eating, and toileting. Illustrations and appendices containing forms to be used for task analyses, instructional plans, and data collection are included.

597. *Our Journey through High Functioning Autism and Asperger Syndrome: A Roadmap.* Andron, Linda, editor. London; Philadelphia: Jessica Kingsley Publishers, 2001. 191 pp. ISBN: 1853029475. Level: Parents.

This book is an excellent travelers' guide because it is a collection of several families' ways of coping with their own experiences with their children who have autism or Asperger's syndrome. Each of the parents offers specific activities and approaches to aspects of socializing and educating children with autism or Asperger's syndrome. In addition, the families provide valuable perspectives of seeing what challenges are faced by other families and how they deal with them. One of the chapters titled "Humor, Imagination and Empathy in Autism," which was written by one of the sets of parents, is very unique, helpful, and interesting because the authors use simple stick-figure cartoons, representing their two sons with autism and Asperger's syndrome, as tools to help their sons understand their daily lives and activities. The appendix, "Thank You for Trusting Me," contains a collection of comments by the children themselves. Includes a very helpful resource list at the end of the book. These insights should be very valuable to anyone caring for, teaching, or interacting with someone who has to struggle with autism or Asperger's syndrome.

598. *The Social Skills Picture Book: Teaching Play, Emotion, and Communication to Children with Autism.* Baker, Jed. Arlington, TX: Future Horizons, 2001. 197 pp. ISBN: 1885477910. Level: Educators/Parents.

Although mainly designed to discuss effective interpersonal relationships in the classroom environment with autistic students and their teachers, the contents of this book should be equally applicable to teaching social skills to all children. The author offers helpful visual aids to teach social skills and positive interaction. With the use of pictures and scripts, the author explains right and wrong ways to handle various social skills, such as play, emotion, conversation, empathy, and so forth. Since proper social skills do not come naturally to autistic children, and must be taught explicitly, the author of this book does that by breaking down social skills into their components and then explaining what to say, behave, and do in social situations. It is an excellent tool that can be used by parents and teachers to teach social skills to children who have difficulty in auditory and language processing, abstract thinking, and maintaining attention.

599. *Asperger Syndrome and Adolescence: Helping Preteens and Teens Get Ready for the Real World.* Bolick, Teresa. Gloucester, MA: Fair Winds, 2004. 192 pp. ISBN: 1931412413. Level: Educators/Parents.

This second edition, written mainly for teachers and parents of young adults with Asperger syndrome, at the middle and high school levels, is unique in that this book is about partnerships between parents and adolescents, between parents and family members, and between professionals and parents. Covered in ten chapters, the main topics are how to work with the school to help the young adult with Asperger syndrome learn and succeed; strategies for turning common

Asperger syndrome traits, such as routines, into positive strengths; how to assist these teenagers to overcome unforeseen glitches; and the most appropriate ways for parents and teachers of these children to talk about friendship, love, romance, and sex. A list of additional resources is also included.

600. *Autism 24/7: A Family Guide to Learning at Home and in the Community.* Bondy, Andy and Lori Frost. Series: Topics in Autism. Bethesda, MD: Woodbine House, 2008. 177 pp. ISBN: 1890627534; ISBN2: 978189062227539. Level: Parents.

Authors Bondy and Frost, the founders of the award-winning Pyramid Approach to educating children with autism, discuss how it is possible to keep family life running smoothly and teach a child with autism to participate in important family events and activities at home and in the neighborhood. Part of the Topics in Autism series, this title covers the following topics: setting goals at home; using motivational strategies to build successful change; important communications goals in and around the home; creating natural opportunities for learning; teaching strategies for the home and community; and dealing with common errors and difficult behaviors. The authors emphasize positive reinforcement and the use of rewards. The last section contains forms and checklists that can be used for evaluating and measuring the strategies parents use and how they effect the child's growth and learning. Black and white illustrations, a bibliography, and an index are included.

601. *100 Ideas for Supporting Pupils on the Autistic Spectrum.* Brower, Francine. London: Continuum International Publishing, 2007. 118 pp. ISBN: 0826494218; ISBN2: 9780826494214. Level: Educators.

Divided into eight sections, this well-organized book covers the following topics pertaining to autism: enhancing understanding; communication; developing social skills; creating the right environment; coping strategies; establishing foundations for learning; tackling the curriculum, and facing the challenges of change. For further understanding of students on the autistic spectrum, a list of recommended books and websites is provided in the appendix. This title should be a helpful book for teachers and support staff who interact with children on the autistic spectrum.

602. *People with Autism Behaving Badly: Helping People with ASD Move on from Behavioral and Emotional Challenges.* Clements, John. London; Philadelphia: Jessica Kingsley Publishers, 2005. 224 pp. ISBN: 1843107651; ISBN2: 9781843107651. Level: Parents.

Written by a clinical psychologist who specializes in the field of developmental disabilities, this book is for the parents, siblings, and other family members of autistic individuals with behavioral problems. The aim of this book is to give families practical ideas that will help reduce the frequency and severity of costly behaviors in physical, social, financial, and emotional situations. The book is divided into four parts. Part 1, "Groundwork," describes the starting points, pinpointing the behaviors to work on. Part 2, "Themes and Supports," lists the things that can be done to make things better based on the understanding of why the behavior occurs. Part 3, "Underlying Issues," looks at the two broader-based contributors—loss of social engagement and loss of personal well-being—and how they affect behavior. Specific suggestions for addressing these issues are also offered. Finally, Part 4, "Think Pieces," contains two sections. The first one reviews the use of psychotropic medications for behavior. The second one discusses the idea of developing an individualized "relationship style" as well as the specific kinds of interventions to effect changes in behavior. This hands-on, practical, and highly recommended book also includes a log book to track what has been tried and what has been learned.

603. *Succeeding with Autism: Hear My Voice.* Cohen, Judith H. London; Philadelphia: Jessica Kingsley Publishers, 2005. 240 pp. ISBN: 1843107937; ISBN2: 9781843107934. Level: Educators/Parents.

This is a positive and inspiring story about Michael, who has autism. The author takes the reader on a journey through the life of Michael, before and during his diagnosis up to the present, covering his growth, his pain, confusion, frustration, and isolation associated with living with autism. Key issues of autism at each stage of development are discussed. Although Michael did not talk during his early childhood, he succeeded at becoming a math and computer science teacher with a master's degree in education. He succeeded in managing his autism and his life, in spite of the fact that the early diagnosis might have predicted only disability and failure in life. The book provides strategies for helping an individual with autism make a successful transition from being a student to an employee. The last chapter in the book, "Reviewing My Life for This Book: An Essay from Michael," is a summary of his life, sharing a personal successful story with the readers. This book offers valuable information and hope to other parents of autistic children as well as the special teachers and professionals who work with autistic children.

604. *Visual Supports for People with Autism: A Guide for Parents and Professionals.* Cohen, Marlene J. and Donna L. Sloan. Series: Topics in Autism. Bethesda, MD: Woodbine House, 2007. 168 pp. ISBN: 9781890627478. Level: Educators/Parents.

Written in a conversational style by two certified behavior analysts, this guide, part of the Topics in Autism series, presents the benefits of visual supports to individuals with autism. The book presents strategies for using visual supports in helping make abstract concepts concrete and therefore capitalizing on the inherent visual learning strengths of individuals with autism. Examples of visual supports are activity schedules, charts, color coding, graphic organizers, nametags, Power Cards, social stories, video modeling, calendars, checklists, flip books, mnemonics, photo boards, scripts, to-do lists, and others. The authors also explain how parents and educators, by incorporating these visual supports, can help autistic individuals improve academic performance, behavior, interaction with others, and self-help skills. Black and white and color illustrations are included. "Adding to the book's many practical suggestions are an informative chapter on how to fade visual supports when appropriate and an extensive list of references and recommended reading." *Library Journal*

605. *Targeting Autism: What We Know, Don't Know, and Can Do to Help Young Children with Autism and Related Disorders.* Cohen, Shirley. Berkeley, CA: University of California Press, 2006. 241 pp. ISBN: 0520248384; ISBN2: 9780520248380. Level: Educators/Parents.

This expanded third edition is an in-depth look into autism. The book is divided into three main parts. Throughout the book, parents, individuals with autism, and professionals use narratives to share with others what they have experienced and learned. Topics that are covered in the first part deal with having autism, life cycles, and families. Part 2 focuses on treating autism. Topics that are covered in this part deal with intervention approaches, including emphasis on equal opportunity to ensure that economic factors do not deprive some children with autism and their families of the intensive support they need in order to achieve a good future. Some thoughts on alternative treatments and other intervention controversies are also presented in this part. The final part looks at cures, recovery, and better lives in the future for autistic individuals, due to more awareness and new technologies in gene research that can allow scientists to better understand the role genes play the development of autism and eventually lead to better treatments. Appendix A lists diagnostic criteria for autistic disorder, and Appendix B lists diagnostic criteria for Asperger's disorder. A comprehensive list of additional resources, including some organizations, is included. Parents, teachers, and professionals should benefit from this book.

606. *The Kid-Friendly ADHD & Autism Cookbook: The Ultimate Guide to the Gluten-Free, Casein-Free Diet.* Compart, Pamela J. and Dana Godbout Laake. Gloucester, MA: Fair Winds, 2008. 256 pp. ISBN: 1592332897; ISBN: 9781592332892. Level: Educators/Professionals.

Written for parents by a pediatrician and a licensed nutritionist, this title is both a cookbook and a guide for addressing the dietary needs of children with attention-deficit/hyperactivity disorder (AD/HD) and autism. The introductory section contains an overview of AD/HD and autistic spectrum disorders and the effect nutrition may have on children diagnosed with these disorders. The seven chapters in the first part address the following nutritional topics: food reactions; risky foods; diets; and strategies that parents can use for implementing optimal eating habits for their children. Each chapter has a chapter summary that enables parents to recognize and enforce key concepts. The second part contains over 200 recipes divided into the following chapters: beverages and healthy shakes; condiments, dressings, and sauces; breads, muffins, waffles, and pancakes; main dishes and one-dish meals; rice and beans; vegetable and side dishes; salads; soups and stews; and fruits, sweets, and treats. Recipes are identified as Quick N Easy or gourmet and contain icons that reflect specific dietary needs. The section on substitutions should be helpful for parents. This unique title provides important information for parents regarding the role that nutrition plays in helping children with AD/HD or autism. Text boxes, tables, an appendix containing additional resources, and an index complete the book.

607. *Asperger Syndrome: A Practical Guide for Teachers.* Cumine, Val, Julia Leach, and Gill Stevenson. Series: Resource Materials for Teachers. London: D. Fulton Publishers, 1998. 90 pp. ISBN: 1853464996; ISBN2: 9781853464997. Level: Educators/Professionals.

Part of the series Resource Materials for Teachers, this book is based on the authors' research on autism and Asperger syndrome after meeting over 100 children with Asperger syndrome in a variety of settings. Although the authors in this book refer to a school system in the United Kingdom, it is a useful source for any parent and teacher of children with Asperger syndrome. The first chapter introduces the readers to Asperger syndrome, followed by assessment and diagnosis. The authors conclude by offering effective educational and behavioral intervention strategies. The appendix lists diagnostic criteria for Asperger syndrome. An index is included.

608. *Autism in the Early Years: A Practical Guide.* Cumine, Val, Julia Leach, and Gill Stevenson. Series: Resource Materials for Teachers. London: David Fulton, 2000. 108 pp. ISBN: 1853465992. Level: Educators/Parents.

Part of the Resource Materials for Teachers series, this guide should help parents as well as teachers of children with autism. The authors define characteristics of autism in the early years, followed by the nature of autism, the issues surrounding assessment and diagnosis, and educational implications of autism. The authors also present a range of practical intervention strategies to promote learning, social development, communication, and appropriate behavior of children with autism. Possibilities for enhancing access to the early years curriculum are explored as well. The authors have included two helpful appendices at the end: "Diagnostic Criteria for Autism" and "Early Learning Goals: Six Areas of Learning."

609. *Teaching Asperger's Students Social Skills through Acting: All Their World's a Stage.* Davies, Amelia. Arlington, TX: Future Horizons, 2004. 191 pp. ISBN: 1932565116. Level: Educators/Parents.

In this unique book, Amelia Davies, an actress, director, and producer, draws her experience both from her background in theater and working with adults and children with autism to provide an easy-to-follow, step-by-step drama curriculum, particularly for parents and professionals without any experience in acting. The book is divided into three parts: 1. Getting started: ideas in regards to space, rules, and requirements of props. 2. The exercises: acting terminology, and list of exercises to help the development of the actor, and 3. The plays: the short plays written by Amelia's husband, John Stamm, which are take-offs of children's fairy tales. Using the theater skills listed in this book, teachers should be able to teach autistic children and adults social and communication skills.

610. *Understanding Autism.* Dodd, Susan. Sydney; New York: Elsevier, 2005. 310 pp. ISBN: 1875897801. Level: Educators/Parents.

This well-researched book is a practical guide that offers insight into the needs and strengths of individuals with autism. The first section of the book is devoted to explaining essential background information about autism, discussing topics such as what autism is, possible causes, diagnosis, current trends in research and treatment, controversies such as some vaccinations (measles, mumps, rubella), and alternative treatments. The next section addresses impairments in communication, social interaction, and patterns of behavior, interests, and activities that are restricted, repetitive, or stereotypic. It also discusses the sensory impairments that affect the ability of autistic individuals to cope and live independently, followed by diagnostic and assessment procedures. The last section offers parents, teachers, health professionals, as well as individuals with autism useful suggestions and practical strategies, which may be individualized and adapted to different situations. It is a valuable guide that will benefit professionals and parents of autistic children. Additional resources, a glossary, and black and white illustrations are included.

611. *A Guide to Asperger Syndrome.* Gillberg, Christopher. Cambridge; New York: Cambridge University Press, 2002. 178 pp. ISBN: 0521001838. Level: Educators/Professionals.

Intended for a wide readership, including parents, teachers, and professionals, this handbook provides an in-depth look at the symptoms, diagnosis, prevalence, background factors, prognosis, and treatment of Asperger syndrome. A chapter titled "What about All Those Famous Geniuses?" looks at a number of famous historical people who might have had Asperger syndrome. In addition, the author shares his observations of some of the case studies of individuals with Asperger syndrome. He concludes that in spite of their difficulties, individuals with Asperger syndrome are an enormous asset to humankind. Three very helpful appendices are included: "The Asperger Syndrome Diagnostic Interview," "The High-Functioning Autism Spectrum Screening Questionnaire," and "Autistic Spectrum Disorders in Adults Screening Questionnaire."

612. *Reaching Out, Joining In: Teaching Social Skills to Young Children with Autism.* Gill-Weiss, Mary Jane and Sandra L. Harris. Series: Topics in Autism. Bethesda, MD: Woodbine House, 2001. 225 pp. ISBN: 1890627240. Level: Educators/Parents.

Part of the Topics in Autism series, this guide introduces social skills programs to parents of children in preschool through early primary grades, diagnosed with any of the pervasive developmental disorders (PDD), including autism and Asperger's syndrome. The authors discuss four broad topics: play skills, the language of social skills, understanding another person's perspective, and functioning within the inclusive classroom. One of the chapters provides a case study using a real-life example of one family's efforts and successes. An index, illustrations, and appendices, which list additional resources such as books, games, and activities, are included.

613. *Right from the Start: Behavioral Intervention for Young Children with Autism.* Harris, Sandra L. and Mary Jane Weiss. Series: Topics in Autism. Bethesda, MD: Woodbine House, 2007. 175 pp. ISBN: 1890627801; ISBN2: 9781890627805. Level: Educators/Parents.

The main objective of this updated edition is to explain how the teaching method known as intensive behavioral intervention (IBI) can benefit young children, mostly preschoolers, with autism and related disorders. Divided into six chapters, the introductory chapters of this second edition emphasize the latest research on the benefits of early IBI, the types of instruction used, home-based professionals including their credentials, and school-based programs. Chapter 3 discusses various models for early IBI in autism, including home-based and center-based models for treatment. Chapter 4 reviews some of the pros and cons in home-based and center-based models and the decisions parents have to make based on these factors. Chapter 5 presents an overview of the early intervention program curriculum, based on the Douglass Developmental Disabilities Center experience. The last chapter presents some guidelines for parents in deciding a quality program for their children. A list of resources for further information and an index are included in this highly recommended guide. A glossary of terms commonly used in autism research and education should be very helpful to the readers.

614. *Siblings of Children with Autism: A Guide for Families.* Harris, Sandra L. and Beth A. Glasberg. Series: Topics in Autism. Bethesda, MD: Woodbine House, 2003. 180 pp. ISBN: 1890627291. Level: Parents.

Written by Sandra Harris, a Board of Governors Distinguished Service Professor at the Graduate School of Applied and Professional Psychology at Rutgers, and by Beth Glasberg, a board certified behavior analyst and two-time recipient of the Lebec Prize for Research in Autism, this volume in the Topics in Autism series is an excellent resource that offers straightforward, authoritative, and instructional advice to family members of autistics. This second updated, well-written book, in addition to addressing questions and concerns regarding autism, explaining autism to siblings, assisting siblings to discuss their feelings, and balancing the needs of the family members, also includes a chapter that discusses concerns and responsibilities of adult siblings. This book helps parents see autism through the eyes of their other children who are not autistic. It is a highly recommended book for siblings, family members, and professionals. A list of additional resources and an index are included.

615. *The Little Class with the Big Personality: Experiences of Teaching a Class of Young Children with Autism.* Hunnisett, Fran. London: Jessica Kingsley, 2005. 152 pp. ISBN: 1843103087; ISBN2: 9781843103080. Level: Educators/Professionals.

This book describes the events that took place at a school in England for children with autism. The author taught in that school, and she wrote these accounts based on her experiences and interviews with the parents of these seven children with autism. The illustrations, drawn by one of her students named Alice, add a child's perspective of the class and its activities. The three appendices list additional resources, websites, and organizations. An index is included.

616. *Asperger Syndrome and Psychotherapy: Understanding Asperger Perspectives.* Jacobsen, Paula. London: Jessica Kingsley Publishers, 2003. 171 pp. ISBN: 1843107430. Level: Educators/Professionals.

The author, a licensed clinical social worker and a psychotherapist, discusses ways to interpret classic analytic and psychodynamic theories in relation to people with Asperger syndrome. She explains how revised theories of mind, executive functioning, and central coherence have helped provide new concepts and language with which to correctly articulate the experiences of those with

Asperger syndrome. Using case studies, she also discusses the importance of the therapeutic relationship, case management, the need for collaboration between professionals, school consultation, and the educational needs of children with Asperger syndrome. One of the appendices lists professional services for children with Asperger syndrome, which should be helpful. The book provides an in-depth analysis of Asperger syndrome from a psychotherapist's perspective, which makes this a useful resource for educators and professionals.

617. *Understanding How Asperger Children and Adolescents Think and Learn: Creating Manageable Environments for AS Students.* Jacobsen, Paula. London; Philadelphia: Jessica Kingsley Publishers, 2005. 120 pp. ISBN: 1843108046; ISBN2: 9781843108047. Level: Educators/Parents.

The main objective of this book is to explain how the learning process takes place in students with Asperger syndrome, and how these individuals can be supported in learning settings. The author provides a view of how students with Asperger syndrome perceive and understand what goes on in the classroom, and how other classmates and teachers perceive them in return. The book is divided into two parts: the first part discusses understanding Asperger thinking and communication. The second part explains how to address and support life and learning during the school years to create a rewarding and supportive learning environment. Examples of behavior commonly observed in children with Asperger syndrome are included. It is a valuable resource for educators and parents of children with Asperger syndrome. Some additional resources and an index are included.

618. *Educational Provision for Children with Autism and Asperger Syndrome: Meeting Their Needs.* Jones, Glenys. London: David Fulton, 2002. 135 pp. ISBN: 1853466697. Level: Educators/Parents.

The focus of this book is to help teachers, professionals, and parents make appropriate decisions when it comes to various educational options and interventions for children with autism and Asperger syndrome. The first two chapters, which follow the glossary of terms, provide a brief summary of knowledge on autistic spectrum disorders, followed by the identification and diagnosis of autistic spectrum disorders. The remaining five chapters discuss education provision and intervention, assessment for planning teaching strategies and managing behavior, support from adults and pupils, and life beyond school. An appendix, titled "Proforma for Tracking the Educational Provision Made for Pupils with Autistic Spectrum Disorders," references, useful websites, and an index are included.

619. *Meeting the Needs of Children with Autistic Spectrum Disorders.* Jordan, Rita and Glenys Jones. London: David Fulton, 1999. 69 pp. ISBN: 1853465828. Level: Educators/Professionals.

The focus throughout this book is to understand how students with autistic spectrum disorders (ASD) experience the world and the implications of this for teachers and other staff members within the mainstream schools. Therefore, it is a good resource for students in teacher training, newly qualified teachers, or anyone teaching children with ASD. The authors, using a case-study approach, help teachers and other staff members identify the meaning behind these students' actions and reactions. They discuss strategies using practical exercises and curriculum suggestions. A list of useful additional references, addresses, and an index are included. Educators will benefit a great deal from this book.

620. *Autism and Pervasive Developmental Disorders Sourcebook: Basic Consumer Health Information about Autism Spectrum and Pervasive Developmental Disorders, such as Classical Autism, Asperger Syndrome, Rett Syndrome, and Childhood Disintegrative Disorder, Including Information about Related Genetic Disorders and Medical Problems and Facts about Causes, Screening Methods, Diagnostic Criteria, Treatments and Interventions, and Family and Education Issues.* Judd, Sandra J., editor. Series: Health Reference. Detroit: Omnigraphics, 2007. 631 pp. ISBN: 078080953X; ISBN: 97807809536. Level: Educators/Parents.

This volume, one of the titles in the Health Reference series, is divided into eight parts, which cover broad areas of interest. Each part is further divided into multiple chapters, which are devoted to specific topics. Several chapters are further subdivided into specific disorders. Part 1 provides an understanding of the autism spectrum and numerous pervasive developmental disorders. The next four parts cover causes, accompanying conditions, diagnoses and evaluations, and treatment options. Parts 6 and 7 cover family, lifestyle, education, and independence issues associated with individuals who have autistic disorders and the impact on their family and friends. The final part contains a glossary, information on how to evaluate Internet health sites, and resources for additional information. An index is included.

621. *Asperger Syndrome: A Gift or a Curse?* Lyons, Viktoria and Michael Fitzgerald. New York: Nova Biomedical Books, 2005. 333 pp. ISBN: 1594543879. Level: Educators/Professionals.

According to the authors, although the majority of cases of individuals with Asperger's syndrome possess extraordinary talents in the areas of memory, mathematics, physics, logic, music, and so forth, the negative view of Asperger's syndrome is wrong and the assets associated with Asperger's syndrome should be viewed from a more positive perspective. Chapter 1 defines the differences between autism and Asperger's syndrome. Chapter 2 addresses the question posed in the title of this book. Chapters 3 through 6 explain the various neurobiological and neuropsychological theories of autism, including various hypotheses. Biographies of nine brilliant individuals who have Asperger's syndrome/autism are discussed in Chapters 7 through 16. It is a well-researched book with in-depth information about the Asperger's syndrome. The book includes an extensive list of additional resources and an index.

622. *Creative Expressive Activities and Asperger's Syndrome: Social and Emotional Skills and Positive Life Goals for Adolescents and Young Adults.* Martinovich, Judith. London; Philadelphia: Jessica Kingsley Publishers, 2006. 287 pp. ISBN: 1843108127; ISBN2: 9781843108122. Level: Educators/ Professionals.

This book integrates cognitive behavioral techniques with alternative ways of learning and processing, which are often nonverbal and congruent with the Asperger way of thinking. With the help of excellent creative activities, including art, drama, music, puppetry, and relaxation techniques, the author presents step-by-step, individualized therapy for individuals who have Asperger's syndrome. Creative activities and interventions are grounded in contemporary principles of positive psychology and social and emotional learning in order to build long-term satisfaction. Activities are designed to adapt to different ages and skill levels, individual or group, in a school setting. It is an excellent comprehensive resource for teachers, parents, social workers, and psychologists who work with those who have Asperger's syndrome. A list of additional reference books and a very helpful subject index are included.

623. *Navigating the Social World: A Curriculum for Individuals with Asperger's Syndrome, High Functioning Autism and Related Disorders.* McAfee, Jeanette L. Arlington, TX: Future Horizons, 2002. 350 pp. ISBN: 1885477821. Level: Educators/Parents.

This book is the result of extensive research done by the author after her daughter was diagnosed as having high functioning autism. It is written primarily for parents, professionals, and paraprofessionals who are in need of specific information on how to provide an intensive social-emotional skills program for their child, client, or student with Asperger's syndrome. The programs within each section have been designed to be taught in the order in which they are presented. Most of the programs in this book can be used either on an individual or in a small group setting. There are five appendices: Appendix A provides a list of additional resources; Appendices B, C, and D contain student handouts, templates, and program tracking forms; and Appendix E is a glossary of terms found this book and in the field of autism.

624. *Asperger Syndrome and Adolescence: Practical Solutions for School Success.* Myles, Brenda and Diane Adreon. Shawnee Mission, KS: Autism

Asperger Publishing, 2001. 227 pp. ISBN: 0967251494. Level: Educators/ Parents.

The main focus of this book is the academic issues of children with Asperger syndrome in middle and high school. This book is a great starting point for helping parents of children with Asperger syndrome to prepare for the transition from elementary to middle school. It should help parents and teachers of these children recognize and deal with stress build up in students with Asperger syndrome before it gets out of control. In addition to some case studies and extensive information and checklists on evaluating the strengths, weaknesses, and needs for accommodations, the author also presents numerous strategies, evaluation tools, and guidance on how and when to use them. The author provides detailed and exhaustive information with the help of tables, graphs, and cartoons.

625. *Asperger Syndrome and Sensory Issues: Practical Solutions for Making Sense of the World.* Myles, Brenda Smith et al.; illustrated by Penny Chiles. Shawnee Mission, KS: Autism Asperger Publishing, 2000. 129 pp. ISBN: 0967251478; ISBN2: 0967251486. Level: Educators/Parents.

The authors explain how children with Asperger syndrome relate to the world through their senses. The first of the five chapters overviews sensory integration terminology, including a discussion of how the sensory systems impact behavior. Chapter 2 discusses sensory characteristics associated with Asperger syndrome. Chapter 3 reviews various assessment tools that are helpful in pinpointing sensory characteristics. A series of interventions in the sensory areas, including specific behaviors and possible reasons for their occurrence, including strategies that may help children with Asperger syndrome, are reviewed in the fourth chapter. The last chapter discusses a sensory processing case study of a 7-year-old boy named Christopher who has Asperger syndrome. An extensive list of resources and organizations and a glossary are included, which should be very helpful for additional information. This book should be of great value to special education teachers, parents, and pediatricians.

626. *Asperger Syndrome and Difficult Moments: Practical Solutions for Tantrums, Rage, and Meltdowns.* Myles, Brenda Smith and Jack Southwick. Shawnee Mission, KS: Autism Asperger Publishing, 2005. 158 pp. ISBN: 1931282706. Level: Educators/Parents.

Divided into five chapters, this revised and expanded edition covers an overview of the characteristics of Asperger syndrome that may impact behavior; tantrums, rage, and meltdowns; functional assessment of behavior; and strategies that promote self-awareness, self-calming, and self-management. The last chapter, coauthored by parents, offers practical suggestions and excellent strategies specifically for parents of children with Asperger syndrome. It also includes suggestions for developing a family plan, special tips for multiparent families, dealing with siblings, bedtime routines, and home-school communication. It is an excellent book that parents and professionals can refer to again and again to understand the characteristics of Asperger syndrome and to use the practical solutions to manage tantrums, rage, and meltdowns displayed by these children. The use of charts and tables listing activities, stress signals, and solutions should be very helpful to the readers. An index and an extensive list of additional reference resources are included in this highly recommended book.

627. *A Parent's Guide to Asperger Syndrome and High-Functioning Autism: How to Meet the Challenges and Help Your Child Thrive.* Ozonoff, Sally, Geraldine Dawson, and James McPartland. New York: Guilford Press, 2002. 278 pp. ISBN: 1572305312; ISBN2: 1572307676. Level: Parents.

This book is written using parents' and children's stories, pain, hopes, and triumphs. The main goal of this book is to help parents give their children, who have Asperger syndrome and high-functioning autism, the best chance possible for a full and happy life. The book is divided into two parts. The first part, "Understanding Asperger Syndrome and High-Functioning Autism," defines these two terms and the diagnostic process used in each case, followed by causes and treatments of both these conditions. The second part, "Living with Asperger Syndrome and High-Functioning Autism," discusses some of the guiding principles that can be used in order to channel the autistic children's strengths. The next three chapters discuss parenting strategies for handling common challenging behaviors that occur in the home as well as in the school, followed by social world of these children. The last chapter discusses critical issues faced by these children during adolescence and adulthood. An extensive list of resources containing books, newsletters, videotapes, software, and websites are included for additional information. "Strongly recommended for public libraries and academic libraries with autism or education collections." *Library Journal*

628. *Enabling Communication in Children with Autism.* Potter, Carol and Chris Whittaker. London: Jessica Kingsley, 2001. 207 pp. ISBN: 1853029564. Level: Educators/Professionals.

Developing communication-enabling environments for children with autism who use little or no speech is the main focus in this book. The introductory chapter provides an overview of autism. The next chapter describes the research project and the findings by the authors. The authors, based on a two-year research project, provide practical advice regarding communication in children with autism. The appendix provides research methods used for this research. In addition to the references, a subject index and an author index are included.

629. *Autism and Learning: A Guide to Good Practice.* Powell, Stuart and Rita Jordan, editors. London: D. Fulton, 1997. 170 pp. ISBN: 185346421X. Level: Educators/Professionals.

This book explains how a psychological perspective on the way in which individuals with autism think and learn may be applied to particular curriculum areas. The objective of this book is making sense of what the child with autism does and how to build a teaching approach based on this understanding. Each of the nine contributors in this book lists practical approaches and kinds of compensatory strategies that can be taught to enable the autistic student to develop intellectually in spite of problems and thereby gain access to new learning and new ways of behaving. The first chapter, "Rationale for the Approach," sets the scene by establishing the broad rationale for the anticipated approach, including the psychological understanding on which it is based. The second chapter sets out the principles by which this understanding can be put into practice. The next five chapters use this approach in the teaching of various subjects, such as science, dance and drama, technology, and others. Chapter 8 discusses assessment procedures used in one of the schools where this approach was taken. This is a highly recommended book for special education teachers.

630. *Children with Autism: A Parent's Guide.* Powers, Michael D., editor. Bethesda, MD: Woodbine House, 2000. 427 pp. ISBN: 1890627046. Level: Parents.

Written by leading researchers, clinicians, educators, attorneys, and parents, this revised and updated book provides comprehensive information regarding autism. It discusses early intervention, educational programs, legal rights, and a look at the years ahead. The authors provide the most updated information on current diagnostic criteria within the spectrum of autism disorder, applied behavior analysis, and the Individuals with Disabilities Education Act (IDEA). A glossary, reading and resource lists, a collection of photographs of children with autism, and an index are included. Quotations from parents who add their reactions and perspectives to the topics should be very useful. "Highly recommended, essential reading for parents and caretakers of autistic children of any age or degree of severity, *Children with Autism* is thoroughly 'reader friendly' and enhanced with a glossary, reading and resource list (including extensive web site listings), and photographs of children with autism." *Internet Book Watch*

631. *Parent Survival Manual: A Guide to Crisis Resolution in Autism and Related Developmental Disorders.* Schopler, Eric, editor. New York: Plenum Press, 1995. 224 pp. ISBN: 0306449773. Level: Parents.

This guide is a collection of solutions that parents have developed as responses to the continual challenges of living with autistic individuals. The anecdotes in this volume were collected over a period of six years at parent meetings and annual conferences of autism societies at the national and state levels. Also, during this time a survey was conducted to see what problems of children with autism or related developmental disorders were found by parents to be most troublesome. The problems cited involved aggression, communication, unusual behaviors, toilet training, eating and sleeping, and difficulties with play and leisure. Each section features accounts by parents of how they found a solution to a particular problem. This allows the reader to look up a specific problem without having to read the entire book. In addition to a list of additional books on the subject, the last chapter lists excellent sources for community support and states and cities with local chapters of the Autism Society of America (ASA). Easy to read, this highly recommended book should be a wonderful aid for families with autistic children.

632. *Creative Therapy for Children with Autism, ADD, and Asperger's: Using Artistic Creativity to Reach, Teach, and Touch Our Children.* Tubbs, Janet. Garden City, NY: Square One Publishers, 2008. 323 pp. ISBN: 0757003001; ISBN: 9780757003004. Level: Educators/Parents.

The main focus of this book is to show how full potential can be reached by a child who has autism through verbal and nonverbal communication and comprehension of the power of creative arts. Written by a therapist, this book is divided into two parts. The first part provides information regarding all aspects of autism and attention-deficit disorder/attention-deficit hyperactivity disorder (ADD/ADHD), such as definitions, diagnosis, causes, and treatments. Diet and nutrition, including the effectiveness of gluten-free, chemical-free diets, and specific supplements are discussed as well. The second part provides a wide variety of exercises, activities, and games to help children with ADD/ADHD reduce hyperactivity, prolong focus, decrease anger, develop fine motor skills, and improve social and verbal skills. Additional resources and an index are included.

633. *Healthcare for Children on the Autism Spectrum: A Guide to Medical, Nutritional, and Behavioral Issues.* Volkmar, Fred R. and Lisa A. Wiesner. Series: Topics in Autism. Bethesda, MD: Woodbine House, 2004. 376 pp. ISBN: 0933149972. Level: Educators/Parents.

Written by leading authorities in the field of autism, mainly for parents of children with autism spectrum disorders (ASDs), this book is part of the Topics in Autism series. The main focus of this book is to provide enough general information about ASDs, thus allowing parents to seek out and recognize quality medical care for their children's general health. The book addresses basic child care issues, such as common medical problems, visits to the emergency room or hospital, growth and nutritional issues, safety concerns, sleep problems, seizure disorders, dental care, sensory issues, common challenging behaviors, medications, adolescence and sexuality, mental deterioration, and complementary and alternative treatments. In addition, the book covers how an evaluation for the spectrum is usually performed and includes useful advice on how to develop a strong parent-doctor partnership. Each of the sixteen chapters concludes by answering questions, asked by parents of children with autism. Two appendices are included: Appendix A lists diagnostic criteria for pervasive developmental disorders, and Appendix B offers advice in dealing with insurance companies. A glossary, resource guide, additional reading material, and an index are included.

634. *Constructive Campaigning for Autism Services: The PACE Parents' Handbook.* Wason, Armorer. London; Philadelphia: Jessica Kingsley Publishers, 2005. 112 pp. ISBN: 1843103877; ISBN2: 9781843103875. Level: Educators/Parents.

PACE (originally Parents Autism Campaign for Education) was founded in 1998 and is now the Policy and Campaigns Team of TreeHouse, the national charity for autism education. This handbook contains in-depth discussions with experienced parent campaigners and with professionals and public authority officers who have developed strong and effective relationships with parents and parent groups. This practical handbook is built on the real-life experiences of parents who have adopted a range of approaches to influencing local agencies and who speak for themselves. It explains how the system works and provides useful information about local authority structures and government policy, which will help with effective campaigning. It also provides a unique opportunity for parents to get involved to make the world a better place for autistic children and their families. An index and a list of helpful resources and websites are included for additional information in this highly recommended book for parents of autistic children.

635. *Educating Students with Autism: A Quick Start Manual.* Webber, Jo and Brenda Scheuermann. Austin, TX: PRO-ED, 2008. 416 pp. ISBN: 1416402551; ISBN: 9781416402558. Level: Educators/Professionals.

Written by two special education professors specifically for educators and other personnel who have the responsibility of teaching children with autism, this book provides guidance and strategies toward planning, organizing, implementing, and monitoring an educational program. The book is divided into sixteen chapters. The introductory chapter gives a brief overview of autism, its characteristics, and implications for educational programming. The topics included are applied behavior analysis, instructional strategies, providing structure in the classroom, supervision of other adults who are working with students who have autism, curriculum development, collecting progress data, teaching language and communication skills, socialization and inclusion, functional behavior assessment, intervention for specific challenging behaviors, and understanding and working with families. Four appendices are included. Appendix A lists resources pertaining to autism, which includes journals and books. Appendix B provides helpful handouts for professional team training. Appendix C covers commercially available curricula, and Appendix D discusses a typical school day at Valdiz Intermediate School. A glossary and a subject index are included.

636. *Asperger Syndrome in the Family: Redefining Normal.* Willey, Liane Holliday. London; Philadelphia: Jessica Kingsley Publishers, 2001. 172 pp. ISBN: 1853028738. Level: Parents.

The author and her daughter both have Asperger syndrome. Written from the perspective of an adult with Asperger syndrome, the author shares her private thoughts and fears and what it means to be married and raise a family when encumbered by a neurological disorder. She explains how the many everyday tasks of raising a family often derail her, and how she, her husband, and her two children have learned to compensate for the Asperger syndrome that she and her daughter share. This is an inspiring story in which the author underscores the importance of family support and respect for the family members with Asperger syndrome and offers practical steps for helping families in similar situations. A list of helpful websites is included. This is an inspiring and helpful book for those who have family members with Asperger syndrome.

637. *How to Live with Autism and Asperger Syndrome: Practical Strategies for Parents and Professionals.* Williams, Chris and Barry Wright; illustrated by Olive Young. London; Philadelphia: Jessica Kingsley Publishers, 2004. 336 pp. ISBN: 184310184X. Level: Educators/Parents.

Written by practicing clinicians with extensive experience in working with children with autism spectrum disorders and their families, this well-organized book is a useful resource for the families of children with autism spectrum disorders and for the professionals who work with them. The book is organized into three parts. Part 1 describes the behaviors that might alert parents to the possibility that their child has autism. It discusses the assessment process, including the emotional impact of a diagnosis. Part 2 gives an overview of how researchers believe children with autism think and experience the world and therefore behave differently. Part 3 uses this understanding to help make sense of the child's behavior and plan strategies to cope with difficult behaviors while encouraging the child's development. A list of additional references and resources is included.

638. *Asperger Syndrome: What Teachers Need to Know.* Winter, Matt. London; New York: Jessica Kingsley Publishers, 2003. 96 pp. ISBN: 1843101432. Level: Educators/Professionals.

Written by an elementary school teacher from New Zealand, this is an easy to understand book. It provides a summary of the information currently available on Asperger syndrome that is relevant to teachers. In addition, it includes all the key issues that may concern teachers of students who have Asperger syndrome, such as social skills, homework, playground behavior, assisting with studies, and so forth. Winter also offers tips and practical ideas that he has personally found successful in a school environment. At the end of the book, a list of recommended additional resources and websites are provided. This book should provide a good initial grounding before pursuing further reading about Asperger syndrome.

639. *Play and Imagination in Children with Autism.* Wolfberg, Pamela J. Series: Special Education. New York: Teacher's College Press, 1999. 193 pp. ISBN: 080773814X. Level: Educators/Professionals.

Part of the Special Education series, this book explores the social and imaginary lives of three extraordinary children who had been diagnosed with autism. The main objective of this book is to merge theory and practice to help children with autism play and form peer relationships. The book is divided into two parts: Part 1, "Perspectives on Autism and Play," examines the problems children with autism experience in social interaction and communication by exploring the nature of the disorder in relation to play's role in childhood development as well as current intervention practices. Part 2, "Passage to Play Culture," presents ethnographic case portraits of three children as they overcome obstacles to enter into the "play culture" of their peers. In order to bring the children's stories to life, the text includes vignettes, dialogue, and samples of children's writing and drawing. An index is included.

640. *Autism: A Holistic Approach.* Woodward, Bob and Marga Hogenboom. Edinburgh: Floris, 2000. 270 pp. ISBN: 086315311. Level: Educators/ Professionals.

Unlike many other books on this subject, this book is based on the philosophical approach of anthroposophy. Using various case studies where curative education, based on a holistic approach, has resulted in marked improvements in the autistic individual's behavior and social integration, the authors challenge the assumption that autism, which is widely assumed to be a condition, places the autistic's inner development beyond the reach of parents and caregivers. In order to back up their theories, the authors cite their own practical experiences along with the findings of other experts in the field. The appendix includes additional anthroposophical background, specific therapies and medical treatments, and useful contact addresses.

641. *Understanding Autism Spectrum Disorders: Frequently Asked Questions.* Yapko, Diane E. London; New York: Jessica Kingsley Publishers, 2003. 224 pp. ISBN: 1843107562. Level: Educators/Parents.

The author provides answers to numerous common questions that are asked primarily by individuals who do not have an expertise in autism spectrum disorders (ASD). Yapko provides the reader with the most current information available on common topics associated with ASD from various perspectives. Since the author uses a question and answer format, it allows her to address precisely those specific issues pertaining to ASD. This easy-to-understand and well-organized book is divided into four main parts: diagnosis and characteristics; causes; medical issues; and treatment, intervention programs, and approaches. The final part in the book includes a useful listing of additional resources, organizations, and websites. The book also has five excellent appendices, which discuss diagnostic criterion, test instruments, and medications.

Down Syndrome

642. *Fine Motor Skills for Children with Down Syndrome: A Guide for Parents and Professionals.* Bruni, Maryanne. Series: Topics in Down Syndrome. Bethesda, MD: Woodbine House, 2006. 241 pp. ISBN: 1890627674. Level: Educators/Parents.

This second expanded edition, part of the Topics in Down Syndrome series, discusses the best practices and procedures for helping children with Down syndrome and for mastering the finger and hand skills needed for home and school activities. An occupational therapist and mother of a teenager with Down syndrome, the author presents a thorough overview of fine motor development. Dozens of easy activities that can be performed at home or at school to help kids learn skills are presented using easy-to-understand instructions, such as cutting with scissors, grasping a pencil, printing, eating, dressing, and grooming. Parents should be able to incorporate these activities into many day-to-day activities. The book has two appendices: the first appendix lists visual motor worksheets using illustrations, and the second appendix lists household items that can be used for hand play. A helpful glossary, a bibliography including additional resources, a list of websites and organizations, and an index are included. It is an excellent resource.

643. *Teaching Math to People with Down Syndrome and Other Hands-On Learners.* Horstmeier, DeAnna. Series: Topics in Down Syndrome.

Bethesda, MD: Woodbine House, 2004. 300 pp. ISBN: 1890627429. Level: Educators/Parents.

This title is the first volume of the Topics in Down Syndrome series. It can be used by teachers and parents to teach practical math skills to kids including adults with Down syndrome or other learning delays. The guide contains twenty-one chapters and is divided into two parts: 1. Basic survival skills; 2. Advanced survival skills. The focus of this book is on teaching essential basic math, such as addition and subtraction, concepts about time, money, counting, and measuring, thus empowering learners to be independent using daily living skills. The author emphasizes frequent use of the calculator as well as hands-on, practical activities, including games that should enable the learners to enjoy math skills. Two excellent appendices are included: the first appendix contains assessment materials, and the second appendix has a list of thirty-five teaching materials with illustrations. It is an easy-to-follow guide and a well-organized teaching aid.

644. *Teaching Math to People with Down Syndrome and Other Hands-On Learners: Book 2. Advanced Survival Skills.* Horstmeier, DeAnna. Series: Topics in Down Syndrome. Bethesda, MD: Woodbine House, 2008. 481 pp. ISBN: 1890627666; ISBN2: 9781890627669. Level: Educators/Parents.

This second volume of the Topics in Down Syndrome series, sequel to the first volume, covers more challenging skills in teaching math to individuals with Down syndrome, such as multiplication and division, fractions, money and banking basics, decimals and percentages, modes of measurement, and others. These skills are usually taught in upper elementary, middle school, high school, and beyond. This volume, like the previous volume, is directed at students who learn through hands-on procedures. Visual supports and worksheets that contain black and white illustrations corresponding to these skills are included and should be effective for teaching. An extensive list of additional resources of teaching materials, including websites, and an index are included. It is an excellent, easy-to-follow aid for parents and teachers. A companion book titled *Hands-On Math Kit*, which includes the manipulatives and teaching aids, is also available.

645. *Common Threads: Celebrating Life with Down Syndrome.* Kidder, Cynthia S. and Brian Skotko; illustrated by Kendra Dew. Rochester Hills, MI: Band of Angels, 2001. 181 pp. ISBN: 1930868049; ISBN2: 9781930868045. Level: Parents.

The main goal of this book, written by a mother of a child with Down syndrome and Band of Angels' founder and CEO Cynthia Kidder, and Brian Skotko, a Harvard-trained physician specializing in genetics, is to reach parents through hospital and physician's office channels, so that this would be the first positive information they receive about the potential of children with Down syndrome. It is an inspiring look at the dreams and goals of children with Down syndrome and their families. Stories from families and people who have made close observations of someone with Down syndrome, opinions on how best to encourage success in a variety of areas, and the most current research on Down syndrome are presented.

646. *Classroom Language Skills for Children with Down Syndrome: A Guide for Parents and Teachers.* Kumin, Libby. Series: Topics in Down Syndrome. Bethesda, MD: Woodbine House, 2001. 339 pp. ISBN: 1890627119. Level: Educators/Parents.

This book, one of the titles in the Topics in Down Syndrome series, is intended to be used by families, teachers, special educators, and speech-language pathologists. The author presents ideas and techniques that can be used for many children with Down syndrome, mainly at elementary and middle school levels, to help them learn the language of the curriculum, language of instruction, language of testing, language of routines, and the language of social interaction. In addition to discussing a variety of resources, materials, and techniques to help children with Down syndrome with classroom language skills, the author also provides information on assistive technology equipment, augmentative and alternative communication materials, and other helpful resources for children who are unable to use speech as their primary communication system. Worksheets that are included at the end of each chapter and in the appendix can be used to help plan the child's individual program to help meet his or her educational goals. The "Resource Guide" lists a directory of organizations, websites, and companies that can provide information, support, and commercial products useful to families of children with Down syndrome.

647. *Early Communication Skills for Children with Down Syndrome: A Guide for Parents and Professionals.* Kumin, Libby. Bethesda, MD: Woodbine House, 2003. 368 pp. ISBN: 1890627275. Level: Educators/Parents.

This updated, expanded, and comprehensive edition focuses on speech and language development and provides many ideas for helping children, from birth to 6 years, with Down syndrome learn to communicate. The author offers some practical suggestions and guidance in helping one's child with Down syndrome learn communication skills at home. Kumin also provides background information about communication and Down syndrome and specific suggestions for home activities and home and community-based language experiences. In addition, the author explains how to work effectively with the child's speech-language pathologist, who can assess and treat the child's communication difficulties. The book includes an extensive guide that lists helpful organizations and websites for additional information. "[B]oth the reading list and the resource section are worth the cost. Essential for most collections." *Library Journal*

Dyslexia and Other Learning Disabilities

648. *Overcoming Dyslexia: A Practical Handbook for the Classroom.* Broomfield, Hilary and Margaret Combley. London: Whurr, 2003. 240 pp. ISBN: 1861562586. Level: Educators/Professionals.

Two practicing teachers in the field of language and literacy authored this second edition based on the feedback received from educators who used the first edition of this book in the classroom. The authors bring together the best of practice in the areas of multisensory teaching, whole language, and phonological awareness training in order to produce a program that integrates skills teaching into real reading and writing. As a result, they have created new clear links with the National Literacy Strategy and applied these to the structure of the Literacy Hour. The book is divided into three parts. The first part provides information regarding the development of literacy skills and the barriers to learning for the dyslexic learner. The second part, "skills into action," describes in detail an integrated approach to literacy skills compatible with the National Literacy Strategy. It includes ideas for developing literacy skills through whole language approaches, such as shared reading and writing. The final part takes the teacher and learner step by step, page by page, through a series of sound-letter links. It includes sample worksheets and games, which can be adapted to the individual's needs and used at different stages of the program. Additional resources are included for more information. This is a highly recommended book.

649. *Learning Disabilities in Children.* Burke, Peter and Katy Cigno. Series: Working Together for Children, Young People, and Their Families. Malden, MA: Blackwell Science, 2000. 176 pp. ISBN: 0632051043. Level: Educators/Parents.

Part of the series Working Together for Children, Young People, and Their Families, this highly recommended book should be a useful resource for professionals specializing in child welfare, social work, health care, and community care. It is based on the experiences of families with children who have learning disabilities. The theory relating to learning disabilities from the family perspective is explained. One of the key features in the book is child development. The authors recommend ways in which an inclusive partnership between children, their families, and professionals can be achieved to help children with learning disabilities. An index and an extensive list of references are included.

650. *The Effective Teacher's Guide to Dyslexia and Other Specific Learning Difficulties: Practical Strategies.* Farrell, Michael. Series: New Directions in Special Educational Needs. London; New York: Routledge, 2006. 88 pp. ISBN: 0415360404. Level: Educators/Professionals.

One of the titles in New Directions in Special Educational Needs series, this volume offers the classroom teacher practical advice, information, and enlightenment that will help them bridge the gap between theory and practice. It provides strategies that deal with everyday classroom situations pertaining to various learning difficulties due to dyslexia, dyspraxia, and dyscalculia. The reader is guided through the legal and policy contexts, an explanation of terms and definitions, interventions and rationale, and approaches related to different curriculum subjects. These steps should allow the reader to understand, encourage, and support children with learning difficulties, so that these children can achieve their full potential in an inclusive environment. A list of various organizations for additional information is included.

651. *Dyslexia in the Early Years: A Practical Guide to Teaching and Learning.* Hartas, Dimitra. London; New York: Routledge, 2006. 102 pp. ISBN: 0415345006; ISBN2: 9780415345002. Level: Educators/Professionals.

Written mainly for teachers of preschool and elementary school children who have dyslexia, this book is divided into seven chapters. The first chapter introduces readers to dyslexia and presents its characteristics and early indicators. Chapter 2 focuses on language development and communication. Chapter 3 examines the social-emotional difficulties associated with dyslexia. Chapter 4 explores issues of identification and assessment of learning and development in early years, and Chapter 5 addresses issues of effectiveness in the early years of teaching and learning by focusing on the curriculum and the National Literacy Strategy. Chapters 6 and 7 discuss the use of information and communication technology (ICT) in teaching young children with dyslexia and provide strategies in which computers and information technology (IT) can help young dyslexic children. The final chapter focuses on collaboration between teachers, parents, and other professionals, including outside agencies. The appendix lists useful websites. Real-life case studies and tasks suggested in this book should be helpful for teachers of young children with dyslexia.

652. *Overcoming Dyslexia: A Straightforward Guide for Families and Teachers.* Hornsby, Bevé. London: Optima, 1995. 182 pp. ISBN: 0356144992. Level: Educators/Parents.

Using her experience as a clinical psychologist, teacher, and speech therapist, the author has written this helpful revised edition for teachers and parents so that the problems of dyslexia can be understood and handled effectively. The first half of the book defines dyslexia and how it can affect every aspect of a child's life, lists its symptoms, and advises parents and school teachers on what practical help they can give. The rest of the chapters explain the diagnostic tests a child with dyslexia might be given how successful specialist teaching can be and provides practical tips on how students and adults can cope with their dyslexia. The author has used case studies for writing this book. Useful addresses are provided.

653. *An Introduction to Dyslexia for Parents and Professionals.* Hultquist, Alan M. London; Philadelphia: Jessica Kingsley Publishers, 2006. 107 pp. ISBN: 184310833X; ISBN2: 9781843108337. Level: Educators/Parents.

This book provides the basic information regarding dyslexia for professionals, teachers, and parents. Using illustrative case studies, the author discusses the causes, types, and subtypes of dyslexia, means of testing, remediation, and the controversial matter of a child "staying back" to repeat a grade. Possible methods of classroom accommodations and modifications for dyslexic students in various subject areas are identified in the appendix. Parents and professionals should be able to use the resources at the back of the book to help them explain dyslexia to children and to find additional information on the subject. A list of professional organizations and a glossary are also included. This is a practical introductory guide that answers frequently asked questions about dyslexia.

654. *What Is Dyslexia? A Book Explaining Dyslexia for Kids and Adults to Use Together.* Hultquist, Alan M. London: Jessica Kingsley Publishers, 2008. 95 pp. ISBN: 1843108828; ISBN2: 9781843108825. Level: Parents.

Written by a licensed school psychologist, this title provides useful information for parents and professionals regarding dyslexia. The author covers basic facts about dyslexia in two parts: Part 1, which is for kids, contains topics such as causes of dyslexia, trouble with sounds and remembering how letters and words look, handling feelings, and bullies. Part 2, which is for kids and adults, contains answers to the questions that kids and parents might ask, including activities that can be done together to help with reading and spelling. Black and white illustrations, a list of additional resources, and an appendix that lists professional organizations, both in the United States and worldwide, are included.

655. *Understanding Dyslexia: A Practical Approach for Parents and Teachers.* Huston, Anne Marshall. Lanham, MD: Madison Books, 1992. 345 pp. ISBN: 0819178047; ISBN2: 0819182494. Level: Educators/Parents.

This well-researched book is written to help parents, classroom teachers, and others understand dyslexia and the many challenges that accompany it. The book is divided into five parts. Part 1 serves as an introduction to dyslexia and provides an overview of the common characteristics of dyslexic individuals. Part 2 explains three general categories of dyslexia: visual, auditory, and the combination of visual and auditory in varying degrees. Part 3 discusses the developmental factors and the dangers of too early diagnosis in young students. Part 4 examines dyslexia in the middle and high schools, followed by adult dyslexia. Part 5 discusses steps that can be taken by parents and teachers to alleviate dyslexia. A glossary, an index, and an extensive bibliography are included. This book is highly recommended.

656. *When Babies Read: A Practical Guide to Help Young Children with Hyper-lexia, Asperger Syndrome and Hugh-Functioning Autism.* Jensen, Audra. London; Philadelphia: Jessica Kingsley Publishers, 2005. 189 pp. ISBN: 1843108038; ISBN2: 9781843108030. Level: Educators/Parents.

The author writes from her personal experiences, describing the joys as well as the challenges of raising her son Isaak. He has autism and hyperlexia, a condition in which an ability to read from an early age is accompanied by a below-aver-age ability to understand spoken language and socialize. Parenting advice and a comprehensive reading curriculum especially designed for young, challenged children to help promote their reading ability are offered by the author. Jensen emphasizes the importance of early diagnosis to ensure that effective teaching strategies are introduced as early as possible, so that the child may be able to enjoy a more typical childhood development. In addition to a subject index and additional resources, the book includes three appendices: Appendix A: "Special Education Law in the United States," Appendix B: "Useful Organizations in the UK," and Appendix C: "Glossary and Diagnostic Criteria."

657. *Spelling, Handwriting and Dyslexia; Overcoming Barriers to Learning.* Montgomery, Diane. London; New York: Routledge, 2007. 208 pp. ISBN: 9780415409247. Level: Educators/Parents.

The main objective of this book is to help teachers understand the valuable contribution spelling and handwriting make to literacy development of children in elementary and secondary schools. The author believes that in dealing with struggling pupils' literacy difficulties in schools, spelling and handwriting are often overlooked, while providing more emphasis to the reading aspect. The first three chapters in the first part examine the nature of spelling, handwriting, and dyslexia and their relationship to becoming literate and to one another. The second part in this book discusses effective links between strategic assessment and strategic interventions in schools, including problem-based learning, underpinned by plenty of case studies and real-life classroom examples. A list of references is included. This book should be of value to teachers who are interested in literacy programs.

658. *100 Ideas for Supporting Pupils with Dyslexia.* Reid, Gavin and Shannon Green. London: Continuum International Publishing, 2007. 123 pp. ISBN: 082649398X; ISBN2: 9780826493989. Level: Educators.

Divided into ten sections, this well-organized book covers the following topics pertaining to dyslexia: teaching strategies; reading and comprehension; spelling; creative writing; learning strategies; planning for learning; memory; getting the teaching right; number work and mathematics; and dyslexia across the curriculum. A list of recommended reading and websites for additional information is included in the appendix.

659. *Dyslexia: A Practical Guide for Teachers and Parents.* Riddick, Barbara, Judith Wolfe, and David Lumsdon. Series: Resource Materials for Teachers. London: David Fulton, 2003. 134 pp. ISBN: 1853467804; ISBN2: 9781853467806. Level: Educators/Parents.

Detailed practical strategies to use when working with children who have dyslexia is the focus of this book, which is one of the titles in the Resource Materials for Teachers series. Topics covered are defining and identifying dyslexia; dyslexia in the early, middle, and secondary school years; raising self-esteem; and working with parents and voluntary organizations. Checklists, assessments, suitable programs, resources, including website addresses and useful books, and an index are included as well. This resource should be helpful for teachers and parents.

660. *Understanding Dyslexia and the Reading Process: A Guide for Educators and Parents.* Sanders, Marion. Boston: Allyn and Bacon, 2001. 210 pp. ISBN: 0205309070. Level: Educators/Parents.

The main objective of this book is to demystify dyslexia by presenting and illustrating its manifestations so that it can be understood by educators, parents, and professionals. Extensive research on helping children who do not learn to read on schedule is provided by the author. Case studies of seven individuals demonstrate the mix of particular personal, family, and situational variables that make each person unique. One of the chapters discusses biological, social, and psychological factors that affect learning. The final two chapters present the history and nature of reading instruction and the steps that can be taken to improve it. A glossary and two appendices are included. Appendix A provides definitions of dyslexia and learning disabilities; Appendix B lists additional resources for parents and teachers, such as organizations and their publications and websites. This is a highly recommended book that contains a wealth of information.

661. *Overcoming Dyslexia: A New and Complete Science-Based Program for Reading Problems at Any Level.* Shaywitz, Sally E. New York: Vintage

Books, 2005. 414 pp. ISBN: 0679781595; ISBN2: 9780679781592. Level: Educators/Parents.

As the winner of two awards, the Margot Marek Book Award from the International Dyslexia Association of New York and Ken Book Award from the National Alliance for the Mentally Ill, this comprehensive, up-to-date book offers parents and educators scientific and human perspectives on a reading problem that troubles one in every five American children. Drawing on scientific research and her own case histories, the author addresses the following topics for parents and teachers who need to help the dyslexic child, based on his or her age, and grade level: what causes dyslexia, and how to identify it at different ages; how to find the right school; and how to work with the child's teacher productively. In addition, exercises to help children use the parts of the brain that control reading, a twenty-minute nightly home program to improve reading, a list of 150 most common problem words that can help the children get a head start, and ways to raise and preserve children's self-esteem using their strengths are included. It is an excellent resource. "Shaywitz's groundbreaking work builds an important bridge from the laboratory to the home and classroom." *Publishers Weekly*

662. *Dyslexia and Reading Difficulties: Research and Resource Guide for Working with All Struggling Readers.* Spafford, Carol A. and George S. Grosser. Boston: Pearson/Ally and Bacon, 2005. 364 pp. ISBN: 0205428568. Level: Educators/Parents.

This book provides a comprehensive overview of one of the most puzzling questions educators and parents face: Why do dyslexics have reading problems and what do we do to help them? These tools are presented in this valuable, informative book: an essential five-hundred-word reading list; practical information for diagnosing dyslexia and reading disabilities; a dyslexia screening checklist and summary with terminology easily referenced and explained for parents and teachers; assessment tools to provide teachers with progress reports about a student's literacy development; and techniques for engaging dyslexic individuals within a balanced literacy program. In addition, the authors address a topic not addressed in too many other resources—the needs of second language learners with learning disabilities—in the chapter titled "Dyslexia: International Perspectives."

Intellectual Disabilities

663. *Sibshops: Workshops for Siblings of Children with Special Needs.* Meyer, Donald J. and Patricia F. Vadasy; illustrated by Cary Pillo Lassen. Baltimore: Paul H. Brookes Publishing, 1994. 237 pp. ISBN: 1557661693. Level: Educators/Professionals.

This excellent workshop guide is written to provide programs, services, and activities for brothers and sisters of individuals with special health and developmental needs. This updated edition will help the siblings to understand specific issues experienced by brothers and sisters with special health and developmental needs and to deal with them. The first part of the book provides an overview of the unusual concerns and opportunities experienced by siblings, as reported in the clinical and research literature and by siblings themselves. The second part is devoted to the Sibshop model, a lively peer support, educational, and recreational program for school-age brothers and sisters. Interesting and enjoyable activities that can be adapted for different disabilities and illnesses as well as ages are also presented. An extensive list of additional resources, including books and organizations, and an index are included.

664. *Parenting Your Complex Child.* Morgan, Peggy Lou. New York: AMACOM, American Management Association, 2006. 220 pp. ISBN: 0814473164. Level: Parents.

Morgan has written this exceptional resource for parents of disabled children based on her personal experience with disabled clients and, more importantly, with her own adopted son with Down syndrome. Part 1 discusses the real world in which a complex child lives. Part 2 helps parents learn about the complex child by reading his behaviors and responses. In addition, this book discusses behavioral disorders, developmental problems, and mental health diagnoses such as autism, Down syndrome, bipolar disorder, schizophrenia, attention-deficit hyperactivity disorder (ADHD), pervasive developmental disorder (PDD), and more. Morgan addresses all of the concerns of the complex child regarding medical, educational, occupational, and social issues. The appendices contain samples of various types of documents, such as routine tracking forms and documentation tools, that can be adapted to individual needs.

665. *Building Blocks for Teaching Preschoolers with Special Needs.* Sandall, Susan Rebecka, Ilene S. Schwartz, with Gail E. Joseph et al. Baltimore: P. H. Brooks, 2002. 214 pp. ISBN: 1557665761. Level: Educators/Professionals.

Practical examples of educational practices that support the inclusion of young children with disabilities and other special needs in community-based classrooms are discussed in this invaluable guide. The three methods teachers can use with any curriculum to include young children with disabilities are: (1) curriculum modifications that allow all children to participate; (2) embedded learning opportunities that are used within typical classroom activities; and (3) child-focused instructional strategies that will help students achieve individual learning objectives. Terms used in the "Building Blocks" model are defined very clearly at the beginning of the book. This is a well-researched book that should be helpful for teachers new to instruction in inclusive classrooms or for those seeking a fresh perspective.

PHYSICAL

Blindness and Visual Impairments

666. *Children with Visual Impairments: A Parents' Guide.* Holbrook, M. Cay, editor. Bethesda, MD: Woodbine House, 1996. 395 pp. ISBN: 0933149360. Level: Parents.

This is a comprehensive guide for parents written by health professionals. The chapter topics include defining visual impairment, daily and family life concerns, legal issues, and the challenges children with multiple and visual disabilities face. This narrative provides practical information in manageable sections. Black and white photographs, a glossary, additional reading resources, an extensive listing of national and state organizations, a list of dog guide schools, and an index are included. This is a highly recommended guide for parents. "Loaded with instructive guidance and concrete support, this fine resource offers a great deal of information and reassurance to parents who have children with visual impairments." *Booklist*

Deafness and Hearing Impairments

667. *Choices in Deafness: A Parents' Guide to Communication Options.* Schwartz, Sue, editor. Bethesda, MD: Woodbine House, 2007. 384 pp. with a CD-ROM. ISBN: 1890627739; ISBN2: 9781890627737. Level: Parents.

This third edition of the preeminent guide for parents is extensively revised and expanded in order to provide a more comprehensive scope of the information regarding deafness or hearing loss. Chapter topics include how the medical profession approaches hearing loss, including assessment, diagnosis, treatment options, cued speech, and the importance of supporting individuals in the deaf community. New third edition sections cover the following topics: universal newborn screening, implemented in thirty-eight states, that identifies children with hearing loss; testing that identifies genetic or hereditary causes; services and devices that enable deaf individuals to communicate; and much more. Many of the chapters use actual scenarios to present the information. The appendices contain a "Systems of Manual Communication," additional reading material, an extensive listing of national organizations serving individuals who are deaf or hard of hearing, and an index. The audio CD contains a demonstration of speech sounds regarding hearing loss. This is highly recommended.

Mobility Impairments

668. *Kids on Wheels: A Guide to Wheelchair Lifestyle for Parents, Teachers, & Professionals.* Dobbs, Jean. Horsham, PA: No Limits Communications, 2004. 155 pp. ISBN: 0971284237. Level: Educators/Parents.

This is the companion volume for *Kids on Wheels: A Young Person's Guide to Wheelchair Lifestyle*. It is a comprehensive resource for parents, teachers, and professionals who need to work with young individuals in need of mobility assistance. Personal experiences are used in illustrating the chapter topics, such as empowering kids, parenting resources, and health and medicine. Practical matters are also addressed, such as insurance issues, personal assistance services, legal questions, transportation and travel concerns, technology products, and clothing. Color and black and white illustrations, bibliographic references, and a directory of resources listed by state are included.

669. *Children with Cerebral Palsy: A Parent's Guide*. Geralis, Elaine, editor. Bethesda, MD: Woodbine House, 1998. 481 pp. ISBN: 0933149824. Level: Parents.

This is the second revised edition of one of the classic works for parents of children with cerebral palsy. Written by professionals, this reassuring and straightforward text is divided into ten chapters that provide comprehensive guidelines for topics such as adjusting to your child's disability, daily care challenges, your legal rights, and hurdles that will be faced. Black and white photographs, an extensive glossary, an extensive list of organizations, additional reading resources, and a listing of special equipment vendors of adaptive equipment, such as wheelchairs, toys, and clothing, are included.

Multiple Physical Disabilities

670. *More Than a Mom: Living a Full and Balanced Life When Your Child Has Special Needs*. Baskin, Amy and Heather Fawcett. Bethesda, MD: Woodbine House, 2006. 487 pp. ISBN: 1890627518; ISBN2: 9781890627515. Level: Parents.

This is a wonderful resource for mothers of special needs children, written by mothers of special needs children based on their own experiences. This resource provides comprehensive information, though informal and humorous at times in order to give the parents some much needed relief during stressful times. Sections and chapters include such topics as taking care of yourself, desperately seeking sleep, finding the help you need, creating a positive future, getting grandparents and the extended family to help, and exploring flexible work options. Additional resources include state leave policies, including a section on Canadian policies, a checklist for child care, sample caregiver interview questions, an extensive list of organizations, additional reading material, and an index.

Chapter 7

Media Resources

Visual resources complement various learning styles in the classroom, and they provide educators, parents, and professionals an alternate means of obtaining information. This chapter includes eighty-eight media resources that are organized alphabetically under the four main headings: General, Emotional, Learning, and Physical. The subheading under Emotional, Learning, and Physical are further divided into specific disorders and disabilities similar to the ones in the first three chapters of this bibliography. There are forty-two entries for educators/parents/professionals and eleven for teens/educators/parents. Twenty-six entries are for high school, five for middle school, and four for elementary school grade levels. There is a disparity of media resources for the elementary grade levels. Due to the unavailability of certain media resources, descriptive media summarizations from print material and websites, as well as reviews from reliable sources, were used to annotate entries. Some of the documentaries can be viewed in segments due to their length and can be adapted for classroom use.

GENERAL

671. *Real Life Teens: Teens and Disabilities.* Princeton, NJ: Films for the Humanities & Sciences, 2007. DVD (18 min.) Grades 8–12.

"This program explores the different ways that disabilities can impact a teen's life and how the general student population can support people with disabilities. Subjects covered include what a disability is; how to understand a disabled student; why those with disabilities are called 'special'; showing respect and helping people with disabilities; and special education. A printable instructor's guide is available online." Films for the Humanities & Sciences

EMOTIONAL

Depression

672. *Childhood Depression.* Princeton, NJ: Films for the Humanities & Sciences, 2000. DVD (29 min.) ISBN: 9781421339900. Level: Educators/Parents.

"Four to eight percent of American children experience bouts of major depression. Among teenage girls, that rate can be as high as sixteen percent. This program . . . emphasizes the importance of early diagnosis and treatment to avoid potential patterns of repeated depression later in life—and to prevent substance abuse and suicide. Children suffering from depression talk about how they cope with it, while child psychiatrist David G. Fassler, author of *Help Me, I'm Sad*, and Steven Atkins, a psychologist at Dartmouth Medical School, provide authoritative insights. A Dartmouth-Hitchcock Medical Center Production." Films for the Humanities & Sciences

673. *From Depression to Discovery: A Teenager's Guidebook.* Princeton, NJ: Films for the Humanities & Sciences, 2006. DVD (25 min.) DVD is subtitled. ISBN: 9781421326924. Grades 9–12.

"This video shatters common misconceptions about depression, helping young viewers recognize its outward and internal symptoms. The latest forms of treatment are also explored. Interviews with teens who are living successfully with the disease, and commentary by renowned adolescent psychologist Dr. Harold S. Koplewicz, are interwoven with eye-catching and informative graphics that reinforce essential points. A printable instructor's guide containing student activities, discussion questions, vocabulary terms, and other helpful features are available online. The result is an honest, youth-centered informational tool that encourages a proactive approach to depression. Correlates to National Health Education Standards. A Cambridge Educational Production." Films for the Humanities & Sciences

674. *Real Life Teens: Teen Depression.* Princeton, NJ: Films for the Humanities & Sciences, 2001. DVD (22 min.) Grades 8–12.

"Depression can be a devastating condition for teens. Through this program, viewers will learn about the real risks of depression, how to identify depression, and how depression interferes with a person's life. Subjects covered include defining depression; the warning signs of depression; identifying the roots of depression; depression and home life; self-medication; self-destructive choices; getting help; and teen suicide. This is real advice for a dangerous and widespread condition among today's teens. A printable instructor's guide is available online." Films for the Humanities & Sciences

Depression-Related Disorders

675. *Nightmare at School.* Montreal, Quebec: The National Film Board of Canada, 2007. DVD (8 min. 43 sec.) Grades 7–9.

"Who hasn't felt apprehensive at the thought of starting high school? This is the central theme of this short animated film. Playing on imagination and humour, the director offers viewers a thought-provoking piece dealing with the transition that young people between the ages of 10 and 13 experience. Inspired by the work of Escher and Magritte, Catherine Arcand has created a graphically rich film through optical illusions and *trompe-l'oeil* effects. Her style aptly illustrates the theme of perceptions and is perfectly suited to conveying the dream world into which the film takes us." *The National Film Board of Canada* This video, which does not contain audio, is available in French: Cauchemar à l'école.

2008 Young Adult Library Services Association (YALSA) award.

Eating Disorders

676. *Battling Eating Disorders.* Princeton, NJ: Films for the Humanities & Sciences, 2006. DVD (29 min.) DVD is subtitled. ISBN: 9781421355740. Teens/Educators/Parents.

"Anorexia and other eating disorders exert a frightening degree of control over millions of teenagers, especially young women. Manifested in so-called Pro-Ana websites sites, which actively promote anorexia, bulimia, and binge eating, the mental and physical grip of these sicknesses can prove impossible to break. This program represents a powerful weapon in the battle against eating disorders, pinpointing their origins in body image and self-esteem issues, illustrating their grim consequences in crystal-clear terms, and offering students, parents, teachers, and counselors a rich source of information and support. Hosted by *The Sopranos'* Jamie-Lynn Sigler, herself a survivor of teenage anorexia, the video explains how to recognize eating disorders, how friends and loved ones should communicate their fears and concerns, and how those who suffer from these often fatal illnesses can find professional help. Special emphasis is placed on identifying anorexia, bulimia, and binge eating as actual diseases, not as misguided lifestyle choices—a realization necessary for effective treatment. A printable instructor's guide is available online." Films for the Humanities & Sciences

677. *Body Image for Boys.* Princeton, NJ: Films for the Humanities & Sciences, 2002. DVD (18 min.) DVD is subtitled. ISBN: 9780736593816. Grades 9–12.

"This topical program explores some of the issues facing young men today as they struggle to define themselves amidst the flood of media-generated images of male physical perfection. Experts as well as a number of young patients grapple with problems such as steroid abuse, eating disorders, exercise addiction, and phony food supplements. A printable instructor's guide is available online." Films for the Humanities & Sciences

2003 Young Adult Library Services Association (YALSA) award.

678. *Dying to Be Thin.* [Boston]: WGBH Video, [2004]. DVD (60 min.) Closed captioned (CC). ISBN: 1593751680. Teens/Educators/Parents.

This NOVA production, narrated by Susan Sarandon, addresses the current epidemic regarding eating disorders that affects eight million women. "Driven by the waif-like images flooding the media of popular actresses, models, dancers and celebrities—who can weigh nearly twenty-five percent less than the average American woman—young girls are obsessed with an unattainable image of perfection. *Dying to Be Thin* introduces you to students, ballet dancers, fashion models and other young women who are seeking recovery or have conquered their disease. Plus, you'll discover how leading eating disorder specialists are making dramatic advances in the diagnosis and treatment of these two devastating diseases." WGBH Video

2002 Young Adult Library Services Association (YALSA) award.

679. *I'm a Child Anorexic.* Princeton, NJ: Films for the Humanities & Sciences, 2007. DVD (57 min.) DVD is subtitled. ISBN: 9781421379432. Teens/ Educators/Parents.

"Therapists in America and Europe have noticed a disturbing trend: anorexia now appears in elementary-school-age children. This film documents the highs and lows of a London clinic's 12-week program, during which malnourished patients must confront and conquer their fears of eating. Girls as young as eight enter the clinic dangerously emaciated and depressed—and although most battle their way back to good health and reunions with loved ones, do their attitudes toward food really change? Once home, will they revert to old ways? The documentary reveals frighteningly distorted beliefs that run rampant among the young patients—one girl even insists that water contains calories—and it offers surprising revelations about the role of idealized body images in the media." Films for the Humanities & Sciences

680. *Real Life Teens: Eating Disorders.* Princeton, NJ: Films for the Humanities & Sciences, 2002. DVD (22 min.) Grades 8–12.

"Complex and dangerous, eating disorders have deep physical, psychological, and emotional roots. In this program, teens of both sexes discuss eating disorders and how to cope with them. Subjects covered include why appearance is important; the difference between anorexia and bulimia; why eating disorders are dangerous; what to do if one suspects an eating disorder; why diet pills and fads are dangerous; good nutrition for teens; and where to turn for help with eating disorders. A printable instructor's guide is available online." Films for the Humanities & Sciences

681. *Slender Existence*. New York: Filmakers Library, 2000. DVD (32 min.) Teens/Educators/Parents.

Told from the point of view of her parents and her best friend, this interesting film is about Laura Murray's ten-year struggle with anorexia nervosa that she developed when she was in the ninth grade. "This compelling film documents Laura's descent from a healthy, attractive teenager into one starving herself to the verge of death, obsessed with exercise, unable to sleep, solitary and secretive." Filmakers Library

2001 Young Adult Library Services Association (YALSA) award.

682. *Thin: Death by Eating Disorder*. Princeton, NJ: Films for the Humanities & Sciences, 2005. DVD (103 min.) DVD is subtitled. ISBN: 9781421358499. Teens/Educators/Parents.

"A form of slow suicide: that is what eating disorders are. Filmed at The Renfrew Center of South Florida, this program closely follows four women, ages 15 to 30, into the weighing room, group and individual therapy sessions, the bedroom, and even the bathroom when the film's subjects relapse and purge. It also examines the evasiveness of restrictive eating behaviors as well as the failure of the health insurance industry to address its clients' needs, while never shifting focus from the women themselves. An intimate and devastating portrait of self-loathing, denial, and depression. A brief status report on the patients' uneven experiences after being discharged concludes the program. Some content may be objectionable." Films for the Humanities & Sciences

683. *Wasting Away: Anorexia Nervosa*. Princeton, NJ: Films for the Humanities & Sciences, 2000. DVD (47 min.) ISBN: 9781421370064. Teens/Educators/Parents.

"This emotionally charged program profiles four young women attempting to recover from anorexia nervosa. Ranging in age from 14 to 25, they struggle to gain weight while dealing with associated conditions such as osteoporosis and depression, family dysfunctionality, and a mind-set that equates starvation with self-control. Filmed at the adolescent eating disorder unit and a private outpatient clinic, the program captures the complexities of a devastating psychological disorder that drives women to continuously lose weight—even if it kills them." Films for the Humanities & Sciences

Mental Illness

684. *Bipolar Disorder in Children: Proper Diagnosis & Treatment Options.* Series: A Keeping Kids Healthy. Sherborn, MA: Aquarius Health Care Media, 2005. DVD (27 min.) Closed captioned (CC). Level: Educators/Parents.

"One minute your child is on top of the world—giddy with laughter, full of energy and confidence. The next, he's raging, or crying, or talking of suicide. There might be tantrums, even threats or acts of violence. What's going on? The answer might be bipolar disorder (formerly called 'manic depression'), a mood disorder that can strike children as well as adults. Hear what leading experts have to say about proper diagnosis and treatment." Aquarius Health Care Media

LEARNING

Attention-Deficit/Hyperactivity Disorder (AD/HD)

685. *ADHD & LD: Powerful Teaching Strategies & Accommodations.* Port Chester, NY: National Professional Resources, Inc. 2008. DVD (52 min.) Level: Educators/Professionals.

"This newly revised 2008 DVD incorporates a Response-to-Intervention (RTI) framework to help teachers address the needs of students who present the characteristics of ADHD and/or LD in their general education classrooms. Sandy Rief, nationally acclaimed author and leading authority on educating students with attention, behavioral and learning difficulties, presents a wide range of proven and successful strategies that can be used in the initial stages of RTI implementation. The most comprehensive resource of its kind on the market today!" National Professional Resources, Inc.

686. *All about Boys.* Series: Brazelton on Parenting. Princeton, NJ: Films for the Humanities & Sciences, 2000. DVD (22 min.) DVD is subtitled. ISBN: 9781421326405. Level: Educators/Professionals.

"This video analyzes the links between biological and cultural development in boys, and addresses problems—such as Attention Deficit Disorder and behavioral difficulties in schools—that tend to involve boys." Films for the Humanities & Sciences

687. *Attention Deficit Disorder: What Teachers Need to Know.* Berg, Barbara. Stafford, TX: World Educational Resources, 2004. DVD (22 min.) Level: Educators/Professionals.

"This is perhaps one of the best programs relating to ADD/HD, as it was designed by Barbara Berg, M.S., M.C.S.W, who has counseled thousands of youngsters with ADD/HD and has also been diagnosed as ADD/HD herself. She understands the difficulty children and teachers have in their daily routine. Barbara provides insight for teachers to understand the illness and what things teachers can do or not do to improve the education and behavioral environment of those children with AD/HD." World Educational Resource

688. *Children in Crisis.* Princeton, NJ: Films for the Humanities & Sciences, 2004. DVD (46 min.) ISBN: 9780736597753. Level: Parents.

"Lillian, a four-year-old with autism, lives in a world all her own. Sixteen-year-old A.D.'s attention-deficit/hyperactivity disorder causes him to proudly proclaim that he does not love his parents anymore. Eleven-year-old Pamela's five different diagnoses stand in the way of her being left alone with her brother. These children are examples of the more than 3 million in the country who have some type of mental and behavioral disorder. This intense program highlights how their lives, as well as the daily routines of their families, are an incessant struggle. Therapists from Vanderbilt University School of Medicine and Center for Child Development and Research assert that with proper diagnosis and treatment, children and families can find a measured quality of life." Films for the Humanities & Sciences

689. *The Drugging of Our Children: Inside the ADHD Controversy.* Princeton, NJ: Films for the Humanities & Sciences, 2005. DVD (104 min.) DVD is subtitled. ISBN: 9781421361017. Level: Educators/Parents.

"Some doctors are wary of prescribing medication for ADD or ADHD, especially when treating young patients—but the majority relies on psychotropic drugs. This program challenges the status quo, supported by a staggering amount of testimony and documentation. Incorporating detailed interviews with psychiatrists, neurologists, and education experts—as well as parents and kids who have suffered because of rigid prescription practices—the program analyzes links between school procedures, the medical establishment, and Big Pharma. Footage from the 1998 Consensus Development Conference on ADD/ADHD raises disturbing questions about how the disorders are diagnosed." Films for the Humanities & Sciences

690. *Living with ADHD.* Princeton, NJ: Films for the Humanities & Sciences, 2004. DVD (50 min.) DVD is subtitled. ISBN: 9781421319629. Level: Parents.

"Children with Attention Deficit Hyperactivity Disorder need not miss out on crucial educational opportunities. This program describes new medical strategies designed specifically for parents struggling to keep ADHD from controlling their households and limiting the prospects and happiness of their children. It also focuses on the challenges of parents who, in addition to their children, are diagnosed with the disorder. While presenting concerns that Ritalin and other drugs have led to overmedication, the video demonstrates that clinical advances are enabling children to learn constructive behavior, build relationships, and lay the foundations of a rewarding life." Films for the Humanities & Sciences

691. *Living with Attention-Deficit/Hyperactivity Disorder.* Princeton, NJ: Films for the Humanities & Sciences, 2000. DVD (53 min.) ISBN: 9780736558853. Level: Educators/Parents.

"Attention-deficit/hyperactivity disorder is characterized by developmentally inappropriate impulsivity, inattentiveness, and, in some cases, hyperactivity. In this program, therapists, teachers, parents, and patients offer their insights into living with and overcoming AD/HD. The benefits of a treatment approach combining ongoing psychological assessment, specialized classes, and carefully monitored use of Ritalin or similar medications are cited. In addition, the brain biochemistry of people with AD/HD is discussed, and anomalous brain development before birth is identified as a likely cause of the disorder." Films for the Humanities & Sciences

692. *Medication for ADHD: YES or NO? A Practical Guide.* Glen Ellyn, IL: Parent-Magic, Inc., 2004. DVD (40 min.) ISBN: 188914018X. Level: Educators/Parents.

"This comprehensive program addresses the critical questions regarding medication in the treatment of ADD or ADHD are addressed through interviews with experts Dr. Jonathan Bloomberg and Dr. Thomas Phelan. Questions addressed: When is medication appropriate; What drugs are available; What benefits can be expected; Can a drug improve social life; Medication 'holidays' and summertime use; The relationship between drug treatment addiction. Special features: Medication Fact Sheets: describing medications available; Medication Hot Line: advice about mornings, sports, homework, ACTs, SATs, family gatherings, discipline, vacations and more; Common Medication Management Mistakes." ParentMagic, Inc.

693. *Troubled Kids: Is Medication the Answer?* Princeton, NJ: Films for the Humanities & Sciences, 2002. DVD (21 min.) DVD is subtitled. ISBN: 9781421318271. Level: Educators/Parents.

"Millions of children in America are being diagnosed with learning disorders and depression. While many say medications such as Ritalin, Dexedrine, and Prozac are the answer, others recommend counseling, social skills training, or dietary changes. How does one distinguish between a child with Attention Deficit Hyperactivity Disorder and a kid who is just being a kid? This program offers parents, teachers, and caregivers a balanced look at options for helping children with learning difficulties or behavioral problems. A viewable/printable instructor's guide is available online." Films for the Humanities & Sciences

Autism Spectrum Disorders

694. *Asperger Syndrome—Living Outside the Bell Curve.* [S.l.]: Attainment Company, Inc.; Cicero, NY: Distributed Program Development Associates, 2008. DVD (17 min.) Closed captioned (CC). Level: Educators/Parents.

"There has been an increase in the diagnoses of Asperger Syndrome in recent years. This video looks at Asperger in general while focusing on 12 year old Andrew. Includes an in-depth interview with Dr. Tina Iyama, MD, University of Wisconsin Children's Hospital. Lyama explains the symptoms, causes of and strategies for coping with Asperger Syndrome. Andrew shows that with successful supports, it's possible to develop skills and behaviors appropriate for the classroom, while maintaining his unique personality. A thoroughly watchable and informative video. Ideal for staff and parents." Program Development Associates

695. *Asperger Syndrome: Success in the Mainstream Classroom.* [Winston-Salem, NC]: Coulter Video, 2000. DVD (44 min.) Level: Educators/Parents.

"This video provides proven techniques and tips to help make mainstreaming a child with Asperger Syndrome a positive learning experience for him or her—AND for teachers and classmates. Whether your child's classroom has one teacher, or the support of special education teachers and aides, these approaches can help make the difference in your child's education. You'll see interviews with psychologist Dr. Jed Baker, parents, regular and special education teachers, an instructional aide and a case manager/social worker—all describing specific steps that have worked for them in guiding and teaching children with AS in elementary through high school classes. You can think of this as 'Asperger Syndrome 101.' At 44 minutes, it's the perfect length to view during an available class period (or to use as a teacher in-service program) and it points the way toward other resources to help generate continued success." Coulter Video

696. *Asperger Syndrome: Transition to College and Work.* [Winston-Salem, NC]: Coulter Video, 2001. DVD (57 min.) Grades 9–12.

This DVD includes interviews with leading experts in the field of learning disabilities. "This video details the things people with Asperger Syndrome need to do to prepare for college and to find and hold a job." Coulter Video

697. *Asperger Syndrome: Transition to Work Video.* [Winston-Salem, NC]: Coulter Video, 2004. VHS (34 min.) Grades 9–12.

"This video details specific things people with Asperger Syndrome need to do to successfully apply for and hold a job. It's relevant for people with a range of challenges and capabilities—and includes sections on finding a job, what makes a good job match, how to approach employers, key workplace skills, disclosure issues and negotiating accommodations to help you succeed in your job." Coulter Video

698. *Asperger's Unplugged: An Interview with Jerry Newport.* Stafford, TX: World Educational Resources: distributed by Program Development Associates, 2005. DVD (38 min.) Teens/Educators/Parents.

"Jerry Newport discovered he has Asperger's Syndrome while watching *Rain Man* and has since become an engaging speaker and self-help organizer. . . . His engaging interview is educational as well as encouraging. An excellent video for teachers, professionals, high school and college students, and anyone who wants to learn about Asperger's Syndrome from a personal perspective." Program Development Associates

699. *Asperger's: What Teachers Need to Know.* Stafford, TX: World Educational Resources, 2005. DVD (27min.) Level: Educators/Professionals.

This program covers the characteristics and diagnosis of Asperger's syndrome, which is one of the least known yet fastest emerging diagnosis for children and adults. Expert Dr. Pauline Filipek explains symptoms and strategies for coping with this disability.

700. *At the Gates of Autism: Emerging into Life.* Princeton, NJ: Films for the Humanities & Sciences, 2000. DVD (59 min.) ISBN: 9781421375588. Level: Educators/Parents.

"As a child, Dr. Temple Grandin was diagnosed as brain-damaged; doctors today would call her autistic. But her condition did not deter her and, with the help of her mother and therapists, she went on to become an expert in animal behavior, designing livestock handling facilities and teaching as an assistant professor at Colorado State University. Much of her expertise with animals comes through lessons learned from her own condition. This program provides the rare opportunity to hear an autistic person discuss her condition and how she deals with life. Dr. Grandin offers many insights into the motivations behind autistic behavior and how parents, teachers, and therapists can better work with autistic children." Films for the Humanities & Sciences

701. *Autism & the New Law: Resources for Treatment.* [Alexandria, VA]: PBS. 2001. DVD (45 min.) Closed captioned (CC). ISBN: 0964616882. Level: Educators/Parents.

"Parents, educators, and healthcare professionals will benefit from this fact-filled documentary about autism, its diagnosis, and treatments. The video explains the Advancement of Pediatric Autism Research Act and discusses new studies and potential cures. Hosted by Anthony Edwards of *ER*." PBS

702. *Autism: Diagnosis, Causes, and Treatments.* Princeton, NJ: Films for the Humanities & Sciences, 2001. DVD (53 min.) ISBN: 9780736557979. Level: Educators/Parents.

"What is it like for people with autism, living among others yet always, in a sense, living alone? And how do their parents cope, as they care for them? Built around several case studies, this program distinguishes between high- and low-functioning autism; illustrates structural and functional differences between autistic and non-autistic brains; considers genetics, neurological diseases, and immune system anomalies as possible contributory factors; and discusses associated conditions, such as mental retardation, epilepsy, and echolalia. Applied behavior analysis, the TEACCH system, multi-sensory stimulation, and dietary interventions are also touched upon." Films for the Humanities & Sciences

703. *Autism Is a World.* Port Chester, NY: CNN Productions and State of the Art, Inc. [distributed by] National Professional Resources Inc., [2005]. DVD (40 min.) Grades 9–12.

"Sue Rubin, who is autistic, was diagnosed and treated for mental retardation until the age of 13, when she began to communicate using a keyboard. In Sue's own words, *Autism Is a World* takes the viewer on a journey into her mind, her daily world, and her life with autism." CNN Productions

704. *Autism Spectrum Disorders.* Verona, WI: IEP Resources, 2001. DVD (39 min.) Closed captioned (CC). ISBN: 1578611512. Level: Educators/Professionals.

"This DVD covers cognitive style, diagnostic characteristics, communication skills, social behaviors and support strategies presented by an educational psychologist. Educational psychologist and author Glenis Benson presents a comprehensive overview of autism spectrum disorders. Her developmental perspective covers major issue areas: Cognitive style, diagnostic characteristics, communication skills and deficits, social behaviors, support strategies and challenging behaviors." IEP Resources

705. *Asperger Syndrome: A Different Mind.* Baron-Cohen, Simon and Catherine Collis. London: Red Green & Blue Company: University of Cambridge; Distributed by Jessica Kingsley Publishers, 2006. DVD (30 min.) ISBN: 1843104717; ISBN2: 9781843104711. Level: Educators/Parents.

"Narrated by Simon Baron-Cohen, a Professor of Developmental Psychopathology at Cambridge University, this interesting DVD provides insight into the lives of six individuals who have Asperger Syndrome, and range in age from Joe, aged 5 to twins Peter and Mathew, aged 22. . . . The video highlights the positive developments that have taken place during the recent years towards a better understanding of children with Asperger Syndrome. Highly recommended for parents, teachers, and other professionals." Red Green & Blue Company

706. *Embracing Play: Teaching Your Child with Autism.* Bethesda, MD: Woodbine House, 2006. DVD (47 min.) ISBN: 0972708014. Level: Parents.

"In this video, parents discuss the importance of play in reaching their child with autism and the rewards that follow. Professionals and parents demonstrate strategies for creating the structure necessary to foster your child's play skills. Teaching your child how to explore and enjoy objects in his/her environment, through 'Object Focused Play,' sets the foundation for your child's communication and social development. Recommended to be used with *Passport to Friendship.* An excellent guide for parents who incorporate applied behavior analysis with their child. With strong production values and informative illustrations, it focuses on using play as a way to interact better with a child with ASD." *Library Journal*

707. *Finding the Words: Case Studies in Autism Treatment.* Princeton, NJ: Films for the Humanities & Sciences, 2005. DVD (53 min.) ISBN: 9781421341200. Level: Educators/Parents.

"Jake and Andrew are two young boys with autism. Diagnosed in preschool, they have been undergoing applied behavioral analysis for several years now, with mixed results. This two-part series from ABC News examines their progress while discussing the benefits and apparent limits of ABA." Films for the Humanities & Sciences

708. *Children and Autism: Time Is Brain.* Hornbein, Marie and Patty Satalia. University Park, PA: Penn State Media Sales; Cicero, NY: Program Development Associates, 2004. DVD (28 min.) Level: Educators/Parents.

"This documentary features two families faced with the daunting challenge of raising a child with autism. Includes family therapists, and a board certified behavior analyst with more than 25 years of experience designing learning environments for people with autism and developmental disabilities. Discussions include identifying the signs and symptoms of autism, and ABA or Applied Behavior Analysis recognized by the Surgeon General." Program Development Associates

709. *Intricate Minds: Understanding Classmates with Asperger Syndrome.* [Winston-Salem, NC]: Coulter Video, 2005. DVD (12 min.) Grades 6–12.

"Candid interviews with teenagers designed to promote positive interactions between classmates and reduce harassment and bullying. Through interviews with students who have Asperger Syndrome (AS), this video offers an inside look at how teenagers with AS act, think and feel—and how they're routinely treated. The students talk about their strengths as well as their challenges and describe how important is it to them to be treated with respect. The program's open includes speculation that Wolfgang Amadeus Mozart, Sir Isaac Newton and Albert Einstein had Asperger Syndrome. After viewing this video, classmates should be less likely to ignore or harass students with AS—and be more willing to treat them as equals. The program is designed for students in high school and middle school and is an excellent staff development tool." Download free discussion guide for *Intricate Minds* in Word for Windows format. Coulter Video

710. *Intricate Minds II: Understanding Elementary School Classmates with Asperger Syndrome.* [Winston-Salem, NC]: Coulter Video, 2006. DVD (16 min.) Grades 3–6.

"This video is an elementary school version of the highly successful 'Intricate Minds' program for middle and high school students. The program includes interviews with boys and girls aged 8 through 12 who describe what it's like to have Asperger Syndrome (AS). They reveal some of the positive qualities classmates will find if they look past the 'different' behaviors that kids with AS sometimes exhibit in school. The program also takes viewers 'inside Asperger Syndrome' with demonstrations to help them see things from the point of view of kids who have AS. *Intricate Minds II* can help classmates avoid the trap of ignoring or teasing kids who have trouble fitting in. Kids who understand the reasons for 'different' students' actions are much more likely to accept them socially and include them in activities. The program is designed for students in elementary grades 3 through 6 and is an excellent staff development tool." Download free discussion guide for *Intricate Minds II* in Word for Windows format. Coulter Video

711. *Intricate Minds III: Understanding Elementary School Classmates.* [Winston-Salem, NC]: Coulter Video, 2006. DVD (17 min.) Grades 3–6.

"The program features interviews with boys and girls aged 8 through 12 who describe what it's like to have conditions that make them act differently from their peers in school. They reveal some of the positive qualities classmates will find if they look past these 'different' behaviors. The program includes 'point of view' demonstrations to show kids how things might seem to them if they perceived the world as some of their classmates do. *Intricate Minds III* can help students avoid the trap of ignoring or teasing kids who have trouble fitting in. Students who understand the reasons for 'different' classmates' actions are much more likely to accept them socially and include them in activities. The program is designed for students in elementary grades 3 through 6 and is an excellent staff development tool." Download free discussion guide for *Intricate Minds III* in Word for Windows format. Coulter Video

712. *The Invisible Wall: Autism.* Princeton, NJ: Films for the Humanities & Sciences, 2001. DVD (51 min.) ISBN: 9781421306865. Level: Educators/ Professionals.

"This program delves into the physiology of autism, a pervasive developmental disorder of the brain that can cause severe deficits in the areas of cognition, communication, socialization, and play. Computer animation reveals the impact of autism on the language center and other parts of the brain, while case studies demonstrate interventions being used to help people with autism live fuller lives. Interviews with Ivar Lovaas, Temple Grandin, and a variety of therapists are featured." Films for the Humanities & Sciences

713. *Talk to Me: Children with Autism.* Kaneshiro, Vanessa. Boston: Fanlight Productions [distributor], 2003. DVD (28 min.) ISBN: 1572959193. Grades 8–12.

"Seven-year-old Adre and Emma, and five-year-old Julian, are in the Autism Program of the Oakland, California, public schools. This engaging documentary takes viewers into their lives at home and at school, and profiles the valiant efforts of their parents and teachers to help them reach their maximum potential. Whatever their incomes, these families struggle to obtain appropriate services for their children, and the film shows realistically that such resources are not always distributed fairly." Fanlight Productions

714. *The Boy Inside.* Kaplan, Marianne. [Boston]: Fanlight Productions [distributor], 2006. DVD (47 min.) Closed captioned (CC). ISBN: 1572958383. Grades 8–12.

"Aspergers is an increasingly common form of autism typically characterized by high intellectual functioning, coupled with emotionally inappropriate behavior and an inability to interact successfully with others. Adam's condition makes life in seventh grade a minefield, a place where he finds himself misunderstood, isolated, and bullied. As he struggles to find a place for himself, he often says or does the wrong thing, and ends up in tears or in fights with other boys. He left his last school after another boy put a knife to his neck. Adam's parents coach him on how to avoid confrontation, and his teachers take extra steps to help the other kids understand him, but his troubles escalate, first at school and then at home." Fanlight Productions

715. *Normal People Scare Me.* [California]: Normal Films, Big Blue Moon Productions [2006]. DVD (90 min.) Grades 9–12.

"17-year-old Taylor Cross captures life and living with autism through interviews with over 65 subjects who have either Asperger's syndrome or autism. Taylor's probing questions and off-beat wit will entertain and educate audiences while shattering the autistic mystic." Big Blue Moon Productions

716. *Passport to Friendship: Facilitating Peer Play for Children with ASD.* S.l: Woodbine House, 2006. DVD (37 min.) ISBN: 0972708022; ISBN2: 9780972708029. Level: Educators/Parents.

This DVD is a follow-up to the previous release, *Embracing Play* (2000). "Using clear examples, insights from parents, and expert commentary by Hilary Baldi of the Behavioral Intervention Association, this illuminating film for parents and educators demonstrates how to build structure and predictability into peer play to help a child with autism. The additional resources (text files accessible by computer) list tried-and-true peer play activities with simple instructions—from rough-and-tumble games to creative ideas for construction play—giving parents ample material for creating fun and instructive play opportunities for their child with autism." Woodbine House "Highly recommended." *Video Librarian*

717. *Autism in the Classroom: What Teachers Need to Know.* Rimland, Bernard. Ft. Lauderdale, FL: World Educational Resources, 2004. DVD (16 min.) Level: Educators/Professionals.

Autism is one of the fastest growing disabilities that affect children in many different and unique ways. Many teachers have not been taught about autism and what special care may be needed to help children with this disability. The program is designed by teachers and parents with autistic children and autistic children in their facilities. Features a short interview with Dr. Bernard Rimland, founder of the Autism Research Institute.

718. *The Spectrum of Autism.* Rosenthal, Heidi. [Boston]: Fanlight Productions [distributor], 2002. VHS (34 min.) ISBN: 1572953446. Teens/Educators/ Parents.

"In this video, we share in the experiences of several families who have struggled to love and care for children who fall at various points on the spectrum of autism. We learn about the symptoms which first alerted them to the possibility of a developmental disorder in their child, and the challenges they faced in obtaining an accurate diagnosis, and then in securing proper treatment and an educational setting appropriate to their children's needs. We hear as well the perspectives of clinicians and educators who explain the difficulties they face in recognizing autism, and point to some of the common developmental signs which may be early signals of the disorder . . . the overriding message of this production is that caring and aware parents and professionals can be extraordinarily effective in enabling children with autism to participate in the world around them." Fanlight Productions

719. *Refrigerator Mothers.* Simpson, David, J. J. Hanley, and Gordon Quinn. [Boston]: Fanlight Productions [distributor], 2002. DVD (53 min.) Closed captioned (CC). ISBN: 1572958286. Level: Parents.

"[S]even women share their poignant stories. All but one were told by psychologists or physicians that they were to blame for their child's autism. The only exception, who is African-American, was told that her son could not be autistic because she did not fit the usual pattern: middle class, highly educated, and white. She was told, instead, that her son must be emotionally disturbed. Yet these courageous women refused to be crushed by the burden of blame. Today, they have strong, supportive relationships with their now adult sons and daughters and, in a variety of ways, have helped them to find their place in the world. Offering fascinating insights into the history of our understanding of mental illness and developmental disabilities, this fascinating and disturbing video raises questions that are of profound relevance today." Fanlight Productions

720. *Struggling with Life: Asperger's Syndrome.* Princeton, NJ: Films for the Humanities & Sciences, 2000. DVD (14 min.) DVD is subtitled. ISBN: 9781421375335. Level: Educators/Professionals.

"Chad is mesmerized by trains. Mikki's passion is washers and dryers. And for Derek, life is a game show, where he is the host and anyone within listening range is a contestant. While these boys might seem like any other children, their intense obsessions are early symptoms of Asperger's syndrome. In this program, ABC News correspondent Jay Schadler reports that neurological disorder, which makes normal interactions with peers virtually impossible. Studies conducted by Yale University's Fred Volkmar shed light on both the compulsive fixations and the difficulties in comprehending facial expressions that characterize Asperger's patients." Films for the Humanities & Sciences

721. *Understanding Brothers and Sisters on the Asperger Syndrome*. [Winston-Salem, NC]: Coulter Video, 2007. DVD (109 min.) Grades 1–12.

"These DVDs are designed to help children of different ages understand and support their siblings on the autism spectrum. One DVD applies to siblings diagnosed with autism, and the other applies to siblings diagnosed with Asperger Syndrome. Each DVD contains four programs; three for siblings of different ages and developmental levels, and one for their parents. The sibling programs are for children ages 4–7, ages 7–12 and ages 12 to adult. While the two DVDs have a similar format, each is unique. For example, we interviewed families dealing with autism for the autism DVD and families dealing with Asperger Syndrome for the Asperger Syndrome DVD. These videos show siblings that other kids are facing the same challenges they face, and explores a range of ways the kids interviewed have learned to get along with and enjoy their brothers and sisters. The videos also can help parents understand the special needs of their neurotypical children. The segments for siblings ages 4–7 feature puppets and the segments for older siblings feature interviews with brothers and sisters. We interviewed mothers and fathers for the parent segments. Overall, we interviewed members of 24 families to create these videos. After viewing these programs, siblings should have a better understanding that their brothers and sisters aren't trying to be difficult, and should be more willing to treat them with tolerance, caring and respect." Coulter Video

722. *Understanding Brothers and Sisters on the Autism Spectrum*. [Winston-Salem, NC]: Coulter Video, 2007. DVD (94 min.) Grades 1–12.

"These DVDs are designed to help children of different ages understand and support their siblings on the autism spectrum. One DVD applies to siblings diagnosed with autism, and the other applies to siblings diagnosed with Asperger Syndrome. Each DVD contains four programs; three for siblings of different ages and developmental levels, and one for their parents. The sibling programs are for children ages 4–7, ages 7–12 and ages 12 to adult. While the two DVDs have a similar format, each is unique. For example, we interviewed families dealing with autism for the autism DVD and families dealing with Asperger Syndrome for the Asperger Syndrome DVD. These videos show sibling kids are facing the same challenges they face, and explores a range of ways the kids interviewed have learned to get along with and enjoy their brothers and sisters. The videos also can help parents understand the special needs of their neurotypical children. The segments for siblings ages 4–7 feature puppets and the segments for older siblings feature interviews with brother and sisters. We interviewed mothers and fathers for the parent segments. Overall, we interviewed members of 24 families to create these videos. After viewing these programs, siblings should have a better understanding that their brothers and sisters aren't trying to be difficult, and should be more willing to treat them with tolerance, caring and respect." Coulter Video

Down Syndrome

723. *Down Syndrome in the Inclusive Classroom.* Princeton, NJ: Films for the Humanities & Sciences, 2001. 2 DVDs (105 min.) ISBN: 9780736566346. Level: Educators/Professionals.

"This compelling two-part series examines the challenges and benefits of educational mainstreaming for children with mental disabilities through the poignant story of Peter Gwasdauskis, a child with Down syndrome. Owing to the extensive classroom footage and many insightful interviews, the series is an indispensable resource for anyone studying or working with Down syndrome, especially within an educational context." Films for the Humanities & Sciences

724. *Educating Peter.* Princeton, NJ: Films for the Humanities & Sciences, 1991. DVD (32 min.) DVD is subtitled. ISBN: 9780736566360. Teens/Educators/ Parents.

"When Peter Gwasdauskis, a child with Down syndrome, was mainstreamed into a public school, he had a lot to learn about dealing with differences—and so did his classmates. Filmed over the course of the third-grade school year, this 1992 Academy Award-winning documentary vividly captures Peter's achievements and frustrations as he makes a place for himself among his peers. The program features interviews with Peter's parents, teachers, fellow students, and aides, and also illustrates how his classmates' wary tolerance grows into sincere acceptance as they actively involve themselves in his process of socialization." Films for the Humanities & Sciences

725. *Downs Syndrome: What Teachers Need to Know.* Glavé, Melody. Ft. Lauderdale, FL: World Educational Resources, 2004. DVD (23 min.) Level: Educators/Professionals.

"This program features Dr. Ruth Smith, PhD., University Researcher, Mental Retardation expert, Susan Carter, a Special Education teacher at Hope University (Anaheim, California) and several Down syndrome children/adults. Most teachers have seen or worked with Down syndrome children, but this program explains some associated problems with DS children and provides tips on how to make their learning experience more productive." World Educational Resources

726. *Graduating Peter.* Princeton, NJ: Films for the Humanities & Sciences, 2001. DVD (76 min.) DVD is subtitled. ISBN: 9780736566384. Teens/Educators/Parents.

"This inspiring and thought-provoking follow-up to the 1992 Academy Award-winning documentary *Educating Peter* highlights the experiences of Peter Gwasdauskis, a child with Down syndrome, in sixth grade, eighth grade, and high school as he adds speech therapy and life skills classes and on-the-job training to his academic coursework. Interviews with Peter's parents, teachers, fellow students, aides, and doctors demonstrate the broad-based, ongoing support mobilized to help him fight depression, improve his ability to communicate, and move ahead in building a meaningful life for himself." Films for the Humanities & Sciences

Dyslexia and Other Learning Disabilities

727. *Classroom Accommodations for Dyslexic Students.* Barton, Susan. San Jose, CA: Bright Solutions for Dyslexia, 2003. DVD (60 min.) with 1 handout. Level: Educators/Professionals.

"In this program, Susan Barton shares 23 practical, no-cost accommodations regular educators should offer to help dyslexic students succeed in the mainstream classroom. Barton shows how to implement these accommodations." *Insight Media*

728. *Could It Be Dyslexia?* Barton, Susan. San Jose, CA: Bright Solutions for Dyslexia, 2000. DVD (45 min.) color with 1 handout. Level: Educators/Parents.

"Presenting research from the National Institutes of Health, this program defines dyslexia and examines the causes of the disorder. It considers warning signs of dyslexia in preschool, elementary, and high school students and adults." *Insight Media*

729. *Dyslexia: Symptoms and Solutions.* Barton, Susan. San Jose, CA: Bright Solutions for Dyslexia, 2006. 2 DVDs (180 min.) Level: Educators/Parents.

"In this program, Susan Barton examines the causes of dyslexia, details warning signs of the disorder in children, and discusses the symptoms of mild dyslexia in adults. She explains that many schools do not test for the disorder, shows how to find a qualified tester, and presents practices for improving school performance." *Insight Media*

730. *Dyslexia: Testing and Teaching.* Barton, Susan. San Jose, CA: Bright Solutions for Dyslexia, 2001. DVD (60 min.) with 1 handout. Level: Educators/ Professionals.

"Susan Barton explains which tests reveal dyslexia and considers who should and should not administer the tests. The program also offers advice for appropriate and inappropriate reading programs to use with dyslexic students." *Insight Media*

731. *Dyslexia: An Unwrapped Gift.* Princeton, NJ: Films for the Humanities & Sciences, 2001. DVD (22 min.). ISBN: 9780736553797. Level: Educators/ Parents.

"This program approaches dyslexia from a new angle, exploring how the so-called disability might prove an advantage in an increasingly image-based world. Educational experts from America and England discuss aptitudes of dyslexics, while video diaries show how dyslexia has affected the lives of young people and how they have harnessed its cognitive differences. Featuring interviews with Tom West, author of *In the Mind's Eye*, this program will boost self-confidence in dyslexics and inspire their teachers and families." Films for the Humanities & Sciences

732. *Dyslexia: What Teachers Need to Know.* Glavé, Melody and Girard J. Sagmiller. Ft. Lauderdale, FL: World Educational Resources, 2004. DVD (16 min.) Level: Educators/Professionals.

"Many youngsters with Dyslexia do not know they have Dyslexia or may not have been diagnosed as Dyslexic. Often, they do not know that there is a different world, they may believe that is the way it is. Gerard Sagmiller is 'the' expert on Dyslexia. He has been living with Dyslexia for most of his life. He is an author and speaks regularly to schools, universities and many other venues on Dyslexia. This program will provide a greater insight for teachers to learn how best to work with and educate people who have Dyslexia." World Educational Resources

733. *Dyslexia.* Guth, Jamie. [Boston]: Fanlight Productions [distributor], 1997. VHS (28 min.) Grades 9–12.

"This outstanding documentary looks at dyslexia, a learning disability that affects millions of Americans. People with dyslexia have minds that are often gifted and productive, but that learn differently from their peers. New approaches to educating children with dyslexia are profiled, and experts such as Dr. Gordon Sherman and Thomas West discuss research into this condition and society's shifting need for these more 'visual' thinkers." Fanlight Productions

734. *Inside Dyslexia.* Princeton, NJ: Films for the Humanities & Sciences, 2007. (57 min.) DVD is subtitled. ISBN: 9781421386379. Level: Educators/Parents.

"This program illustrates the challenges faced by Amanda, Carmen, and Gio—three young people living with dyslexia—through personal interviews with them and those close to them. Viewers are guided into their unique and often overlooked world, made clear through eye-opening scenes at school and home. Produced by filmmakers who are themselves dyslexic, the film serves as a tool for educating others about dyslexia, dyscalculia, and dysgraphia, and for identifying a common vocabulary that can bridge the gap between those with and without learning disabilities. A printable instructor's guide is available online." Films for the Humanities & Sciences

735. *Teach Me Different: Successful Strategies for Teaching Children Who Learn Differently.* Alexandria, VA: PBS Video, 2001. 2 VHS tapes (222 min.) ISBN: 0793691540; ISBN2: 9780793691548. Level: Educators/Professionals.

"All children with learning disabilities can be classroom successes. Sally L. Smith, founder-director of the renowned Lab School of Washington, D.C., demonstrates simple, effective techniques one can immediately use to guide children to academic excellence." The catalog record states: "Sally L. Smith, founder of The Lab School of Washington, distills her classroom and research findings in four special tutorials. Set includes Abilities and Disabilities, Visual Concrete Teaching, Prizing Diversity, and Problem Solving and Self-Advocacy. Winner of the 1993 LDA Award from the Learning Disabilities Association of America, Smith is known for her pioneering approaches to educating children and adults with learning disabilities." PBS website

Intellectual Disabilities

736. *How Difficult Can This Be? F.A.T. City—Understanding Learning.* Lavoie, Richard. [Alexandria, VA]: Artwork PBS. 2004. DVD (70 min.) ISBN: 0793642620. Level: Educators/Parents.

This classic program, originally produced in 1989, continues to be indispensable for those preparing to work with children with learning disabilities. "This unique program lets viewers experience the frustration, anxiety, and tension faced by children with learning disabilities. Workshop facilitator Richard Lavoie presents a series of striking simulations emulating daily experience of LD children. Teachers, social workers, and parents, workshop participants, reflect upon how the workshop changed their approach to LD children." PBS

737. *Beyond F.A.T. City: A Look Back, a Look Ahead.* Lavoie, Richard D., Niki Vettel, and Dennis Allen. [Alexandria, VA]: PBS Video, 2005. DVD (90 min.) Closed captioned (CC). ISBN: 0793690102. Level: Educators/Parents.

This DVD is a continuation of the classic program, *How Difficult Can This Be?* "City Workshop reviews the history and philosophy of the project, the major trends and issues in the field of learning disabilities since 1987, and the challenges ahead for parents and educators." PBS

PHYSICAL

Blindness and Visual Impairments

738. *Acting Blind.* Duckworth, Martin. [Boston]: Fanlight Productions [distributor], 2006. DVD (52 min.) Closed captioned (CC). ISBN: 1572958340. Grades 8–12.

"*Acting Blind* takes audiences behind the scenes as a company of nonprofessional actors rehearse Dancing to Beethoven, a play about blind characters negotiating their way through the emotional and physical maze of life without sight. Most of the performers have no problem imagining themselves in these roles—they are blind themselves. All but one of them lost their sight later in life. In this spirited documentary, we hear their own stories about losing their vision and learning to cope with the world of blindness." Fanlight Productions

739. *Edges of Perception.* Kutner, Eric. [Boston]: Fanlight Productions [distributor], 2007. DVD (14 min.) Closed captioned (CC). ISBN: 1572959010. Grades 8–12.

"Eleven-year-old Jessica Perk thinks she might be a photographer, a gymnast, a soccer player—or maybe the first girl president of the United States. 'We'll just have to wait and see,' she says. But seeing is a problem for Jessica, who has Stargardt's, an inherited form of macular degeneration which usually appears between the ages of six and twenty and causes loss of sharpness of vision, decreased color vision, and blind spots. It's estimated that over 25,000 Americans have the disease, and there's no cure." Fanlight Productions

Deafness and Hearing Impairments

740. *Outside: The Life and Art of Judith Scott.* Bayha, Betsy. [Boston]: Fanlight Productions [distributor], 2006. DVD (26 min.) Closed captioned (CC). ISBN: 1572958529. Grades 8–12.

"For more than a decade, Judith Scott has been deeply involved in making large, colorful body-like sculptures out of found objects and yarn. Her works are abstract, dense, multilayered and, ultimately, a mystery, yet she cannot tell us what they mean, or what inspires her to create these objects. Judith has Down syndrome, is deaf, and does not speak. These sculptures are her most complex means of communication. Judith spent thirty-five years institutionalized, with no creative outlet. Because of her deafness, she had been misdiagnosed as having an IQ of only 30; . . . Today her work sells for thousands of dollars, and has captured the attention of collectors and museums worldwide. Though never fully aware of it herself, Judith had become a famous 'outsider artist.'" Fanlight Productions

741. *Communication Options for Deaf Children: A Family Decision.* [Oklahoma]: Oklahoma Department of Rehabilitation Services; Cicero, NY: Distributed by Program Development Associates, 2002. DVD (18 min.) Closed captioned (CC). Level: Educators/Parents.

"This video helps parents, service providers, and college students understand that there is no 'one right way' of communicating with deaf children that will meet the needs of all families. The emphasis is on researching the various communication options, choosing what is best for a family, and starting the communication process early." Program Development Associates

742. *See What I'm Saying.* Kaufman, Thomas. [Boston]: Fanlight Productions [distributor], 1992. DVD (31 min.) ISBN: 1572958812. Grades 8–12.

This slightly older film has a unique perspective on the challenges facing a deaf child and family. "This illuminating documentary follows Patricia, a deaf child from a hearing, Spanish-speaking family, through her first year at the Kendall Elementary School of Gallaudet University. It dramatically illustrates how the acquisition of communication skills, particularly sign language, enhances a child's self-esteem, confidence, and family relationships. *See What I'm Saying* affords viewers the opportunity to witness exceptional teaching, and Patricia's remarkable progress will reassure parents and teachers that deaf children can become successful communicators and active learners whether or not they learn to speak. This program is not only open-captioned, but signed, dubbed and, when needed, translated from Spanish." Fanlight Productions

743. *Summer's Story.* [Alachua, FL]: Munroe MultiMedia, 2002. VHS (27 min.) Teens/Educators/Parents.

Summer Crider lost her hearing at age 3 and later received a cochlear implant. Until she was 15 she was mainstreamed into a hearing world, but then she was exposed to the deaf community and entered the Florida School for the Deaf and Blind. This is the story of a teenager's growing up in the hearing and deaf worlds.

Sign Language

744. *I Want to Learn Sign Language: Everyday Sign Language Lessons for Children, Ages 5–12.* Ft. Lauderdale, FL: World Educational Resources, 2001. 2 DVDs (120 min.) ISBN: 9781888147759 (Vol. 1); 9781888147766 (Vol. 2). Grades 1–5.

"In fun, real-life scenarios children can learn signing for letters, numbers, favorite foods, hobbies, greetings, favorite expressions, family members, animals, fruits, colors, sports, holidays, and much more. Children can learn about the deaf culture, particularly special telephone devices that let people with hearing impairments talk on the phone, and discover the origins of American Sign Language." World Educational Resources

Mobility Impairments

745. *Mister Spazzman.* Girot, Suzanne. [Boston]: Fanlight Productions [distributor], 2006. DVD (47 min.) ISBN: 1572959045. Grades 8–12.

"At the age of 40, Robert fell out of a tree and broke his neck, becoming a quadriplegic. A professional musician and political activist before the accident, today he expresses his frustrations and passions through the music he writes using a voice-activated computer. Poignant, funny, sometimes downright raunchy, Robert's songs form the central metaphor for his life. Faith and his church; sex and lovers; relationships with friends, family and caretakers are all woven into the musical tapestry he creates. . . . Robert lives in a skilled nursing facility and must come to terms with a life of near-constant pain and 24-hour a day care. Yet he has a wide and supportive network of friends." Fanlight Productions

746. *Cerebral Palsy: What Teachers Need to Know.* Glavé, Melody, Susie Rodde, and Dena Schott. Stafford, TX: World Educational Resources, 2004. DVD (18 min.) Level: Educators/Professionals.

"Children with Cerebral Palsy have unique and distinct wants and needs in the child care and educational environment. This program features Susie Rodde, who has Cerebral Palsy. Susie shares her world and explains what teachers can do to assist children with this disability, which enhances their learning environment. Susie has a disability, but she also leads a productive life. Her story is inspiring, but also educational for anyone working or educating children with Cerebral Palsy." World Educational Resources

747. *Kiss My Wheels.* Grunstein, Miguel and Dale Kruzic. [Boston]: Fanlight Productions [distributor], 2003. DVD (56 min.) Closed captioned (CC). ISBN: 1572958774. Grades 8–12.

"*Kiss My Wheels* follows the Zia Hot Shots, a nationally ranked junior wheelchair basketball team, through a season of training and tournament competition. This spunky, diverse, co-ed group of adolescent athletes bring a special meaning to the idea of teamwork. . . . And we do see them deal with some thorny and difficult issues, from gender conflicts to injury, illness and thoughts of death. . . . This is a great film about living with a disability, but it's an even better film about living with yourself." Fanlight Productions

748. *How Come You Walk Funny?* Hahn, Tina and James Weyman. [Boston]: Fanlight Productions [distributor], 2004. DVD (47 min.) Closed captioned (CC). ISBN: 1572958847. Grades 8–12.

"This video profiles a unique experiment in early childhood education. At Toronto's Bloorview MacMillan Children's Center, 21 four- to six-year-olds, half of whom use walkers, crutches, or wheelchairs, take part in a 'reverse integration' kindergarten classroom. Here, wheelchairs and other mobility equipment compete for space with scooters and trikes in the halls; computer voices from communication devices mix with excited children's chatter. In this program, a group of parents have chosen to enroll their non-disabled kids in a school designed for children with physical disabilities. Its goals are to promote inclusive behavior in the non-disabled children and self-advocacy skills in those with disabilities. Over the course of one academic year, the documentary follows several families who have a variety of motivations for choosing the Center. . . . *How Come You Walk Funny?* explores the challenges, surprises, and inspirations that confront these parents and their 'kindergarten crusaders' as they tackle their differences and discover common ground through 'finding a way that all can play.'" Fanlight Productions

749. *One Strong Arm.* Mendell, Loren and Tiller Russell. [Boston]: Fanlight Productions [distributor], 2004. DVD (19 min.) ISBN: 1572958855. Grades 8–12.

"This is an inspiring and funny portrait of an extraordinary young man. When he was eighteen months old, Cody Wagner was diagnosed with a brain tumor. During surgery, he suffered a series of strokes that paralyzed one side of his brain and body. His doctors told his mother that he would never recover, but they were wrong. He survived and, with the help of dedicated parents and friends, he seemed to thrive. . . . Sixteen years later, he discovers arm wrestling. In his first serious competition, he confronts a taller, heavier, more experienced opponent, who's 'able-bodied' besides." Fanlight Productions

750. *Safe and Courteous Wheelchair Handling: Helping People Using a Wheelchair.* Aquarius Health Care Videos (Firm); Vancouver Island Health Authority (BC) 2006. DVD (14 min.) Grades 8–12.

"Knowing how to help someone in a wheelchair is so important. People with challenges want to feel secure and safe when being helped. This program provides insights on types of wheelchairs, planning for outings, handling a wheelchair inside and outside of a facility and how to relate to a person in a wheelchair. This program will help volunteers to feel more confident in helping others." Aquarius Health Care Media

751. *Pushin' Forward.* Tanaka, Izumi. [Boston]: Fanlight Productions [distributor], 2007. DVD (39 min.) Closed captioned (CC). ISBN: 1572958871. Grades 8–12.

"Growing up poor and Latino in Chicago, James Lilly dreamed of becoming a professional athlete, but he got sidetracked into the world of drugs and gangs. At the age of fifteen, he was shot in the back and paralyzed, but even that didn't put an immediate end to his involvement in drug dealing and fights. Four years later he decided to get away from the gang scene, but on a final visit to the old neighborhood he was attacked and nearly killed. This time, when he recovered, he began to turn his life around. Now, he helps others to do the same thing. James works to help inner city school kids stay on the right track by sharing his story, and by talking about one thing that helped him move on—wheelchair racing. James started racing in 1990. . . . He is an inspiration for at-risk youth, people with disabilities, and anyone struggling to push forward through what seem to be overwhelming difficulties in their lives." Fanlight Productions

Multiple Physical Disabilities

752. *Deafblind: A World without Sight and Sound.* Princeton, NJ: Films for the Humanities & Sciences, 2004. DVD (60 min.) ISBN: 9780736581905. Teens/ Educators/Parents.

"Adam and Mark are 12-year-old boys born deaf and blind. With no exposure to language, how do they communicate with their parents? This fascinating program provides a window into the world of those who are deafblind. Gaela and Graham, two remarkable deafblind adults who lost their hearing after childhood, describe their lives and experiences—including how Graham jet skis." Films for the Humanities & Sciences

753. *Able to Laugh.* Dougan, Michael J. [Boston]: Fanlight Productions [distributor], 1993 DVD (27 min.) Closed captioned (CC). ISBN: 1572958804. Grades 8–12.

This video, originally produced in 1993, is still unique in that actual disabled individuals are portrayed. "Enter the world of disability as interpreted by six professional comics, who happen to be disabled. This video is about the awkward ways disabled and able-bodied people relate to each other, and how humor can remove barriers of fear, guilt, vulnerability and misunderstanding. This will be an outstanding discussion starter for classes in psychology, social work, nursing, and rehabilitation, as well as for healthcare and corporate settings." Fanlight Productions

754. *Mothers of Courage.* Dransfield, Rosie. [Boston]: Fanlight Productions [distributor], 2003. DVD (48 min.) Closed captioned (CC). ISBN: 1572959053. Grades 8–12.

"This insightful video is a tribute to dedicated mothers and fathers throughout North America who fight and organize for their children to get the medical and social services they need. . . . *Mothers of Courage* remains an uplifting story of the best that can happen when parents, school, and community are able to work together to support children with special needs." Fanlight Productions

755. *We are PHAMALY.* Junge, Daniel and Henry Ansbaacher. Boston: Fanlight Productions [distributor], 2003. DVD (19 min.) ISBN: 1572928820. Grades 8–12.

"This engaging and entertaining documentary follows three cast members from their initial auditions through intensive and challenging rehearsals, to opening night, as they take the stage for a remarkable performance of Once Upon a Mattress. Troy Willis (Jester) became legally blind . . . Tara Cowan (Queen Aggravain) uses a motorized wheelchair after a spinal injury. Stephen Hahn (Sir Harry), who was born with Spina Bifida, wears leg braces and has increasing mobility difficulties. 'It's OK to be disabled,' he says. 'It's not OK to be disabled and use it as an excuse to not do everything you can to contribute, and to be the best person you can be. But everybody in PHAMALY gives it everything they've got, every day.'" Fanlight Productions

756. *KidAbility Special.* Cicero, NY: Program Development Associates, 2001. DVD (49 min.) Grades 5–12.

This two-part program, KidAbility 1999 and KidAbility Two 2001, is on one DVD. "Part 1 provides general disability etiquette guidelines that both children and adults can benefit from through profiling adults and children who talk candidly about their disabilities. Part 2 is designed as an introduction to assistive technology for kids, with and without disabilities, to increase the understanding and sensitively towards people with disabilities." Program Development Associates "Overall, a useful tool for raising disability awareness." *Booklist*

757. *Kids with Differences: The Series.* Lake Oswego, OR: Arnold Creek Productions. 2005. DVD (25 min.) Grades K–12.

This upbeat thought-provoking three part program, running about eight minutes each, helps break down stereotypes of children and teens with physical and nonvisible health differences such as, cerebral palsy, hearing loss, and so forth. The program promotes discussion focusing on differences rather than handicaps or disabilities. Part 1: "More Alike Than Different," which is recommended for grades three to six, features children and teens with nonvisible health differences. Part 2: "Kids Just Want to Have Fun," which is recommended for grades kindergarten through five, features children and teens with physical differences. Part 3: "What's the Difference?" which is recommended for middle and high school, features teens with physical differences and stresses educating their peers on disabilities.

758. *With Pity: A Film about Abilities.* Princeton, NJ: Films for the Humanities & Sciences. 1996. DVD (56 min.) Grades 8–12.

Originally produced in 1996, this film is still an excellent portrayal of disabilities. "This HBO documentary, narrated by Christopher Reeve, celebrates the efforts of people with disabilities to live full, productive lives. We meet a cross-section of Americans. . . . This program applauds the resilience and potential of people turning disabilities into 'diff-abilities' in their determination to be self-sufficient." Films for the Humanities & Science

Chapter 8

Internet Resources

This chapter, which encompasses ninety-nine entries, is organized alphabetically under four main headings: General, Emotional, Learning, and Physical. The majority of the entries are for educators/parents/professionals and there are two for teens/educators/parents. Three entries are for high school, six for middle school, and two for elementary school grade levels. Although the majority of these resources are for educators, parents, and professionals, some of the features within the websites can be adapted to meet the curricular needs of children at different grade levels. Several of the websites, although identified for educators, parents, and professionals, contain sections for specific grade levels. Grade levels have been noted within the entries. Websites that focus primarily on social networking have not been included.

GENERAL

759. Girls Health. www.girlshealth.gov/. Grades 5–10.

This excellent website, maintained by the Office on Women's Health in the United States, U.S. Department of Health and Human Services, promotes healthy, positive behaviors in teenage girls. The tagline "Be Happy, Be Healthy. Be You. Beautiful" illustrates the emphasis of this well-designed website. Useful and reliable information regarding health issues is divided into the categories of body, fitness, nutrition, illness and disability, drugs, alcohol and smoking, emotions, relationships, bullying, safety, and the future. Under the illness and disability section, in-depth information is provided pertaining to learning disabilities, spinal cord injuries, traumatic brain injuries, living with an illness or disability, rehabilitation using games and activities, and medical issues. By using the link

"Partners and Friends of girlshealth.gov," additional information on these topics can be accessed. A comprehensive glossary is included. Some of the sections are available in Spanish as well.

EMOTIONAL

Depression

760. Family Aware. www.familyaware.org/

This website provides excellent coverage of depression. It defines and identifies symptoms and signs and offers suggestions for helping someone who is depressed. In addition, it has a section that lists strategies and suggestions to help in coping after a tragedy. Other subsections containing valuable information are devoted to teens and children and parents. Some of the resources, such as flyers and videos, can be downloaded. Special features include online confidential tests for depression and bipolar disorders and a form for completing a mental health family tree.

Depression-Related Disorders

761. Anxiety Disorders Association of America (ADAA). www.adaa.org/

This site provides information and background on a variety of disorders, such as anxiety, depression, bipolar, eating, and much more. The resources section lists advice for locating therapists, treatment options, clinical trials, frequently asked questions, glossary, and excellent links to organizations, treatment centers, and self-help resources. Special features include online self-tests for parents, children, and teens, and family members; statistics and facts; and online resources including websites. A free e-newsletter titled *Triumph* is available.

Eating Disorders

762. Bulimia Treatment. www.bulimia-treatment.net

This website provides excellent coverage on bulimia, its symptoms, causes, and treatment. Other eating disorders are explained, such as anorexia, binge eating, compulsive eating, and several more. A confidential online assessment, including a list of additional websites, can be accessed.

763. National Association of Anorexia Nervosa and Associated Disorders (ANAD). www.anad.org

The ANAD, the oldest eating disorder organization in the nation, is a nonprofit corporation that educates the general public and health care professionals in the area of eating disorders, especially anorexia nervosa and bulimia nervosa. The strength of this website lies in its identification of treatment facilities that sponsor ANAD. Updated news, how to locate therapists, treatment programs, as well as online documents concerning eating disorders are included. ANAD maintains a mirror website in Spanish.

764. National Eating Disorders Association (NEDA). www.nationaleatingdisorders .org

The NEDA, established in 2001, is the largest not-for-profit organization in the United States, and it works to prevent eating disorders and provide treatment referrals to those suffering from anorexia, bulimia, and binge eating disorder. Features include a listing of registered coordinators and events in each state that support the National Eating Disorders week; substantial online resources for specific groups, such as girls and women, boys and men, parents, friends, students, and educators and coaches. In addition to an excellent section titled Eating Disorders Survival Guide, the website also addresses insurance issues, as well as assessment and appropriate care. Some of the sections are available in Spanish as well.

765. Something Fishy: Website on Eating Disorders. www.something-fishy.org

This excellent comprehensive website covers anorexia, bulimia, compulsive eating, binge eating, and ED-NOS (eating disorder not otherwise specified). It has an outstanding list of online resources in the section titled Associated Mental Health Conditions and Addictions. An online questionnaire can be completed and used for consultation with a doctor or a therapist. One of the sections contains information that educators can use in discussing websites that promote destructive eating disorders. Noteworthy features are societal factors that encourage eating disorders, detailed information regarding prescribed medications, and a listing of organizations, additional websites, hotlines, and research links. The site has received numerous awards.

766. Overeaters Anonymous (OA). www.overeatersanonymous.org

OA is a fellowship of individuals recovering from compulsive overeating. This organization, originally composed of adults, has shown an increased interest in addressing the needs of children and young adults. OA's website now contains a section for specifically for youth. Youth in OA newsletter and publications are available online. Two exceptional e-booklets, The Twelve Steps and Twelve Traditions of Overeaters Anonymous: A Kid's View and Billy's Story, can be printed and used with younger children.

Mental Illness

767. Bipolar Significant Other (BPSO). www.bpso.org

The members in this informal organization exchange support and information about bipolar disorder using email and discuss the impact of bipolar disorder issues on their family members. The major sections on BPSO's website include diagnosis and treatment, medications, self-care, the role of the family and caregivers, organizations, and the latest research. Other sections address bipolar disorder in children and adolescents, including personal reflections from those individuals who have bipolar disorder. An extensive bibliography is included.

768. BP Children. www.bpchildren.com

This website is maintained by psychologists, a medical doctor, and authors who have written about bipolar disorder in children. Fun for Kids section contains stories from kids dealing with bipolar disorder, an online sibling story, My Special Brother Turtle, printable mood charts, downloadable coloring and discussion pages for Tracy Anglada's book, Brandon and the Bipolar Bear, and a free e-newsletter for kids. The section about school contains online resources that help children with bipolar disorder succeed in school, and the section for parents provides contact information for support organizations.

769. Child & Adolescent Bipolar Foundation (CABF). www.bpkids.org

The CABF is a parent-led, web-based membership, not-for-profit organization. The Learning Center section contains online resources for parents, including excellent descriptions and historical highlights of bipolar disorders and support groups. Additional resources and chat rooms require registration. A free e-bulletin is accessible. Some sections are available in Spanish.

770. CopeCareDeal: A Mental Health Site for Teens. www.copecaredeal.org. Grades 7–10.

This excellent website for teens is sponsored by the Adolescent Mental Health Initiative created by the Annenberg Foundation Trust at Sunnylands. The Initiative's mission as reflected in this website is to inform teenagers about the prevention and treatment of mental disorders in adolescents. Each of the three main sections, Cope, Care, and Deal, provides positive strategies for dealing with mental health issues. The Mind Zone provides facts about mental disorders, such as depression, bipolar disorder, anxiety, schizophrenia, and suicide. Additional features include helpful online resources, a glossary, myths versus facts, and frequently asked questions about mental illness.

771. Depression and Bipolar Support Alliance (DBSA). www.ndmda.org

This website is sponsored by the DBSA, a leading patient-directed, not-for-profit, national organization that focuses on mental illnesses, particularly mood disorders such as depression, bipolar disorder, anxiety disorder, and many more. Noteworthy features include current news available via podcasts and blogs, numerous free educational materials that can be downloaded, confidential online mood disorders screening tests, and advice for helping someone with a mood disorder. There is a mirror site in Spanish.

772. National Alliance on Mental Illness (NAMI). www.nami.org

NAMI is the nation's largest grassroots mental health organization dedicated to improving the lives of persons living with serious mental illness and their families. This website contains three major sections: (1) Inform Yourself, which includes information about attention-deficit/hyperactivity disorder, eating disorders, general information about medications, recovery, and research; (2) Find Support, which includes information regarding state, local, education and support groups, child and adolescent as well as multicultural needs; (3) Take Action, which includes information pertaining to legislation advocacy and fighting the stigma of mental illness. The *Advocate*, an e-newsletter, is available. Some sections are available in Spanish.

773. Pendulum. www.pendulum.org

Since 1994, Pendulum.org, a leading nonprofit web community, has been providing quality information, support, and education to the family members, caregivers, and individuals whose lives have been impacted by bipolar disorder. This comprehensive and in-depth website provides information in a multilayered format. Topics regarding bipolar disorder include symptoms, causes, diagnosis, treatments, medications and medication side effects, complementary treatments, childhood bipolar disorder, and bipolar education. The website contains over fifty bipolar disorder–related audio and video files ready for immediate listening and viewing. These files are divided into categories such as causes, diagnosis, treatment, family, society, rehabilitation, specific treatments such as medication, psychotherapy, and electroconvulsive therapy, legislation and advocacy for the mentally ill, special patient populations, interviews with bipolar authors and researchers, and more.

774. Schizophrenia. schizophrenia.com

Schizophrenia.com is a leading nonprofit web community, established in 1995, and dedicated to providing quality information, support, and education to family members, caregivers, and individuals whose lives have been impacted by this disorder. This comprehensive and in-depth website provides information in a multilayered format. Topics regarding schizophrenia include symptoms, causes, treatments, recovery tips, facts and statistics, and frequently asked questions. The website contains over 120 schizophrenia-related audio and video files ready for immediate listening and viewing. These files are divided into categories such as causes, diagnosis, treatment, family, society, rehabilitation, specific treatments, prevention, and more.

Multiple Emotional Disabilities

775. Columbia University Teen Screen Program Mental Health Check-Ups for Youth. www.teenscreen.org. Teens/Educators/Parents.

Teen Screen is a program that encourages adults and teens to learn more about mental health issues using screening tests. The following topics are found on this website: fact sheets about mental health, current research, frequently asked questions concerning the importance of mental health screening, specific frequently asked questions for parents and school administrators and staff. Teen Screen affiliates across the country can be located. Online resources are divided into general information and information for parents and teens. New updates, profile stories, tips, and best practices from the mental health community are featured in Teen Screen's e-newsletter.

776. Musicians for Mental Health. www.mpoweryouth.org/411.htm. Grades 9–12.

This website addresses a wide range of mental health issues, including depression, anxiety, eating disorders, and other related issues for teenagers. Special sections list crisis hotlines and suggestions for getting help. Over one hundred artists have lent their names, their personal stories, and MP3 songs to support mental health awareness.

777. National Mental Health Consumers' Self-Help Clearinghouse. www.mhself help.org

The National Mental Health Consumers' Self-Help Clearinghouse is the nation's first national consumer technical assistance center that collects information regarding all aspects of mental health. In addition to consumer resources, educators and professionals can use the resources section, which contains online materials regarding mental health concerns about disorders and disabilities such as anxiety disorders, schizophrenia, autism, Asperger's syndrome, and more. This Clearinghouse also contains information on other disorders and disabilities such as vision and hearing impairments, as they pertain to mental health. An e-newsletter titled *Key Update* is available.

LEARNING

Attention-Deficit/Hyperactivity Disorder (AD/HD)

778. ADDvance. www.addvance.com

Internationally recognized authorities on attention deficit disorder (ADD) and authors of several books about ADD (AD/HD) for children, teens, and adults are the founders of this website, which addresses a variety of needs of all people with ADD (AD/HD). The special feature, Answers to Your Questions, is categorized according to age level, such as parents, teens, young adults, adults, women and girls, and professionals. Another noteworthy section, ADD-Friendly Living, covers tools, tips, and strategies to create a more friendly lifestyle. An extensive list of additional websites on this subject is provided in the resources section. A free e-newsletter is available.

779. Children and Adults with Attention-Deficit/Hyperactivity Disorder (CHADD). www.chadd.org

CHADD is a national nonprofit organization that provides education, advocacy, and support for individuals with AD/HD. This website contains sections for parents, adults with AD/HD, those new to AD/HD, and professionals. CHADD publishes a variety of printed materials to keep members and professionals current on research advances, medications, and treatments affecting individuals with AD/HD. One of CHADD's most helpful publications is *Attention!* magazine, which is available with a membership to CHADD. Also includes tips and resources for schools as well as information such as myths and misunderstandings about AD/HD. This website contains a wealth of information. A free e-newsletter and blog are available.

780. National Resource Center for AD/HD. Children and Adults with Attention-Deficit/Hyperactivity Disorder (CHADD). www.help4adhd.org

The National Resource Center on AD/HD is the nation's clearinghouse for science-based information about all aspects of attention-deficit/hyperactivity disorder (AD/HD). This website meets the information needs of professionals and the general public. Sections include symptoms, medications, doctors, behavior, and schools, including a special section that deals with educational issues such as scholarships, financial aid, and so forth. Each of these sections has links for additional information. This site is available in Spanish.

Autism and Spectrum Disorders

781. Association for Science in Autism Treatment (ASAT). www.asatonline.org

Established in 1998, the ASAT, a not-for-profit organization of parents and professionals, maintains this website for improving the education, treatment, and care of people with autism. The major sections include how to define autism; what families and professionals need to do; which conferences to attend; and what additional resources are available.

782. The Autism Research Institute (ARI). www.autism.com

The ARI, a nonprofit organization, was founded in 1967 by Bernard Rimland, Ph.D., an internationally recognized authority on autism. ARI continues to be the hub of a worldwide network of parents and professionals concerned with all aspects of autism. The sections for individuals, families, and providers contain numerous links to online documents and additional sites. For example, the section For Families addresses the following topics: living with autistic spectrum disorders, educational therapies, sensory integration, siblings, insurance issues, medical concerns, and advocacy. A free e-newsletter is available.

783. Autism Society of America (ASA). www.autism-society.org

The ASA is the nation's leading grassroots autism organization. This website is one of the means by which ASA increases the public awareness about issues faced by individuals with an autistic spectrum disorder. Special sections include research and programs, the autism community, frequently asked questions, free downloads available upon free registration, and tips of the day. The website is available in Spanish.

784. Autism Source. Autism Society of America (ASA). www.autismsource.org

Autism Source is the ASA's free online referral database of local resources, services, and support that individuals can access. This comprehensive database, created in 2004, is searchable by location or service type. Service providers include ASA chapters, support groups, medical professionals, educational facilities, legal services, government agencies, research centers, and more. This website can be accessed from the ASA website, www.autism-society.org.

785. First Signs. www.firstsigns.org/resources/index.htm

First Signs is a nonprofit organization dedicated to educating parents and professionals about the early warning sign of autism and other development disorders. Specific sections address concerns regarding autistic children, various screening tools, diagnosis, and treatment. There is a list of resources containing articles, books, and media sources. Noteworthy is the extensive list of websites that address a wide range of needs, such as information and strategies that may be used at home, at school, and in the community.

786. National Autism Association. www.nationalautismassociation.org

The National Autism Association educates and empowers families affected by autism and other neurological disorders. This website provides excellent coverage of autism that includes definitions, causes, diagnosis, treatment options, safety issues, and myths. Especially noteworthy is the brief online video that describes the symptoms of autism. Other sections provide information regarding financial assistance and resources for families, particularly military families. This website is highly recommended for parents.

787. O.A.S.I.S. Online Asperger Syndrome Information and Support. www.udel .edu/bkirby/asperger/

Supported by parents of children who have been diagnosed with Asperger syndrome, OASIS is a volunteer organization. Some of the sections on this website are message boards, chats, and support group information; research papers and descriptions of Asperger syndrome; educational implications and ideas for classroom management; diagnostic scales for Asperger syndrome; related disorders; and social implications and strategies. International websites include translated documents in various languages, such as Spanish, German, and French. In addition, the Kids's Corner section contains contributions from kids with Asperger syndrome and related disorders. A print and e-newsletter are available.

Down Syndrome

788. Club NDSS. National Down Syndrome Society. www.clubndss.org. Grades 5–8.

This relatively new site, sponsored by the National Down Syndrome Society (www.ndss.org), is aimed toward young teenagers. Several interactive sections allow users to access information regarding living healthy, school and free time, sports, movies and television, and much more. Television personality Chris Burke, who has Down syndrome, is featured. Teenagers will enjoy this colorful website that provides some games, social networking, and encourages self-advocacy.

789. Down Syndrome: For New Parents. www.downsyn.com

This website provides support and information for both new and experienced parents. Noteworthy features include sections for relatives, a recommended reading list, particularly for siblings, and stories, poetry, and music that have special meaning for parents of children with Down syndrome. The website contains a forum for parents to share their experiences and feelings.

790. National Association for Down Syndrome (NADS). www.nads.org

Since its inception in 1961, NADS has always believed that parents helping parents is a very powerful concept, and most parents find that some of their greatest resources are other parents. This website fulfills this mission. Down syndrome facts that can be downloaded, links to other online resources, sections for teens, and human interest stories are just a few of the features available on this site. Some of the sections on this website are available in Spanish.

791. National Down Syndrome Congress. www.ndsccenter.org

This site provides resources for parents new to Down syndrome as well as links to chapter members that offer inclusion resources. News and events, resources, as well as information for new parents are included. One of the most noteworthy features on this website is the section titled Self-Advocate, which contains information on the Woo-Hoo Award, and an online video profiling several individuals with Down syndrome and their personal accomplishments. A mirror site in Spanish is available.

792. National Down Syndrome Society. www.ndss.org

This is the largest organization providing support, research dollars, and information on Down syndrome. In addition to a wide range of activities, the Information Topics section provides an extensive wealth of information regarding health, development, education and schooling, as well as publications that can be downloaded. Additional information requires registration. One of the unique features on this website is the ability to locate state-specific organizations and support groups on the Affiliates link. The National Down Syndrome Society operates Club NDSS for teens and its corresponding website (www.clubndss.org). Some sections of this website provide information in Spanish.

Dyslexia and Other Learning Disabilities

793. Brain Connection. www.brainconnection.com

This is a web resource from Scientific Learning, which was founded over thirty years ago by some noted research scientists who were responsible for creating reading intervention products. The Education section contains articles related to effective reading instruction. The Library section lists articles, news, interviews, reviews, and interactive resources into the following categories: general, education, clinical, and brain basics. The Clinical Topics and the Brain Teasers sections are especially noteworthy. Clinical Topics section lists attention-deficit disorder (ADD/ADHD), autism, mood disorders, and more. Over twenty-two online interactive games that address the skills needed for memory attention and sound discrimination can be accessed under the Brain Teasers section. One can subscribe to the biweekly e-newsletter, *Brain Buzz*.

794. Child Development Institute. www.childdevelopmentinfo.com/index.htm

This website is maintained by the Child Development Institute, founded by renowned clinical child psychologist Robert Myers, Ph.D. It provides general information for parents and teachers about learning disabilities and genetic disorders, such as attention-deficit/hyperactivity disorder, anxiety disorders, Asperger's syndrome, autism, bipolar disorder, and depression. Three of the major sections address health/safety, learning, and parenting issues. The Health/Safety section provides comprehensive information regarding medical, dental, nutrition, physical fitness, and sleep issues. The Learning section covers study habits, preparing for school conferences, establishing parent/teacher relationship, and more. The Parenting section offers information regarding self-esteem, organization of one's home, selecting a babysitter, tips for new parents, and parenting teenagers.

795. Do2Learn. www.do2learn.com

The main focus of this outstanding website is to provide tools and solutions, based on scientific research and clinical experience, for parents, educators, and health professionals who deal with children who have learning difficulties. The five main sections, Disabilities, Activities, Songs and Games, Get Organized, and Picture Cards, are further subdivided. For example, color/number games, emotion games, and sequence games are listed under the Songs and Games section. These interactive games are free. The Mall Safety, Street Safety, and Fire Safety animated streaming videos are exceptionally valuable resources for parents and teachers.

796. Dyslexia Parents Resource. www.dyslexia-teacher.com

This is a comprehensive website that provides information regarding all aspects of dyslexia. Sections offer parents dyslexia resources, including a variety of printable fact sheets, and offer educators information regarding teaching methods, assessment, frequently asked questions, and individualized dyslexia programs. Most noteworthy are the distance learning multimedia courses for teachers and parents, under the direction of John Bradford, who has over thirty years' experience of working with dyslexic individuals. The courses are Dyslexia

Parents' course, Dyslexia Certificate course, and the Synthetic Phonics Certificate course. *The World of Dyslexia* e-newsletter and *Dyslexia Online Magazine* are available.

797. The International Dyslexia Association (IDA). www.interdys.org

The IDA, an international organization that addresses some of the complex issues of dyslexia, sponsors this helpful website. Special sections contain fact sheets, some of which are available in Spanish and Italian, frequently asked questions, and career information. In addition, the IDA's Resources section provides a comprehensive list of online resources regarding dyslexia and learning disabilities materials. The calendar of IDA events and activities in various states can be accessed. Registration is required for IDA's newsletter.

798. LD Online. www.ldonline.org

This is one of the largest websites on learning disabilities and attention-deficit/ hyperactivity disorder. LD Online is a national educational service of WETA-TV, the PBS station in Washington, D.C. The website provides information and resources to adolescents and young adults regarding transitional issues from school to college as well as from school to work. There are separate sections for educators, parents, and kids. The Kids section contains an art gallery, a story place, and an annotated book list. An extensive glossary, a free newsletter, streaming videos and web casts, and hundreds of expert-reviewed articles and resources are available. A few of the sections can be accessed in Spanish.

799. Learning Disabilities Association of America (LDA). www.ldanatl.org

The LDA has provided support to individuals with learning disabilities, teachers, parents, and other professionals since 1963. Currently, LDA is the largest nonprofit volunteer organization advocating for individuals with learning disabilities. There are specific sections on its website for parents, teachers, and professionals. One of the noteworthy features is a four-hour online IDEA (Individuals with Disabilities Education Act) training course for parents, which can be taken at one's own pace. Sections for teachers have online resources to help with understand learning disabilities. The Resources section contains helpful booklets that can be downloaded; several of these are available in Spanish.

800. Learning Disabilities Worldwide (LDW). www.ldworldwide.org/default.html

LDW, founded in 1965, is a nonprofit organization that works to enhance the lives of individuals with learning disabilities. Sections for parents, kids, teens, young adults, educators, clinicians, and researchers contain additional online resources. Kids, teens, and young adults will find online documents that will help them with study skills, writing assistance, and so forth. The section under Educators is further divided into additional subsections: Teachers, Administrators, Guidance Counselors, and more. The section under Teachers has articles, handouts and teaching materials, and additional online resources. Registration is required to access some of these sections. A free e-newsletter is available.

801. National Center for Learning Disabilities (NCLD). www.ncld.org

The NCLD, founded in 1977, provides essential information to parents, professionals, and individuals with learning disabilities. The website contains informational sections for parents and professionals that address specific age groups, such as PreK, K–8, and Grades 9 and above. These sections lead to additional online resources. Helpful resources for parents and educators include LD InfoZone, which highlights LD news; LD Talk, which has transcripts and interviews with leading LD experts. Educators will welcome the comprehensive section that includes Early Education tools, K–8 success strategies, and a LD checklist of signs and symptoms. A free e-newsletter is available.

802. SparkTop. Schwab Learning. www.Sparktop.org. Grades 3–6.

This very interactive and visually pleasing website was originally created by Schwab Learning. Currently it is maintained by the Professor Garfield Foundation (PGF). Children at various grade levels can benefit from the social networking and games offered by PGF. Registration is required, although there is no cost. There are links for parents and teachers that lead to additional helpful online resources and activities.

Intellectual Disabilities

803. The Arc. www.thearc.org

The Arc is probably the best known association working for the benefit of intellectually disabled persons. The Links section provides educators and parents a wealth of information regarding a wide range of disabilities and disorders, such as disability resources, information about specific conditions, support for community living, general information for families, special education, health promotion, and national organizations. The Resources section contains numerous education-related fact sheets, such as the Individuals with Disabilities Educations Act (IDEA) and Individualized Education Program (IEP).

PHYSICAL

Blindness and Visual Impairments

804. American Council for the Blind (ACB). www.acb.org

The nation's leading membership organization of blind and visually impaired people is the ACB, which was founded in 1961. The alphabetical list of websites provides users with comprehensive sources of services and support available on the Internet. Noteworthy features include *Braille Forum*, a monthly magazine, available in podcast and email formats; ACB's four radio channels; text and sound files on a variety of issues related to blindness and visual impairments; and numerous articles and documents regarding pedestrian safety. Information on state and special-interest organizations that are affiliated with ACB is accessible.

805. American Foundation for the Blind (AFB). www.afb.org

The AFB is a national nonprofit that offers support to people with vision loss. Its exceptional website can benefit family members, seniors, kids, and professionals. Numerous e-newsletters to keep members informed regarding the latest developments about technology related to visual impairment are available. There are two outstanding sections: Helen Keller; and the Braille Bug. Under the Helen Keller section, young readers will find excellent coverage about her entire life, such as photographs and her correspondence and writings, including the e-version of her book *The Story of My Life*. The Braille Bug is an excellent source for children in grades three to five to learn about Braille. It contains games, puzzles, rhymes and riddles, and jumbles. A Message to Teachers provides suggestions for using this section and for classroom activities that involve Braille.

806. National Association for Parents of Children with Visual Impairments (NAPVI). www.spedex.com/napvi/

The NAPVI is a nonprofit organization whose members provide support to the parents of children who have visual impairments. The unique feature on this website is the section Links to Other Resources, which offers a listing of over one hundred websites, subdivided into the following categories: private and government links, diagnosis specific links, parenting links, school for the blind U.S. links, and listservs and chat rooms. State and local NAPVI chapters and Parent Directory, a virtual place for support and informational networking, can also be accessed. Some sections are available in Spanish.

807. National Center for Blind Youth in Science (NCBYS). www.blindscience .org/ncbys/Default.asp

The NCBYS, sponsored by the National Federation of the Blind, is a resource that helps blind teenagers investigate educational opportunities and career possibilities. This website contains portals for Students and Teachers and Parents. NCBYS's various programs, such as the National Federation of the Blind Youth Slam, are detailed in the Students portal. The Youth Slam science program brings blind children into laboratories to engage in hands-on science and engineering projects. Additional information regarding programs and online resources is included for parents and teachers. The Resources section includes tactile materials and online resources that are divided into four categories: Science, Technology, Engineering, and Mathematics. These four categories are further subdivided into specific disciplines, such as Astronomy, Biology, and Chemistry, which are under Science.

808. Prevent Blindness America. www.preventblindness.org

As the nation's leading volunteer eye health and safety organization, Prevent Blindness America, founded in 1908, is dedicated to fighting blindness and saving sight. The main focus of its website is to promote vision care. One of the sections, mainly for parents, is titled Your Child's Sight, which includes online home eye tests, tips for taking one's child to the eye doctor, and suggestions to prevent eye accidents at home. Additional information regarding first aid for eye emergencies, safe toy checklist, sports eye safety, and fireworks safety is included as well. Current news is available via really simple syndication (RSS) news feed and public service podcasts. Some of the sections are available in Spanish.

Deafness and Hearing Impairments

809. Alexander Graham Bell Association for the Deaf and Hard of Hearing. www.agbell.org

The Alexander Graham Bell Association for the Deaf and Hard of Hearing, a nonprofit organization, can trace its origins to 1880 when Alexander Graham Bell set up Volta Laboratory Association. This website fulfills the Association's mission in helping families, health care providers, and educators understand childhood hearing loss and the importance of early diagnosis and treatment. It has excellent information for parents and educators. Most noteworthy are the resources for educators, which includes a message board, advocacy materials, and management articles. In addition, there is a downloadable sixty-nine-page PDF titled "Mainstreaming the Student Who Is Deaf or Hard-of-Hearing: A Guide for Professionals, Teachers, and Parents." Through membership, numerous e-publications can be accessed.

810. De@fchild International. www.deafchild.org

De@fchild International provides opportunities for deaf and hearing children to communicate with one another throughout the world. This website uses bright colors and cartoon figures to appeal to its young audience, ages 7 to 9. The Kids in Youth section contains a Fun Club, which has online games, a poetry page, and Cool Links to other websites for additional games and activities. In addition, users will find Deaf Role Models, Favourite Teachers, and Events under this section. This is a free website; however, it requires registration.

811. Deaf Resource Library. www.deaflibrary.org

Developed and maintained by Yale professor and ethno-photographer Karen Nakamura, this exceptional and extensive collection of websites provides information about deaf cultures in Japan and the United States. The deaf related network resources are subdivided into twenty-three specific categories, such as national/state organizations of the deaf, schools and universities, deaf kids and their parents, Americans with Disabilities Act (ADA), resources for the hard of hearing and late deafened, and many more.

812. Laurent Clerc National Deaf Education Center: Information on Deafness. clerccenter.gallaudet.edu/InfoToGo/index.html

The Laurent Clerc National Deaf Education Center is maintained by Gallaudet University, founded by an Act of Congress in 1864 and whose charter was signed by President Abraham Lincoln. This is the only university in the entire world that designs and provides programs and services specifically for deaf and hard-of-hearing students. The information is organized under the topics assistive devices and hearing aids; careers and employment; and communication and sign language. Additional information is provided in sections for children, their teachers, and parents. Educators can access fact sheets, printable handouts for classroom use, and lists of online resources. An email newsletter titled *News and Notables Flash* is available.

813. Listen to Your Buds! American Speech-Language-Hearing Association (ASHA). www.listentoyourbuds.org

The main focus of Listen to Your Buds, created by the American Speech-Language-Hearing Association, is to make consumers aware of the potential risk of hearing loss from unsafe usage of personal audio technology. The Kids section contains games to enforce the consequences of exposure to loud sounds. The Parents section provides excellent information regarding protecting children's ears, warning signs and getting help, other types of causes of hearing loss, and additional resources. The Educators section contains information regarding what to do when students have hearing loss, three things educators can do, and lesson plans and classroom activities. The Media section offers facts, figures, and more and information regarding MP3 players and much more. There is a mirror site in Spanish.

814. The National Association of the Deaf (NAD). www.nad.org

The NAD, which has a long history of defending the rights of deaf and hard-of-hearing people, was established in Cincinnati in 1880. NAD also supports the Junior National Association of the Deaf (Junior NAD), a coalition founded in 1961, of individual chapters at junior high and high schools all over the nation. This website contains several sections on legal rights and advocacy issues. The Youth section contains information about Junior NAD, membership frequently asked questions, Junior NAD blog, details regarding the Miss Deaf America Pageant and Youth Leadership Camp, as well as information about College Bowl, a contest that pits teams of top students against one another in a war of knowledge and quick wits. *NADezine*, an e-magazine, is available.

815. National Institute on Deafness and other Communication Disorders (NIDCD). www.nidcd.nih.gov/index.asp

The NIDCD was established in 1988 as one of the divisions of the National Institutes of Health (NIH), part of the U.S. Department of Health and Human Services. NIDCD conducts and supports biomedical and behavioral research regarding hearing, balance, smell, taste, voice, speech, and language. In addition to the Research and Funding for Research sections, this website has an entire section devoted to Health Information and Health Resources. Under the latter section, educators can access free publications, a directory of national communication disorders organizations, student and teacher online activities, which contain video clips and classroom guides, and links to more health information. Several sections are available in Spanish also. The text on the website can be changed to a larger font size.

816. OtiKids. www.otikids.com

OtiKids is maintained by the Eriksholm Research Centre. This independent facility, which was established in Denmark in 1977, focuses on hearing as well as technology. The five main sections on this website are Understanding (Discovery and recognition), Concerns (The effects on your and your child's life), Helping (How can you help your child?), Networking (Share experiences), and Solutions (Hearing aids for your child). The Kids Corner section provides information about hearing and hearing loss and stories written by hearing-impaired children from all over the world. Kids will also enjoy the free, interactive puzzles and games.

817. Raising Deaf Kids: A World of Information about Children with Hearing Loss. www.raisingdeafkids.org

The Deafness and Family Communication Center (DFCC) at the Children's Hospital of Philadelphia has designed this website to offer information and resources to parents who have deaf and hard-of-hearing children and teenagers. The four main sections—(1) newborn hearing concerns including screening test options, (2) early intervention guidelines, (3) young child communications needs, and (4) challenges of the deaf teenager—contain in-depth online resources. Additional features offer information about growing up with hearing loss, communicating, and special needs for children with attention-deficit/hyperactivity disorder, autism, bipolar disorder, depression, learning disabilities, and many more. The excellent resources section contains organizations, additional websites, and an annotated list of books on deafness. A very good glossary is also provided. There is a mirror site in Spanish. This is an excellent website for parents.

818. Unitron Hearing: Kids Klub. www.kidsklub.unitron.com/kidsklub.html. Grades 2–4.

This website, created by Unitron Hearing in 1993, is an online support tool that helps children with hearing loss, their parents, and other caregivers learn about hearing loss as well as caring for their hearing aids. There are two sections full of bright color cartoon illustrations: Enter the Klub, where children can access downloadable puzzles and tips regarding hearing and hearing aids and play several interactive games; Meet Moki and Pip, where children can read an interesting story about Moki's use of his hearing aid. The Parents Corner has a section regarding hearing loss, causes, symptoms, and suggestions to help their children succeed in school.

Sign Language

819. ASL PRO. www.aslpro.com

This website was created by educators and sign language interpreters as a free resource for classroom teachers to use as a facilitating resource to enhance the teaching of American Sign Language (ASL). The website contains video dictionaries, ASL learning tools, and quizzes. The video dictionaries, categorized under main, religious, conversational, and ASL for babies, contain streaming video clips that depict individuals signing words and phrases. The section featuring quizzes allows individuals to take interactive streaming video quizzes. In addition, the online ASL learning tools provide streaming video clips for "The Star-Spangled Banner," "The Pledge of Allegiance," several Christmas songs, and many more.

820. Signing Time. www.signingtime.com

This exceptional website was developed by a family whose daughter was born profoundly deaf. The information is divided into manageable sections. Enjoyable online resources, such as coloring books, signing activity guides, and games for young children, can be located under the Fun Stuff section. The Learning Centers section contains resources for parents, teachers, speech/hearing professionals, and child care professionals. Each of these sections provides fun activities and online resources to help children learn how to sign. There is a streaming video of signs that teachers can learn and use in their classrooms. Free e-newsletters are available.

Mobility Impairments

821. 4MyChild. www.cerebralpalsy.org

4MyChild Foundation was founded in 1997 by Ken Stern who provided legal counsel for families of special needs children for more than twenty-six years. This website fulfills Stern's mission of providing and assisting families with receiving adaptive equipment, medical treatment and therapy, and financial security for their children with cerebral palsy, Erb'spalsy, and other neurological injuries. This is an excellent website that provides comprehensive resources about cerebral palsy: its diagnosis, history, types and causes, coping with, treatments, and therapies. In addition, a glossary, frequently asked questions, inspirational stories for all ages, and a list of organizations are included. Parents have access to specialists using live chat or email. A resource blog and really simple syndication (RSS) feed are available.

822. Dizabled: The Heartwarming Episodes of Leeder O.Men. www.dizabled .com. Grades 3–12.

This website, maintained by John and Claire Lytle, contains their cartoon, "The Heartwarming Episodes of Leeder O.Men." This cartoon strip covers the fantastic adventures of Leeder O.Men as he wheels through his life. The Resources section lists links to activities and speakers, camps, children's magazines, sports, and much more. An excellent section titled Able-bodied offers helpful suggestions regarding interaction with a person who uses a wheelchair.

823. Paralysis Resource Center. www.paralysis.org

This website is maintained by the Christopher and Dana Reeve Foundation Paralysis Resource Center (PRC). The main purpose of PRC is to promote health and the well-being of individuals living with spinal cord injury, mobility impairment, and paralysis. This well-organized website has an extensive list of resources that cover a wide range of topics related to all aspects of paralysis. Sections provide information regarding health issues, rehabilitation options, active living including travel and sports, and rights and benefits. Websites, articles, and organizations can be located under specific states. This website is available in Spanish, Chinese, Korean, and Vietnamese as well.

824. Spina Bifida Association of America (SBA). www.sbaa.org

The SBA, established in 1973, is the only national voluntary health agency solely dedicated to enhancing the lives of individuals who live with the challenges of spina bifida by education, advocacy, research, and service. This website contains frequently asked questions, numerous downloadable fact sheets that provide in-depth information regarding health, and other topics related to spina bifida. In addition, extensive links to domestic and international websites are provided. Some sections are available in Spanish.

Multiple Physical Disabilities

825. Center for Implementing Technology in Education (CITed). www.cited.org/index.aspx

CITed is funded by the U.S. Department of Education, Office of Special Education Programs. The main purpose of this website is to help educators, administrators, technology coordinators, and professional development coordinators. This website's three main sections, Learn Center, Action Center, and Research Center, contain hundreds of resources, such as lesson plans, websites, case studies, articles, online courses and training, and guidebooks related to education technology. These resources provide a comprehensive look at technology planning and budgeting, managing instruction and assessment, addressing social, legal and ethical issues, and setting up a technology infrastructure. Registration, at no cost, is required to access some of the resources. The Learn Center and Action Center enable users to access the resources based on their specific role as educators, administrators, technology coordinators, or professional development coordinators. This is a very useful website.

826. Information Access Laboratory: Technology, Opportunity and Education. www.ece.udel.edu/InfoAccess/

The purpose of this website, sponsored by the National Science Foundation (NSF), is to encourage students with disabilities to pursue their educational goals in the sciences through the development of innovative new technologies, outreach programs, and accessibility to appropriate curriculum. The website covers three main sections: Technology, which highlights research and the development of new assistive technologies; Opportunities, which model outreach projects for high school and university students; and Education, which addresses professional development programs for parents and educators. Students can access a list of e-magazines in the Scientopia Resources section under the Opportunities section.

827. Ivy Green. www.helenkellerbirthplace.org

Maintained by the Helen Keller Birthplace Foundation, this website helps individuals prepare for an actual visit to the birthplace of Helen Keller, Tuscumbia, Alabama. Sections include The Grounds, The House, and Artifacts. There is a section of links to additional information regarding Helen Keller.

Multiple Disabilities

828. Able Data: Your Source for Assistive Technology. www.abledata.com

Sponsored by the National Institute on Disability and Rehabilitation Research (NIDRR), part of the Office of Special Education and Rehabilitative Services (OSERS) of the U.S. Department of Education, Able Data provides objective information about assistive technology products and rehabilitation equipment. The major sections include Products, a database that classifies assistive technology products and its intended function; Resources, which lists Internet resources by state and by company; and Library, which provides numerous free and printable publications, such as fact sheets, guides, and articles. The website's search engine allows users to locate bibliographic citations and abstracts of articles that evaluate various software products for use in the classroom.

829. Adolescent Health Transition Project (AHTP). http://depts.washington.edu/ healthtr/Teens/Educators/Parents.

This website, developed by the Center on Human Development and Disability at the University of Washington and the Washington State Department of Health, is an excellent resource for adolescents with special health care needs, chronic illnesses, or physical or developmental disabilities. The information section is organized for teens and young adults, parents and families, health care providers, and educators. Some of the other noteworthy sections are Health History Summary for Teens, a self-assessment tool; Medical Summaries, which allows users to build an individual care journal; Health Insurance Options for Young Adults with Disabilities and Special Health Care Needs; and Tips for Choosing and Talking with a Health Care Provider. Downloadable forms are available in most of the sections.

830. American Association of People with Disabilities (AAPD). www.aapd.com

The main focus of the AAPD, the largest national nonprofit cross-disability member organization in the United States established in 1995, is to ensure that individuals with disabilities can be self-sufficient and able to contribute as full participants in all aspects of society and government. This website provides a calendar of events from across the country as well as policies and activities. In addition, the section Disability Mentoring Day provides students with important information regarding career and employment opportunities. Another section, Disability Resources, is divided into several categories, such as adaptive mobility, blind/visually impaired and deaf/hard of hearing, education, health, magazines/publications, and news sites.

831. American Psychological Association (APA). www.apa.org

The APA, the largest scientific and professional organization of psychologists worldwide, maintains this website as a service to psychology students and the general public. Individuals can access current and expert information regarding several disabilities and disorders such as attention-deficit/hyperactivity disorder, anxiety, autism, bipolar disorder, depression, eating disorders, emotional health, obesity, parenting, schizophrenia, and stress. Each topic provides press releases, psychology news, books and videos, journals, and additional links.

832. Bandaids and Blackboards. www.lehman.cuny.edu/faculty/jfleitas/bandaides. Grades K–12.

The author and manager of this colorful site, Joan Fleitas, is on the nursing faculty of Lehman College of the City University of New York. This website is about growing up with any type of medical problems such as cerebral palsy, bipolar disorder, attention-deficit disorder, attention-deficit/hyperactivity disorder, Down syndrome, autism, and many more. The information is organized into three groups, Kids, Teens, and Adults. In addition, there are online resources especially for teachers that include tips and lesson plans. Parents and siblings can access sections containing beneficial resources, such as personal stories and activities, to help family members cope with various medical and health challenges. This comprehensive website has received numerous awards.

833. Centers for Disease Control and Prevention (CDC). www.cdc.gov

Currently named as Centers for Disease Control and Prevention, the CDC was originally founded as the Communicable Disease Center in 1946 in Atlanta, Georgia. The CDC, the nation's leader in public health, sponsored by the Department of Health and Human Services, uses its comprehensive and informative website to promote health and quality of life by preventing and controlling disease, injury, and disability. Definitions, statistics, articles, support and contact information, resources, publications, and research about disabilities and disorders are provided under the Diseases and Conditions section. These disabilities and disorders are attention-deficit hyperactivity disorder, autism, obesity, cerebral palsy, Down syndrome, hearing loss in children, mental health, mental retardation, and vision impairment. There is a section for student and educators that includes online resources for teachers, K–12 students, and parents. Some of the sections are available in German, Italian, Russian, Vietnamese, Chinese, French, and Korean. The CDC provides a mirror site in Spanish. Information is also available in podcasts and really simple syndication (RSS) feeds.

834. The Council for Exceptional Children (CEC). www.cec.sped.org

Dedicated to improve educational outcomes for individuals with exceptionalities, students with disabilities, and the gifted, the CEC is a nonprofit international professional organization. The history of CEC can be traced back to 1922 when the International Council for the Education of Exceptional Children was organized at Teachers College, Columbia University. CEC's seventeen divisions for specialized information provide services for teachers, administrators, students, parents, and paraprofessionals. Some of these divisions focus on deafness, developmental disabilities, learning disabilities, and physical and visual impairments. The News and Issues section on this website provides the most current information affecting the field of special education. The Teaching and Learning Center offers comprehensive coverage of information for individuals interested in pursuing a job in special education, including accreditation and licensure details and instructional strategies in various disciplines. Teachers who are new to the classroom will find the CEC blog very helpful.

835. DisabilityInfo. http://DisabilityInfo.gov

This website was created by a presidential initiative in 2002, as a collaborative effort among twenty-two federal agencies, to help individuals with disabilities achieve their personal and professional ambitions. In addition to the main sections that provide information about employment, housing, health, and community life, this website has important features under the Education section, such as online resources regarding early childhood and elementary, middle and high school, special education, parents, educators, and youth programs. The Civil Rights section has links for education laws and regulations. Resources can be located by state and by region.

836. The Families and Advocates Partnership for Education (FAPE). www.fape. org

Originally funded as one of the four projects by the U.S. Department of Education to assist parents, administrators, service providers, and policy makers nationwide, the FAPE focuses on improving the educational outcomes for children with disabilities. One of the projects that FAPE supports is the dissemination of information about Individuals with Disabilities Education Act (IDEA '04) for families. The Research section contains excellent links to online resources regarding research-based practices. An extensive list of downloadable files about IDEA can be accessed in the Publications section. Some sections are available in Spanish as well.

837. Family Center on Technology and Disability. www.fctd.info

The Family Center on Technology and Disability is entirely supported by the U.S. Department of Education's Office of Special Education Programs (OSEP). This website features family information guides and assistive technology (AT) fact sheets that include a glossary. Some of these resources are available in Spanish as well. The online resources are divided into three areas: (1) Assistive Technology Categories, such as early intervention and parenting; (2) Material Types, such as books, tools, newsletters, and websites; (3) Disability Categories, such as attention-deficit hyperactivity disorder/attention-deficit disorder, autism, bipolar disorder, cerebral palsy, developmental disabilities, dyslexia, hearing impairments/deaf, learning disabilities, mental health impairment, mental retardation, and visual impairment/blind. In addition, success stories featuring children and young adults are included.

838. Family Village: A Global Community of Disability-Related Resources. www .familyvillage.wisc.edu

Sponsored by the Waisman Center at the University of Wisconsin–Madison and founded in 1996, the Family Village website is for children and adults with disabilities, their families, and their friends. The website has an easy-to-use directory with colorful icons to connect to different sections such as Library, Research, Living with a Disability, School, and Family Resources. The Library section can be used to find information on specific disabilities and diagnoses, such as attention-deficit disorder, Asperger syndrome, autism, blindness, cerebral palsy, deaf/blind, Down syndrome, dyslexia, depression, learning disabilities, mental health issues, schizophrenia, and visual impairments. The Village School section has instructional and educational related resources for children with disabilities that can be shared with parents or teachers. In addition, contact information for support groups and websites are provided. This website should be enjoyable to use because of its card catalog graphics.

839. Films Involving Disabilities. www.disabilityfilms.co.uk

A detailed list of over 2,500 feature films involving various disabilities is presented on this site. The films, dating from the late 1940s to 2001, are divided into disability categories, such as autism, blind, deaf, learning difficulty/retardation, mental disability, and many more. Documentaries regarding disabilities are also identified. Each category is further subdivided into major and minor films and includes box office and made for television movies. In addition, this website provides recommended articles, books, and essays pertaining to films involving disabilities.

840. Internet Special Education Resources (ISER). www.iser.com

ISER is a nationwide online directory of professionals, organizations, and schools that offers special needs teacher training programs and job opportunities, special needs software and assistive technology, and travel assistance for disabled individuals. Learning disabilities or special education help can be accessed by using one of the six main sections: (1) LD, Autism, Dyslexia, and ADD/ADHD Assessment; (2) LD, Autism, Dyslexia, and ADD/ADHD Schools, Treatment, Therapy; (3) LD and ADD/ADHD Rights; (4) At-Risk Teens—Programs and Treatment; (5) Camps and Special Programs; and (6) Special Education Software and Assistive Technology. In addition to information regarding Special Education Learning Centers, Therapy, and College Programs, which is accessible by state, online resources for advocacy programs, homeschooling, and distance learning are included.

841. K12 Academics. http://k12academics.com

Using a community-based approach, K12 Academics is a complete education resource website that provides teachers, parents, students, professionals, and district officials in the K–12 education system, extensive information on various topics in education and disabilities. The main categories on this website are related to education, school, teachers, and students. Other sections list after-school programs, camps, colleges and universities, organizations, and libraries. The section on disabilities and disorders contains definitions, characteristics, causes, diagnosis, books, media, and support services related to attention-deficit disorder, Asperger syndrome, autism, bipolar disorder, blindness, cerebral palsy, deafness, depression, Down syndrome, dyslexia, mental retardation, and more.

842. Kid's Health for Kids. www.kidshealth.org. Grades 3–12.

The Nemours Center for Children's Health Media, founded in 1995, sponsors this colorful, fun-to-use website that provides free, jargon-free, up-to-date health information to children and families. Asperger syndrome, cerebral palsy, autism, Down syndrome, attention-deficit hyperactivity disorder, eating disorders, and anxiety are some of the topics covered. This website has separate areas specifically for kids, teenagers, and parents, each with its own design, age-appropriate content, and tone. Included are over 1,000 in-depth features, articles, animations, interactive games and activities, and resources developed by medical experts. The Parents' site contains topics such as infections, emotions and behaviors, growth and development, nutrition and fitness, positive parenting, first aid and safety, and doctors and hospitals. The Kids' site covers dealing with feelings; staying healthy; recipes; people, places, and things that help; a glossary; how the body works; games; and enjoyable animated video clips. The Teens' site provides information regarding the body, the mind, food and fitness, recipes, and questions and answers. This exceptional, award-winning website also provides links to other related articles and websites and is available in Spanish.

843. MedlinePlus. http://medlineplus.gov

Developed by the National Library of Medicine and the National Institutes of Health, MedlinePlus is a comprehensive reference source pertaining to medication information that can be used by parents, educators, and young adults for research. The main sections are listed under health topics; drugs and supplements; medical encyclopedia and dictionary; and directories and other resources. Individuals can access information about attention-deficit disorder, eating disorders, autism, Asperger syndrome, visual impairment and blindness, cerebral palsy, child mental health, depression, bipolar disorder, dyslexia and learning disorders, and hearing disorders and deafness. Over 165 interactive health tutorials with slide shows with sound and pictures, email updates, really simple syndication (RSS) feed, and several listservs are available. MedlinePlus has a mirror site in Spanish.

844. National Center on Birth Defects and Developmental Disabilities (NCBDDD). www.cdc.gov/ncbddd/

The NCBDDD is a subsection of the Centers for Disease Control and Prevention (CDC). The mission of the NCBDDD is to promote the health of babies, children, and adults by identifying the causes of and preventing birth defects and developmental disabilities. The NCBDDD section of the CDC website contains in-depth resources regarding specific disabilities and disorders, such as autism spectrum disorders, hearing loss, attention-deficit hyperactivity disorder, and vision impairment. In addition, there are numerous noteworthy features, such as the one designed for students in grades four to six, titled Kids' Quest, which provides information regarding disabilities awareness. Parents and educators can modify the resources to meet various learning styles.

845. National Center on Secondary Education and Transition (NCSET). www .ncset.org Grades 9–12.

The NCSET, created in 2005, coordinates national resources pertaining to youth with disabilities. The main emphasis of this website is to engage youth through various activities designed to help youth learn more about a specific topic, enhance their knowledge base, and engage with and assimilate materials on a personal level. Publications such as briefs, articles, and policy updates summarizing recent laws and federal regulations can be accessed. The main topics are teaching and learning and national events, which can be located by state or by territory. Numerous websites and newsletters are available; however, in order to access all the resources, free registration is recommended.

846. National Dissemination Center for Children with Disabilities (NICHCY). www.nichcy.org

NICHCY, founded in 2003, is sponsored by the Academy for Educational Development (AED) and the Office of Special Education Programs (OSEP), U.S. Department of Education. NICHCY serves the nation as a central source of information regarding disabilities in infants, toddlers, children, and youth; the Individuals with Disabilities Education Act (IDEA); No Child Left Behind; and research-based information on effective educational practices. The Research section has a searchable database for online articles. Some of the topics covered in the A–Z Topics section of web resource pages include attention-deficit hyperactivity disorder, Asperger syndrome, autism, blindness/visual impairments, cerebral palsy, deafness/hearing impairments, Down syndrome, and learning disabilities. Various free publications, frequently asked questions, and disability related resources in each state are available. A section titled Zigawhat is a fun website of online resources designed for children to learn, connect, grow, and cope. Zigawhat also contains a section titled Fun and Games. This website has a mirror site in Spanish.

847. National Institute on Disability and Rehabilitation Research (NIDRR). www.ed.gov/about/offices/list/osers/nidrr/index.html

The NIDRR is one of the three components of the Office of Special Education and Rehabilitative Services (OSERS) at the U.S. Department of Education that was created in 1978. It serves as a national leader in sponsoring research by generating new knowledge and by promoting its effective use to improve the abilities of people with disabilities. The main sections on this website are Programs and Projects, Grants and Funding, Legislation and Policy, Publications, Research and Statistics, Frequently Asked Questions, and Additional Resources. The online resources in each of these sections are further subdivided into four categories: students, parents, teachers, and administrators.

848. National Youth Leadership Network (NYLN). www.nyln.org

First held in 1997, the National Conference for Youth with Disabilities evolved into NYLN in 2001. The mission of NYLN is to promote leadership development, education, and health and wellness and to foster the inclusion of young leaders with disabilities into various aspects of society. In addition, this organization communicates about matters that are vital to youth with disabilities. NYLN's website provides information under the Resources section regarding the topics Education, Healthcare, Disability History/Disability Culture, and Material by and for young people with disabilities. Another helpful section, Youth Experts, has a list of young leaders who are available to speak at conferences, to mentor, to provide technical assistance to organizations and agencies, and to serve on advisory boards and committees. A free e-newsletter is available.

849. Our-Kids. www.our-kids.org

The Our-Kids network, formed in 1993 by a parent on behalf of her child who had a disability, provides global support for parents, caregivers, and others who work with children with physical and/or mental disabilities. This network has members from countries such as Australia, Canada, and England. This website lists recommended books, including online magazines, for parents and for kids, by age. Specific disabilities that are addressed include attention-deficit disorder, autism, cerebral palsy, deafness, Down syndrome, mental health, and visual impairments.

850. PACER Kids against Bullying. www.pacerkidsagainstbullying.org. Grades 2–6.

This colorful and enjoyable interactive website, created by Parents and Children Education Resources (PACER) in 2006, provides valuable information on an important topic that affects many children, particularly those who have disabilities—bullying. The Games and Fun section has stories and printable coloring pages and word games. The Watch This section, using streaming videos, defines bullying and what to do about it. Other sections offer some additional information and tips about how to cope with bullies. The Parents and Professionals section links to the PACER website where information is provided regarding bullying in general.

851. Parents and Children Education Resources (PACER). www.pacer.org

Founded in 1977, PACER Center is a parent-training and information center for families of children and youth with various disabilities from birth to 21 years old. This nonprofit organization's mission is to offer opportunities and to improve the quality of life for children and young adults with disabilities, including their families. One of the main sections on this website is Programs and Resources, which list programs, publications, translated materials, and websites. In addition, the Simon Technology Center (STC) section, which is committed to making the benefits of assistive technology more accessible to individuals with disabilities, provides publications and resources pertaining to technology issues. Several e-newsletters can be accessed. Some sections are available in Spanish.

852. PsychCentral. http://psychcentral.com

This website was established and maintained by author, researcher, and clinical psychologist John M. Grohol, Psy.D., one of the premier pioneers of online mental health. Since its inception in 1995, Dr. Grohol has personally evaluated each resource listed in this award-winning multifaceted website. Online resources are provided for the following childhood and young adult disorders: anxiety, Asperger's disorder, attention-deficit/hyperactivity disorder (AD/HD/ADD), autistic disorder, bipolar disorder, depression, eating disorders, schizophrenia, and more. Educators and parents would benefit from the section that contains psychological tests and quizzes. These free, scientifically reviewed quizzes, which can be instantly and automatically scored, are available with free registration. Free e-newsletter and blog are available.

853. Seeing disABILITIES from a Different Perspective. http://library.thinkquest .org/5852/homepg.htm. Grades 4–5.

Created in 1999 by elementary students in Illinois, this award-winning website offers young students a perspective on living or being at school with students who have disabilities. The focus of this website is on autism, blindness, cerebral palsy, and deafness. Each of these topics has links to additional websites. Activities and simulations are provided for kids who have wondered what it is like to have a disability. A quiz about disabilities, a glossary, and a bibliography are included.

854. Sibling Support Project. www.siblingsupport.org

The Sibling Support Project, founded 1990, addresses the needs and concerns of brothers and sisters of people who have special health, developmental, or mental health issues. This website has links to related websites including sibling-related books and sibling support efforts in other countries, such as Iceland, Belgium, New Zealand, Australia, the United Kingdom, Japan, and Italy. SibKids listserv, a valuable feature on this website, is a great place for young brothers and sisters to meet and get support from others whose siblings have special needs. A free e-newsletter is available.

855. Technical Assistance Alliance for Parent Centers (TAAlliance). www .taalliance.org

Funded by the U.S. Department of Education, Office of Special Education Programs, the TAAlliance consists of one national center and six regional centers. This innovative project supports a unified technical assistance system to develop, assist, and coordinate Parent Training and Information Centers (PTIs), and Community Parent Resource Centers (CPRCs). Its website leads to online resources regarding the following topics: No Child Left Behind (NCLB); Individuals with Disabilities Education Act (IDEA); scientifically based research; helpful resources, many of which are in Spanish; and publications and translated materials.

856. Wrightslaw. www.wrightslaw.com

Pete and Pam Wright, an attorney and psychotherapist, respectively, created this website in 1998 in order to provide parents, advocates, educators, and attorneys with accurate and the most current information regarding special education law and advocacy. Individuals can access resources in the form of articles, cases, and newsletters on various topics such as assessment and testing, autism, Asperger syndrome, Individualized Education Program (IEP), medication, parental protections, self-advocacy, teachers, principals, and paraprofessionals, and more. Advice for preparing oneself for legal consultation, a glossary of special education and legal terms, and downloadable flyers for educating others are included. Publications regarding autism and other disabilities, as well as the *Special Ed Advocate*, a free e-newsletter, are available. This website can be accessed in Spanish.

857. Yellow Pages for Kids with Disabilities. www.yellowpagesforkids.com

This website, maintained by Wrightslaw, helps individuals locate the following professionals by state or U.S. territory: educational consultants, psychologists, educational diagnosticians, health care providers, academic therapists, tutors, speech language therapists, occupational therapists, coaches, advocates, and attorneys for children with disabilities. In addition, special education schools, learning centers, treatment programs, parent groups, respite care, community centers, grassroots organizations, and government programs for children with disabilities can also be located by state or U.S. territory. International resources, *Special Ed Advocate*, a free e-newsletter, legal and advocacy resources, and best school websites can be accessed.

Chapter 9

Journals/Magazines

This chapter lists eighty-nine titles of various journals and magazines that are organized alphabetically under the four main headings: General, Emotional, Learning, and Physical. The General section is subdivided into the categories Education; Health, Exercise, and Rehabilitation; and News, Culture, and Lifestyle. The remaining sections, Emotional, Learning, and Physical, are organized under subtitles similar to the ones in the first three chapters of this bibliography. There are fifty-one entries for educators/professionals, one for parents, and five for educators/parents, and thirty for teens/educators/parents. One entry is for high school and one is for middle school grade levels. Research revealed a disparity of journals and magazines for the elementary, middle, and high school grade levels. Quotes within the entries are from the publisher or website for the magazine cited unless otherwise noted.

Journals/magazines identified for educators/professionals are valuable resources for obtaining scientifically based research and professional wisdom. Both of these elements comprise evidence-based education (EBE). According to the current policy of the U.S. Department of Education, educators must employ evidence-based practices in their classrooms.

Information regarding the indexing of current and archived issues is included when available. In addition, free indexing services for the journal titles are noted in the entries. For example, Education Resources Information Center (ERIC) (http://eric.ed.gov), PubMed (http://www.pubmed.gov), Scirus (http://www.scirus.com), and Ingenta (http://www.ingentaconnect.com) enable individuals to access articles in numerous journals simultaneously. ERIC provides a link to open access (no cost) journals or articles indexed in its database.

GENERAL

Education

858. *Art Therapy: Journal of the American Art Therapy Association.* American Art
    Therapy Association. www.arttherapyjournal.org/. ISSN: 0742-1656. Level:
    Educators/Professionals.

"[*Art Therapy*] presents a broad spectrum of ideas in art therapy, practice,
professional issues, and research with an emphasis placed on the use of the visual arts in therapy." Research articles cover the use of art therapy in a variety
of circumstances. A recent issue had the topic of traumatic stress situations and
the therapy efficacy. Issues are available online for review. By paid subscription
in print, but also available free on ERIC as an open access journal beginning in
2004. The latest issue can be accessed on the journal home page.

859. *Educational and Psychological Measurement.* American College Personnel
    Association. epm.sagepub.com/. ISSN: 0013-1644; Online ISSN: 1552-
    3888. Level: Educators/Professionals.

This is a professional peer reviewed journal specializing in measurement and
assessment. This is accessible to individuals with a master's degree or above and/
or experience in research and statistics methods. Because this journal evaluates
and theorizes about testing and assessment in education and psychology, it has
some use for experienced readers. It has been indexed in ERIC since 1984 and
more recently on its website.

860. *European Journal of Special Needs Education.* Routledge. www.tandf.co
    .uk/journals/routledge/08856257.html. ISSN: 0885-6257. Level: Educators/
    Professionals.

This journal has been indexed in ERIC continuously since 2004. The *European
Journal of Special Needs Education* reflects the dynamic growth of the theory
and practice of special needs education as it is emerging worldwide. Written for
teachers and researchers, it provides a forum for reporting and reviewing scholarly research and significant developments in the field of special educational
needs. Each issue includes contributions from a variety of different countries
dealing with special needs at all levels of education from primary to adult.

861. *Exceptional Children.* Council for Exceptional Children. www.cec.sped.org/
    Content/NavigationMenu/Publications2/ExceptionalChildren/. ISSN: 0014-
    4029. Level: Educators/Professionals.

This journal covers gifted and disabled children in education. It has been indexed in ERIC since 1970. This is the official journal of the Council. It publishes research on general standards in schools and on the effectiveness of programs and practices in the classroom relative to a wide range of exceptional children such as "Effects of Preventative Tutoring on the Mathematical Problem Solving of Third-Grade Students with Math and Reading Difficulties" and "Effects on Science Summarization of a Reading Comprehension Intervention for Adolescents with Behavior and Attention Disorders."

862. *Exceptionality.* Council for Exceptional Children. Division for Research. www.leaonline.com/loi/ex or www.informaworld.com/ampp/rss~content= 0936-2835. ISSN: 0936-2835. Level: Educators/Professionals.

Generally each issue of this quarterly journal covers some major topic in special education from administration organization and ethics, autism identification and learning needs, to labels, attitudes, and outcomes. It does have special topic issues such as "Effective Practices for Children and Youth with Autism Spectrum Disorder" and "The Changing Landscape of Special Education Administration." The materials cover all ages. Indexed in ERIC.

863. *Focus on Exceptional Children.* Love Publishing. www.lovepublishing.com/ journals.html. ISSN: 0015-511X. Level: Educators/Parents.

This is a trade magazine aimed at teachers and covers a single topic in each issue. The topics covered generally focus on some area of theory to practice in the classroom or in the administrative office, such as "Framing the Progress of Collaborative Teacher Education" and "Students with Disabilities in Charter Schools: What We Now Know." For the most part the articles are based on current research rather than looking at issues from a historical perspective. There is a bibliography with each article. Indexing is available in ERIC.

864. *Journal of Positive Behavior Interventions (JPBI).* Association for Positive Behavior Support. http://pbi.sagepub.com/archive/. ISSN: 1098-3007; Online ISSN: 1538-4772. Level: Educators/Professionals.

The JPBI offers sound, research-based principles of positive behavior support for use in school, home, and community settings with people with challenges in behavioral adaptation. Regular features of JPBI include empirical research and detailed case studies; descriptive, survey, and qualitative research; discussion, literature review, and conceptual papers; programs, practices, and innovations; program descriptions and research-to-practice forum; perspectives on controversial issues, responses to published material, and personal experiences; book and material reviews. Articles include "A Descriptive Analysis of Intervention Research Published in the Journal of Positive Behavior Interventions: 1999 Through 2005" and "Implementing Visually Cued Imitation Training with Children with Autism Spectrum Disorders and Developmental Delays." The journal can be searched on its website.

865. *Journal of School Psychology.* Ohio Department of Education and Elsevier Publishing. www.sciencedirect.com/science/journal/00224405. ISSN: 0022-4405. Level: Educators/Professionals.

"The *Journal of School Psychology* publishes original empirical articles and critical reviews of the literature on research and practices relevant to psychological and behavioral processes in school settings. JSP presents research on intervention mechanisms and approaches; schooling effects on the development of social, cognitive, mental-health, and achievement-related outcomes; assessment; and consultation." Articles include "The Effect of Classroom Environment on Problem Behaviors: A Twin Study," "Gender Differences in Severity of Writing and Reading Disabilities," and "Writing Problems in Developmental Dyslexia: Under-Recognized and Under-Treated." About a one-fourth of the articles deal with disabilities or disorders directly. This journal has been indexed in ERIC since 1970 and more recently on its website.

866. *Journal of Special Education (JSE).* Council for Exceptional Children (CEC). Division for Research (DR). sed.sagepub.com/. ISSN: 0022-4669; Online ISSN: 1538-4764. Level: Educators/Professionals.

This is a professional journal that is indexed in ERIC for the years 1969 to 2005. Ingenta has the issues from 2002 and on its website. "The *Journal of Special Education* (JSE) . . . provides research articles and scholarly reviews by expert authors in all sub-specialties of special education for individuals with disabilities ranging from mild to severe." Literature critiques as well as the empirical research articles will be especially useful. "Examining the Influence of Teacher Behavior and Classroom Context on the Behavioral and Academic Outcomes for Students with Emotional or Behavioral Disorders," "Classroom-Based Research in the Field of Emotional and Behavioral Disorders: Methodological Issues and Future Research Directions," and "Orton-Gillingham and Orton-Gillingham–Based Reading Instruction: A Review of the Literature" are some examples.

867. *Journal of Special Education Technology (JSET).* Council for Exceptional Children. Technology and Media Division. jset.unlv.edu/shared/volsmenu .html. ISSN: 0162-6434. Level: Educators/Professionals.

This is a professional journal covering computer-assisted instruction in special education. It has been indexed in ERIC since 1985. It is also an open access journal for issues, from volume 15, 2000 up to two years from the present. Articles include "Establishing and Maintaining an Early Childhood Emergent Literacy Technology Curriculum," "The Universal Design for Play Tool: Establishing Validity and Reliability," and "School Web Sites: Are They Accessible to All?" *"Journal of Special Education Technology* is a refereed professional journal that presents up-to-date information and opinions about issues, research, policy, and practice related to the use of technology in the field of special education. JSET supports the publication of research and development activities, provides technological information and resources, and presents important information and discussion concerning important issues in the field of special education technology to scholars, teacher educators, and practitioners."

868. *Psychology in the Schools.* Wiley Publishing. www3.interscience.wiley.com/journal/32084/home. ISSN: 0033-3085; Online ISSN: 1520-6807. Level: Educators/Professionals.

This journal has been indexed in ERIC since 1970. It covers theoretical and practical issues confronting school psychologists and administrators. It contains research and opinion articles that particularly describe implications for practice. It has an annual topic issue with topics such as "Linking Psychological Research with Schools and Education," "School-Based Health Promotion: An Introduction to the Practitioner's Edition," and "Autism Spectrum Disorders." Also there are articles such as "Considerations in the Identification, Assessment, and Intervention Process for Deaf and Hard of Hearing Students with Reading Difficulties" and "Examining the Relationship between Treatment Outcomes for Academic Achievement and Social Skills in School-Age Children with Attention-Deficit Hyperactivity Disorder."

869. *Reading and Writing Quarterly.* Taylor and Francis Publishing. www.informa world.com/smpp/title~db=all~content=g789033204~tab=summary. ISSN: 1057-3569. Level: Educators/Professionals.

"Reading and Writing Quarterly provides direction in educating a mainstreamed population for literacy. . . . the journal addresses the causes, prevention, evaluation, and remediation of reading and writing difficulties in regular and special education settings. . . . Possible topics include adjustments for language-learning style, literature-based reading programs, teaching reading and writing in the mainstream, study strategies, language-centered computer curricula, oral language connections to literacy, cooperative learning approaches to reading and writing, direct instruction, curriculum-based assessment, the impact of environmental factors on instructional effectiveness, and improvement of self-esteem."

Each issue has a topic such as reading and writing and incarcerated youth or assessment or learning disabilities. One issue had "Enhancing the Oral Narratives of Children with Learning Disabilities," "Achtung Maybe: A Case Study of the Role of Personal Connection and Art in the Literary Engagement of Students with Attentional Difficulties," and "Thinking, Writing, Talking: A Discourse Analysis of Writing Instruction for Boys with Dyslexia," except for a book review, as the only articles.

870. *School Psychology Quarterly.* American Psychological Association (APA). Division of School Psychology. www.apa.org/journals/spq/description.html. ISSN: 1045-3830; Online ISSN: 1939-1560. Level: Educators/Professionals.

This journal, published by the APA, generally covers children, youth, families, and the adults who serve children, research, evaluation, and service for those individuals. It also accepts data-based manuscripts on research for all age groups with relevance to schooling. In addition to its emphasis on the educational enterprise, the journal publishes articles about school psychological services in nontraditional settings. This journal has been indexed in ERIC since 1992 and in PsycARTI-CLES. This division of APA also publishes *School Psychology* for members.

871. *Teaching Exceptional Children.* Council for Exceptional Children. www.cec .sped.org/Content/NavigationMenu/Publications2/TEACHINGExceptional Children/. ISSN: 0040-0599. Level: Educators/Professionals.

"*Teaching Exceptional Children*, TEC, an official publication of the Council for Exceptional Children, is published specifically for teachers and administrators of children with disabilities and children who are gifted. TEC features practical articles that present methods and materials for classroom use as well as current issues in special education teaching and learning. TEC also brings its readers the latest data on technology, assistive technology, and procedures and techniques with applications to students with exceptionalities. The focus of its practical content is on immediate application." Not surprisingly articles such as "CEC's Position on Response to Intervention (RTI): The Unique Role of Special Education and Special Educators" can be found here. In addition, approaches to policy, "Developing Standards-Based Individualized Education Program Objectives for Students with Significant Needs," and practice, "Facilitating Reading Comprehension for Students on the Autism Spectrum," are examples of the journal's content and focus. Indexed in the subscription database EbscoHOST Education Research Complete and H.W. Wilson Education Index and Fulltext. *Teaching Exceptional Children PLUS* is the online version with abstracts of TEC research articles.

872. *Teaching Exceptional Children PLUS.* Council for Exceptional Children. escholarship.bc.edu/education/tecplus/. ISSN: 1553-9318. Level: Educators/ Parents.

This is an online open access (read free) professional journal where all of the past issues are browseable beginning with volume 1, issue 1, 1994. It is also indexed in the subscription database EbscoHOST Education Research Complete. *"Teaching Exceptional Children Plus* publishes material which is of particular interest to individuals who work with children with special needs. The content of a typical issue may include: feature articles on instruction and services for exceptional children, some of which may have additional multimedia content, including podcasts of selected articles and videos; case studies and case stories which help to document the success of practitioners working with exceptional children; abstracts of the articles appearing in the print journal *Teaching Exceptional Children*; book reviews; and software and technology reviews." Feature articles are presented such as "Teaching Data Analysis to Elementary Students with Mild Disabilities." Case studies are included such as "Reality Lessons in Traumatic Brain Injury" and "Four Seventh Grade Students Who Qualify for Academic Intervention Services in Mathematics Learning Multi-Digit Multiplication with the Montessori Checkerboard."

873. *Topics in Early Childhood Special Education.* Hammill Institute on Disabilities/Sage Publishing. tec.sagepub.com/. ISSN: 0271-1214; Online ISSN: 1538-4845. Level: Educators/Professionals.

   "Topics in Early Childhood Special Education* (TECSE) communicates information about early intervention, which is defined broadly and includes services provided to (a) infants, toddlers, and preschoolers who are at risk for or display developmental delays and disabilities and (b) the families of such youngsters. TECSE includes articles on personnel preparation, policy issues, and operation of intervention programs. The intent is to publish information that will improve the lives of young children and their families." Articles such as "Learning to Listen: Teaching an Active Listening Strategy to Preservice Education Professionals" and "A Protocol for Assessing Early Communication of Young Children with Autism and Other Developmental Disabilities" have been publish here recently. This journal has been indexed in ERIC since 1984 and is indexed on publisher's journal page from 1879.

Health, Exercise, and Rehabilitation

874. *Active Living: The Health, Fitness and Recreation Magazine for People with a Disability.* Disability Today Publishing Group. Canada. www.activeliving magazine.com/. ISSN: 1206-0941. Level: Teens/Educators/Parents.

   This is a subscription magazine, which is indexed in the subscription database SportDiscus. "Focusing on fitness, sport and recreation opportunities for healthy living, the publication has steadily redefined what physical activity means for those with disabilities. *Active Living* serves a very distinct readership one that shares the ambitions of their able-bodied peers, but looks to the publication for adaptive ways to achieve those goals—with the informational tools to attain and maintain a healthy lifestyle, regardless of age, stage or station in life. *Active Living* magazine is a one-stop source for the healthy lifestyle information." The CripWorld section of the magazine is the print extension of the magazines members blog site, www.cripworld.com.

875. *Adapted Physical Activity Quarterly.* International Federation of Adapted Physical Activity. www.humankinetics.com/APAQ/journalAbout.cfm. ISSN: 0736-5829; Online ISSN: 1543-2777. Level: Teens/Educators/Parents.

Adapted Physical Activity Quarterly (APAQ) is an international, multidisciplinary journal designed to stimulate and communicate high scholarly inquiry related to physical activity for special needs populations. Articles appearing in APAQ are informed by a range of disciplines, including corrective therapy, gerontology, health care, occupational therapy, pediatrics, physical education, dance, sports medicine, physical therapy, recreation, and rehabilitation. The official journal of the International Federation of Adapted Physical Activity. Indexed on the publication's website.

876. *American Journal of Physical Medicine & Rehabilitation.* Association of Academic Physiatrists (AAP). www.amjphysmedrehab.com/pt/re/ajpmr/home.htm. ISSN: 0894-9115; Online ISSN: 1537-7385. Level: Educators/Professionals.

"*American Journal of Physical Medicine & Rehabilitation* focuses on the practice, research and educational aspects of physical medicine and rehabilitation." The journal is a leading peer-reviewed serial of a highly technical nature. It covers the current thinking in often extremely narrow and detailed aspects of physical rehabilitation. It is worthwhile knowing about this journal simply because of that. From scanning the journal the reader can become aware of what is being tested, researched, and applied as possible, or not, in the areas of musculoskeletal conditions, brain injury, spinal cord injury, cardiopulmonary disease, trauma, acute and chronic pain, amputation, prosthetics and orthotics, mobility, gait, and pediatrics. By subscription. Indexed on its website.

877. *Challenge.* Disabled Sports USA. www.dsusa.org/about-overview.html. ISSN: 1940-526X; Online ISSN: 1940-5294. Level: Teens/Educators/Parents.

This magazine of the Disabled Sports USA organization is a free webzine and current and archived copies are available online. *Challenge* informs readers about opportunities for competition for individuals with permanent neuromuscular and/or orthopedic disabilities. Feature articles cover athletes and competitions and outcomes for many different sports.

878. *Journal of the American Dietetic Association Online.* American Dietetic Association (ADA). www.adajournal.org/. ISSN: 0002-8223. Level: Teens/Educators/Parents.

Journal of the American Dietetic Association Online offers complete coverage of the journal, with full-text articles starting from 1993 to the present. Indexed in PubMed. Since nutrition and dietetics are a common approach to home treatment for many disorders and disabilities, the association issues position papers in areas such as "nutrition intervention in the treatment of anorexia nervosa, bulimia nervosa, and other eating disorders" and "food and nutrition misinformation." There are also research articles in areas of specific disorders such as diabetes, metabolic disorders, cystic fibrosis, and others. Access to the full-text is available to ADA members and personal subscribers. Access to tables of contents and abstracts is complimentary. ADA members access the journal content by logging onto the ADA website.

879. *Research and Practice for Persons with Severe Disabilities (RPSD).* TASH (Organization). www.tash.org/publications/RPSD/RPSD.html. ISSN: 1540-7969. Level: Educators/Professionals.

"[RPSD] emphasizes articles that report original research, authoritative and comprehensive reviews, conceptual and practical position papers that offer new directions, and effective assessment and intervention methodologies and service delivery model program descriptions." The journal publishes research that is covered in the mission of TASH, which is the "support and further quality of life for individuals with severe disabilities and their families." Articles such as "Rallying Relationships: The Role of Positive Visions and Possible Actions in Person-Centered Planning," "The Modifier Model of Autism and Social Development in Higher Functioning Children," and "Review of Studies with Students with Significant Cognitive Disabilities which Link to Science Standards" are found in this journal. So this journal would also be of interest to parents and advanced readers in high school. Indexed in ERIC from 2003.

News, Culture, and Lifestyle

880. *Abilities Magazine.* Enable Link Organization of Canada. www.enablelink .org/abilities/current.html?showabilities=1. ISSN: 1910-9210; Online ISSN: 0845-4469. Level: Teens/Educators/Parents.

This is the information vehicle for the Enable Link Organization of Canada. There is a fee for print subscription is available in print. This trade magazine comes out quarterly. While this magazine is Canadian, much of what is in it can apply anywhere. A recent issue covered attention-deficit hyperactivity disorder coaching, fitness training with aqua exercise, and sign language for any kid. Enable Link has an excellent website with links to informational and social networking opportunities for all ages and abilities related to disability and illness. The magazine is indexed on the Enable website.

881. *Ability Magazine.* C. R. Cooper Publishing. www.abilitymagazine.com. ISSN: 1062-5321. Level: Teens/Educators/Parents.

This trade magazine has a wide range of personalities as their feature stories, not all of whom have a disability, so the audience for this is general. Nicely written, the topics range from grief recovery through the latest therapeutic technologies. Portions of current and past issues are available on the website listed, but this is a subscription magazine. Available online and in print, tables of contents for past issues are at their website and past issues are available for purchase. The website also features current news about child health issues and disabilities.

882. *Able News.* ablenews.com. Level: Teens/Educators/Parents.

This New York–based newspaper has been around for a number of years and provides current and important news relating to the disability community. Available online or in paper for a modest price. Samples of articles and tables of content for past issues are on their website.

883. *Disability Nation.* www.disabilitynation.net/. Level: Teens/Educators/ Parents.

This audio magazine is produced by people with disabilities. Its thrust is that there is not anything special about being disabled, it is simply life. Inclusion Daily Express is its main current news source. The magazine is an excellent resource for finding people and websites on, about, and for inclusion. The national political scene and its major candidates and their policies and covered in voice and text. Personalities are interviewed as well. It uses a variety of connection speeds for accessibility and sends out announcements of new "issues" through email. The site archives past issues.

884. *Disabilities Studies Quarterly: DQS.* Society for Disability Studies. www .dsq-sds.org/. ISSN: 1041-5718. Level: Educators/Professionals.

DQS, an open access journal that is indexed in IngentaConnect and Ebsco-HOST Education Research Complete, brings together diverse sections of commentary, creative writing, book and film reviews with peer review articles and a themed issue section. Some of the past topics are "Disability and Humor," "Disability and History," and "Disability Studies in the Undergraduate Classroom." This journal is not just for academics; material here can be used in high school curriculum as well. Courses in history, peace, and justice would be interested as well. Not just for disability studies.

885. *Inclusion Daily Express.* Inonit Publishing. www.inclusiondaily.com/. Level: Teens/Educators/Parents.

This is a subscription service providing international news on the state of disability rights. This up-to-date news service has an audio component as well. The writing is at a tenth-grade reading level so it is at a higher level than most general newspapers. It is featured on the Ragged Edge and Disability Nation websites. Some of the articles in recent issues of *Inclusion Daily Express* were "Appeals Panel Sympathizes with Killer's 'Unique' Situation; Grants Robert Latimer Day Parole (Metchosin, British Columbia)"; "We Can All Celebrate in Wrestler's Journey (Chillicothe, Ohio)"; "Petitioners Call for Investigation into Accident Involving Patrol Car and Wheelchair (Charlottesville, Virginia)"; "Authorities Resort to Saddam-Era Laws to Detain 'Street People' (Baghdad, Iraq)"; "Officials: Terrorists Used Women with Disabilities to Kill Dozens at Pet Markets (Baghdad, Iraq)"; and "SuperBowl Ad Invites Viewers into 'Deaf World' (Los Angeles, California)."

886. *Journal of Disability Policy Studies (JDPS).* Hammill Institute on Disabilities and others. dps.sagepub.com/. ISSN: 1044-2073; Online ISSN: 1538-4802. Level: Educators/Professionals.

The JDPS addresses compelling, variable issues in ethics, policy, and law related to individuals with disabilities. Regular features include "From My Perspective," which provides discussions of issues currently confronting a particular disability discipline or area, and "Disability Policy Newsbreak!" which offers commentary on disability policy and advocacy activities from disability organizations. Indexed for member access at: http://www.ingentaconnect.com/content/proedcw/jdps and at the website listed above.

887. *Logan.* Logan Magazine, Inc. www.loganmagazine.com/. Grades 5–12.

Logan was started by a young woman with disabilities and her mother for the teen and preteen audience to provide an active positive image for "young people with disabilities about how to lead a lifestyle that is productive, purposeful and pleasurable." The eye popping colorful photo packed magazine that we looked at had fifteen different departments. The interviews were with two male athletes and a young woman who has found genuine strength in "embracing the turtle" to forge success. The clothing and gadgets articles may be more than a boy can take, but the cooking and Microsoft Vista article are kinds of articles boys will come back for. Excellent school transition, leadership, and resources sections. *Logan* could be anybody's cool sister.

888. *Ouch!* British Broadcasting Company. www.bbc.co.uk/ouch/. Level: Teens/
      Educators/Parents.

Ouch puts the imp into impairment. This award-winning weekly radio/podcast-
ing/e-zine is very hip and mildly edgy—honest. It leads the way for Disability
Nation and it also has games. For teens and older. This is an example of where
many print magazines are going. They describe themselves a little differently:
"*Ouch* is a website from the BBC that reflects the lives and experiences of
disabled people. It has regular columns, features, quizzes, a monthly near-cult
podcast, a blog or two and a community message board amongst other stuff.
All contributors, well, 99% of them, are disabled—and *Ouch*'s editorial team is
rather wonky and deserve big fat special diversity badges too."

889. *Reach Out.* http://reachoutmag.com. Level: Teens/Educators/Parents.

"*Reach Out* Magazine is more than just a Web magazine, it's a meeting place
for people with disABILITIES all over the world. In addition to a complete online version of *Reach Out* Magazine, the Subscribers area also contains live chat,
personals, message boards, members only mailing list and more!"

890. *Review of Disability Studies: An International Journal.* Center on Disability
      Studies at the University of Hawai'i at Manoa. http://www.rds.hawaii.edu.
      ISSN: 1553-3697. Level: Educators/Professionals.

This quarterly journal began in 2004 and is available online. This is a serious
periodical that offers a thoughtful forum on disability issues and culture in general
and a good source for reviews, research, and commentary for mature researchers
and beginning explorer of high school age. Browsing is the only access to the
journal at this point, since no indexing could be found including using the standard
web browsers. "The *Review* . . . is a peer-reviewed, multidisciplinary, international
journal." It contains not only research articles but also poetry, reviews, and commentary. Four research articles in the latest issue reviewed the invisibility of disabled women in major psychology research, college preparation and experiences,
nonprofit organizations and their impact on civil rights, and the Dutch social support system. The journal also supports a listserv and blog. Paid subscriptions for
print are also available; online is available gratis but donations are encouraged.

891. *SNAP Report.* Special Needs Advocate for Parents (SNAP). www.snapinfo
      .org/our_report.html. Level: Teens/Educators/Parents.

Available online, this is a forum providing information about advocacy for
special needs children and how they can be supported. The quarterly newsletter,
as of November 2007, is behind at least a half year. The archive, which is searchable, begins in summer 1997.

892. *SpeciaLiving Magazine.* SpeciaLiving Magazine. www.specialiving.com/ index.asp. ISSN: 1537-0747. Level: Teens/Educators/Parents.

SpeciaLiving is a consumer style magazine for mobility-impaired consumers. The focus is on people, products, health, inspiration, accessibility, travel, and more. This is a fee subscription print magazine.

EMOTIONAL

Depression-Related Disorders

893. *Anxiety, Stress, and Coping.* Stress and Anxiety Research Society. www .tandf.co.uk/journals/titles/10615806.asp. ISSN: 1061-5806; Online ISSN: 1477-2205. Level: Educators/Professionals.

Anxiety, Stress, and Coping "deals not only with the assessment of anxiety, stress, and coping, and with experimental and field studies on anxiety dimensions and stress and coping processes, but also with related topics such as the antecedents and consequences of stress and emoting." This refereed journal specializes in research articles and case studies as well as literature reviews and analysis that contribute to practice and education. Obsessive-compulsive disorder, eating disorders and posttraumatic stress syndrome are subjects of articles in the journal. Indexed on its website and in PubMed.

894. *PTSD Research Quarterly.* National Center for Posttraumatic Stress Disorder. www.ncptsd.va.gov/ncmain/publications/publications/ncpbl_rq.jsp. ISSN: 1050-1835. Level: Educators/Professionals.

"[The National Center for PTSD] produces the newsletter: *PTSD Research Quarterly* (RQ). Each RQ issue contains a single review article written by guest experts on specific topics related to PTSD. The article also has a selective bibliography with abstracts and a supplementary list of annotated citations." Sadly this disorder, which one would think is one that affects adults only, is also evidenced in children, as is shown in "Impact of Mass Shootings on Survivors, Families and Communities" and other articles. Each article has an extensive annotated abstract and is written at an early college level.

Eating Disorders

895. *e-Lifeline Magazine.* Overeaters Anonymous (OA). secure.yourmis.com/ oa.org/subscribe_online.html. Level: Teens/Educators/Parents.

Lifeline magazine, written by and for OA members, is available in two versions: a 30-page, printed magazine and an electronic online magazine, called *e-Lifeline.*

Both contain the same content. *Lifeline* is published ten months a year, with the combined March/April issue published March 1 and September/October published September 1. Combined issues are thirty-four printed pages. OA offers an Alcoholics Anonymous style self-help approach to managing eating disorders. A sample can be seen at http://www.oa.org/Lifeline/sample/index.html

896. *International Journal of Eating Disorders.* Academy for Eating Disorders. www.aedweb.org/. ISSN: 0276-3478. Level: Teens/Educators/Parents.

Free access to key articles in this journal are available online through a link on the Academy's homepage. The topics covered are generally of a clinical and diagnostic nature, though there are also articles that explore cultural issues that affect those with eating disorders. Among some of the issues covered are articles such as "The Influence of Reported Trauma and Adverse Events on Eating Disturbance in Young Adults," "Geographical Clustering of Eating Disordered Behaviors in U.S. High School Students," and "Evidence-Based Treatment of Anorexia Nervosa."

Mental Illness

897. *Advocate.* National Alliance on Mental Illness (NAMI). www.nami.org/ ADVtemplate.cfm?section=Advocate_Magazine. Level: Teens/Educators/ Parents.

This quarterly magazine is the information and newsletter for the NAMI. It is free with membership in the organization and issues are available online to anyone who registers on the website. The *Advocate* has articles on issues of research and policy interest to persons with mental disabilities and their families, such as organization legal actions and positions on civil rights, reports on drug studies, bipolar disorder, schizophrenia, and borderline personality disorders. The December issue lists the NAMI best of the year books and films. There is also an e-newsletter available on the site. Not found to be indexed except for members on the website.

898. *The Key Update: e-newsletter.* National Mental Health Consumers' Self-Help Clearinghouse. www.mhselfhelp.org/pubs/list.php. Level: Teens/Educators/ Parents.

"*The Key Update* is a monthly e-newsletter that focuses on late-breaking news and notes on important mental health issues. Its supplement, *The Key Assistance Report*, is published quarterly, to provide technical assistance for products designed to help consumers get what they need. Both the *Key Update* and the *Key Assistance Report* have evolved out of *The Key* newsletter. *The Key* and [an] in-depth Technical Assistance Guides are still valuable sources of technical assistance for mental health consumers and consumer groups throughout the country." Some of the recent news articles are "FDA Will Require That Drug Trials Include Information on Suicidal Behavior"; "Advocacy Groups Join Forces to Have Impact on Presidential Race"; "National Commission to Address Disparities in U.S. Mortality Rates"; and "Scientists Can Predict Psychotic Illness in up to 80 Percent of High-Risk Youth." There is also a blog.

Multiple Emotional Disabilities

899. *American Psychologist.* American Psychological Association. www.apa.org/ journals/amp/. ISSN: 0003-066X; Online ISSN: 1935-990X. Level: Teens/ Educators/Parents.

This journal has been indexed in ERIC since 1970 and on its own website. "The *American Psychologist* is the official journal of the American Psychological Association. As such, the journal contains archival documents and articles covering current issues in psychology, the science and practice of psychology, and psychology's contribution to public policy." While much of this journal is aimed at practitioners, some articles are understandable to the general public, including high school students. Special topic issues, such as eating disorders, are often of interest to a broader public other than psychologists.

900. *Developmental Psychology.* American Psychological Association. www.apa .org/journals/dev/. ISSN: 0012-1649; Online ISSN: 1939-0599. Level: Educators/Professionals.

This journal has been indexed in ERIC since 1984, as well as on PubMed and its own website in PsychARTICLES. The journal covers all aspects of psychology growth and change for all ages. From the perspective of this book, it covers disabilities and disorders not found in great numbers. In the past there were more articles on learning disabilities and developmental disabilities, but the focus has shifted to eating disorders, self-esteem, anxiety, and perception of disabilities and disorders. The journal is worth mentioning here because of its authority.

901. *Journal of Abnormal Child Psychology.* Springer Netherlands. www.springer link.com/content/104756/. ISSN: 0091-0627; Online ISSN: 1573-2835. Level: Educators/Professionals.

This journal is indexed in PubMed and on its own website. The journal covers a wide range of research on accurate evaluation and understanding of emotional, learning, and mental disabilities, some of which would find application in the classroom and school in the areas of socialization, reading, writing, and language acquisition. Recent articles include "Children with Autism and Their Friends: A Multidimensional Study of Friendship in High-Functioning Autism Spectrum Disorder," "Violent Victimization in the Community and Children's Subsequent Peer Rejection: The Mediating Role of Emotion Dysregulation," and "Person–Group Dissimilarity in Involvement in Bullying and Its Relation with Social Status."

902. *Journal of Applied Behavior Analysis.* Society for the Experimental Analysis of Behavior. www.pubmedcentral.nih.gov/tocrender.fcgi?journal=309& action=archive. ISSN: 0021-8855. Level: Educators/Professionals.

This journal has been indexed in PubMed since 1968. Back issues are available online through PubMed. This journal describes itself as "a psychology journal that publishes research about applications of the experimental analysis of behavior to problems of social importance." The types of information in the journal can be used to develop learning strategies for students with intellectual, behavioral, or learning disabilities. Methods for training parents with children with disabilities are also discussed.

903. *Journal of Clinical Child and Adolescent Psychology (JCCAP).* American Psychological Association. Society of Clinical Child and Adolescent Psychology. www.leaonline.com/loi/jccp. ISSN: 1537-4416; Online ISSN: 1537-4424. Level: Educators/Professionals.

This journal has been indexed in ERIC from 2004 to 2006. More current issues can be browsed or searched on its website. This is the official journal for the Society of Clinical Child and Adolescent Psychology. While it covers materials perhaps of more interest to clinical and family therapist, it will also have some topics of interest to school psychologists and parents. All would have interest in articles on child advocacy.

904. *Journal of Emotional and Behavioral Disorders.* Hammill Institute on Disabilities and Sage Publishing. ebx.sagepub.com/. ISSN: 1063-4266; Online ISSN: 1538-4799. Level: Educators/Professionals.

This journal has been indexed in ERIC since 2005 and on its site from 1999. "The *Journal of Emotional and Behavioral Disorders* (JEBD) presents quality interdisciplinary research, practice, and commentary related to individuals with emotional and behavioral disabilities." Current articles of interest might be "Ethnic Disparities in Special Education Labeling" or "Mother and Adolescent Reports of Interparental Discord among Parents of Adolescents with and without AD/HD," as well as many others related to school and home, test reliability and validity, or the long-term well-being of students are covered in this journal.

905. *Organized Chaos.* Obsessive Compulsive Foundation (OCF). www.oc foundation.org. Level: Teens/Educators/Parents.

Organized Chaos is only a portion of this website. At the time of this writing, there have been nine volumes of material collected. Each has some relevant technical issues, treatment topics, personal stories, among other things. The Foundation site also has the usual frequently asked questions such as What is it? This site is very helpful in defining habits and rituals as opposed to compulsions and obsessions. The site takes a more biological approach in presenting the origins of these disorders. OCF also publishes a bimonthly newsletter, *OCD Newsletter.* *Kidscope* is a semiannual newsletter for children and teens with OCD and related disorders.

LEARNING

Attention-Deficit/Hyperactivity Disorders (AD/HD)

906. *ADDitude.* Additude Foundation. www.additudemag.com/. ISSN: 1529-1014. Level: Parents.

This journal is available in print, online, or on the website. Created by parents of children with ADD, *ADDitude* provides lifestyle and self-help articles to its readers. Its motto is "Living Well with ADD and Learning Disabilities." There is a feature section, in a recent issue: "It's Not too Early to Plan for Summer Camp"; an inspiration section; and a health living section, which promotes exercise as a way to manage ADD. The website offers advice on "What to do for parents of a child who has been newly diagnosed with a learning disability," treatment, schooling, and parenting. You can join the ADDitude group as well.

907. *Journal of Attention Disorders.* Multi-Health Systems Inc. jad.sagepub.com/. ISSN: 1087-0547; Online ISSN: 1557-1246. Level: Educators/Professionals.

This journal covers attention disorders and related issues across age groups. Among those issues that might be of interest to teachers are behavior assessment and classroom management. Parent training is also covered in the journal. Articles included recently are "Improving School Outcomes for Students with ADHD: Using the Right Strategies in the Context of the Right Relationships," "Identifying, Evaluating, Diagnosing, and Treating ADHD in Minority Youth," and "Current Literature in ADHD." The abstracts on this site clearly cover the objective, method, results, and conclusions. This publication can be browsed on the website and has been indexed on PubMed since 1996.

Autistic Spectrum Disorder

908. *Autism: The International Journal of Research and Practice.* National Autistic Society. www.sagepub.co.uk/journalsProdDesc.nav?prodId=Journal 200822. ISSN: 1362-3613; Online ISSN: 1461-7005. Level: Educators/Professionals.

This journal is indexed in ERIC and PubMed as well as on its website. "*Autism* provides a major international forum for research of direct and practical relevance to improving the quality of life for individuals with autism or autism-related disorders. The journal's success and popularity reflect the recent worldwide growth in the research and understanding of autistic spectrum disorders, and the consequent impact on the provision of treatment and care. *Autism* is interdisciplinary in nature, focusing on evaluative research in all areas, including: diagnosis; case study analyses of therapy; education; quality of life issues, family issues and family services [and other areas of scientific interest.]" Articles like the recent one by Humphreys and Lewis, "'Make Me Normal': The Views and Experiences of Pupils on the Autistic Spectrum in Mainstream Secondary Schools," and other such research make this an important journal for teachers, parents, and students. Most of the recent articles focus on children and adolescents.

909. *Autism-Asperger Digest Magazine.* Future Horizons. www.autismdigest .com/rl. Level: Teens/Educators/Parents.

This consumer style magazine is similar to *Autism Spectrum Quarterly.* Both have highly respected board members and have articles written by specialists and top notch researchers. The content is readable at a tenth-grade level for the most part, so it would be understandable by a wide audience. Both feature articles by, for, and about individuals who have a spectrum disorder. The *Digest Magazine* has archived issues available to subscribers only. The tables of contents are exhibited on the website. The magazine does not seem to be indexed in an indexing service. The magazine has won several awards, including a National Parenting Publication Gold Award.

910. *The Autism Perspective (TAP) Magazine.* www.theautismperspective.org/ index.htm. Level: Teens/Educators/Parents.

This consumer magazine presents many aspects of autism and persuasive developmental disorders. It is not indexed anywhere, but if you are interested in back issues there are tables of contents that go back to 2006, and at some point there will be one for the previous first year. These are easy to read articles and of interest. Starting with the summer 2007 issue, the magazine is available free in a very slick electronic edition.

911. *Autism Spectrum Quarterly.* Starfish Specialty Press. www.asquarterly.com/welcome.html. ISSN: 1551-448X. Level: Teens/Educators/Parents.

Presenting itself as a "MagaJournal," the *Autism Spectrum Quarterly* is similar to the *Autism-Asperger Digest Magazine.* Both have well-known board members and expert researchers summarizing current research and practice. There is general news and personal articles by individuals who have a spectrum disorder or who are in close relationship with someone who does. Includes book reviews. There are also a "Kids on the Cover" photo contest and a poster contest. Not indexed anywhere, and there are no tables of contents for back issues. Available only in print through a paid subscription.

912. *Focus on Autism and Other Developmental Disabilities.* Council for Exceptional Children. Division on Developmental Disabilities. foa.sagepub.com/. ISSN: 1088-3576; Online ISSN: 1538-4829. Level: Educators/Professionals.

"In each issue of *Focus*, there are practical educational and treatment suggestions for teachers, trainers, and parents of persons with autism or other pervasive developmental disabilities. It covers persons with autism or other pervasive developmental disorders [such as fetal alcohol syndrome and hearing impairment]. Articles reflect a wide range of disciplines, including education, speech language pathology, physical therapy, occupational therapy, psychology, medicine, social work, and related areas." Some examples of practical suggestions would be "Promoting Social Interactions between Students with Autism Spectrum Disorders and Their Peers in Inclusive School Settings" or "Use of Strategy Instruction to Improve the Story Writing Skills of a Student with Asperger Syndrome." Indexed in ERIC since 1996 as well as its website.

913. *Journal of Autism and Developmental Disorders.* Springer Netherlands. www.springerlink.com/content/104757/. ISSN: 0162-3257; Online ISSN: 1573-3432. Level: Educators/Professionals.

This journal has been indexed in ERIC since 1979. While covering empirical research, case studies, and literature meta-analysis, the journal also reviews books and media in the subject area of autistic spectrum disorder. About a third of the research covers children and young adults. These are the first three articles in the March 2008 issue: "Growth of Head Circumference in Autistic Infants During the First Year of Life," "Clinical Utility of Autism Spectrum Disorder Scoring Algorithms for the Child Symptom Inventory-4," and "WISC-IV and WIAT-II Profiles in Children with High-Functioning Autism."

914. *Research in Autism Spectrum Disorders.* Elsevier Publishing. http://www.sciencedirect.com/science/journal/17509467. ISSN: 1750-9467. Level: Educators/Professionals.

The journal includes, but is not "limited to diagnosis, incidence and prevalence, methods of evaluating treatment effects, educational, pharmacological, and psychological interventions across the life span." At the present time, the majority of articles focus on infant, preadolescent, and adolescent age groups, with some instruction intervention discussed, such as "The Effects of Instructions, Rehearsal, Modeling, and Feedback on Acquisition and Generalization of Staff Use of Discrete Trial Teaching and Student Correct Responses." Begun in 2007, this journal can be searched at the above website. An email article alert service is available for tables of content.

Down Syndrome

915. *Down Syndrome Research and Practice.* European Down Syndrome Association. www.down-syndrome.org/research-practice/. ISSN: 0968-7912. Level: Educators/Professionals/Parents.

"First published in 1993, *Down Syndrome Research and Practice* publishes original research reports, reviews and case studies, with particular emphasis on the practical implications of research for people living with Down syndrome. *Down Syndrome Research and Practice* has recently been re-launched to offer a broader range of research, practice, reviews and news in a more accessible format. The journal has also adopted an Open Access publishing policy and all articles are now freely accessible online." Most articles are relatively short and the coverage of each issue ranges from case studies of individuals to issues of bruxism. It is also international in scope. Indexed currently in PubMed.

Dyslexia and Other Learning Disabilities

916. *Annals of Dyslexia.* International Dyslexia Association. www.springerlink .com/content/0736-9387. ISSN: 0736-9387. Level: Educators/Professionals.

ERIC has indexed this journal regularly since 1997 and it is indexed on the website listed here. The journal includes articles on the results of empirical studies of theoretical practice for individuals with dyslexia and its complex conditions as well as articles examining its origins and effects. Emergent literacy, reading development, and dyslexia are topics of the latest issue of the journal as well as the results of a longitudinal study of twins with reading disability.

917. *The British Journal of Developmental Disabilities (BJDD).* British Society for Developmental Disabilities. www.bjdd.org/new/index.htm. ISSN: 0969-7950. Level: Educators/Professionals.

"The BJDD provides an international forum for a multidisciplinary approach to the problems posed by mental handicap/learning disability in all countries. Emphasis is put on the practical implications of the work of educationists, instructors, nurses, occupational and other therapists, psychiatrists, psychologists, social workers, whether taking place in a hospital setting or in community care." Articles are browseable on the website and open access is available for issues after two years.

918. *British Journal of Learning Disabilities (London, England)*. British Institute of Learning Disabilities. www.blackwell-synergy.com/loi/BLD. ISSN: 1354-4187; Online ISSN: 1468-3156. Level: Educators/Professionals.

This journal is indexed in ERIC, PubMed, and on its website. "The *British Journal of Learning Disabilities* is an international peer-reviewed journal with a multidisciplinary approach. The focus of the journal is on practical issues, with current debates and research reports. Its readers and authors are academics, practitioners, and others interested in learning disability from a personal or professional perspective. The aim of the Journal is to promote better lifestyles and high quality services for adults and children with intellectual disabilities worldwide." Largely done in a European context, the bulk of the research focuses on adults. However, issues on disabilities, regardless of where they exist, have relevance and can be thought provoking, inspirational, and forceful in any case. The greater focus on adults becomes meaningful in that that is who students become and what they are being schooled for. Worth the occasional perusal just for that.

919. *Child Language Teaching and Therapy*. Edward Arnold Publishing. www.sagepub.com/journalsProdDesc.nav?prodId=Journal201804. ISSN: 0265-6590; Online ISSN: 1477-0865. Level: Educators/Professionals.

Indexed in ERIC and also at the Sage Publishing website under "View Fulltext" link. "*Child Language Teaching and Therapy* is a peer-reviewed journal with articles of high practical relevance on all aspects of spoken or written language needs of children, whatever their causes and influences. Research and practice in this field are at a point where linguistics, psychology, speech and language pathology, education and social sciences meet and overlap. Articles focus on practitioner research, action research, case studies and small-scale studies, together with papers discussing professional, theoretical, methodological or philosophical issues in the field of child language teaching and/or therapy." The three most read articles from the site are "Teaching Grammar to School-Aged Children with Specific Language Impairment Using Shape Coding," "Intensive Dysarthria Therapy for Older Children with Cerebral Palsy: Findings from Six Cases," and "The Assessment and Identification of Language Impairment in Asperger's Syndrome: A Case Study."

920. *Education and Training in Developmental Disabilities*. Council for Exceptional Children (CEC). Division on Developmental Disabilities. www.dddcec.org/etmrddv/TOC/etddv42n4.htm ISSN: 1547-0350. Level: Educators/Parents.

Education and Training in Developmental Disabilities is the professional journal published quarterly by the CEC Division on Developmental Disabilities. The most recent issue has a summary of ideas and practice for implementing research to practice in cognitive disabilities/mental retardation, autism, and related disabilities and an article on facilitating student achievement with assistive technology.

921. *Intervention in School and Clinic.* Council for Learning Disabilities. isc.sagepub.com/. ISSN: 1053-4512; Online ISSN: 1538-4810. Level: Educators/ Professionals.

"*Intervention* equips teachers and clinicians with hands-on tips, techniques, methods, and ideas for improving assessment, instruction, and management for individuals with learning disabilities or behavior disorders. Articles focus on curricular, instructional, social, behavioral, assessment, and vocational strategies and techniques that have a direct application to the classroom setting." Teaching and learning strategies for an effective curriculum in straightforward language from the page to the classroom is the goal of the journal. Indexed in ERIC and on its website.

922. *Journal of Communication Disorders.* Elsevier Publishing. http://www.science direct.com/science/journal/00219924. ISSN: 0021-9924. Level: Educators/ Professionals.

"The *Journal of Communication Disorders* publishes original articles on topics related to disorders of speech, language and hearing. Authors are encouraged to submit reports of experimental or descriptive investigations, theoretical or tutorial papers, case reports, or brief communications to the editor. Special topic issues titled Clinics in Communication Disorders provide clinicians with essential information on the assessment, diagnosis, and treatment of communication disorders." Recent articles included "Working Memory Limitations in Children with Severe Language Impairment," "Auditory Processing Disorders: Acquisition and Treatment," and "Listeners' Perceptions of Speech and Language Disorders." This journal has been indexed in ERIC since 1986, also it is can be searched on Scirus or its own website.

923. *Journal of Fluency Disorders.* Elsevier Publishing. http://www.sciencedirect .com/science/journal/0094730X. ISSN: 0094-730X. Level: Educators/ Professionals.

The *Journal of Fluency Disorders* provides comprehensive coverage of clinical, experimental, and theoretical aspects of stuttering, including the latest remediation techniques. As the official journal of the International Fluency Association, the journal features full-length research and clinical reports; methodological, theoretical, and philosophical articles; reviews; short communications, and much more, all readily accessible and tailored to the needs of the professional. This journal has been indexed in PubMed since 2002, as well as on its own website.

924. *Journal of Learning Disabilities (Austin, TX)*. Hammill Institute on Disabilities. ldx.sagepub.com/. ISSN: 0022-2194; Online ISSN: 1538-4780. Level: Educators/Professionals.

This is one of the leading publications in the area of learning disabilities. Articles cover such fields as education, psychology, neurology, medicine, law, and counseling. This journal has been indexed in ERIC since 1970 and is searchable on the publisher's website.

925. *Learning Disabilities Research & Practice (LDRP)*. Council for Exceptional Children. Division for Learning Disabilities. www.blackwell-synergy.com/loi/LDRP. ISSN: 0938-8982; Online ISSN: 1540-5826. Level: Educators/Professionals.

LDRP provides research articles for special education teachers, school psychologists, administrators, and other practitioners. Issues cover topics such as transition to college, international concepts and practices in LD, and individual differences in LD and testing. This journal from the CEC Division for Learning Disabilities has been indexed in ERIC since 1993, though there is a keyword search engine on one of the journal's websites (www.teachingld.org/ld_resources/ldrp/search_form.cfm) and the website shown above.

926. *Learning Disability Quarterly*. Council for Learning Disabilities. www.cld international.org/Publications/LDQ.asp. ISSN: 0731-9487. Level: Educators/Professionals.

This journal has been indexed in ERIC since 1978. In keeping with the goals of the Council, the journal publishes articles on evaluation of effective teaching methods and policies. One of the topic issues centers entirely around mathematics learning, teaching, and resources, with such articles as "Self-Regulation Strategies to Improve Mathematical Problem Solving for Students with Learning Disabilities." Other articles in other issues include the topics self-determination, peer mediation, and early intervention. The focus is on the quality of lifespan development.

927. *Remedial and Special Education (RASE)*. Hammill Institute on Disabilities. rse.sagepub.com/. ISSN: 0741-9325; Online ISSN: 1538-4756. Level: Educators/Professionals.

"Remedial and Special Education (RASE) is devoted to the discussion of issues involving the education of persons for whom typical instruction is not effective. Emphasis is on the interpretation of research literature and recommendations for the practice of remedial and special education. . . . RASE is rated in the top 10 most frequently cited journals in the Special Education category of the 2004 JCR Social Science Edition of the Institute for Scientific Information." The content of the journal is more focused on remediation than on special education, though many of the strategies for remediation can be used in special education situations. The topic issues, such as the one on mathematics, has at least one article directly relating to students with learning disabilities. Other issues include articles such as "Views of Inclusion: A Comparative Study of Parents' Perceptions in South Africa and the United States," "A Social–Behavioral Learning Strategy Intervention for a Child with Asperger Syndrome," and "Effects of GO 4 IT . . . NOW! Strategy Instruction on the Written IEP Goal Articulation and Paragraph-Writing Skills of Middle School Students with Disabilities."

928. *Research in Developmental Disabilities.* Elsevier Publishing. http://www .sciencedirect.com/science/journal/08914222. ISSN: 0891-4222; Online ISSN: 1873-3379. Level: Educators/Professionals.

This journal averages a minimum of one article per issue about children with disabilities; the majority of those are about autism, but others include visual, language, or hearing impairments. In a recent issue, "Nonverbal Social Interaction Skills of Children with Learning Disabilities," "Do Contacts Make a Difference? The Effects of Mainstreaming on Student Attitudes toward People with Disabilities," and "An Evaluation of a Stimulus Preference Assessment of Auditory Stimuli for Adolescents with Developmental Disabilities" could be found; the remaining six articles covered young adults, adult employment issues, and test validity.

929. *Topics in Language Disorders.* Lippincott Williams & Wilkins. www.topicsin languagedisorders.com/pt/re/tld/home.htm. ISSN: 0271-8294; Online ISSN: 1550-3259. Level: Educators/Professionals.

This journal has been indexed in ERIC since 1983 and is searchable on its website. *"Topics in Language Disorders* (TLD) has the dual purposes: (1) to serve as a scholarly resource for researchers and clinicians who share an interest in spoken and written language development and disorders across the lifespan, with a focus on interdisciplinary and international concerns; and (2) to provide relevant information to support theoretically sound, culturally sensitive, research-based clinical practices." As the title implies, each issue has a particular topic related to language disorders. Issues have covered evaluations of language and communication norms in societies and within the profession as well as within specific disability situations such as aphasia, dyslexia, Asperger's syndrome, and others.

930. *Word of Mouth.* Hammill Institute on Disabilities. wom.sagepub.com/. ISSN: 1048-3950. Level: Educators/Parents.

"This is a newsletter with practical solutions and careful thoughts on daily issues for teachers of students with speech and/or language disorders." This newsletter contains short articles such as "Promoting Syntactic Skills through Sentence-Combining," "Effectiveness of Social Skills Programs for Children with Autism," and "Genetic Etiology in Stuttering." There are two regular columns, Shot Bits and Idea Swap! The latter offers ideas for the classroom. Indexed in the subscription database, Cumulated Index of Nursing and Health Literature (CINAHL).

Intellectual Disabilities

931. *Intellectual and Developmental Disabilities (previously Mental Retardation).* Association on Intellectual and Developmental Disabilities. aaidd .allenpress.com/aamronline/?request=get-archive. ISSN: 1934-9556; Online ISSN: 1934-9491. Level: Educators/Professionals.

This research journal covers policy and treatment issues, but also occasionally teaching approaches. As a result, this would be useful to anyone who is involved with those who have intellectual and developmental disabilities, including parents. "Parental Bereavement and the Loss of a Child with Intellectual Disabilities: A Review of the Literature" and "Concepts of Illness in Children: A Comparison between Children with and without Intellectual Disability" are examples of research articles. The article by Liz Cameron, "The Maine Effect, or How I Finally Embraced the Social Model of Disability," is an example of the more editorial and informative pieces found in the journal.

932. *Journal of Intellectual Disability Research (JIDR).* MENCAP and the International Association for the Scientific Study of Intellectual Disabilities. www.blackwell-synergy.com/loi/JIR. ISSN: 0964-2633. Level: Educators/Professionals.

This important British-based journal publishes original research on a broad range of topics related to intellectual disabilities and is of interest to those involved in special education and rehabilitation. "Coping over Time: The Parents of Children with Autism" and "Siblings of Individuals with Autism or Down Syndrome: Effects on Adult Lives" are examples of some of the articles found here. This journal has been indexed in ERIC since 2004 and is searchable on its own website.

PHYSICAL

Blindness and Visual Impairments

933. *Journal of Visual Impairment & Blindness (JVIB)*. American Foundation
for the Blind. www.afb.org/Section.asp?SectionID=54. ISSN: 0145-482X.
Level: Teens/Educators/Parents.

This journal has been indexed in ERIC since 1994 and on its own website. This
subscription journal has a wide area of interest, since it has professional level
articles, a forum, and research news from the field of vision impairment. "Three
sections of JVIB are available free online to the public: Speaker's Corner, Perspectives, and This Mattered to Me. These columns are platforms for members of
the blindness field who are invited to express their points of view about timely,
important, and controversial issues, or to share their passion for meaningful JVIB
articles that remain relevant today. Readers of these columns are encouraged to
visit the JVIB online message board, and voice their opinions on these important
topics." Research articles include "E-Learning and Blindness: A Comparative
Study of the Quality of an E-Learning Experience," "Caregivers with Visual
Impairments: A Preliminary Study," and "Program Accountability for Students
Who Are Visually Impaired." Each article is preceded by a single word description such as "Employment," "Braille," or "Research Report." The link to the print
requires a username and password.

934. *RE:view*. Association for Education and Rehabilitation of the Blind and
Visually Impaired. www.heldref.org/review.php. ISSN: 0899-1510; Online
ISSN: 1940-4018. Level: Educators/Professionals.

"Articles dealing with useful practices, research findings, investigations,
professional experiences and controversial issues in education, rehabilitation
teaching and counseling, orientation and mobility and other services for the visually handicapped." (*EbscoHOST*) "*RE:view* serves professionals concerned with
assisting individuals of all ages with visual disabilities, including those with multiple disabilities and deaf-blindness. Articles deal with useful practices, research
findings, experiments, professional experiences, and controversial issues; they
address education and rehabilitation topics such as philosophy, trends, administrative practices, teaching, counseling, technology, and other services to people
with visual disabilities. *RE:view* is published in conjunction with the Association
for Education and Rehabilitation of the Blind and Visually Impaired."

Deafness and Hearing Impairments

935. *American Annals of the Deaf.* Executive Committee of the Convention of
American Instructors of the Deaf. gupress.gallaudet.edu/annals/. ISSN: 0002-
726X; Online ISSN: 1543-0375. Level: Educators/Professionals/Parents.

This is one of the oldest research journals in the world dedicated to the education of the deaf and hearing impaired as well as services for them. The journal has research articles covering deaf identity, communications, writing, language skills, employment outcomes from a variety of education circumstances and other social interactions. There is an annual reference issue (no. 2) that has two to four research articles and a list of dissertations relating to persons who are deaf or hearing impaired, but also has substantial directories of services, schools, educational, and advocacy programs. The directory on colleges and universities covers teacher training programs and advance degree programs for teachers of people who are deaf or hearing impaired. This is readable for advanced teen readers. This journal is indexed in ERIC.

936. *DeafLife.* MSM Productions. www.deaf.com. ISSN: 0898-719X. Level: Teens/ Educators/Parents.

Deaf Life, the deaf community's number one magazine, is written and produced by deaf people for the deaf and hearing communities. The magazine has a lead feature about some famous or influential person or persons who are deaf, or on an organization or conference related to hearing impairment. The next column is HPO with topics of discussion or speculation about the deaf community or deaf culture such as "If Deaf Parents Only Want to Have Deaf Kids, What Happens if They End Up Having Hearing Kids?" Friends of Deaf People and Deaf Person of the Month are what they seem. DeafView looks at legal and social issues within the overall community and deaf persons, such as "It's Been 17 Years Since the ADA Was Signed into Law. Has There Been a Major Improvement?" This is a fee subscription for a print magazine. The publisher runs an online community forum, DeafNotes.com, and a chat service, DeafChat.com. It is not indexed anywhere outside the website; back issues are browseable.

937. *Sign Language Studies.* Gallaudet University Press. gupress.gallaudet.edu/ SLS.html. ISSN: 0302-1475; Online ISSN: 1533-6263. Level: Educators/ Professionals.

This peer review research journal has some very interesting topics relating to language and interpersonal communication from an anthropological or linguistic point of view. The journal covers the varieties of signing where they appear in the world and under what circumstances. These articles could be turned into classroom discussions about what language is, where language comes from, and what is it supposed to do. Tables of content and abstracts can be viewed on their website.

938. *The Volta Review.* Alexander Graham Bell Association for the Deaf. www .agbell.org/DesktopDefault.aspx?p=The_Volta_Review. ISSN: 0042-8639. Level: Educators/Professionals.

This is the peer-reviewed companion to *Volta Voices*. This has three issues per year, one of which is a special topic issue. This is the official research journal of the Association and is aimed at researchers and practitioners who work with persons who are deaf or otherwise hearing impaired. In volume 107, the first issue, the editor marks a change in the research focus of the journal more toward children and youth. Examples of that change in the journal are reflected in the articles "Facilitators and Barriers to the Integration of Orally Educated Children and Youth with Hearing Loss into Their Families and Communities," "Outcomes of an Auditory-Verbal Program for Children with Hearing Loss: A Comparative Study with a Matched Group of Children with Normal Hearing," and "An Analysis of Phonological Process Use in Young Children with Cochlear Implants." Indexed in subscription databases, CINAHL and Education Fulltext, and at the publication's website.

939. *Volta Voices.* Alexander Graham Bell Association for the Deaf. www.agbell .org/DesktopDefault.aspx?p=Volta_Voices. ISSN: 1074-8016. Level: Teens/ Educators/Parents.

This magazine has current news and research summaries relevant to hearing loss and impairment. Articles range from political, social, and economic issues to personalities, news, technology, and lifestyle stories. Some topics include "Investing in Family Support," "Dispelling the Myths of Auditory Deprivation," "Picture It! The Language-Literacy Connection," and "Setting the Stage for Culturally Responsive Intervention." When available, the editors include articles in both Spanish and English. It is indexed on the publication's website.

Mobility Impairments

940. *New Mobility.* Miramar Communications. www.newmobility.com. ISSN: 1086-4741. Level: Teens/Educators/Parents.

"*New Mobility* encourages the integration of active-lifestyle wheelchair users into mainstream society, while simultaneously reflecting the vibrant world of disability-related arts, media, advocacy and philosophy. [The] stories foster a sense of community and empower readers to participate in all areas of life, including education, work, love, sex, home ownership, parenting, sports, recreation, travel and entertainment, be informed of and take charge of health concerns, obtain appropriate technology, [and] assert legal rights." The current issue has feature articles centering around stem cell research, as well as an interview with Hollywood writer Allan Rucker. "Rehab Today: Better or Worse?" "My Town: Chicago," "Adventure Rec DVDs," and "When Your Kids Are Taken . . ." are other examples of articles. There are also regular feature columns covering social, cultural, lifestyle, and health issues. Subscription fee.

941. *Paralinks: Wheelchair Nation.* www.paralinks.net. Level: Teens/Educators/ Parents.

Paralinks: Wheelchair Nation is an online news and resources periodical. It changes feature articles monthly, such as "Independence through Technology" and covers topics that range from the Americans with Disabilities Act issues to reports of recent spinal cord injury research. The *SCI Daily News* links to spinal cord–related articles in major papers and other news outlets. *Paralinks: Wheelchair Nation* is a conflation of two sites and includes the archives of both. The site has links to other organizations and social networking sites related to issues of mobility impairments.

942. *PN/Paraplegia News.* Paralyzed Veterans of America (PVA). www.pva magazines.com/pnnews/#. ISSN: 0031-1766. Level: Teens/Educators/ Parents.

"PN is packed with timely information on spinal-cord-injury research, new products, legislation that impacts people with disabilities, accessible travel, computer options, car/van adaptations, news for veterans, housing, employment, health care and all issues affecting wheelers and caregivers around the world." This is a well-designed and thoughtful magazine. Its personal tone and relevant topics, such as travel issues from wheelchair travelers of a wide varieties of disability issues, legal topics and the clear goals of legislative needs, or the update on a growing family highlighted years before, make this an interesting and useful magazine.

943. *SCI Life.* National Spinal Cord Injury Association. www.spinalcord.org/ members/news.php?dep=0&page=21&list=314. Level: Teens/Educators/ Parents.

SCI Life is a bimonthly newsletter that specializes in news and issues of the disabled community. Available in print or electronically at the website to those who register as a member, which is free, the magazine covers civil rights, health, personalities, and media issues. The latest issue has a summary of survey responses from democratic presidential candidates as well as a lengthy article about EndeavorFreedomTV, a web-based information channel. The clear and succinct writing makes the newsletter very readable. As a resource in class, articles can easily be used to refocus community and social issues with a different voice. Not indexed anywhere, back issues are browseable in PDF or html formats.

944. *Sports n' Spokes.* Sports n' Spin. www.pvamagazines.com/resources/index. php?pub=0. ISSN: 0161-6706. Level: Teens/Educators/Parents.

This magazine is the one to go to when you want to know about all out sports in wheels and the people who take and make the challenge. Issues contain articles such as "Rugby: Demolition Derby," "Shooting 'Birds' Fly in Arizona," "Hunting Something for Everyone," "Basketball Camp Info," "Fishing Tournaments of Champions," "Power Soccer When Dreams Become Reality," and large number of other sports and health topics as well as interviews with players.

945. *YaZ: Youth Amputee e-Zine*. Amputee Coalition of America (ACA). www .amputee-coalition.org/yaz/index.asp. Grades 4-7, 10–16.

This is a free online e-zine with stories, puzzles and games for teens and the slightly younger kids. Registration is required for full access. It is not clear from the website how often things are updated, but it is appealing and has relatively recent dates on materials. The parent association, ACA, also offers curriculum materials, Limb Loss Education and Awareness Program (www.amputee-coalition .org) under publications, see the link marked "LLEAP."

Multiple Physical Disabilities

946. *Neurology Now*. American Academy of Neurology. https://www.aan.com/ go/elibrary/neurologynow. ISSN: 1553-3271; Online ISSN: 1553-328X. Level: Educators/Parents.

This publication offers current information resources from physicians, researchers, and medical writers in the area of the brain and nervous system. The general articles define and summarize a wide range of current issues in neurological disorders. Lifestyle issues relative to neurological disorders are covered; particularly of interest to readers would be cerebral palsy, epilepsy, Guillain-Barre, migraine headaches, but also fibroneuralgia, and spinal cord injuries. The reading level for the magazine is undergraduate, so the audience would be advanced reading teens, adults, parents, and teachers.

Appendix A

Book and Media Awards

Educators use established awards, for both book and media, to identify quality literature on specific subjects, for specific grade levels, as well as quality visual representation in both print and nonprint materials. There are two book awards given specifically to authors and illustrators of literature pertaining to disabilities: the Schneider Family Book Awards and the Dolly Gray Award for Children's Literature in Developmental Disabilities. In addition, other book awards mentioned have given honors to individuals who have authored books about disabilities and disorders. These are the Newbery Medal, the Pura Belpré Award, and the Michael Printz Award. Although not an award, the International Board on Books for Young People (IBBY) identifies outstanding books for young people with disabilities. Awards are also given to quality media resources.

THE SCHNEIDER FAMILY BOOK AWARDS

The Schneider Family Book Awards honor an author or illustrator for a book that embodies an artistic expression of the disability experience for children and adolescent audiences. The book must portray some aspect of living with a disability or that of a friend or family member, whether the disability is physical, mental, or emotional. Three annual awards are announced at the American Library Association (ALA) mid-winter meeting in each of the following categories: birth through grade school (age 0–8), middle school (age 9–13), and teens (age 14–18) (www .ala.org/ala/awardsbucket/schneideraward/schneiderawardrecipients.htm).

The following is a list of the Schneider Family Book Awards that are listed in this book.

Young Children grade school (age 0–8)

2009 *Piano Starts Here: The Young Art Tatum* written and illustrated by Robert Andrew Parker

2008 *Kami and the Yaks* by Andrea Stenn Stryer; illustrated by Bert Dodson

2007 *The Deaf Musicians* by Pete Seeger and Paul DuBois Jacobs; illustrated by R. Gregory Christie

2006 *Dad, Jackie, and Me* written by Myron Uhlberg; illustrated by Colin Bootman

2005 *My Pal Victor/Mi amigo, Victor* by Diane Diane Gonzales Bertrand; illustrated by Robert L. Sweetland

2004 *Looking Out For Sarah* written and illustrated by Glenna Lang

Middle School Grade (age 9–13)

2009 *Waiting for Normal* by Leslie Connor

2008 *Reaching for Sun* by Tracie Vaughn Zimmer

2007 *Rules* by Cynthia Lord

2006 *Tending to Grace* by Kimberly Newton Fusco*

2005 *Becoming Naomi León* by Pam Muñoz Ryan

2004 *A Mango Shaped Space* by Wendy Mass

Teens (age 14–18)

2009 *Jerk, California* by Jonathan Friesen

2008 *Hurt Go Happy* by Ginny Rorby

2007 *Small Steps* by Louis Sachar

2006 *Under the Wolf, Under the Dog* by Adam Rapp

2005 *My Thirteenth Winter: A Memoir* by Samantha Abeel

2004 *Things Not Seen* by Andrew Clements

THE DOLLY GRAY AWARD FOR CHILDREN'S LITERATURE IN DEVELOPMENTAL DISABILITIES

The Dolly Gray Award for Children's Literature in Developmental Disabilities, initiated in 2000, recognizes authors, illustrators, and publishers of high quality fictional children's books that appropriately portray individuals with developmental disabilities. The Division of Developmental Disabilities (DDD) of the Council for Exceptional Children (CEC) and Special Needs Project (a distributor

*Denotes a title that does not fall into the disabilities or disorders included in this book.

of books related to disability issues) sponsor this award. An award is presented to an author and illustrator of a children's picture book and/or a juvenile/young adult chapter book in every even year (www.dddcec.org/secondarypages/dollygray/ Dolly_Gray_Children's_Literature_Award.html).

2008   *A Small White Scar* by K. A. Nuzum
2006   *Keeping up with Roo* by Sharlee Glenn; illustrated by Dan Andreason
2006   *So B. It* by Sarah Weeks
2004   *The Curious Incident of the Dog in the Night-time* by Mark Haddon
2002   *Me and Rupert Goody* by Barbara O'Connor
2002   *My Brother Sammy* by Becky Edwards; illustrated by David Armitage
2000   *Tru Confessions* by Janet Tashjian
2000   *Ian's Walk* by Laurie Lears; illustrated by Karen Ritz

ADDITIONAL BOOKS AWARDS

The Newbery Medal

The Newbery Medal, established in 1922, is awarded at the American Library Association (ALA) annual mid-winter meeting by the Association for Library Service to Children (ALSC), a division of the American Library Association, to the author of the most distinguished contribution to American literature for children (www.ala.org/ala/alsc/awardsscholarships/literaryawds/newberymedal/ newberymedal.cfm).

2007   Newbery Honor Book, *Rules*
2005   Newbery Honor Book, *Al Capone Does My Shirts*
2003   Newbery Honor Book, *A Corner of the Universe*
2001   Newbery Honor Book, *Joey Pigza Loses Control*

The Pura Belpré Award

The Pura Belpré Award, established in 1996, is presented to a Latino/Latina writer and illustrator whose work best portrays, affirms, and celebrates the Latino cultural experience in an outstanding work of literature for children and youth. It is cosponsored by the Association for Library Service to Children (ALSC), a division of the American Library Association (ALA), and the National Association to Promote Library and Information Services to Latinos and the Spanish-Speaking (REFORMA), an ALA Affiliate (www.ala.org/ala/alsc/ awardsscholarships/literaryawds/belpremedal/belprmedal.htm).

2006 Pura Belpré Honor Book, *Becoming Naomi Leon*

The Michael Printz Award

The Michael L. Printz Award, an award for a book that exemplifies literary excellence in young adult literature, was established in 2000 by the Young Adult Library Services Association (YALSA), a division of the American Library Association (ALA). This award is named for a Topeka, Kansas, school librarian who was a longtime active member of YALSA. The award is sponsored by *Booklist*, a publication of the American Library Association (ALA).

2009 Michael L. Printz Medal Winner, *Jellicoe Road*
2005 Michael L. Printz Medal Winner, *How I Live Now*

OUTSTANDING BOOKS FOR YOUNG PEOPLE WITH DISABILITIES

The International Board on Books for Young People (IBBY) is a nonprofit, international organization of individuals who bring books and children together. In 1997 IBBY began identifying quality literature for young people with disabilities. The 2009 volume represents the third in a series of biennial annotated catalogues that IBBY hopes will encourage publishers to produce new books and translations for parents and educators to share with disabled young people. The 2009 volume lists fifty outstanding books from various countries that were published in 2004 and later, except one outstanding title that was published in 1998 (www .ibby.org).

The following IBBY Outstanding Books for Young People with Disabilities 2009 are listed in this book:

The London Eye Mystery by Siobhan Dowd
Rules by Cynthia Lord
Small Steps by Louis Sachar

The 2007 volume lists sixty-two outstanding books from twenty-three countries that were published in 2002 or later, except five outstanding titles that were published earlier than 2002. The following IBBY Outstanding Books for Young People with Disabilities 2007 are listed in this book:

Dad, Jackie, and Me by Myron Uhlberg; illustrated by Colin Bootman
From Charlie's Point of View by Richard Scrimger
The Hangashore by Geoff Butler
I Can, Can You? by Marjorie W. Pitzer
Lily and the Mixed-Up Letters by Deborah Hodge; illustrated by France Brassard
Moses Sees a Play by Isaac Millman
Nathan's Wish by Laurie Lears; illustrated by Stacey Schuett

Sosu's Call by Meshack Asare
Zoom! by Robert N. Munsch; illustrated by Michael Martchenko

FABULOUS FILMS FOR YOUNG ADULTS

The Young Adult Library Services Association (YALSA), a division of the American Library Association (ALA), identifies Fabulous Films for Young Adults annually. By identifying titles of quality and effect in their presentation, YALSA assists librarians and educators in collecting multimedia that accommodates the varied interest of young adults (www.ala.org/ala/yalsa/yalsa.cfm).

Body Image for Boys; 2003 Young Adult Library Services Association (YALSA) award

Dying to Be Thin; 2002 Young Adult Library Services Association (YALSA) award

Slender Existence; 2001 Young Adult Library Services Association (YALSA) award

Appendix B

Calendar of Events

Educators traditionally use occasions, particularly holidays and observances, for lesson planning and enhancing curriculum activities. The following observances can be used with the resources listed in this book to develop lesson plans and build comprehensive units centered on specific disorders and disabilities.

The observances that are sponsored by various organizations and associations throughout the calendar year are listed below. If available, websites for these observances are included. During the months of January, June, July, August, and November, there was no documentation of any observances related to the disorders and disabilities that have been covered in this book.

February: AMD/Low Vision Awareness Month (www.preventblindness.org/news/observe.html)

National Eating Disorders Awareness Week (www.nationaleatingdisorders.org/)

March: Mental Retardation Awareness Month (www.arcfc.org/mramonth04.html)

Save Your Vision Week: This is an annual proclamation that began by a joint resolution of Congress in 1963.

April: National Autism Awareness Month (www.autism-society.org/site/)

National Stress Awareness Day (www.stresscure.com/hrn/april.html)

May: Mental Health Month (http://www.ffcmh.org/)

National Children's Mental Health Awareness Week (http://www.ffcmh.org/)

Better Hearing and Speech Month (www.asha.org/bhsm/)

Healthy Vision Month (www.aoa.org/x5086.xml)

September: ADHD Month

Deaf Awareness Week (www.nad.org/site/pp.asp?c=foINKQMBF&b=180409)

October: Disability Awareness Month (www.cdc.gov/Features/Disability
  Awareness/)
National Depression Education and Awareness Month
National Down Syndrome Awareness Month (www.ndss.org)
World Blindness Awareness Month (http://www.eyecareamerica.org/eyecare/
  news/20071010.cfm)
December: National Stress-Free Family Holidays Month

The government sponsored website, National Health Information Center,
which lists its 2008 observances, offers information regarding other health-
related issues. Some of the topics are anxiety disorders, autism, Down syndrome,
eating disorders, mental health, and vision. The following website provides additional information regarding the National Health observations (www.health
finder.gov/library/nho/nho.asp#m6).*

---

* Source: 2008 National Health Observances, National Health Information Center, Office of Disease Prevention and Health Promotion. Washington, D.C.: U.S. Department of Health and Human
Services.

Author Index

The numbers refer to entries, not pages.

Illustrator/Photographer Index

The numbers refer to entries, not pages.

Title Index

Numbers indicate entry numbers, not pages.

Series Index

Numbers indicate entry numbers, not pages.

Book and Media Award Index

Grade/Level Index

The numbers refer to entries, not pages.

Subject Index

The numbers refer to entries, not pages.

About the Authors

Alice Crosetto received her BA in Latin and Greek from Kent State University, Ohio. In addition, she received a master of arts in English, a master of science in education with emphasis in curriculum and instruction/educational media, and a master of science in library science from Kent State University. She has been an educator and a librarian in Ohio for over thirty years. In 2005, she accepted a faculty position at The University of Toledo Libraries and is currently the acquisitions librarian and coordinator of collection development. She is a member of the Academic Library Association of Ohio (ALAO), the American Library Association (ALA), and the Italian American War Veterans of the United States. She has made several presentations at the local, state, and national levels. She has also written several articles, including reviews for *American Reference Books Annual* (ARBA).

Rajinder Garcha, born and raised in Tanzania, received her associate degree from Highridge Teachers' College in Nairobi, Kenya, and taught elementary school for six years in Dar es Salaam, Tanzania. She received her BS in educational studies and her master of library and information science from Kent State University, Ohio. She worked at Kent State University Libraries for several years prior to becoming a faculty member at The University of Toledo. From 2001 to 2002, she was the interim dean of the University Libraries at The University of Toledo. She is currently a professor emerita. She has made several presentations at the local, state, and national levels. In addition, she has published extensively in refereed journals. This is her second book. Her first book, titled *The World of Islam in Literature for Youth: A Selective Annotated Bibliography for K–12*, was published by Scarecrow Press in 2006. She has a daughter, a son, and two grandsons.

Mark Horan received a BA in general literature from Syracuse University, New York, a master of arts in English literature from Slippery Rock State College, Pennsylvania, and a master of library science from the University of Pittsburgh. He has held a variety of positions in academic libraries throughout his twenty-eight years of experience. He worked as a consultant, an electronic services librarian, and a head librarian. In 2001, he accepted a faculty position at The University of Toledo Libraries and is currently the college librarian for the Judith Herb College of Education at The University of Toledo. He is an active member of the American Library Association (ALA). He has published several articles and has made presentations locally, nationally, and internationally.